H
C
C
S

Harvard Contemporary China Series, 13

The Harvard Contemporary China Series is designed to
present new research that deals with present-day issues
against the background of Chinese history and society. The
focus is on interdisciplinary research intended to convey
the significance of the rapidly changing Chinese scene.

Changing Meanings of Citizenship in Modern China

Edited by

Merle Goldman

and

Elizabeth J. Perry

Harvard University Press

Cambridge, Massachusetts

London, England   2002

Library of Congress Cataloging-in-Publication Data

Changing meanings of citizenship in modern China / edited by Merle Goldman,
Elizabeth J. Perry.

    p. cm. — (Harvard contemporary China series ; 13)

  Based on a conference held at the Fairbank Center for East Asian Research,
Harvard University, in the fall of 1999.

  Includes bibliographical references.

  ISBN 0-674-00766-2 (cloth : alk. paper) — ISBN 0-674-00843-X (paper : alk.
paper)

1. Citizenship—China—History—20th century.

2. China—Politics and government—20th century.

I. Goldman, Merle. II. Perry, Elizabeth J. III. Series.

JQ1517.A2 C53 2002

323.6'0951—dc21   2001059351

Contents

III Taiwan

Preface

This volume derives from a conference held at the Fairbank Center for East Asian Research at Harvard University in the fall of 1999. The impetus for the conference arose in part from the individual interests of the two editors, and in part in reaction to the discussion of civil society in China that seemed to us increasingly removed from an emphasis on its connection to the state. We were surprised and gratified to find so many colleagues in our field who were also working on the meaning of citizenship in modern China. Although there are numerous definitions of what it means to be a citizen, based on gender, religion, education, ethnicity, and other criteria, we define citizenship in this volume primarily as political, civil, and legal relations between members of society and the state, and we trace changes in the conceptualization and implementation of these relations during China's cataclysmic twentieth century.

In addition to the authors of the essays, many others contributed to this volume in their roles as discussants, critics, readers, editors, and organizers. Among them, we must thank Stefanie Van Pelt, Assistant Director of the Fairbank Center, who mobilized the Center staff to handle all the arrangements for the conference. We also are grateful to the discussants, William Kirby, Alan Wachman, William Joseph, and William Alford. We want to thank in particular Paul Cohen, who was not only a discussant but also a very critical and constructive reader of the volume. We want to express our appreciation to Theresa Lee, whose conference paper on Liang Qichao set the tone for the discussion on the meaning of citizenship in the late imperial period. Thanks also go to Zhou Xiaohong for his contribution on rural citizenship under Mao. Once again, we must thank Nancy Hearst, the librarian of the Fairbank Center, who has corrected our mistakes, filled in our blanks, and thereby saved us from many an embarrassing slip. To these and others who attended the conference and participated in the discussion, we are very grateful.

Merle Goldman
Elizabeth J. Perry
December 2001

Changing Meanings of Citizenship
in Modern China

MERLE GOLDMAN
ELIZABETH J. PERRY

Introduction: Political Citizenship in Modern China

The establishment of the European Union and the dissolution of much of the formerly Communist world revived interest in the concept of citizenship among Western scholars. Dramatic changes in political sovereignty led quite naturally to a reexamination of the fundamental meanings of citizenship, specifically the relations between members of a political community and their government.

The Chinese experience merits a central place in any comparative discussion of political citizenship for a number of different reasons: the pressing questions surrounding Chinese sovereignty in the wake of the return of Hong Kong and Macau; the quest for an alternative political identity on Taiwan; international attention to human rights in China, galvanized by the Tiananmen Uprising of 1989; the democratization of Taiwan and the implementation of village elections in rural China. Chinese citizenship is noteworthy in its own right because of its long— and markedly different—historical patterns in contrast to those that have characterized the European and Anglo-American experiences.

Political citizenship is a multivalent concept. On the one hand, it can refer simply to *membership* in a political community (be it a city or a nation-state)—whether acquired by birth, migration, immigration, or naturalization. On the other hand, it can refer to the *quality of the relationship* between individual members and the larger political community to which they belong. Membership is determined sometimes by community consensus, sometimes by legal decree. The quality of that membership has even more complex social, political, economic, and cultural determinants and consequences—not to mention interpretations.

T. H. Marshall pointed out in his classic studies of citizenship in Western Europe that the past three centuries have seen the development of three distinct permutations of the concept. In the eighteenth century, what Marshall terms "civil citizenship" ensured individual rights to property, personal liberty, and justice. During the nineteenth century, a notion of "political citizenship" underscored the right to participate in the exercise of political power. In the twentieth century, "social citizenship" has implied a right to economic welfare and social security.[1] Each of these connotations spread rapidly from one European nation to the next, creating an escalation of entitlement expectations. Although Marshall believed that the third type of citizenship (as embodied in the modern European welfare state) represented the final stage of development, in recent years other scholars have identified additional variants designed to cope with the challenges of the twenty-first century: "cultural citizenship," "race-neutral citizenship," "gender-neutral citizenship," "European citizenship," "global citizenship," "ecological citizenship," and the like.[2]

The concept of political citizenship directs our attention squarely at state-society relations by highlighting the duties, obligations, claims, and/or rights that connect members of society to the state. While these ties may have assumed a distinctive form in the modern European context, they are by no means limited to that particular pattern. Citizenship exists in authoritarian as well as in democratic polities, and can refer to a range of legal, political, social, and economic links between the state and members of society. As opposed to civil society, which is often interpreted to mean a sphere of associational activity that is relatively autonomous from state control, citizenship presupposes nothing about the autonomy of either state or society and instead spotlights the specific interconnections between them. Moreover, again in contrast to some interpretations of civil society, the term "citizenship" need not connote a teleological movement toward a liberal democratic regime. Although we focus in this volume on the concept of *political* citizenship—or the demands for greater participation and inclusion in the polity by various elements of the population—we leave open the sort of political system that may result from such claims. Citizenship, in other words, is not just another term for democratization—and the study of political citizenship in modern China invites us to examine seriously a whole range of reform initiatives, both top-down and bottom-up, from late imperial days to the Republican era, through the Maoist period to the contemporary scene, on Taiwan as well as in the People's Republic of China (PRC).

In defining and delimiting the boundaries of political membership, citizenship implies exclusion as well as inclusion. The answer to the question of who enjoys the full prerogatives of community membership (and who is relegated to the categories of second-class citizen and non-citizen) affords considerable insight into the basic nature of any political system. The borders of citizenship are subject to change, of course. They may be redrawn by pressures from below—as the women's suffrage movement and the Civil Rights movement demonstrated in the course of American history. Or they may be altered by state fiat, as various Immigration and Naturalization Service regulations in effect have done for the United States.

In the case of twentieth-century China, the plethora of political authorities who have claimed jurisdiction at various times over various parts of the country has resulted in bewildering fluctuations in the boundaries of citizenship. The Manchus, warlords, foreign imperialists, Nationalists, and Communists (under Maoist and post-Mao regimes) tried to impose quite different conceptions of citizenship upon the populations living under their control. But they did not enjoy a free hand in such efforts; non-official interpretations of citizenship—espoused by ordinary people as well as by intellectuals—also played an important role in the process of boundary definition.

For Westerners studying this confusing century in Chinese history, the situation is further complicated by the fact that several distinctive Chinese concepts—which gained widespread currency during this period—are all rendered into English as "citizen." The terms *shimin* (literally "city people"), *guomin* ("nation-state people"), and *gongmin* ("public people"), all usually translated as "citizen," refer to membership in rather different communities. They include and exclude people on the basis of different territorial and political principles. But even within each of these delimited rubrics, which all have their own complicated etymology, Chinese have argued vehemently about the criteria and consequences of membership.

The term *guomin,* for example, was used more than 2,000 years ago in pre-Qin texts to refer to inhabitants of rival warring states. But when the late Qing reformer Liang Qichao reintroduced the term at the turn of the twentieth century, he borrowed the Chinese characters back from Meiji Japan.[3] The Japanese had adopted the term to capture the new ideas of citizenship imported from the West. Although Liang embraced the term as a vehicle for criticizing Confucian political culture, his aim was not the development of autonomous individuals, but rather the cultivation of full-fledged participants in the modern nation-state.[4] By what principles were people to be included within this new nationality? Some anti-Manchu writers, such as Zhang Taiyan, stressed race as the key criterion. Moderates such as Kang Youwei preferred to emphasize morals and culture over blood and descent. The mature Liang Qichao, disillusioned with both race and culture as means of unifying China, began to propose state-conferred membership.[5] These polemics had an impact that spread well beyond the rarefied world of intellectual debate. As Leo Lee has noted, the subject of the national citizen—rendered into Chinese as *guomin*—entered state-sponsored textbooks (which themselves had only just been introduced to Chinese classrooms) around the time of the 1911 Revolution.[6]

Over the course of the twentieth century, the term *gongmin* largely replaced *guomin* in both official and popular parlance as the accepted designation to refer to those persons who are legally recognized as members of a state. The origins of the term *gongmin* lie in the Confucian celebration of public service. The character *gong,* or public, has a history that can be traced back for thousands of years. It was often counterposed in Confucian discourse to *si,* or private, which implied selfishness. According to the Japanese sinologist Mizoguchi Yūzō, by the seventeenth century the meaning of the character *gong* had lost much of its original connection to the state or government, and carried instead the connotation of a burgeoning zone of "communal" or "collective" activity.[7] This growing "extra-bureaucratic public sphere" may have begun in the area of water conservancy.[8] Regardless of its origins, Mary Rankin and William Rowe have both argued that there developed in late imperial China a wide-ranging elite tradition of local activism, subsumed under the rubric of *gong,* which could be interpreted as a Chinese counterpart to the Habermasian "public sphere."[9] Subsequent adoption of the term *gongmin* to refer to legally recognized members of nation-states thus suggested the two-way linkages between state and society that modern polities were expected to exhibit.

The term *shimin* (city people) is evidently of fairly recent vintage, linked to the rise of new urban classes—capitalists, professionals, and industrial laborers—after the Opium Wars of the mid-nineteenth century.[10] Nevertheless, it has figured prominently in the discourse of twentieth-century political activism. Urban reformers and revolutionaries, seeking to bring about a new form of municipal governance, staked a claim as *shimin* to the right of self-rule. The growing commercial and industrial wealth being generated in cities like Shanghai prompted a desire for increased social and political capital as well. From the urban uprisings accompanying the Revolution of 1911 to the protests of 1989, manifestos demanding greater popular participation and local control have been issued in the name of the *shimin.* Similarly, governments have regularly called upon urban dwellers as *shimin* to maintain social stability and uphold civic virtues.

These terms, along with a number of others, highlight distinct aspects of state-society relations: nationalism in the case of *guomin,* public spirit in the case of *gongmin,* and urban rights and responsibilities in the case of *shimin.* Their deployment in dissimilar ways by different parties for divergent political purposes suggests the richness of the citizenship debate in modern China.

Although in premodern times most Chinese probably felt a strong sense of belonging to a family, lineage, locality, or dynasty, such identifications did not usually imply a voice in deciding the affairs of these communities. Managerial authority lay with officials and gentry. Community membership did often carry a claim to certain basic welfare guarantees (a cornerstone of Confucian social theory), but was seldom accompanied by a right to political participation. In other words, T. H. Marshall's evolutionary scenario was essentially reversed in the case of China, where a commitment to social citizenship predated political citizenship by many centuries.[11]

With increasing encroachment from the Western powers around the turn of the twentieth century, intellectuals and officials deployed the term *guomin* (nationals) to express their new understanding of citizenship. Although a reaction to Western influence, the resurrection of this ancient Chinese term carried a meaning that was distinct from contemporary Western connotations of citizenship. In adopting the term *guomin*, late Qing and Republican-era elites revealed their preoccupation with asserting China's position vis-à-vis the foreign imperialist powers, rather than with ensuring the rights of individuals vis-à-vis the state. Political rights were viewed primarily as a means of promoting the interests of the state over those of the individual. Chinese governments—and political activists—during most of the twentieth century have considered rights not as inherent and inalienable natural endowments, but as revocable privileges conferred by the state.[12] Reformers in the late Qing and Republican periods wrote proposals, organized groups, and founded newspapers and journals demanding political rights for the purpose of rendering their country "rich and powerful."

One of those reformers, Liang Qichao, was the preeminent Chinese intellectual of the early twentieth century. His influential views exerted a profound impact on the understandings of citizenship in modern China.[13] Theresa Lee has described Liang's efforts to integrate Chinese and Western ideas of citizenship.[14] Confronted with Western imperialism and Social Darwinism and particularly concerned about China's survival among competitive nation-states, Liang urged his countrymen to reorganize themselves around nationalism. In place of the use of race or culture to unify China, he exhorted them to "renew" themselves as nationals, or *guomin*. In Liang's view, the lack of a sense of obligation—to pay taxes and serve in the military, for example—rather than the lack of rights, constituted the root cause of China's problems. In one respect, Liang uses the term *gongmin*, public people, to argue that participation in the polity should be the right of anyone born in a national state. The ultimate goal of his ideas, Lee points out, was to transform the imperial state into a modern nation-state, in which subjects would be replaced by citizens (as in the French Enlightenment project). But since the Chinese people were not yet deemed ready for Western-style democracy, Liang believed that China required authoritarian leadership during the transition, a view that would be echoed by Chinese leaders as well as intellectuals throughout the twentieth century.

These ideas (along with those of Lenin) set the stage for the emergence of the mobilizational state on the Chinese political horizon. Since the late 1920s, Chinese governments (and their Bolshevik-style parties) have viewed the cultivation of a committed citizenry as a pressing responsibility. First the Nationalists and then the Communists devoted substantial attention and resources to the task of political education. Massive campaigns, such as the New Life Movement of the 1930s and the Cultural Revolution of the 1960s, encouraged popular political participation along lines dictated by state authorities. But not everyone was welcomed into the ranks of the nascent citizenry. In the People's Republic of China, the concept of the "people" *(renmin)* explicitly excluded and targeted for criticism certain elements of the populace who were considered enemies of the state.[15] The exclusion or inclusion of various social categories—whether based upon political consciousness, economic class, ethnicity, gender, or other criteria—by the authoritarian state has been a notable feature of Chinese citizenship over the past century.

Joan Judge's chapter in this volume links the creation of a modern citizenry in China to the integration of women into the modern polity and their involvement in the task of national strengthening. Because women were the source of social and cultural reproduction, their participation as female *guomin,* that is, as mothers of citizens, would help to build a new national identity, strengthen the race, and inculcate their children with the values of becoming good patriots. Therefore it was necessary for women to be educated so that they could assume their national duties. Though the definition of citizenship in the late Qing dynasty was constructed and imposed from above, the resulting education of women and space for new social and cultural practices challenged long-standing Chinese views of citizenship as the preserve of a male-educated elite.

Another means for broadening citizenship in the late nineteenth and early twentieth centuries, David Strand points out in his chapter, was through public speaking. The leaders of the Hundred Days of

Reform, Kang Youwei as well as Liang Qichao, used speech-making to form public opinion and as a new weapon in their political battles to reform China. While Liang turned to public speaking in his early days to reconcile nationalism with citizenship under a constitutional monarchy, Sun Yat-sen used it to bring people into the political process. Hurling anti-Manchu slogans against the Qing dynasty, Sun exhorted the Chinese people to transform themselves from subjects into nationals *(guomin)*. While an emerging sense of citizenship in the early decades of the twentieth century did not lead to electoral accountability, it did force officials, Strand insists, to face the people in the rhetorical realm. Although the idea of citizenship promoted by such different leaders as Liang and Sun emphasized the importance of a mobilized populace in support of a powerful state, the actual practice of citizenship was more disorderly. Because Sun and the early Communist leaders reached out to diverse audiences that became part of the political process, they found that the spoken word was a powerful—though, as Strand stresses, an unpredictable—tool for mobilizing support.

Bryna Goodman and Jeffrey Wasserstrom write in their chapters about public protests, a burgeoning press, the establishment of a variety of associations, and the beginning of the electoral process in Shanghai during the late teens and early 1920s. Although Shanghai was anything but a typical Chinese city, its cultural influence in the Republican period was enormous. As China's most cosmopolitan metropolis, Shanghai's political experiments captured national attention. These halting efforts at political reform were diffuse, episodic, and ephemeral and did not take the form of a fully institutionalized democracy. They were, however, the beginnings of the articulation of citizens' rights *(shimin quan)* in an urban setting. Associations that were formed in this period drafted constitutions, improvised electoral procedures, and claimed to represent "the public." Like village elections in China today, these Republican-era developments were examples of local democratic procedures taking place in the absence of a functioning democratic state.

Goodman highlights the democratic innovations in several key Shanghai institutions and voluntary associations until the ascendancy of party-dominated politics in the mid-1920s. Throughout most of the twentieth century, there was a gap between the democratic rhetoric of citizenship and civil rights, on the one hand, and actual practice, on the other. As Goodman points out, there were conflicts between "the numerical rationality of electoral procedures" and traditional considerations based on seniority and stability. Nevertheless, there was also a gradual transformation of ideas and practices in some organizations, such as the Shanghai Chamber of Commerce and the Commoners' Chamber of Commerce consisting of smaller shopkeepers, whose rallying cry was "no taxation without representation." These organizations, along with major native-place and commercial associations, expanded the meaning of the "public" and encouraged limited voting procedures. Concepts of citizenship, civil rights, and political representation were articulated and practiced by these groups.

Wasserstrom, by contrast, emphasizes the limited nature of these efforts. Taking place in a semi-colonial context, such political experiments were infused with racism and anti-democratic tendencies toward the native Chinese population. He shows that with a few exceptions, the Chinese who paid taxes in Shanghai's International Settlement could not participate in governing the enclave or in using the public parks that their taxes helped to maintain. Nevertheless, the Chinese demands to enter the parks and to be included on the governing board of the Settlement helped to foster an emerging civic consciousness. Those involved in these efforts claimed legal, political, and social rights. With a sense of being disenfranchised, they demanded to be recognized as active members of the community. As Marshall has observed, groups excluded from the category of citizen are likely to demand an expansion of its definition to permit their own inclusion. By 1928, some headway had been made in Chinese efforts to gain representation on the governing board and in the use of the parks, but this citizenship covered only a small number of tax-paying residents; the overwhelming majority of the population of the Settlement did not attain such rights. Nevertheless, as both Wasserstrom and Goodman show, the struggle for citizenship— even when less than fully successful—affords valuable experience that may be put to work at another time and in another context.

Beyond the realm of intellectuals and political elites, most studies of early twentieth-century China tend to deal fleetingly, if at all, with what ordinary people may have had in mind when they began to demand entry to the political system as "citizens."[16] John Fitzgerald's study of the Nationalist Revolution does stress the newfound identities of citizen and patriot as a major element in the "political awakening" of early twentieth-century China, but his discussion of the issue is largely confined to the ideas of influential turn-of-the-century political thinkers.[17] David Strand's *Rickshaw Beijing,* a colorful portrait of street politics in the 1920s, offers an insightful introduction to the world of an expanding citizenry in Republican China. Strand reveals the ways in which city dwellers—merchants, policemen, and rickshaw pullers alike—began to assume new political roles and to press new claims.[18]

Similarly, Elizabeth Perry's chapter in this volume spotlights the entry of industrial workers into the ranks of the urban citizenry. Workers figure prominently in a series of political confrontations that changed the face of modern China, from the May Fourth Movement of 1919 through the crackdown on demonstrators in Tiananmen Square on June 4, 1989. Though these confrontations are usually regarded as student protests, workers also joined—not only as workers, but also as citizens *(shimin).* Perry describes the workers' participation as part of a larger transnational process. Like Chinese intellectuals in 1919, the workers were influenced by the political thought of the French Revolution and the French Enlightenment. Moreover, only when students reached out to form coalitions with workers did their combined quest for citizenship become a significant political force.

Whereas the landmark protests of the Republican era involved coordination between labor and intellectuals, workers in Communist China have acted mostly without guidance from intellectuals. Moreover, during the Mao era (1949–1976), the discourse of citizenship gave way to a discourse of class, the terms of which were defined by the party leadership.[19] Depending on the party's line or factional configuration at a given time, groups and individuals were classified as either friends or enemies. So-called enemies or reactionaries could be landlords, nonconformist intellectuals, or anyone whom Mao disliked.

While in the first half of the twentieth century the opportunity of becoming a citizen with substantial political rights as well as responsibilities had seemed possible, during the Maoist era one aspired to be a "comrade" *(tongzhi)*. The historian Irene Bloom has observed that the term *tongzhi* was originally used in the Han dynasty to denote a group committed to a common purpose. And the sociologist Ezra Vogel has pointed out that in the wartime Communist base areas and in the early 1950s, to address someone as "comrade" was to imply a fundamental equality among faithful and trusted followers.[20] Though theoretically connoting equality, as the Communist party-state became entrenched and political campaigns accelerated from the late 1950s until Mao's death in 1976, the understanding of *tongzhi* increasingly demanded strict subservience to party orders and allegiance to party principles.

An indication of the degree to which the party-state repressed and rechanneled the impulse toward citizen activism that had developed in earlier decades is encapsulated in Strand's description of speech-making. Whereas Chinese Communist leaders had made fiery speeches before 1949, speech-making afterwards evolved into the drone of long policy reports to selected audiences. Not only could no one claim the right to speak as a citizen, but audiences were less free to exercise their independent political judgment or to display the corrosive power of bad manners. These potentially critical functions, evident in the Chinese political culture of earlier decades, were superseded in mid-century by the party leadership's assumption of the authority to "speak for and to the people."

In the post-Mao era, during the last decades of the twentieth century, a gradual emergence of new forms of citizenship has occurred alongside a revival of some pre-1949 practices. The reform effort launched in the late 1970s sparked renewed interest in the question of citizenship in contemporary China. Many young Chinese intellectuals became intrigued with the issue, writing articles and holding forums on the subject. Yet, as Andrew Nathan has pointed out, the state-centric view of citizenship that had prevailed among Chinese intellectuals and political leaders since the late nineteenth century continued to inhibit would-be democrats from developing a more radical critique.[21]

Furthermore, the difficulties of fostering democratic citizenship in contemporary China are not limited to the intellectual and political elites. Dorothy Solinger's book on the floating population of migrants from the countryside paints a gloomy picture of the state of citizenship in contemporary China. Commercialization and urbanization, Solinger cautions, do not lead inexorably to political liberalization or political inclusion. Instead she finds that "citizenship does not come easily to those outside the political community whose arrival coincides with deepening and unaccustomed marketization."[22] The arduous plight of millions of peasants living on the margins of the Chinese political system is graphic testimony to the problems inherent in the construction of modern citizenship.

Despite these tremendous barriers on both the elite and the popular levels, some individuals and groups have sought to assert political rights and express independent political views. What is more significant, they presumed these rights rather than waiting for them to be granted by the government. The first evidence of this change in the post-Mao period was the Democracy Wall movement of 1978–1979. Merle Goldman's chapter describes this movement of ex–Red Guards, workers, and youth, who would have been students but for the Cultural Revolution. Mobilized by Mao's injunction that "to rebel is justified," they were instilled early on with the idea of the right to protest against official misconduct. Although repressed in Mao's later years, in the fall of 1978, only two years after Mao's death, they used the skills acquired in the Cultural Revolution—putting up posters, distributing pamphlets, delivering speeches, and engaging in debates—to demand, among other things, political rights as citizens *(gongmin quan)*. Their goal was to ensure that never again would they, their families, their colleagues, and the Chinese people be subjected to the arbitrary persecution they had suffered in the Cultural Revolution. This was the first mass movement in the People's Republic in which the participants sought not only to strengthen the nation, but also to protect and enlarge their own individual and collective political rights.

The gradual development in the late 1970s of "rights consciousness" was partly a response to the enormity of the Cultural Revolution. The Democracy Wall participants framed their demands in familiar Marxist terminology, but their language was also influenced by an increasing awareness of dissident movements in Eastern Europe and the Soviet Union. Several of their posters, for example, urged President Jimmy Carter to pay as much attention to their demands for human rights as he was devoting to Soviet dissidents' demands. Moreover, unlike most Chinese intellectuals and political leaders, the Democracy Wall activists as a result of their experience in the Cultural Revolution did not regard rights as a gift from the state, with which they had become disillusioned, but as prerogatives they must achieve on their own.

Although this grassroots movement demanding human rights was crushed by the early 1980s, some of the Democracy Wall demands for political reforms and freedom of expression were carried on by a small number of establishment intellectuals associated with the brain trusts surrounding Deng's presumed successors, first Hu Yaobang and then Zhao Ziyang. Among the most outspoken was the editor and journalist Hu Jiwei, the subject of Judy Polumbaum's chapter. Polumbaum depicts Hu before the Cultural Revolution as having acted in the tradition of a Confucian scholar-bureaucrat. This represented a limited form of citizenship, in which the scholar-bureaucrat accepted the duties and perquisites of official position along with an idealized obligation to remonstrate against official wrongdoing. Hu became involved in the movement for revolution in 1936 at age 20 and became a journalist and later an editor in the Yan'an revolutionary base area. Like his scholar-bureaucrat predecessors, he accepted the fundamental legitimacy of the political system and worked to consolidate its basic institutions.

It was not until the Cultural Revolution, when Hu and other obedient party colleagues suffered severe persecution, that he began to question the party's authority. In its aftermath, Hu publicly and repeatedly criticized the Communist Party at meetings and in articles. He emphasized that when the party's interests and the public's interests diverge, as they did in the Cultural Revolution, the media have the responsibility to side with the public over the party. Although Hu served as editor-in-chief of the party's premier newspaper, *People's Daily,* in the late 1970s and early 1980s, he was dismissed in 1983 for defying party orders. He then sought to establish a national press law to guarantee freedom of expression. In opposition to the party's position that freedom of the press would encourage social turmoil, Polumbaum quotes Hu as arguing that, on the contrary, press freedom would minimize unrest by providing a safe outlet for people to vent their dissatisfaction. In addition, as a member of the Standing Committee of the National People's Congress (NPC), Hu sought to use that institution to negotiate an end to the 1989 demonstrations in order to avoid the use of military force. Polumbaum sums up the transformation in Hu's conception of a good citizen *(gongmin)* in the aftermath of the Cultural Revolution: when faced with official wrongdoing, one acts according to individual conscience and does not defer to authority.

Although few other groups and individuals in post-Mao China articulated such a coherent view of citizenship, they expressed similar ideas through their actions. Kevin O'Brien, in his chapter on village elections, points out that ordinary Chinese are adept at taking advantage of government commitments and legitimating myths for their own purposes. They have long seized on official rhetoric, whether framed in Confucian or democratic terms, to press claims against abusive power holders. Even in the imperial period, rural people objected to taxes when they felt that local authorities ignored proper collection procedures. Such objections rested on appeals to equity and fairness. As village elections spread through the Chinese countryside in the 1990s, O'Brien notes that villagers likewise pressed for free and fair elections.

Despite the urban connotations of citizenship in both European and Republican Chinese discourse, O'Brien observes that in the West citizenship first appeared in relatively small towns that were more rural than urban. Long before the industrial revolution, rural dwellers sought community autonomy with a high degree of association and participation. O'Brien points out, however, that Chinese villagers do not consider rights as inherent, natural, or inalienable, nor do they disagree with the common Chinese view that rights are granted by the state for societal purposes rather than to protect the individual. They see citizenship *(gongmin quan)* more as a claim to community membership than as a claim to political rights. The expectation is that officials should fulfill their obligations to those below, whereupon those below will reciprocate with loyalty to those above. O'Brien explains that villagers display a specific sense of citizenship rights in dispensing with corrupt officials and demanding accountability in their elected leaders. As a consequence, leaders find that in order to win villagers' support, they must open the account books to show how taxes are spent. Even more significant, as villagers have become aware of the Organic Law of 1987 that approved village elections, and of local regulations granting certain protections, they have increasingly challenged improper electoral procedures, using the vocabulary of rights discourse. At present, villagers mainly demand entry into local politics; they seldom press for wider civil and political rights to association, expression, and participation. Nevertheless, while Chinese villagers may not regard such rights as inherent, O'Brien concludes that in their practice they are creating the status of citizens.

The development of a sense of citizenship in rural China becomes even more complicated when we consider minority areas. The chapter by Chih-yu Shih illustrates the wide variation in minority responses to recent state-sponsored initiatives. Looking first at three sites in Yunnan province (Xishuangbanna, Dali, and Lijiang), Shih shows how the effort to instill "citizenship"—in the form of state-imposed education—may create alienation, rather than assimilation, among target populations. The Wuzhong Muslims present a contrasting case, however, in which ethnic identity has proved remarkably compatible with both the economic and the political goals of the state's "civilizing" effort. In Yongshun, the Communist state has actively revived previously dormant ethnic identities among the Miao and Tujia through its policy of providing special privileges to minorities. Finally, in Taiwan a new sense of ethnic awareness has been stimulated by political initiatives from aspiring politicians anxious to create a basis for Taiwan's independence.

Private entrepreneurs are another group for whom a nascent sense of rights represents a practical response to state initiatives. Their emergence with China's move to the market is responsible for much of China's economic growth and job creation in the late twentieth century. As with other social groups, the state has created a variety of business associations to ensure that private entrepreneurs will act as agents of the state. Although some studies suggest that crony or bureaucratic capitalism is the main form of business organization in post-Mao China,[23] Bruce Dickson shows in his chapter on private entrepreneurs that certain entrepreneurial organizations have also become effective advocates for their members' interests. Businessmen are still closely interconnected with the state, particularly in partnerships with local officials, and have no legally enforced rights. Nevertheless, Dickson shows that while entrepreneurs cooperate with local party and government officials, they do not necessarily share the beliefs of those officials. They have not converted their economic influence into political power, but they express an evolving concept of organized interests and a willingness to use their associations to address specific business concerns. Dickson concludes that it is not yet clear whether private entrepreneurs will also use their associations to promote collective action on political issues, or whether they will confine their purview to purely economic interests.

The legal system is another arena in which state-initiated reforms have created new space for grassroots activism. Margaret Woo's chapter focuses on the interrelation of gender, law, and citizenship to show how the legal system has helped some women to achieve citizens' rights. The move to the market has led to a decline in benefits and protection for many Chinese women. Nevertheless, Woo points out that changes in the legal system accompanying marketization have generated opportunities for women to assert their legal rights and heighten their "rights consciousness." In contrast to the instrumental considerations that underlie the recent assertion of rights by villagers, entrepreneurs, and minority groups (as described by O'Brien, Dickson, and Shih), Chinese women appear to be motivated more by social concerns. The women involved in this process are more financially independent and more urban than rural. Yet, as with other groups, their nascent rights consciousness is in jeopardy, Woo fears, because it depends on the development of further institutional and legal support. Still, the increased use of the courts, in which problems are defined and solutions determined, makes women's litigation a potentially important route for expanding citizens' rights. So far, Woo explains, women are more likely to turn to the courts as a means to assert personal rights, as in marriage or personal injury, than to assert broader economic rights in such matters as labor protection and land use. Nevertheless, the very fact that women look to the courts for redress is the beginning, Woo believes, of a broader rights consciousness.

Yu Xingzhong points out in his chapter on law and citizenship that the notion of equal political rights, consciously claimed and enjoyed by all members of the community, is weak in contemporary China. This is both a result of China's historical heritage, which had no concept of individual rights, and a result of the imposition in the Maoist era of strong state control over virtually all activities. China has yet to establish laws and regulations, Yu notes, that effectively protect citizens' rights. Nevertheless, he detects a few moves in that direction. China's 1982 constitution, for example, placed a section on citizens' rights before the section on the state, whereas the previous constitution of 1975 had put the section on citizens' rights near the end. More important, those rights have been enlarged. The 1982 constitution lists such political and civil rights as electoral rights, freedom of speech, public assembly, association, demonstration, and personal and religious freedom. Since the 1990s, the state has also allowed ordinary people to sue local officials as stipulated in the Administrative Litigation Law. Yu concludes, however, that the legal framework that would enable genuine citizen participation in the management of political and social life remains largely on paper. Thus, although China is moving steadily toward a legal system intended to buttress its new market economy, its population still lacks a developed sense of individual rights and a legal system capable of enforcing them.

In his chapter on the National People's Congress, Michael Dowdle adopts an institutional approach to citizenship. Dowdle describes the structures and incentives in the NPC that he believes encourage new political norms, including citizenship. Although a rubber-stamp legislature in the Mao era, the NPC has gradually become more asssertive and innovative under strong leaders in the post-Mao era. Dowdle details various procedures used by the NPC, such as committee hearings and advisory groups, which encourage input from private or non-governmental actors into legislative drafting. Such procedures, Dowdle asserts, help foster new norms for political participation. Even though these procedures have developed more for utilitarian than for ideological reasons, they have inadvertently encouraged wider participation in political activities.

In the case of Taiwan, Shelley Rigger points out that institutional reforms have been accompanied by changes in political culture and civil society. As Taiwan gradually dismantled the emergency provisions that the Guomindang had used to restrict democracy, and as a powerful movement coalesced to seek political citizenship for the Taiwanese, the Guomindang leadership in 1987 recognized an opposition political party. These changes built on competitive local elections, begun in the 1950s, brought the Taiwanese into the political system and reinforced the community solidarity and self-reliance that characterize Taiwan's civil society. They also created a sense of entitlement that encouraged the Taiwanese, voters as well as candidates, to think of their participation in elections and policy-making on the local level as rights that expanded to the national level by the late 1980s. Thus, the Guomindang authoritarian government gradually enlarged and transformed institutions that had once limited freedom and popular participation. By the end of the twentieth century, the people of Taiwan viewed citizenship *(gongmin quan)* as incorporating substantive political rights.

Whereas people on Taiwan at the beginning of the twenty-first century had to some degree laid claim to all three kinds of citizenship described by Marshall, the essays in this volume suggest that in the People's Republic of China, civil and political citizenship still lag behind social citizenship. In any political system, enlarging the scope of citizenship requires prolonged popular struggle and top-down as well as bottom-up pressure. Although Chinese political thought has generally conceived of rights as concessions rather than as entitlements, that view shows some signs of change in the post-Mao era. Certain groups, including a small number of intellectuals and some members of the Cultural Revolution generation, have begun to think of citizenship *(gongmin quan)* as the assertion of political and civil rights. Equally significant is the fact that many for whom citizenship may not hold this meaning are managing through their concrete actions in village elections, entrepreneurial organizations, and lawsuits to exercise and expand such rights.

As the chapters in this volume indicate, both the meaning and the practice of citizenship are highly susceptible to redefinition and renegotiation by state and societal actors alike. Rather than seeing this as an evolutionary development that progresses from one stage to the next, as Marshall's depiction of citizenship in Western Europe would suggest, we might better approach it as an uncertain and irregular process which is shaped by past history, contemporary challenges, and international influences—but whose future is never entirely predictable on the basis of any of these factors.

Historical developments over the last century have at various junctures encouraged ordinary people in China to confront power in order to improve their standing vis-à-vis the state. Today, as during the

Republican period, changes in popular consciousness and a growing sense of entitlement as exhibited through actions, more than words, suggest that important elements of the Chinese populace are adopting a definition of citizenship that includes the exercise of political rights, determined not only by the state but also by their own initiatives. If one looks at another Chinese society, namely Hong Kong, one finds that its inhabitants achieved a degree of citizenship based on legal rights. Although introduced by the British, these rights were sustained after their departure by an independent judiciary through the efforts of indigenous citizens. By contrast, in Taiwan the legal system is far from autonomous. There, as shown in Shelley Rigger's chapter, people have acquired citizenship by means of popular protest, competitive elections, a multi-party system, and a free press.

Yet as China's experience of the past century makes all too clear, participatory stirrings do not necessarily imply democratic outcomes. The discourse and practice of citizenship have buttressed nationalist agendas as well as democratic ones. Moreover, exclusionary lines have been drawn on the basis of gender, ethnicity, class, political loyalty, urban residency, and other factors. The variations that we discover in the case of China stand as a stark reminder that "modern citizenship" is a highly protean phenomenon, capable of assuming many different forms. Developments during the Republican era and more recently on Taiwan demonstrate that Chinese political culture does not pose an insuperable barrier to democratic conceptions of citizenship. Nevertheless, China's past century of rapid change and regional variation cautions against any facile assumption that the practice of citizenship must lead inevitably or uniformly in liberal democratic directions.

I | Imperial and Republican China

1 | Citizens or Mothers of Citizens? Gender and the Meaning of Modern Chinese Citizenship

Once women's schools were initiated,
the embryo of our nation's citizens was created.
—Wuben nüshu, school song, c. 1902

Modern Chinese conceptions of citizenship were consciously and inextricably connected to notions of gender. In contrast to Western societies, where issues of women's rights and female education were not fully addressed until almost a century after modern ideas of citizenship were put forward, in China "the women's question" and "the citizenship question" were treated simultaneously.[1] This was largely because Chinese political and cultural elites had imported the entire trajectory of Western rights thinking—from the Enlightenment through the late nineteenth century—into China at once and at a time of national crisis. Directly linking the problem of creating a modern citizenry to the problem of integrating women into the modern polity, these elites considered both to be integral to the early twentieth-century project of national strengthening.

These late Qing elites attempted to mobilize women both as concrete historical actors whose abilities were needed in this effort of national strengthening, and as a potent symbol capable of integrating the two competing "knowledge cultures" which served as the basis of modern Chinese notions of citizenship.[2] These knowledge cultures, which I will call "modern nationalism" and "Confucian familism," came into contact when Western rights thinking was introduced into China in the late nineteenth and early twentieth centuries. Giving rise to a contested sense of what was historically possible and culturally desirable in early twentieth-century China, they fueled the dual and often contradictory objectives of the late Qing reform project: the need to assert China's political position in the international arena while preserving its cultural integrity.

As historical actors, Chinese women would play a central role in reconciling these contradictions. Because they were virgin political actors in the early twentieth century, their new role as "female citizens" was open to limitless manipulations. And because they remained the fundamental source of social and cultural reproduction, their participation as feminine *guomin* (citizens) lent authenticity to the uncertain process of forging new national identities. The timeless symbol of Woman was also central to the process of integrating the spatial and temporal economies of family and nation, "Confucian" and "modern" values. This would bring a new cohesiveness to an empire that had been rigidly divided into domestic and public spheres by linking home and the world, and it would harmonize uneven cultural tempos as Western ideas were adopted and elements of China's past reappropriated in the process of building the new Chinese nation.

The unrealistic burden placed on China's new female citizen is most evident in the objectives of late Qing female education: the transformative project that would mold China's girls and women into citizens or mothers of citizens. Promoters of female education called on young women to practice reproductive and physical education in order to strengthen the race, and to expand their knowledge of the nation in order to become good patriots. Textbooks encouraged young female students to emulate foreign and Chinese women, to model themselves on exemplars of civil and military, past and present values. Late Qing cultural and educational authorities instructed young students to shed reprehensible past practices and restore China's cultural greatness, calling on the "new women" to fashion—and signal—a respectable modernity for all of China's future citizens.

In the pages that follow, I will examine the strategies that educators and political elites used to integrate women into the new citizenship ideal, focusing on how diverse late Qing prescriptions for women's roles illuminate the tensions and ambiguities in the meaning of modern Chinese citizenship. The sources of my analysis include late Qing textbooks for females and males, citizens' readers, official documents, and essays written from a broad spectrum of political positions on female education and citizenship.

Competing Representations of Women and the Nation

Notions of both citizenship and gender roles were widely contested in early twentieth-century China. For heuristic purposes, I will isolate three groups—conservative officials, moderate reformers, and radical revolutionaries—who dominated the late Qing political-cultural field. Their conceptual universes reflected the two predominant knowledge cultures of the period. The conservatives' perspective could be defined as "Confucian familism," the moderates' as "Confucian nationalism," and the radicals' as "revolutionary nationalism." Members of these groups were distinguished, in part, by their divergent conceptions of female roles, specifically, the degree to which they believed women should be integrated into the new citizenry. Whereas conservatives advocated that women should serve exclusively as "good wives and wise mothers" *(liangqi xianmu)* who would be principally concerned with the domestic realm, moderates promoted the formation of "mothers of citizens" *(guomin zhi mu)* who would be indirectly involved in national politics, and the more radical visionaries called directly for the acceptance of women as "female citizens" *(nü guomin or nüzi guomin)*.[3]

The conservative position was revealed in official documents related to female education. Two of the most important of these were a 1904 memorial put forward by the officials Rong-qing, Zhang Baixi, and Zhang Zhidong entitled "Regulations for Early Training Schools and for Education on Household Matters," and the 1907 official regulations sanctioning the establishment of elementary and normal female schools for the first time in Chinese history. Both the memorial and the regulations voiced opposition to the idea of females becoming citizens with national rights and obligations. They particularly objected to females participating in politics, forming associations, or lecturing in public. As the 1907 regulations stated, women should only receive an education that would enable them to maintain the household and educate their children. They had no need for superfluous knowledge, nor should they "become involved in external matters or form important opinions."[4]

While the conservatives were most concerned with preserving the way of the women as it had existed "since the time of the Three Dynasties," both male and female radical activists called for a categorical break with all past notions of womanhood. The term for "female citizens" signified this rupture with the past. "From the time when Cang Jie invented Chinese characters four to five thousand years ago," the female editor of a radical women's journal wrote, "the four characters *nüzi guomin* (female citizen) have never been used together."[5] This new title signified unprecedented political and social roles for Chinese women, roles which radical female nationalists had already begun to assume. He Xiangning, for example, was the first woman to join Sun Yat-sen's Tongmeng hui in 1905; Lü Bicheng became the head teacher at the Beiyang Women's Academy *(nüzi gongxue tang);* and Lin Zongsu, who was active in the Fujian Women's Study Society, would become a leader of the women's suffrage movement in 1912. These radical women all called for the recognition of women's rights and national responsibilities as equal to men's.[6]

The reformists, whose position was in between that of the conservatives and that of the radicals, called for women to play a mediated and indirect role in the polity as mothers of citizens. This formulation simultaneously relegated women to the margins of the nationalist project, by not directly naming them as citizens, and placed them at the heart of the new nation as the biological and moral progenitors of a new citizenry. The inherent ambivalence of this concept also made it the most flexible and usable. It served, therefore, as the dominant representation of women at this time, becoming the "applied gender ideology" in textbooks of the period.[7] I will focus my analysis in this chapter on the concept of "mothers of citizens" both because it was the dominant representation of the period, and because I believe it most effectively highlights the tensions between family and nation, "Confucian" and "Western" values which infused modern Chinese ideas of citizenship.

Defining the relationship between women and the nation in terms of motherhood—mothers of citizens—the late Qing reformists simultaneously naturalized the woman's new political role and politicized her natural maternal role.[8] Integrating citizenship into the female life cycle, they gave the most intimate of human relationships—that of mother to child—a political meaning. A late Qing textbook for girls and women explained that women could best fulfill their responsibilities as citizens by assuming—rather than abandoning—their relational domestic roles. The text criticized elite women in the treaty port cities, who had become unnaturally politicized. Consumed with "extravagant conversations about patriotism and eloquent discussions of the salvation of the collective," these women neglected their household and maternal obligations, not realizing that the nation was nothing more than "an aggregation of families." The text warned that "if women did not treat their household and children as priorities," the nation would never be sufficiently strengthened and unified to survive.[9]

The Chinese concept of mothers of citizens thus emphasized the public ramifications of women's private roles, a principle that was central to the post-revolutionary French and American ideal of Republican Motherhood.[10] Both the Chinese and Western formulations served as devices which integrated domesticity and politics, and inserted women into historical time and political theory. The linkage of motherhood and citizenship was nonetheless rife with paradoxes, which, in the Chinese case, arose from the reformists' efforts to negotiate a position between the conservative and radical factions. On the one hand, the politicization of motherhood marked new possibilities for women as national actors, allowing Chinese reformists to open up the question of the status of women in twentieth-century society despite conservative resistance. On the other hand, it foreclosed the option of full female political participation, making it possible for the reformists to circumvent the radical concept of *nü guomin*.[11]

The Transformative Power of Education: Making Mothers into Mothers of Citizens

Despite the profound differences in the conservative, reformist, and radical conceptions of women's roles in the new national polity, all three groups considered education to be the key to preparing women for these new roles. The reformer Liang Qichao made the most celebrated and direct plea for women's education in 1897, arguing that it would eliminate female economic dependence on men.[12] Even the conservative officials Rong-qing, Zhang Baixi, and Zhang Zhidong put forward a proposal—albeit very restricted—for the education of girls and women in their 1904 memorial as a means of strengthening the Chinese citizenry.[13] Radical authors like Liu Yazi articulated the most far-reaching objectives for female education, which they heralded as a means of restoring rights that women had ostensibly possessed in primitive Chinese society.[14]

This shared commitment to education reflects, in part, the enduring influence of the Confucian knowledge culture on modern Chinese conceptions of citizenship: since the time of Confucius, Chinese culture had privileged education as the most effective means of personal, social, and political transformation.[15] In the context of late Qing nationalism, this Confucian emphasis on education was evident in modern conceptions of rights: Chinese elites contended that political rights presupposed abilities which were the product of a certain degree of education. In the Chinese world view, rights were not natural and inherent in individual personhood but rather were contingent, to be granted in accordance with the individual's demonstrated ability to excercise them effectively. An author named Dan Chen wrote in a women's journal that it was less worrisome that Chinese women lacked rights than it was that they lacked the education which would qualify them to use effectively whatever rights they might be granted. Using language representative of rights thinking in this period, Dan asserted that "to speak to uneducated women of rights is like speaking to children about freedom, or to farmers about popular empowerment."[16]

The reformists used this argument for the predication of rights on abilities to justify their limited appeals for women's rights. Late Qing textbooks presented equal rights as a distant foreign phenomenon enjoyed by Western women but not yet attainable by Chinese. While women "in England and America have freedom of speech and freedom of action," one text explained, Chinese women could not expect to enjoy these freedoms until they became qualified to do so. Before they could "seek freedom they had to attempt to understand principles. And in order to understand principles, they had to study."[17] The right to free marriage was also presented as contingent on a certain level of education. One textbook explained that free marriage was possible in the West because "both men and women were learned and literate." In China, however, illiterate women would be easily deceived by profligates, and the practice would degenerate into "dissolution and debauchery."[18]

Reformists and radicals who were at least rhetorically committed to the expansion of women's rights thus considered education to be the crucial first step in preparing Chinese women to exercise those rights enjoyed by female citizens in the West. Members of these two groups were responsible for establishing the first Chinese-run women's schools in Shanghai in the last years of the nineteenth century. These schools were progressive by definition, one of their prime objectives being the integration of women into the new Chinese citizenry. A number of these schools—most notably the Aiguo nüxue (Patriotic Women's School) founded by Cai Yuanpei and others in 1902—had revolutionary leanings.[19] The Wuben nüshu, which was established by Wu Xin (Huijiu) in 1902, also had radical young women among its students despite its emphasis on household education and the cultivation of good wives and wise mothers.[20] Associations for female education that were founded in Shanghai, Fujian, Guangdong, and Zhejiang in this early period were also generally associated with radical groups who supported the promotion of women's rights.[21]

The Qing government finally sanctioned the implementation of a formal system of elementary and normal education for girls and women in 1907 in order to co-opt this growing and radicalized movement for female education.[22] The government's educational objective was to preserve "the way of daughters, wives, mothers" rather than to prepare women for the assumption of political rights.[23] Their sanctioning of female education, nonetheless, helped to open up new spaces where reformists and radicals could promote their conceptions of female citizenship. The number of Chinese-run women's schools rose dramatically in this period, from 6 schools in 1903 to 512 in 1908, while the number of female students increased from some 40 in 1903, to 20,557 in 1908, and to 141,130 by 1912.[24] There was still a tremendous difference between the number of girls and boys being educated, however: in 1907 there were some 37,672 boys' schools and 1,013,571 male students, and in 1912 there were 2,790,000 boys attending school.[25]

The late Qing commitment to education as the transformative process that would prepare young students to assume the rights and duties of citizenship is manifest in private and government-approved teaching materials produced in this period. Most notable is the new genre of vernacular texts called *guomin bidu* or citizens' readers. One of the earlier texts—entitled *Guomin bidu*—was written in the vernacular by Chen Baoquan and Gao Buying and published in 1905. Targeting a general audience, it defined basic terms such as *guomin* and *guojia* (nation-state) and emphasized such principles as loyalty to the ruler and devotion to the national cause.[26] In 1908 and 1909 the Shanghai-based Constitutional Preparation Association (Yubei lixian gonghui) published two editions of a *Gongmin bidu* (Citizens' reader) which was aimed at individuals with a higher level of education than the readers of Chen and Gao's text—local self-government deputies, local managers, and provincial assembly deputies—which probably explains the use of the term *gongmin* rather than *guomin*.[27] The government also became involved in this process in 1908 when the Board of Education announced the publication of its own citizens' reader in keeping with the dynasty's 1906 Nine-Year Constitutional Preparation Program.[28] These texts did not explicitly target a female audience,[29] nor were they listed in any of the curricula for female schools from the period. They were, however, read by both males and females. The scholar and writer Chen Hengzhe (1890–1976) recorded, for example, that she had studied a text entitled *Guomin duben* (Citizens' reader) with a progressive uncle in Guangdong in 1903 before she enrolled in one of the new schools for girls in Shanghai.[30]

Although no late Qing texts were specifically labeled as citizens' readers for women, female ethics textbooks *(nüzi xiushen jiaokeshu)* and readers *(duben)* published in the early twentieth century all promoted ideas related to female citizenship.[31] The primary objective of these texts was to raise the readers' awareness of the connection between women and the nation. This is reflected in their standard opening line: "Women are the mothers of citizens." A 1906 ethics textbook stated in its first lesson, for example, that "China will

only produce quality children if its mothers are of high quality."
Since these children would become members of the Chinese citizenry, "what could be more important than the education of females?"[32] Women were the crucial link between the domestic sphere
where China's future citizens would be raised and the international
arena where these citizens would eventually defend China's national
honor. "If female education is developed," the textbook continued,
"human talent increases. And when human talent increases, the nation is strong."[33]

Citizens or Nationals?

This brief introduction to the content of late Qing textbooks for
girls and women reveals the extent to which the reformists' anxieties about China's place in the international arena informed the
concept of *guomin zhi mu*. Convinced that the weakness and ignorance of China's women was one of the sources of its national weakness, these reformists also believed that "the prosperity of Japan and
the Western nations could be attributed to the advanced state of female education in those countries."[34] This global contextualization
of female citizenship points to one of the key features of modern
Chinese citizenship. Whereas Western ideas of citizenship were, from
the seventeenth century, defined within the national arena—that is,
the concept of citizenship developed only as national citizenship—
and the local arena is now being considered as a crucial forum for
the development of ideas of rights, in early twentieth-century China,
by contrast, the international context was most crucial in framing
ideas of Chinese citizenship, male and female.[35] China's future citizens were not viewed as separate individuals endowed with the right
to press particular claims against the nation-state, but as a group of
individuals obliged to defend the nation's rights in the international
arena. This is reflected in the use of the term *guomin*—literally, people of the nation—to denote the Western concept of citizenry in this
period.[36] Unlike the terms later and more properly used for citizen
such as *gongmin* (public persons), or *shimin* (urban or city persons),
the term *guomin* did not signify an individual within the nation but
rather a collective entity whose identity was virtually conflated with
that of the nation.[37] As Chen and Gao's 1905 *Citizens' Reader* ex-

plained, the *guomin* and the nation *(guojia)* "cannot be separated from one another. The reputations, interests, honor, and dishonor of the nation and the people are one."[38]

This intimate connection between notions of citizenship and the existence of the nation as a physical entity is highlighted by the discourse on mothers of citizens. According to this discourse, the woman's connection to the citizenry was first and foremost biological and racial, and thus fundamentally pre-political. A female ethics textbook explained that, as mothers of citizens, women alone had the ability to "elevate [the Chinese] race to the highest level" and ensure its position "in the ranks of the superior nations." The physical state of Chinese women would determine the fate of the nation and the quality of the race.[39] The "quality of the race" was clearly defined in this discourse in physiological rather than in moral or intellectual terms. Even the devoted female educator Lü Bicheng asserted that the quality of citizens had less to do with the mother's moral or intellectual influence on her children than it did with reproductive education.[40]

This ideal of female citizenship as biological and racial in content gave rise to a new conception of the female body and to new feminine physical practices in the late Qing period. Women were no longer valued for their delicacy, weakness, and refined adornment, but for their robust healthiness, rosy cheeks, and dignified bearing. In order to achieve this new feminine physicality, late Qing educators promoted physical education for girls and women and advocated the abolition of footbinding. The early Chinese women's schools generally included some form of physical education in their curricula, and some even held athletic meets with foot races.[41] The Board of Education also recognized the importance of female physical health and included physical education classes as part of the curricula outlined in the 1907 regulations.[42]

Late Qing textbooks for girls and women all included lessons on physical education which explicitly tied feminine physical improvement to national strengthening. According to one textbook, while "physical education is important for both males and females, women are the mothers of citizens. The superiority or inferiority of their physical health is thus linked to the strength or weakness of the citizenry."[43] In addition to general textbooks, specialized texts exclusively devoted to female physical education were also published in this period. Underlining the foreignness of the concept of female physical education, many of these texts were translations. The *Nüzi ticao jiaokeshu* (Girls' physical training), for example, was written by an English woman, Alice R. James; it was first translated into Japanese by Shirai Kikurō and then into Chinese by Cai Yun. By 1908, however, the Chinese were less dependent on foreign expertise in this area. They were able to train their own physical education teachers at schools such as the Nüzi ticao xuexiao (Girl's school for physical training), founded in Shanghai by an ex-overseas female student in Japan, Tang Linren.[44]

This emphasis on physical education as part of the new female citizenship ideal served as an important impetus to the late Qing anti-footbinding movement. The early, private schools for girls and women broadly promoted this movement.[45] The Wuben Women's School had an anti-footbinding policy which was said to have attracted many students, for example, and some schools popularized songs with titles like "Song of Unbinding Feet" (Fangzu ge).[46] Textbooks of the period drew a direct link between footbinding and national weakness. Because women bound their feet, one text explained, their bodies were weak. And because these weak-bodied women bore sons, their sons were also weak, and ultimately, the entire population was enfeebled.[47] In addition to presenting these general admonitions against the practice of footbinding, a number of textbooks offered concrete advice to young women who wanted to unbind their feet. One included a special supplement with precise instructions on the unbinding process, for example.[48] The Manchu government (which had never supported the practice because its own women had no tradition of binding their feet) also contributed to the movement by prohibiting footbinding in its 1907 regulations on women's schools.

China's new mothers of citizens were expected to have more than an embodied and biological link to the nation, however. They were also expected to cultivate a sense of national pride and an understanding of fundamental national issues. "Females are also citizens and should understand the meaning of patriotism," one ethics textbook explained.[49] This sense of patriotism would be founded first of all on an understanding of the international context. One ethics textbook used a map to situate China in the world for the students. The text accompanying the illustration explained that although the "Chinese often call China all under heaven, it is only one country in East Asia."[50] In a similar fashion, another text stated that "China is not alone in the world." In dealing with foreigners, it must learn to "study their good methods and not become their slaves."[51] Other texts attempted to foster a sense of China's place in the world by providing lessons in world geography.[52]

The textbooks also instructed their readers, the future mothers of China's future citizens, on China's own geography and history. One textbook author explained that local regions were connected to the greater national entity called China. While I am from Nanxun, he noted, "Nanxun is in the county of Wucheng which is in the prefecture of Huzhou which is in the province of Zhejiang which is in the nation, China." As a result of this geographic embeddedness, "the glory or the shame of China is mine. [Regardless of whether] I am a woman [or a man] I have a responsibility to protect China."[53] Another text provided its female readers with an overview of the various regions of China, from the coast to the hinterland, in the guise of the account of a traveler.[54] A number of textbooks also introduced chapters from China's national history. One presented a series of detailed lessons on consecutive periods of Chinese history, from the ancient through the modern era. The more recent accounts included critical discussions of such sensitive issues as the 1894–1895 Sino-Japanese War, the 1898 reforms, and the Boxer Rebellion.[55]

The late Qing textbooks for girls and women also attempted to include their female readers in the "community of consciousness" that would serve as the cement of the new Chinese nation and the basis for unified action. They provided a thorough introduction to the new constitutional idiom and the new discourse on nationalism. One text, for example, provided detailed explanations of the meaning of the terms "nation" and "society," the differences between political systems, the role of an assembly, and the need for laws, taxes, and military service.[56] The textbooks also explained terms relevant to new understandings of society, such as public and private.[57]

The introduction of female readers to this vast store of new knowledge would certainly improve their understanding of national issues. Its ultimate target was not the women themselves, however, but their future offspring: a female patriot was one who transmitted patriotic values to her sons.[58] An essay on female education explained that patriotism began in the home. "The most important aspect of education in the home" was the inculcation of "national thinking" and a "conception of the collective." When young men who were reared in this kind of household went out into the world, they would certainly have much to contribute to the nation.[59] Many authors used the classic formulation of the Spartan mother to describe the woman's responsibility to raise sons prepared to sacrifice themselves for the nation.[60]

In addition to promoting these indirect expressions of female patriotism through the transmission of national values or biological reproduction, some proponents of the late Qing discourse on mothers of citizens encouraged informal political participation by appealing to women to take part in specific regional and national political struggles. This participation was not understood in terms of women's assertion of their own political rights, however. Rather, it was represented as their contribution to the defense of China's national rights. In a lesson on "Aiguo xin tuanli" (Patriotism through group strength) in one of the ethics textbooks, for example, the accompanying illustration placed women directly in the public political domain. It depicted both men and women at a meeting of a commerce association, flanked by two banners that read "Wanhui guoshi zai jie tuanti" (Restore national strength by forming organizations) and "Buyong Meihuo jianchi daodi" (Hold out against using American products until the end).[61] In a lesson written in the form of a letter and entitled "Quan tongxue jiemei gou tielu gupiao shu" (Exhortation to fellow female students to buy stock in the railway), another text appealed to its readers to join the Nüjie baolu hui (Women's Railway Protection Association) in order to recover China's rights to the Suzhou-Hangzhou-Ningbo Railway.[62] One reader for girls and women appended its call to patriotic action to an account of the life of Florence Nightingale. The final lines of the biography and, rather dramatically, of the reader itself are as follows: "Alas, Florence died some five years ago. The people of Western Europe have been enriched by her kindness and Japanese women are continuing her work [in East Asia]. At this time, mighty and crafty Russia is again extending its claws into the east, ensuring that the north of China will be a bloody battlefield in the future. The women of China have risen up on hearing the news and embrace Florence's ambition." The author thus encouraged his female readers to join their sisters—in China, students at Aiguo nüxuexiao, and, in Japan, members of the Gongaihui (Humanitarian Association)—who had organized to protest the massing of Russian troops in Manchuria after the Boxer Rebellion.[63]

Late Qing women were also called upon to express their allegiance to the nation by making contributions of money or personal belongings to the national cause.[64] The locus classicus for such action was a tale about Mencius's mother (Meng Mu). In a lesson on female acts of bravery, a reader recorded how Mencius's mother sold her hairpins and ear ornaments in order to buy meat for her son, thus contributing to his ability to study and, ultimately, to the national cultural heritage.[65] Late Qing writers also used more current examples to attempt to encourage this mode of informal female political participation. "In the face of the current Russian challenge," Liu Yazi wrote, "lower-level Japanese prostitutes willingly pawned their clothing and jewelry in order to contribute funds to the government. Why is it our Chinese women are not as devoted as Japanese prostitutes?"[66] A number of late Qing women did respond to this challenge. One reader documented how "women went so far as to sell their hairpins, ear ornaments, and clothing in order to buy stock in the Suzhou-Hangzhou-Ningbo Railway."[67]

Female political citizenship was thus construed in terms of national duties rather than personal rights. The same was true for female social citizenship, which focused on the woman's obligation to make a contribution to society rather than on her rights to work or to consumption. Reformists and radicals argued that in order for women to become patriotic citizens, they had to be economically independent. As noted earlier, Liang Qichao made this argument first in his essay "Lun nüxue" in 1897. Establishing what would become a common trope in later essays on women's education, Liang claimed that women had to be transformed from parasites to producers, from helpless creatures who lived off the labor of their fathers or husbands to economically independent individuals. Ignoring the important role that women had actually played in the family economy in the past, Liang thus established clear links between the state of female education, women's ability to contribute to the national economy, and the state of the nation.[68]

Despite these general calls for Chinese women to follow their Western counterparts and become economically more productive, there was great resistance in the late Qing period, by reformists as well as conservatives, to female vocational education. With the exception of fledgling schools established by radicals—such as the Nüzi shiye xuetang (Female Occupational School) founded by the Cantonese doctor and revolutionary Zhang Zhujun in Guangdong early in the twentieth century—the only vocational schools for women were normal schools. The scope of sanctioned women's work in the early twentieth century was thus limited to teaching.[69] The reason for this resistance is evident. Late Qing cultural and political authorities recognized—as did radical women like Zhang Zhujun and Lü Bicheng, and as Mary Wollstonecraft had in the *Vindication of the Rights of Woman* in 1792—that women's economic independence was a precondition of female political independence.[70]

The Female Citizen as Source of Integration

The reformists did not view mothers of citizens as individual actors who would further disperse the political and social field through their economic or political independence, but as the unifiers of foreign and Chinese cultural practices, past and present values, private and public spheres.

The concept of mothers of citizens was itself derived from a culturally hybrid range of sources. Writers of the period claimed that the term *guomin zhi mu* had originated in the West.[71] And a number of Western heroines—from queens to anarchists, from Joan of Arc and Florence Nightingale to Charlotte Corday and Louise Michel—were featured in textbooks and essays of the time as models for China's new female citizens. These exotic and "modern" Western models were, however, presented in tandem with legendary and historical Chinese exemplars dating back to the Han dynasty.[72] The editor of a textbook which combined the biographies of Chinese women with Western heroines explained the rationale for using this method. While the Chinese historical exemplars highlighted in the text would serve as "the past leaders of our new Chinese women citizens," he stated, the foreign women would represent "their future image."[73] The objective of this strategy was thus to create a universal category of female citizen which would incorporate the dualities of East and West, the essential and the evolving.[74]

The highly different ways in which the Western and Chinese heroines functioned in the late Qing ideal of female citizenship reveal the competing forces the new Chinese woman was expected to embody: family and nation, "Confucian" and "Western" values. No Chinese women were celebrated for their political roles—with the exception of Huang Chonggu of the kingdom of Shu (908–925), who had to disguise herself as a man to do so, and Wu Zetian, who is presented as a licentious usurper[75]—and no foreign women were featured for their role within the family. The Western models, who were almost exclusively heralded for their bold interventions in the public sphere, helped to expand the imagined possibilities for young Chinese women into the realms of direct social action and political participation. Chinese heroines, on the other hand, who were mostly celebrated for their ability to influence public affairs through their private actions, represented the restriction of feminine conduct to roles defined by the female life cycle: daughter, wife, and most significantly, mother. Demonstrating the overriding importance of female domesticity even in the new global context, Mencius's mother, the quintessential Chinese maternal exemplar, was the most celebrated presence in the late Qing textbooks—at least one and more frequently two or three chapters were devoted to her in almost all of these texts—and in essays from across the political spectrum.[76]

Mencius's mother was not only celebrated for linking the private and public spheres by judiciously raising one of the most prominent figures in the Chinese cultural heritage, however. She also symbolized the relevance of China's cultural past to the nationalist present. As mentioned earlier, one late Qing text described how she sold her hairpins and ear ornaments—details which do not appear in the original story—in order to buy meat for her son. This representation of Mencius's mother engaged in a practice which had become recognized as an expression of early twentieth-century female patriotism —the sale of personal effects to benefit the public welfare—was a means of linking this cultural heroine to the nationalist movement.[77]

The practice of using ancient feminine images to define the modern female citizen was a prevalent strategy in reformist texts of this period. It was a means of reconciling the dual objectives of nationalism by mobilizing resources from China's cultural past to create a new political identity in the present.[78] The author of one ethics textbook admonished his readers for not being as patriotic as the daughter of Qi Shi celebrated in the Han dynasty text, the *Lienü zhuan,* for the deep concern she expressed for her "nation," the state of Lu.[79] Another textbook author linked past to present by explaining that as "mothers of citizens" women must "cultivate a self-respecting ethical nature worthy of those the ancients called the paragons of the great families." He declared that in the present, as in the distant past, ethically principled women were the source of national greatness. "The culture of the Zhou was rooted in the inner chambers," he declared, thus linking the women's role in the domestic sphere to one of the most glorious dynasties in Chinese history.[80] In order to qualify as patriots, early twentieth-century Chinese women had to understand not only the ways but the history of the ancient past. "The territory of our nation is Shenzhou, the largest nation in the world," the author of an ethics textbook declared. "Our race is the flourishing *Hua* race which from ancient times was superior to all barbarian races. Patriotic women should also understand this."[81]

The reformists also called upon the future mothers of China's citizens to integrate old and new ethical practices, to serve as both the custodians of the Chinese moral order and the source of a new public morality. Many of the late Qing textbooks for girls and women combined lessons on long-standing Confucian ethical principles— serving one's husband and in-laws, chastity, and righteousness, for example—with a new concern for community, society, and nation. In accordance with the prevailing ethos of the time, they claimed that the preservation of China's unique ethical system which had been "passed on from the ancient sages" was crucial to China's survival as a nation in the early twentieth century. "If the morality of the five relationships is not maintained," one text warned, "the special essence of the nation would be imperiled. Could such a nation be expected to survive?"[82] This long-standing ethical system had to be supplemented, however, by a new sense of public morality *(gongde)* relevant to the demands of the present. The reformists called upon women to play the crucial role of linking the old and new ethical systems. A lesson in a 1908 women's reader on the need for Chinese citizens to develop a sense of public virtue, for example, ended with the statement that, as mothers of citizens, women in particular must grasp the importance of public morality.[83]

This new morality would not only supplement what was of value in China's ancient system of ethics, it would also replace superstitious and religious practices which were considered wasteful, harmful to the collective, and incompatible with the rational, scientific ethos of a "modern" nation. Almost all of the late Qing textbooks included lessons on eliminating "superstition," which was defined as including *fengshui,* the principles of *yin* and *yang,* belief in ghosts and spirits, and folk customs such as the annual festival celebrating the story of the cowherd and the weaver.[84] Buddhist and Daoist religious practices were also targeted.[85] Lessons in the various textbooks ridiculed women who burned incense, visited temples, and worshipped wooden and clay idols in the form of bodhisattvas. They taught that superstition harmed the greater society and the nation by eliminating human responsibility and distracting women from their more pressing practical duties.[86] As one textbook declared, Buddhist priests, Daoist priests, nuns, and practicing Buddhists, together with those who told fortunes, used geomancy, and dissected the meaning of characters and recombined them for predicting the future, were all like grubs in the wood of the nation.[87]

Integrator of public and private virtues, past and present values, the figure of women was also used to bridge the civil and military cultures of *wen* and *wu.* Many of the exemplars—both Chinese and foreign—that the new mothers of citizens were called upon to emulate were more martial than maternal. However, the way these martial heroines were presented ultimately reinforced, rather than undermined, the gender specificity of the fundamental notion of citizenship.[88] Women noted for their military prowess in late Qing reformist texts were not represented as natural women but rather as surrogate men. Just as men had to rid themselves of all effeminate characteristics in order to become citizens, so did women have to be masculinized in order to become heroic. "Without a martial spirit citizens are effeminate, unsoldierly, and useless," a textbook for young boys explained. "If they allow their nature to become effeminate, they will never be capable of defending themselves."[89] In a similar vein, a textbook for girls and women maintained that "a female hero is one who knows what males know and does what males do. A female leader is one who knows what ordinary females cannot know and does what ordinary females cannot do; who knows what ordinary males cannot know and does what ordinary males cannot do."[90]

Courageous feminine exemplars celebrated in late Qing texts were generally represented as either stand-ins for, or disguised as, men. Ti Ying of the Han dynasty, who submitted a petition to free her father from a cruel punishment, spoke out because she had no brothers who could defend her father. Hua Mulan (c. 500 C.E.), the legendary warrior first celebrated in a sixth-century Chinese poem, fought in her father's place when he was ill and could not respond to the emperor's call to arms.[91] Pang E of the Tang dynasty courageously avenged her father's death because her three brothers had died, leaving her to defend the family honor.[92] Women of the past who disguised themselves as men in order to replace their fathers, defend their nations, or serve as officials included—in addition to Hua Mulan and Huang Chonggu[93]—Joan of Arc (1412–1431), who disguised herself in order to lead her French countrymen into battle against the British, and the French anarchist Louise Michel (1830–1905), who fought against the Russians in a soldier's uniform.[94]

Women who served heroically as women to defend the honor of family, community, or nation generally did so in tandem with their husbands. Liang Furen, a female officer of the Southern Song, fought with her husband against the Jin invaders; Xi Furen joined her husband in battle and continued to struggle after his death to defend the "Lingnan minority" in the Southern dynasties; the wife of Li Kan judiciously advised her husband on military strategy; Anita Garibaldi fought with her husband in South America and Italy; and Madame Roland proved herself to be more courageous than her husband and political partner.[95]

When the late Qing texts addressed the issue of militarism in practical rather than idealized terms, they did not appeal to women to take on military roles, but rather to encourage the male members of their families to do so. A lesson in a women's reader on the citizen's duty to serve as a soldier, for example, ended by admonishing "all mothers to encourage their sons, and all wives to rouse their husbands to sacrifice themselves for the army and exert their duties."[96]

Women who did take up arms in the late Qing period were not re-
warded with citizenship. The Republican government refused to recognize the women who served as soldiers in the 1911 Revolution.[97]

Conclusion

Conceptions of Chinese female citizenship did not emerge out of
claims for political participation from below, or struggles for local
economic or legal rights.[98] Rather, they were formulated by cultural
and political elites from above and framed by nationalist and Social
Darwinist concerns. The nature of this driving impetus behind the
late Qing ideal of female citizenship sheds light not only on notions
of female citizenship in this period but on the meaning of modern
Chinese citizenship.

First and foremost, the early twentieth-century idea of citizenship
in China—male or female—was not singular but fractured and multiple, a corollary of the divisions in the late Qing political field. Second, the international arena was the defining context for understandings of late Qing citizenship. The very term used for citizen in
this period, *guomin,* reveals the preoccupation of late Qing elites
with asserting China's position vis-à-vis the foreign powers rather
than ensuring the rights of individual citizens vis-à-vis the nation-
state. Political rights, for example, were construed as rights to act in
the national, rather than the personal, interest. Third, late Qing
elites did not conceive of rights as inherent in individual personhood but as predicated on individual abilities. Advocates of female
education were not concerned with promoting the woman's right to
education per se; rather, they sought to provide women with the
knowledge necessary to assume their national duties. Finally, as the
cultural and historical mix of exemplars and values in representa-
tions of the new female citizenship ideal demonstrates, modern Chinese citizenship was the product of an often discordant merging of
past and present, indigenous and foreign principles.

Although notions of citizenship were defined and imposed from
above—through official documents, school textbooks, and polemi-
cal essays—they nonetheless opened up the space for new social and
cultural practices which would challenge elite conceptions of the individual's role. In the case of women, efforts to prepare young girls

for roles as citizens or mothers of citizens required the establishment of new schools, the encouragement of new fields like physical education, and the elimination of restrictive practices like footbinding. The need to mobilize female energies for the national project further allowed for female participation in patriotic movements, such as the struggle for the recovery of rights to China's railways or the campaign against Russia's encroachment in Manchuria. This participation would have unintended consequences, inspiring women to pursue new forms of unsanctioned political knowledge and offering them firsthand experience of the power of political organization and cooperation. It also provided these women with the opportunity to develop their own subjectivities and their own conception of citizenship, which would continue to be bound, nonetheless, by the confining context of twentieth-century Chinese nationalism.

DAVID STRAND

2 | Citizens in the Audience and at the Podium

On January 1, 1912, four hundred million Chinese subjects of the Qing dynasty became citizens of a republic. Although many, perhaps millions, had participated in events leading up to and including the Wuchang uprising on October 10, 1911, and its revolutionary aftermath, the reality of citizenship took time to sink in.[1] Most were unaware for some weeks, months, or even years that this change had taken place. To some extent, the details involved must have been reassuringly (or disappointingly) familiar. Citizens would continue to pay taxes and obey the law as imperial subjects had done. Other expected behaviors such as voting were less familiar, despite the Qing government's last-minute willingness to hold elections and convene legislative assemblies. The cutting of the Qing queue worn by men may have been the most widespread sign of republican citizenship.[2] What seems certain is that the process whereby subjects became citizens was for the most part uneven and piecemeal. Citizenship emerged in scattered settings where the role of citizen for a moment eclipsed other, more familiar ways of thinking and feeling about the individual's and the group's relationship to the state and to power.

One practice common to both periods and the condition of citizenship that spread unevenly, but also continuously, in turn-of-the-century China was public speaking (*yanshuo*). There is something inevitable, and therefore universal, about the connection between citizenship as a multiform role and this very public form of political communication. Public speaking can flourish under a monarchy. But it is hard to imagine a republic bereft of oratory. Silent conformity may be a typical, if somewhat depressing, feature of most kinds of modern citizenship. But an audience—silent or restive—that listens to a speaker and later claps or heckles or drifts away adds sound and a broader panorama to politics.

As natural and universal as human speech is, the practice of getting up and giving an address to an audience has a distinct Western coloration, especially as this seemingly inevitable act (how else to rally the troops, quiet the mob, or admonish the wicked?) is applied to politics. The line from Pericles to Cicero to Edmund Burke to Abraham Lincoln to a range of twentieth-century practitioners beyond Europe and North America also traces the evolution of democratic, republican, and populist traditions tied to the West. The spread of these traditions throughout the world has carried public speaking and allied practices like debates and the public discussion of issues along with them, and one result is that few modern leaders can refrain from speaking in public. And few citizens can avoid serving in audiences. The relative importance of such practices is bound to vary and in particular cases may well underline the dictatorial, quasi-monarchical, and elitist basis of a regime. But public speaking by its nature also carries a prospect of dissent, contention, and public accountability that can be suppressed and controlled but never expunged.[3] Furthermore, however Western the form that modern oratory initially takes, it is also one of the more plastic and accessible forms of public political engagement.

The history of speech-making in twentieth-century China suggests ways in which both the coercive capacity of political organization and the social capacity of citizenship have collided and intermeshed. Persuading people to pay taxes, serve in the military, or follow new rules and laws required a large investment in propaganda and other forms of persuasion. While Chinese republicanism did not lead inevitably to electoral accountability, it did require that politicians and officials face the people both in the realm of rhetorical abstraction and in concrete settings. Facing citizens in city squares, auditoriums, theaters, playing fields, and village lanes meant injecting the unpredictable element of audience reaction into the political process. Elites had reason to try to limit this uncertainty, and citizens often had cause to try to expand the repertoire of response beyond polite applause. Controversies over who should speak and when and where helped determine the dimensions and content of public life as well as when and how this relatively free and turbulent sphere might be converted into a more regimented and orderly institution.

One might object that public speaking in China, weakly supported as it was by law and constitutional norms, was more form than substance, more a pose than a viable role. Censorship, arrest, or even assassination might cut short an attempt to speak in public. Electoral campaign trails, where speakers might convert words into votes, were few, faint, and dead-ended. Parliaments and assemblies, where words might shape policy, were institutionally hollow or under the close control of extra-parliamentary forces increasingly expert at scripting what was said at such meetings. But for things to look right in the new China, someone had to get up and make a speech and someone had to listen. This imperative was often more a matter of political aesthetics—the criteria that elites and the public used to judge the look and feel of modern Chinese politics—than of law and constitution. The political aesthetics of citizenship and republicanism brought elites and the public together in novel and unpredictable ways that sometimes filled hollow institutions with contention, undermined political control, and changed the script.[4]

How New Was Public Speaking?

There is little doubt that late Qing and early Republican political figures and activists shared the view that public speaking was a new weapon in the political wars they were engaged in. How new the practice of *yanshuo* actually was, or how indebted to (or at odds with) Chinese traditions, is a more complicated question. Promoters of public speaking as a civic activity acknowledged that both the Chinese classics and vernacular traditions were hostile to oratory. In the preface to a 1946 primer on public speaking, Sun Qimeng recalled:

> When I was a small child, I studied the *Analects* and had great respect for Old Master Kong. But when I studied the part that says

"The gentleman is slow in speech but quick in action," I was not inclined in my own mind to consider that natural.[5]

Sun could understand why a gentleman must act quickly but not why he must be slow of speech or suspicious of "fine words" *(qiaoyan)*. Nor was he convinced by his teacher, who explained that the passages in the *Analects* in effect warned that "if a man only talks and does not act he will become a purveyor of empty talk" *(kongtan jia)*. Sun also claimed that the very village elders who reinforced Confucian strictures against glibness with admonitions like "Don't use careless speech or giggle without cause" actually "said quite a lot and spoke quite well."[6] Besides, if Confucius was so dead set against the spoken word, why does the *Analects* contain the continual refrain "The Master said"?[7] How could he have communicated with his seventy-two disciples and three thousand followers if he had not been adept at public speaking?

Some Chinese advocates of public speaking saw little or no precedent for it in Chinese tradition. Mu Jinyuan, in a preface to a translated American textbook on the subject, was adamant:

In the whole history of our literature there is not a single page of *yanshuo*. In four thousand years our literary circles have not produced a single public speaker *(yanshuo jia)*.[8]

Mu acknowledged that, of course, people speak in Chinese history. "But these are only conversations *(tanhua)*, not public speaking *(yanshuo)*, only speech *(shuo)*, not public speech *(gongkai de shuo)*." Mu agreed that the historical record includes numerous examples of speech suggestive of elements of the rhetoric of a Demosthenes or Burke. He cites the roving propagandists *(youshuo jia)* of the Warring States period who "criss-crossed [China] making trouble and settling disputes," theoreticians *(qingtan jia)* of the Six dynasties, the practice of "haranguing troops" *(shishi)* before battle, and the discourses *(jiangxue)* of Song dynasty scholars. Ordinarily, state oppression precluded the development of these professions and practices into a settled tradition of oratory; for example, "those who talk together [end up at] the public execution ground" and "they signified their anger with their looks as they met on the road—not daring to speak openly about government oppression."[9]

While prejudices against public speaking as an intemperate and seditious form of behavior were real enough, others have seen Chinese rhetorical tradition and elite and community practice as offering stronger analogies to modern oratory. J. I. Crump, covering some of the ground sketched out by Mu Jinyuan, has observed that

> we know of no early oratorical tradition in China—that is, one which involves exhorting groups of people to certain actions or attitudes—but [we] have almost numberless examples of the adviser exhorting a single person (a ruler) to undertake actions, to revise or adopt certain attitudes . . . [and] the basic devices of diction and style are the same for Western oratory and the Chinese persuasion [*shuo*].[10]

Although China lacked a Pericles or a Cicero, there was no shortage of rhetoricians to direct their arguments and persuasive skills upward to the ruler or out to students and disciples. The encounters could be just as dramatic. The roving persuaders or propagandists discounted by Mu used words to prevent (or start) wars or win allies by playing to an audience of one. When Mencius trapped King Xuan of Qi into admitting that he would be as culpable for bad government as a faithless friend or a corrupt official, the ruler "looked to the left and the right and spoke of other matters."[11] The ancient art of oral persuasion—a form Crump characterizes as "private speaking" (Mu's *shuo*) rather than public speaking[12]—could stir emotions and draw blood as surely as a contemporary or Western orator, leaving a ruler to try to deflect stinging words and a broad readership to study the rhetorical techniques embedded in the classics. This roving persuader or quick-tongued adviser role did not disappear in the twentieth century. In fact, the political history of the twentieth-century Chinese Republic includes examples closely patterned after heroes of the Warring States period as the diplomats and agents of warlords and politicians carried out missions of peace and war.[13] But the most significant change in the structure of political rhetoric involved the rerouting and redirecting of speech-making from adviser to ruler to the republican audience of the many or the one people. Instead of gaining power by seeking an audience with the ruler, one had to find, reach, and persuade "the people."

Direct appeals to the people in the contexts of reform and revolution gave a novel cast to behaviors that could also grow out of preexisting patterns of political speech. Just as Sun Qimeng's villagers might be both disapproving of loquaciousness—or the wrong person speaking—and eloquent after their own fashion, the lack of a formal tradition of oratory did not prevent certain individuals, including literati who were fully versed in classical rhetoric, from making speeches, particularly at moments of great stress or crisis. Rebels gave speeches, but so did certified defenders of the social order. Literati were pressed into service by the state as public lecturers on the imperial edicts that formed the content of the "village covenant" *(xiangyue)* institution. "Exposition pavilions" were built in some areas for the purpose, and officials were told to "take every opportunity to instruct villagers in Confucian moral precepts, employing local dialects and colloquial speech, so that all could comprehend."[14]

A vivid description of literati speech-making that mixes the roles of rebel and defender of community values in an intriguing fashion is found in Li Boyuan's turn-of-the-century novel *Wenming xiaoshi* (A Short History of Civilization or, Modern Times).[15] One segment of the novel opens in rural Hunan, where residents are coming to grips with Western influences in the form of a reform-minded prefect and foreign mining company officials collaborating to exploit the remote area's mineral wealth. The local people are convinced that their officials are conspiring to "sell our land to foreigners who will [then] exterminate the common people."[16] When the prefect, who has already published a circular explaining that no such precipitous action will take place, complains about being the victim of a misunderstanding, a local teacher comments in realistic and conventional fashion: "Those who can read are few while those who engage in empty talk are numerous."[17] Meanwhile, four or five thousand people have congregated at a local school to hear a local degree-holder named Huang, of whom it was said that "in the prefectural capital there was not one who was not afraid of him." Huang enters the school, parts the crowd, and climbs up on a table to deliver a hair-raising speech on the need to defend to the death land that belongs to the emperor and to "us."[18] Huang's status and his reputation equip him to speak in a direct and spontaneous fashion to and for his community, putting the well-intentioned prefect to flight in comic disarray.

Public speaking as an extension of elite status and the foundational mastery of the written word can also be glimpsed in Kang Youwei's stirring speech, given in fluent, heavily Cantonese-accented Mandarin, to examination candidates in Beijing in the aftermath of the Treaty of Shimonoseki.[19] Kang's words caused many in the crowd of literati from all over the empire to cry out and weep and thirteen hundred of them to sign a petition of protest to the throne. The emotional impact of what Kang had to say seems not very different from that felt by a nineteenth-century American who, upon hearing an address by the famous orator Daniel Webster, "thought my temples would burst with the gush of blood."[20] Kang shared the fictional degree-holder Huang's talent for spontaneous oratory. In fact, lecturing and speaking at banquets and in schools and academies was very much a part of the literati tradition of socializing for civic and political purposes.[21]

If literati were surprisingly well-equipped to speak in public, despite Confucian doubt about the propriety of speech and speech-making, the new conditions of reform and revolutionary politics would broaden the range of speakers and audiences. When the action in Li Boyuan's novel shifts to Shanghai, public speaking is encountered in the newly fabricated settings of reform clubs and political meetings. A provincial visitor, when invited to attend a rally at a "Protect the Country and Strengthen the Race Anti-Footbinding Society," enthuses: "Great! I've often heard people talk of the kind of public-speaking societies (yanshuohui). I imagine this is one of them."[22] What surprised the visitors, however, was the lack of spontaneity in the speeches they heard.

> What was said was nothing but the talk you read in newspapers, nothing strange or out-of-the-ordinary. Moreover, before the sound of applause had left their ears, the society's secretary had prepared [a draft of the proceedings] to be sent to a newspaper [for publication].[23]

The uncertainty and drama associated with spoken yanshuo, so much in play in degree-holder Huang's harangue, could be reduced and muted by the assembly-line atmosphere of a yanshuohui and the predictable messages contained in cliché-ridden newspaper copy. However, when the patron of the anti-footbinding society, Wei Bangxian, is obliged to give an address at another rally held at the Xu Gardens (a well-known site of public meetings and orations),[24] he experiences a type of unwonted sensation familiar to public speakers everywhere. In a promising opening, Wei compares in graphic terms embattled China to his own body. Wei then pauses suddenly, shuts his eyes, and, to calm his nerves, takes two deep breaths. The audience, sensing a high point of Wei's stirring speech, applauds and settles in for more. But then "Wei Bangxian suddenly began groping at his body for some considerable length of time, and searching the floor as if he had lost something there. He searched for a long time and found nothing. In his anxiousness, beads of sweat dripped from his head . . . [and] his whole body was seized with turmoil and he could not speak one word."[25] Both the boredom produced by boilerplate speeches and the stage fright that results from losing your text or simply forgetting what you intended to say spread with the growing popularity of *yanshuo,* along with the emotional and unpredictable reactions that speech-making as a rhetorical form carried. Further emphasizing the unpredictable nature of public oratory, in the contexts of reformist and revolutionary passions and movements, one did not need to be a degree-holder to get up and give a speech. Political groups engaged in "revolutionary harangues" *(gaotan geming)* in schools and public parks.[26] And, as Li Boyuan's novel suggests, these speeches were often immediately transcribed and published in the hope of influencing public opinion.[27] For example, the revolutionary, anti-Qing newspaper *Subao* regularly and prominently published lectures given in Zhang Park, one of Shanghai's most famous recreation complexes.[28] In other cases, readers of revolutionary magazines and newspapers were moved to found societies dedicated to lecturing on topics related to social and political reform.[29]

Some individuals spoke naturally, without any apparent concern for *yanshuo* as an art or area of expertise. Tan Sitong spoke on the need for reform in Hunan and Beijing in 1898 and, after his arrest, gave his last speech on the execution ground, fulfilling the ancient admonition about public utterances.[30] Tan's heroism and the growing power of speech-making as a political act made his last words an incitement to further orations and actions. Other revolutionaries, like Cai Yuanpei, viewed public speaking as a foreign import to be mastered. Cai used Japanese texts on the subject to reform school curricula and established a *yanshuohui* to provide opportunities to practice.[31] During the repression that followed the failure of the 1898 reforms, the Qing government actively prohibited public speech.[32] This ban was gradually rescinded after the proclamation of the Qing reformist "New Policies" in January 1901. Deep public interest in events of national moment expanded the practice. For example, during March and April of 1901 the "Resist Russia" campaign against that country's aggression in Manchuria caused hundreds of people to gather in Shanghai and Hangzhou to listen to patriotic speeches.[33] The term "public speaking" (*yanshuo*) itself began to be used more openly, and by 1902 editorialists in some newspapers were calling for more speeches as a way of strengthening China. The *Impartial Daily (Dagong bao)* declared:

> Nowadays if one wishes to raise morale high and low and target the soul of the nation, a dead language [classical, written Chinese] certainly cannot rival the immediacy of the living language [vernacular, spoken Chinese]. Henceforth and in order to rouse patriotic worthies, we must pay close attention to the art of public speaking.[34]

The Hangzhou *Vernacular Post (Baihua bao)* agreed and proposed the establishment of academies for public speaking (*yanshuo tang*) which, unlike regular schools, could serve literate and illiterate people alike, so that "the emotions and [patriotic] love of officials and people high and low will gradually spread."[35]

Independent political organizations dedicated to causes like anti-footbinding and anti-opium smoking as well as reform-minded government agencies concerned with reaching the public made heavy use of public speaking in their campaigns and projects.[36] Expatriate and exile communities in places like Tokyo also offered fertile ground for these potent mixtures of the written and spoken word. The Tokyo history of Sun Yat-sen's Revolutionary Alliance (Tongmeng hui) and its struggles with rival exile organizations led by Kang Youwei and Liang Qichao is filled with stirring speeches, heckling by opponents, and even fist fights among audience members.[37] Speaking on incendiary subjects in Chinese communities at home and abroad had immediate and unsettling effects on preexisting patterns of elite interaction and popular politics. This was due partly to the nature of the issues discussed but also to volatile relations between and among speakers and audiences. The 1902 charter of a political society in Yangzhou insisted that members "wait until the person speaking is finished before the next person begins so as to avoid raising a hue and cry and causing turmoil."[38]

Fusing rebel speech and the appeal for a new kind of social order based on citizenship defined a distinct realm of political innovation. Initially the literati, despite increasingly radical anti-government positions, were reluctant to embrace speaking to the broader populace because of the bad and rebellious connotations associated with "inciting" the people.[39] Perhaps this is why one movement which carried speech-making the furthest in an institutional sense was the Taiping Rebellion. Taiping rebel leaders, influenced in part by missionary practice, preached to large open-air assemblies long before this was commonplace in late Qing and early Republican political life.[40] A panorama of large crowds and enthusiastic speakers looked and felt right to these millenarian rebels. Literati deviations from Confucian and government warnings about the dangers of speech-making only went so far in enabling leaders to reach beyond smaller communities of friends and students to massed conventions and collections of citizens. Was anyone who got up and gave a speech or sat or stood in the audience a fully qualified citizen? The entry of women into public life pressed the point with considerable force and volatility.

Women as Speakers, Hecklers, and Citizens

The fact that anyone could get up and speak, even if one lacked access to the printed page or the proper social credentials, gave public speaking an air of possibility and radicalness. The intrinsic ability of public speakers to appeal to the majority of Chinese who could not read or who were otherwise kept to the margins of public life also generated considerable excitement and anxiety. It is not surprising that one of the earliest essays on the possibilities inherent in oratory was written by a woman who realized this potential for portability and universality. Qiu Jin, famous for her defiance of convention, desperate courage, and martyr's death, published a 1904 essay entitled

"The Advantages of Public Speaking." Qiu Jin did not claim that China lacked a tradition of oratory, but only that the Chinese have "regarded public speaking too lightly."[41]

> [They] consider it just talk. What use could it have? Why would it be necessary to train for it? At the sites of speech-making they talk simply as they wish without regard for the correct way [of doing it]. This is not sufficient to move people. How can it be called public speaking?

Advancing an argument made often by proponents of *yanshuo,* Qiu Jin complains that too few Chinese can read well enough to make buying a newspaper worth their while. By conveying the "knowledge [held by] civilized people" through public speaking, "everyone can understand, even illiterate women and children." According to Qiu Jin, "one can give a speech anytime, any place" without elaborate preparations or financial resources. Since no admission will be charged, the audience will be huge. Public speaking offered a simple solution to the daunting problem of how to reach and move the Chinese nation. Armed only with an "eloquent and honest tongue," speech-makers would make the mobilization of military and financial resources unnecessary. Beginning with the overseas students who were her immediate audience in Tokyo in 1904, Qiu Jin hoped to form a training society to prepare her fellow revolutionaries for the deployment of this potent new weapon in the struggle to "awaken the citizenry."[42] This she did, along with a *Vernacular Post (Baihua bao)* which promoted the value of public speaking.[43]

Qiu Jin eventually chose armed rebellion rather than oratory alone as a means of carrying out revolution. When she returned to China, at a meeting of students in Zhejiang, Qiu Jin dramatically drew the two modes of action together when she "thrust the dagger she always carried on her person into the podium" and advised her audience to "stab me with this dagger" if she ever betrayed China.[44] Rather than dominating the new politics of revolution and reform, public speaking expanded the repertoire of possible actions one could take and the gestures one could make.

Qiu Jin's friend and associate Tang Qunying lived long enough to put some of Qiu Jin's ideas into practice. Tang, a Hunan province native and the daughter of a Xiang Army general who doted on her,

was an accomplished poet and essayist who retained an early fascina-
tion with the Mulan story of a daughter who dresses as a man and
takes the place of her father as a soldier.[45] She was married after the
death of her father to a cousin of the great statesman Zeng Guofan,
but early widowhood freed her to return to her natal home and
eventually accompany Qiu Jin to Japan for study. In addition to organizing the hundred or so female Chinese students in Tokyo, Tang,
under the influence of Sun Yat-sen, become the first female member
of Sun's Revolutionary Alliance. Along with Qiu Jin, she helped out
in a bomb factory in Yokohama run by Sun's organization.[46] The
women's groups with which Tang was associated directly expressed
the desire to achieve full citizenship along with men while recognizing that "[we] lack education and lack organization and it follows
that in lacking education we lack knowledge and in lacking organization we lack justice. No wonder for endless millennia [we have lived]
like slaves and like sand."[47] "Although China formally has a majority
of female citizens (nü guomin), the spirit is lacking and the result is
the same as having a 'people' without a people."[48] Conceding that in
the past Chinese women "did not know what a nation (guojia) is or
what the relationship between the nation and women is," Tang argues that women as "a source of education and the basis of modern
civilization (wenming)" are needed as citizens to save China from disaster.

> In the world of East Asia permit us to soar with women's journals
> everywhere, catching every ear in the name of progress, raising a
> great cry with the mountains echoing in support. Sweet dreams
> awaken, motivation is born, severe illness is cured, and bodies are
> strengthened. [Women] will take the opportunity to progress and
> firm up their independent will, simply and honestly relying on
> their female compatriots as a second nature, simple and unaffected
> as a child. Female citizens bravely and honestly stride forward,
> countenances shining, heir to the mother of Mencius and Mulan.[49]

Tang Qunying's politics may have been more radical, but her vision
of the new, female citizen seems fully consistent with Liang Qichao's
"way of the citizen" (xinmin zhi dao).[50] Liang declared in 1902 that
"We must have citizens!" Tang and her "female compatriots" were
ready in 1911 to accommodate him by word and deed.

When Tang Qunying returned to China in 1911, she threw herself into revolutionary activities and helped to organize a number of military and political bodies led and staffed by women. Although the number of women involved in such organizations was small, branches and networks of activists were to be found in every major city. Along with political parties like the Revolutionary Alliance, various organizations seeking social and economic reform, and groups like the Manchus who feared losing the status they had clung to under the Qing, women's organizations were among the most politically active groups in the year following the revolution.[51] In the immediate aftermath of the Wuchang uprising, many women joined military brigades. A former student of Qiu Jin's led a women's detachment in the battle for Hangzhou.[52] Tang herself was a captain in a "Women's Northern Expedition Brigade."[53] Women's brigades were later disbanded by the provisional government in Nanjing, and many of these activists joined a nationwide movement for women's suffrage.[54] Tang Qunying and others, representing the more radical wing of the women's movement, demanded full citizenship even before the provisional government was formed at the end of 1911.[55] One of their statements read in part: "Happily China has been revived in glory with a dictatorship now transformed into a republic. With political revolution comes social revolution. If we wish to end the social tragedy, we must seek social equality. If we wish social equality we must first have equal rights for men and women. We must first have the right to vote and be elected."[56]

However, when the legislative assembly promulgated a Provisional Constitution on March 11, there was no stipulation for male-female equality, and those involved in the suffrage movement reacted indignantly. On March 19 Tang Qunying led a group of women armed with pistols into the parliament building in Nanjing to protest the reluctance of representatives to make women's equality and suffrage an explicit part of the new Provisional Constitution.[57] Seating themselves among the delegates, the band of women waited for the debate over women's suffrage to begin and then "jeered so loudly that the proceedings could not continue." In subsequent days, confrontations involving women protesters led to broken windows and assaults on guards who tried to keep them out of the building. The women engaged male delegates in spontaneous debates as the men tried to enter the building and searched their sleeves for what they thought might be incriminating documents. The violence of the protests was both real and symbolic, reflecting the militant and military background of many of the women and the deep sense of betrayal they felt when the full citizenship they had been promised was denied. If they were refused the legal status of voting citizens they could still act like citizens, and not in the more sedate and pliable form favored by many conservatively-minded politicians. Women who cut their hair short, walked unaccompanied in public, smoked cigarettes, and engaged in political acts like making speeches were liable to be stared at or worse. Brandishing weapons, shouting slogans, and laying hands on male delegates broke every Confucian taboo imaginable.

In April Tang Qunying helped to combine five different women's organizations into a single "Women's Political Alliance" based in Nanjing with branches in five other major cities.[58] The new group's agenda included social as well as political reforms and suffrage.[59] In a letter to Sun Yat-sen, the organization observed in an exasperated tone that the legislators had acted almost "as if they openly desired an intense, emotional struggle with we women" when all "our party" wants is the addition of two characters, "male-female," to the article currently banning discrimination on the basis of "race, class, or religion."

A famous photograph of Qiu Jin shows her dressed as a man. A female citizen or speaker dressed like a woman was just as provocative. In principle, public speaking was a pragmatic way of reaching women and men who could not read. But for many female revolutionaries of this era, the medium, the pose, and the form of speaking out in public was also a good portion of the message. Under the circumstances, women might have reasons to delay domesticating the more theatrical and even violent aspects of republican rhetoric.

The 1912 Nationalist Party Convention

In the conventional language of the time, 1911 had been a year of "destruction" *(pohuai)*, including the destruction of empire and the imperial idea as well as violence and damage done to people and property caught up in the turmoil of revolution. 1912, the first year of the Republic, was to be the beginning of "construction" or "reconstruction" (*jianshe*). If citizenship was to be more than violent words and deeds and conspiratorial politics, institutions needed to be built and revolutionary organizations redesigned to better fit the demands of public life in a republic. It must have appeared to even the casual observer that events like political meetings, legislative sessions, and party conventions needed to be planned and choreographed with some care so as to avoid a return to either revolutionary violence or imperial autocracy. But what kind of preparation was necessary or possible? Two thousand years of monarchy had established public ritual for emperor, court, officialdom, and commoners within an intelligible and enforceable set of strictures. A few months of a republic and more than a decade of revolutionary politics did not offer anything comparable in the way of rituals and rules. As would be expected, revolutionaries were more expert at corroding authority than consolidating it. If any stability or decorum was emerging, it seemed to come spontaneously from the crowds who greeted political figures like Sun Yat-sen with brass bands, polite applause, hat-doffing (which was as new to China as brass bands), and the quasi-monarchical cry of "Long live!"

The problem of how public events associated with republicanism fitted or clashed with the calculations of elites came to a head in the summer of 1912. With President Yuan Shikai in power in Beijing, leaders of the Revolutionary Alliance were engaged in converting a revolutionary and conspiratorial party into a political body capable of contesting the upcoming elections to the national parliament. The key figure in this transformation was not Sun Yat-sen, who had been forced to resign in early 1912 as provisional president based in Nanjing in favor of the militarily stronger Yuan Shikai, but Song Jiaoren. Song, steeled in the political brawls and wars of revolutionary politics, now offered a vision of a democratic China rooted in parliamentary institutions. Part of this new political order was hammered out behind the scenes. Song brokered a deal whereby the Revolutionary Alliance and several smaller parties would join together in a new Nationalist Party (Guomindang). In order for this merger to take place, Song agreed to demands to drop the Revolutionary Alliance's support for male-female equal rights. This compromise on the revolutionary agenda set the stage for public confrontation with Tang Qunying and other women, who were already deeply suspicious of the male leaders of the Revolutionary Alliance.

The Nationalist Party's inaugural meeting took place in Beijing on August 25, 1912. The titular leader of the new party, Sun Yat-sen, had arrived with great ceremony in the capital the day before in order to enter into negotiations with Yuan Shikai. Yuan had arranged for Sun to be transported from the railway station to his residence in an ornate carriage once owned by a Manchu prince, drawn by white horses and accompanied by thirty mounted escorts.[60] A crowd of several thousand, many of whom had been waiting more than eight hours, doffed their hats and shouted greetings. The Nationalist Party convention itself took place in a provincial hostel for natives of Hubei and Hunan, the Huguang Huiguan, which had a great hall capable of accommodating the several hundred representatives and several thousand spectators who attended.[61] The meeting opened on the morning of August 25 with a tribute to Sun Yat-sen sponsored by the Revolutionary Alliance. Since resigning as president Sun had been traveling around China speaking to crowds, who welcomed him as a revolutionary hero. Sun Yat-sen had honed his skills as a speaker during long years of exile and in the course of numerous fund-raising and organizing speeches to overseas Chinese communities and exile groups. His fondness for oratory and reputation for ambitious schemes led fellow Cantonese to nickname him "Sun the Cannon" (Sun Dapao).[62] This referred both to Sun's predilection for the "empty talk" that old-fashioned school masters warned against and to an ability to "lay down heavy artillery fire" *(kai dapao)* in his speeches and writings in a style that appealed to a nation in crisis.

The large audience at the Huguang Huiguan was attributed to the fact that in Beijing, as in the other cities and towns Sun had visited, "the struggle to pay respects" to the famous leader was "keen."[63] Reflecting a widespread interest in public affairs and in oratory, Sun and other politicians and public figures were much in demand as speakers by merchants, students, and miscellaneous citizen groups throughout urban China. On this particular morning, Sun gave a speech on the importance of the Revolutionary Alliance's transition to a new, more open, inclusive party. In order to broaden the party's appeal, he stressed the need to abandon the mentality of treating outsiders as enemies. Sun's remarks were greeted by thunderous applause.

The next speaker was Song Jiaoren, well known for his eloquence, who was followed by the meeting's chairman, Zhang Ji. But before

Zhang could complete his report on the party merger, three women, Shen Peizhen, Wang Changguo, and Tang Qunying, suddenly got up on the stage and interrupted the proceedings.[64] One of the women gave an impromptu speech about how the new party constitution betrayed women. She argued that eliminating the original clause guaranteeing women's rights showed that "you have no regard for the Revolutionary Alliance and no regard for the Chinese Republic." Shen struck out at the men on the platform with her fan. (Another account had Wang grabbing Song by the throat and threatening to shoot him.)[65] The women attacked Song and Zhang and appealed to the audience to oppose removing the original clause. After attempts to mediate the dispute on stage failed, Zhang Ji declared that the morning's meeting was not after all a plenary session. Shouting "Long live the Republic!" three times, Zhang adjourned the convention until the afternoon. In the past, kingly decorum had enabled King Xuan of Qi to look to the left and the right and speak of other matters when confronted with Mencius's corrosive comments. Zhang Ji fashioned a different kind of evasive maneuver out of parliamentary procedure and sloganeering. As had happened before in such political meetings, oratory and fisticuffs competed at the podium. Only a few months earlier Song Jiaoren had received a black eye from a delegate during a session of the National Assembly in Nanjing, when Song had opposed sending troops to Beijing to force Yuan Shikai to cooperate with the Nanjing government.[66] On this occasion Song knew his assailants well, and not just from the earlier altercations in Nanjing. He and Tang, combatants at the podium in 1912 in Beijing, had likely spent a number of pleasant afternoons or evenings together listening to lectures and discussing the art of oratory at Qiu Jin's Public-Speaking Training Society in Tokyo in 1905.[67]

The afternoon session opened with Zhang Ji again in the chair. He gave a speech that appealed for unity and declared that "in one nation there can only be one center," and the same was true for a nation's political parties. With the formation of the Nationalist Party, six parties would become "one great political party." Then several women again made speeches on the question of rights and equality, this time apparently by prearrangement. Zhang Ji permitted a formal petition to restore the excised clause to be brought before the convention.[68] Wang Changguo spoke in terms even harsher than

Tang Qunying's remarks at the morning session. Zhang Ji and other speakers responded by arguing that "inasmuch as even members of the Revolutionary Alliance are not equal, it is only natural that voting rights for men and women not be equal."[69] These remarks further inflamed women's rights advocates and, "as a result, the order of the meeting became one of chaos."[70] As Zhang Ji and others attempted without effect to resolve things, a woman shouted from the gallery: "You are abolishing equal rights for men and women. Which of you was not born of [both] a father and a mother?" Seeing Song Jiaoren on the stage, Tang Qunying attempted to strike him with her fan but was prevented from doing so by Zhang.[71] Tang, with a bobbed-hair young woman at her side, declared that abandoning the equal rights clause "showed contempt for women's circles." At this point those in favor of women's rights began clapping, but they were drowned out by "snorts of contempt" (*chi zhi yibi*) from the overwhelmingly male audience (only about twenty of those in attendance were women).[72] To quiet the crowd, Zhang rang a bell and called for a show of hands on the question, the precise nature of which he underlined by holding up a sign with big characters reading "Male-Female Equality."[73]

Supporters of women's rights managed to muster only thirty or forty votes to hundreds against. After the vote, Tang Qunying and other women continued to condemn the outcome. When Sun arrived for the afternoon session, Tang was still visibly angry. Another delegate, in a gesture perhaps intended to mollify her and chasten his colleagues, declared that although the attempt to reinsert the equal rights clause had failed, he intended to vote for Tang Qunying for an official position in the party leadership. He then took out a ballot and wrote her name on it. The raucous atmosphere of the convention continued through a dispute over balloting procedures. Zhang Ji, in what a reporter characterized as "extremely painful words," appealed to the audience for calm: "If you gentlemen wish to establish a Nationalist Party, please cast aside your personal feelings and your abstract arguments" (in favor, presumably, of shared sentiments and a common agenda).

Finally, Sun Yat-sen reentered the hall to huge applause and the audience removed their hats in respect. (Henrietta Harrison has drawn our attention to hats as a key prop in Republican political life.)[74] Sun gave another speech lasting two hours, which addressed, among other issues, the question of women's rights. In order to achieve party unification, he supported leaving out the women's rights clause. While equal rights was "still something very much to be hoped for, not even foreign countries have been able to reach this goal."[75] But he promised that "one day" these rights would be secured. After all, how could men demand freedom for themselves and not accept equality with women? At that point Tang Qunying, after a parting verbal shot, walked out in protest.

The next day Shen Peizhen and Tang Qunying went to see Sun at his residence. According to a newspaper account, Tang wept so loudly that the sound "shook the room." The women "stuck fiercely to their position" and cited the many women who had risked or lost their lives for the revolution. Although Sun attempted to console them and was said to be "much moved," Shen and Tang left the meeting furious.[76]

While the Nationalist Party convention alienated feminists and their supporters, Song Jiaoren did lead the party to victory in parliamentary elections held in late 1912 and early 1913 after a rousing speaking tour of his own through central China. Early in 1913, Song was murdered on a railway platform in Shanghai with the connivance of Yuan Shikai and his followers. Parliamentary institutions were crushed and the Nationalists were broken by Yuan's superior military power in the "Second Revolution" they launched in response. Beaten on the battlefield, Sun and his close supporters, including Tang Qunying, withdrew to exile in Japan.

The rejection of women's rights at the Beijing party meeting in 1912 was not a factor in the defeat of the Nationalist Party. But the drama enacted by speakers and the audience over that and other issues suggests both the power and the vulnerability of political speech in this formative period of modern Chinese public life. The events of August 25, 1912, represented the intersection of several lines of political activity which, for similar reasons, surfaced in public view. Republicanism and republican citizenship implied publicity of a particular kind. Song Jiaoren's behind-the-scenes factional negotiations required public affirmation. His commitment to a parliamentary regime and electoral politics led inevitably to open meetings, press coverage, and public scrutiny. However, this opening from the sub-

terranean to the pellucid exposed him and the larger political organization he planned to construct to opposition by those not included in his brokered agreements. Throughout the remainder of
1912 and up until Song's death in 1913, Song's formula of political
organizing, public meetings, and speech-making attracted many imi-
tators. The Democratic Party's "Electoral Guidelines" included "preparing public-speaking materials for the political stage" and using
them "at various communications points" across the country.[77] One
political leader recalled later that during "electoral activities at that
time, aside from a few people secretly buying votes, most everyone
else chose the mode of making speeches. I myself [when visiting
Jiangsu] . . . gave over forty election speeches. Most speeches by candidates were given in teahouses or other public places."[78] Other politicians gave speeches as they traveled by boat up the Yangtze River.
Song himself "mounted the podium with gusto" to give speeches in
Shanghai, Nanjing, Changsha, and Hangzhou in the fall of 1912.[79]

Chinese women activists had not only been involved for years as
republican revolutionaries, but also more recently had continually
challenged the new institutions of Republican China to live up to the
ideals of liberty and equality. At the Huguang Hostel in Beijing,
Shen, Wang, and Tang, as women, were vastly outnumbered. But any
female presence at a public event drew attention because of its novel
character. Press accounts of Sun's arrival in Beijing estimated the
crowd present to meet him at three to five thousand and described
how the mass of onlookers stretched from the station outside Qian
Gate to Dazhalan Street, but also counted the fourteen members of
"women's circles" in that crowd and the twenty women in the contingent of diplomatic and foreign greeters.[80] In her recent book on political and social change in late Qing and Republican Chengdu,
Kristin Stapleton notes the importance of whether and how women
appeared in public as an issue for reformers, who celebrated that
presence as a symbol of progress, and for conservatives, who bridled
at what they saw as a breach of propriety.[81] Transnational connections also influenced and strengthened the impact of women's politics in China. The willingness of women to mix violence and verbal
protests reflected both their frustration and anger and the example
offered by fellow suffragists in Britain, who were making increasing
use of direct action and force. In actions widely reported in the Chi-

nese press, British suffragists broke windows, went on hunger strikes in prison, and even committed suicide in public. In return, radical actions by Chinese women received public support from English activists.[82]

Through the lens provided by the practice of public speaking, we can see that a woman at the podium was both a logical extension of republican politics and citizenship and provocative to the point of riot. Like men, women contributed to the visual imagery of citizenship. If men had their hats, women had their bobbed hair. In this aesthetic sense, citizenship was a work-in-progress in which the word-picture of the Chinese polity drawn by the drafters of constitutions and political tracts was challenged and expanded in a turbulent panorama of more spontaneous words and deeds, gestures and fashions. The minority status of women in political gatherings made that presence, carefully costumed and armed with words and (sometimes) weapons, all the more striking, but it also left them vulnerable to majority votes and the sound of snorting contempt.

For his part, Sun Yat-sen was less interested in electoral politics or the fate of any particular issue like women's rights than in his quest for some larger means of moving China toward wealth and power as a nation. As suggested by his speeches of this period, and their brass band accompaniment, Sun used public events to represent a larger national unity beyond organizational or factional politics. At the same time, when controversy erupted, he responded directly and sought to use his oratorical skills to mediate and resolve division. Like Song Jiaoren, Chinese suffragists, and other political actors in this transitional period, Sun found in the spoken word a powerful, if unstable, tool for mobilizing support.

Oratory and the Rise of Propaganda

By the time of the early Republic, despite an aura of novelty that still surrounded speech-making, politicians and leaders had become accustomed to giving orations, and people who assembled in political conventions, chambers of commerce, reform societies, and all manner of other organizations expected to be addressed.[83] Formulaic and inspirational speeches helped in the welding of consensus. Dissent and disturbances exposed the cracks formed by disputes over leaders, policies, and identity. Because the Republic did not stabilize on the basis of an electoral mandate or representative institutions, whatever latent capacity for civic activity or political support there might be tended to emerge in public assemblies like the Nationalist Party convention or lesser gatherings convened by a province or community. In these large and small workshops of leadership, policy, and sentiment, speeches often formed the pivot around which civic action was taken and citizenship exercised. As Mu Jinyuan observed in his advocacy role in 1929, in modern China "everyone must hold meetings and when meetings are held there must be *yanshuo*."[84]

The men and women who gave speeches and reports at the 1912 Nationalist Party convention and those who applauded, jeered, and questioned what they heard were acting within this complex set of inheritances, borrowed forms, and improvisations. Political meetings were sites where the new worthies of Republican political life established a direct relationship with supporters and the citizenry. Joining speaker to audience, both in the institutional settings of a convention, school, guild, or army camp and also during mass protest rallies, served the immediate goal of conveying a message and mobilizing support. Movements like May Fourth and May Thirtieth in the teens and 1920s spread the sites of speech-making, at least temporarily, to places like temples, train stations, docks, and public parks.[85] The sight of a speaker on a podium or stage and an audience in chairs, on stools, or standing in a city square also graphically represented the new polity that was emerging in early twentieth-century China. Speakers and audiences, singly and as a sequence of constituencies, helped model and lend concreteness to the notion of a national "people." The newness of leaders facing followers in the expectation of applause (or negative gestures like hurling stools or cigarette canisters or making catcalls) was striking. Leaders invoked the needs or interests of the people just as emperors and officials had. But they also sought out and actually faced the people. Admittedly, the percentage of citizens reached in this way was limited by the size of assembly halls and stadiums as well as by the undeveloped state of modern communications. However, the act of public speaking itself implied interaction beyond older ritual expectations. Citizens faced leaders and waved their hats or even shouted "10,000 years!" But they did not kowtow to them. And, as the 1912 Nationalist Party convention demonstrated, an impressive range of responses was possible in an upright position.

Leninism rather than parliamentary procedure eventually became the basis for mass mobilization and the more routine organizational settings of speech-making. However, midway between the classically-influenced and revolution-tempered *yanshuo* and the Leninist and bureaucratic realm of cadre "reporting" *(baogao)*[86] fell a concerted effort to turn public speaking (increasingly termed *yanjiang*) into a coherent discipline that could be taught and replicated. Public speaking was accepted as a subject in school, and prizes were given in speech competitions.[87] Famous lecturers drew large crowds. When Rabindranath Tagore visited Shanghai on a speaking tour, Beijing students cut classes and rushed south to hear him.[88] Luminaries like Hu Shi, who had given a well-received lecture at his school in Shanghai at the age of sixteen and had witnessed two presidential campaigns in the United States, went on speaking tours of Chinese cities.[89] The art of public speaking also became a more fixed and disciplined part of China's nation-building effort. Lecturing was praised as a technique for fostering "citizen education," along with newspapers, movies, radio, and exhibitions.[90] Lecture halls could be found in most cities as a distinctive form of public architecture. An article entitled "The Relationship Between Architectural Design and Urban Aesthetics" listed examples of typical public architecture as "municipal offices, lecture halls, schools, libraries, churches, and parks."[91] In this way public speaking and its formal and informal venues formed part of an infrastructure that enthusiasts identified as a basis for "training citizens" in "local facilities like public lecture halls, parks, theaters, savings banks, athletic societies, local self-government training societies, citizen schools, and commoner schools."[92] Public speaking attracted the attention of anyone interested in engineering consent and support for particular nation-building projects. For example, in the 1930s the Fuzhou Electrical Company, as part of its effort to test the prospects for rural electrification, made lectures the main component of its public education effort.[93]

Advocates of public speaking as a civic art and discipline like Mu Jinyuan stressed the importance of rich content, the appropriate turns of phrase, and effective gesturing. Mu observed that one was more likely to be "moved" or "inspired" *(gandong)* by a play than a (silent) movie because the play has the spoken word. Both plays and movies are more stirring than novels because they have gestures.[94] As other witnesses to the rise of speech-making had concluded, "Everyone knows that public speaking is a quicker way of inciting people than reading."[95] Properly trained, according to Mu, one would be able to gain control over one's audience: "You instruct him to laugh and he'll laugh. You instruct him to cry and he'll cry. When the audience leaves the site of the speech, they won't forget the points you have made. After one, ten, and twenty years, they still won't forget."[96] This kind of skill also presupposes a knowledge of one's audience. A manual on propaganda from the 1940s advised: "Before a propagandist speaks or writes an essay he must understand who is the object of the propaganda. What kind of lives do they live? What is their intellectual level? What kind of past history and experiences have they had? What things do they care most about? What things pain them the most? Whom do they hate? Whom do they love?"[97] The best speeches merged appeals both to logic and to powerful feelings held by audiences.[98] The attractiveness of public life to many participants seems to have been related in part to the opportunities these new rituals and practices offered for expressing powerful and otherwise private emotions.[99] Politicians and parties sought to accommodate and channel this highly charged politics by appearing to speak from the heart to the hearts of the Chinese people.

Conclusion

The legacy of late Qing and early Republican speech-making as reasoned argument and emotional appeal can be seen in the growing and increasingly formal role played by addresses, speeches, and reports in the organizational life of the state and society.

> Speech-making today [the 1930s] is an extremely common thing. At the opening of commemorative meetings or celebrations we often hear speeches. Sometimes we give speeches ourselves. This word *yanjiang* is already quite widespread in society. And this is not just so among adults. Even among seven- or eight-year-old elementary school students it is a common thing.[100]

The Nationalist and Communist party-states absorbed this style of public address into their civic rituals and political campaigns.[101] And so on Women's Day in 1943 Zhang Ji could give a speech on "The

Chinese Revolution and Women" in which he could recall the sacrifices of female martyrs like Qiu Jin and "other nameless female heroes . . . sitting in sedan chairs carrying bombs, or carrying small children in order to transport bombs . . . who at that time lacked the language of women's liberation [and had only that of] national liberation and racial liberation."[102] Tang Qunying, who, in fact, never lacked for words in print or on the podium on the issue of women's liberation, had spent the remainder of her family fortune on women's education and died in difficult circumstances in 1938.[103] There was no one in Zhang Ji's audience able or willing to correct his account or challenge his authority.

Republicanism and citizenship, increasingly domesticated and scripted, thus acquired a vocal and visible presence that avoided the direct accountability of elections and a critical press. The ability of the Communists in particular to undermine the autonomy of social groups like workers and students made it less likely that audiences would have the wherewithal or the will to resist official speakers. Few things better expressed Song Jiaoren's commitment to democracy than his willingness to expose himself to criticism, questioning, and even blows at the podium as he tried to create a new republican political authority. Few practices better convey the party-state's different agenda than the Communist Party's evolution from fiery speech-making to the drone of leaders reporting on policy to cadres and the people. Under communism, regular speech-making by political elites continued along with the deployment of large numbers of "report personnel" (baogao yuan) assigned to hold forth on official matters at the basic-unit level.[104] New social and political credentials for speakers were enforced. It was no longer the case that anyone could claim the right to speak as a citizen. Audiences were less free to exercise either independent political judgment or the corrosive power of bad manners. Of course, the success of the party-state in imposing uniform scripts and policing audience behavior came at the price of colorless oratory and bland reactions. Occasionally, in the Hundred Flowers Movement, the Cultural Revolution, and the democracy movements of the 1970s and 1980s, spontaneous speech of a critical and emotionally charged kind buckled or broke through the party boiler-plate.[105] Under these conditions, a "good" speech would almost have to carry with it the mark of dissent or rebellion. And it was

still possible to lose an audience with a bad speech, as the Nationalists discovered throughout the 1930s and 1940s and the Communists
have experienced more recently. The power of speech-making, and
heckling, as spontaneous acts of criticism or defiance remained
available in the repertoire of the heirs of Mencius, Qiu Jin, and
Tang Qunying, although often "many people dared be angry but
didn't dare speak."[106] Creating regimented public spheres from a
controlled press and an officially scripted oratory can be ultimately
self-defeating if and when speakers again frankly address public issues, "target the soul of the nation," or stir private passions. Since
these potentially critical and corrosive functions have been embedded in Chinese political culture for a century or more and involve a
logical response to leaders who "speak to the people" no matter how
cynically intended that speech and appeal may be, the periodic reappearance of an independent-minded, emotionally aroused citizenry
should not be marveled at.

3 | Democratic Calisthenics: The Culture of Urban Associations in the New Republic

It is hard to read Shanghai newspapers in the late teens and early 1920s without being struck by the radical play of democratic ideas and practices. The public protests and burgeoning press of the May Fourth era have, of course, been recognized. Debates over civil society and a public sphere have provided a recent context for renewed interest in the mobilization of urban residents and their articulation of citizens' rights in this era. Scholarly discussion, nonetheless, tends to view the social mobilization of this period as a froth on the surface of society, that is, as episodic, spontaneous, diffuse, and ephemeral. Popular spontaneity—rather than any institutionalized democratization of society—characterizes the era, and, more broadly, Chinese democracy movements in the twentieth century.[1]

This chapter focuses on institutions rather than popular spontaneity, sketching changes in relatively enduring voluntary associations and social institutions which spanned this period. It is possible to trace a pattern of institutional transformation by following the path of a group of social activists who were involved in a series of reforms, public meetings, and political movements, all of which addressed the practical problem of creating more democratic and representative structures in Chinese social organizations. By following such threads of interconnection, it is possible to characterize understandings of citizenship and experiences of democratic organization in associational life—in the absence of a functioning democratic state—in the early Republican period.

In response to the discrediting of the Qing order and the establishment in 1912 of a Chinese Republic, public associations recognized a societal imperative to reconstitute themselves along more democratic and republican lines. Ideas and practices of democracy circulated in translated texts, in the Republican-era press, and in an increasingly abundant variety of public associations. Internally, associations drafted constitutions and improvised public elections and more democratic governance. Externally, associations legitimated themselves by demonstrating that they represented "the public." These transformations in the nature of public associations, together with the expansion of associational life city-wide, testify to the ubiquitous circulation of democractic ideals in the Republic. Of course, it is easier to take on new rhetoric and new organizational overlays than to change daily behavior and habits of mind. This chapter focuses, therefore, on the ways in which democratic changes translated into practice. The associational transformations described here serve to map some of the complexities of a process of intercultural translation or reconfiguration—questions similar to those raised by Lydia Liu in her study of "translingual practice."[2]

Imported into a Chinese context, and in the absence of a working model of representative democracy in the Chinese Republic, the ideas of democracy which circulated in urban areas were denaturalized from their European origins, unbounded by conventions, and uncodified by Chinese practice. Moreover, the aspiring democratic citizens who would deploy these ideas in early Republican Shanghai lacked access to state power. In these ways, the conceptions of democracy in this period may be described as "free-floating." (They were not entirely free-floating, of course, because of the way in which Western associational forms and concepts were immediately bonded to Chinese associations and ideas of local self-government, the predominant conceptual idiom for local activism at the time.)[3] Models of democratic procedures were similarly free-floating, lacking concretization in working practice. On the other hand, because of the multinational character of treaty-port cities like Shanghai, a number of particular local models of government institutions and associational forms readily presented themselves for emulation.

Shanghai's semicolonial character and the nationalist aspirations of Chinese residents for equal rights in the foreign settlements also influenced urban residents to adopt certain forms, rhetoric, and rules of association rather than others.

This confluence of factors suggests that it is unwise to make assumptions about the necessary form, content, or apparent familiarity of democratic impulses and institutions in early Republican urban society. Indeed, observation of the practices of the period helps to problematize "democracy" and reveals the contradictions of democratic concepts set loose from their historical moorings. In what was called an "urban citizens' rights movement"[4] in this period, one cannot help observing a fanciful, redundant, and grandiose variety of associational forms and political initiatives, including a Chamber of Commerce *(Zong shanghui)*, a Commercial Federation *(Shangjie lianhehui)*, a National Federation of Chambers of Commerce *(Quanguo shanghui lianhehui)*, a Federation of Commercial Street Unions *(Shanghai gelu shangjie zong lianhehui)*, a co-existing New Federation of Commercial Street Unions *(Shanghai gelu shangjie lianhe zonghui)*, a National Citizens' Convention *(Guomin huiyi)*, a Citizens' National Affairs Conference *(Guoshi huiyi)*, a Citizens' United Association for Foreign Affairs *(Guomin waijiao lianhe dahui)*, a Conference of National Educational Associations and National Chambers of Commerce *(Quanguo shang-jiao lianxi hui)*, and a United Association of National Representative Interests *(Quanguo gejie lianhehui)*.[5] A look at the overwhelmingly republican rhetoric of the period reveals a similar multiplicity of strategies, possibilities, problems, and contradictions in the articulation of democracy in discourse and practice. By focusing on these "democratic calisthenics"—exercises in the practice of citizenship—I do not mean to suggest a teleological framework. The experiences described here should not be understood as warm-up exercises for something identified as "real democracy." Rather than engage in an attempt to measure democracy or assess whether democracy (with an assumed content) was correctly understood or misunderstood, I will focus instead on how the problem of democracy was integrated into the context of early Republican Shanghai society, and how democracy worked in Chinese practice.

In terms of the public practices of urban residents, what did it mean to have a republic and to try to organize on a democratic basis as citizens? How were the twin imperatives of being public and representing the public expressed? What problems developed in the realization of local democratic forms, particularly in the absence of a successfully functioning republican state?

A series of highly publicized and interrelated democratic challenges and reform movements took place within several key Shanghai institutions and voluntary associations in the period between the "age of Republican innocence"[6] and the ascendance of party-dominated politics in 1924. This chapter examines moments in the organizational redefinition of, in turn, a native-place association, the Shanghai General Chamber of Commerce, the grassroots Commercial Street Unions *(gelu shangjie lianhehui)*, and the Shanghai Ratepayers' Association *(Shanghai gonggong zujie nashui huarenhui)*. Despite the variety of associational or institutional forms and ideas these organizations represented, in their storms and their reforms they reflected overlapping personnel, strategies of struggle, and common problems of definition of democracy and citizenship.

The Reformulation of Shanghai Public Associations: A Brief Overview

The Guang-Zhao Gongsuo Reform. In 1918, a faction within the Guang-Zhao *gongsuo* (the native-place association of sojourners from Guangzhou and Zhaoqing prefectures) contested the traditional administrative structure and practices of the association and advocated a series of modernizing reforms. Contemporary accounts of the crisis that developed delineate a struggle between conservative power-holders and a reform group, based on an existing democratic language of group governance through a board of directors *(dongshihui)*. The *gongsuo* had been governed oligarchically by wealthy Guangdong merchants in Shanghai. Less powerful directors on the board deferred to those whom everyone recognized informally as the authoritative leaders of the association. Although at times a temporary chairman was designated for a particular purpose, normally no individual held a supreme executive post. Instead the *gongsuo* had a designated secretary *(xixi)* who administered the decisions of the group.[7] Despite the existence of a language of elections and set of practices described as "voting," the governing group of directors enjoyed remarkable stability. At the time of the 1918 crisis, most of the older *dongshi* had served for decades.[8]

The reform group was composed of younger businessmen, several of whom had been educated abroad. This "new faction" advocated the reorganization of administrative and electoral procedures, accounting, and an expansion of specific social welfare projects. A major point of contention was a proposal to create permanent leadership positions (a chair and vice-chair) with specified terms of office. Related tensions involved criticism of former directors for insufficient accountability and proposals for (1) a regularized contribution by directors for charitable works; (2) raising the rent on *gongsuo* properties to fund charitable education; and (3) making education and medical services accessible to the broad sojourning community.

The reform proposals highlight problems of governance and self-definition that emerged within the *gongsuo* in the course of the transformation of the national polity from an empire to a republic. In a process of political mirroring, as popular conceptions of legitimacy in government changed at the national level, local associations altered their governing rhetoric in accordance with the ideal images of the new nation and its constituent citizens. Activists within local associations then seized upon the spaces which opened up between rhetoric and practice and expressed the imperative for democratic reform.

Prior to 1912, a handful of directors managed the Guang-Zhao *gongsuo*. In a gesture toward democratization, after the Revolution the number of directors increased from nine to thirty-one.[9] Elections for directors became increasingly salient after the Revolution, but conflicts developed between a modern emphasis on the numerical rationality of electoral procedure and an older cultural calculus that favored seniority and stability. Therefore, despite the formal existence of voting procedures, they were frequently not followed.

After 1911 a generalized republicanism infused the rhetoric of native-place associations. The gap between republican rhetoric and actual practice lent itself to democratic critique. As the reformers put it:

Since the *gongsuo* belongs to the public, its agents should be publicly voted in by the public. . . . Regarding today's so-called *dongshi*

. . . May we ask on which day of which year they were selected, as well as by what sort of election? Does the public publicly elect them by ballot? . . . [The first] directors set up this *gongsuo* with great hardship. They didn't expect that afterward two or three wicked persons would occupy it and make the *gongsuo* their private place *(sisuo)*.[10]

Arguing that it was necessary to "accord with civilized procedures,"[11] in a strategic move on August 11, 1918, the small new faction took advantage of the lax attendance of the directors at meetings to pass a resolution to elect a chair and vice-chair. Seizing the opportunity of the moment (and exhibiting little delicacy of their own in regard to procedures), they called an election on the spot. The conservative directors (most of whom had not been present at the August 11 meeting) were outraged. In the end, despite conservative resistance, the reform faction took control of the *gongsuo*.

The outcome of the Guang-Zhao *gongsuo* crisis was not, in retrospect, surprising. The victory of the reform faction resulted from transformations in ideas and social practice that were expanding the meaning of the "public" and practices of democracy in public culture at the time. Native-place "community" traditionally depended upon the delicate balancing of a form of leadership that was elitist and oligarchic with a rhetoric of inclusive membership.[12] The new legitimacy of a republican rhetoric that advocated electoral rationalization, democracy, progress, and citizenship provided an opportune vocabulary with which the reform faction could stake its claim to participate in the exercise of power.

The careers of three young activists—Tang Jiezhi, Feng Shaoshan, and Huo Shouhua—who rose to positions of prominence in the reformed Guang-Zhao *gongsuo* link this 1918 reform to the subsequent May Fourth and post–May Fourth political agitation in Shanghai. Connections may also be drawn in terms of the ideas and tactics which informed their struggles in 1918 and their political activities a year later over the issue of who could appropriately represent the public and how the public should be represented. The reformed Guang-Zhao *gongsuo* itself, together with a similarly democratized Ningbo native-place association, was also prominent in the May Fourth and the post–May Fourth struggle over citizens' rights *(shimin quan)* in Shanghai.[13]

Challenges to the Shanghai General Chamber of Commerce. In the summer of 1919, Tang Jiezhi, Feng Shaoshan, and Huo Shouhua were vocal among a considerably larger group of activists of diverse provincial backgrounds who engineered a reform movement in the Shanghai General Chamber of Commerce. The immediate catalyst for this "storm within the Chamber" was the May 10 publication of a notorious telegram sent to the Beijing government in the name of the Shanghai Chamber of Commerce, advocating direct negotiations between China and Japan in regard to Qingdao. In indignation, more than fifty Shanghai commercial organizations united in a Commercial Federation and repudiated the telegram as capitulating to Japanese interests and "violating the will of the people."[14]

The reform activists did not stop with the resignations of the chair and vice-chair of the Chamber (Zhu Baosan and Shen Lianfang) and the retraction of the telegram. Rather, they seized upon the public discussion opened by the telegram scandal to air their grievances with the structure and administration of the Chamber of Commerce itself, as an institution representing Chinese commercial interests. In this sense, the Chamber reform movement had less to do with the events of May Fourth and more to do with broader changes in the structure of Shanghai commerce and in social understandings of the responsibilities of representative institutions. When it was revealed that the telegram had not been approved by the board of directors, activists denounced the Chamber as aristocratic, elitist, and unrepresentative. The activists advocated enlarging the membership and lowering fees, as well as creating specialized sections within the Chamber to conduct research and create scientific knowledge of commerce and trade conditions. Despite the relatively smaller size of the reform faction, its challenge bore fruit in 1920 when an expanded base of voters elected an almost entirely new board of directors, among them Tang Jiezhi, Huo Shouhua, and Feng Shaoshan, the very men who had played leading roles in the Guang-Zhao *gongsuo* reform.[15]

The "Commoners' Chamber" and Street Union Movements. At the same time that pressure for democratic reform emerged in the Shanghai General Chamber of Commerce, smaller merchants and shop-owners who were excluded from membership challenged the preeminent role of the Chamber as a representative organ of the Chinese community. By the end of June shop-owners coordinated their efforts to create a "Commoners' Chamber of Commerce" *(pingmin shanghui),* based on the "masses" who were excluded from the General Chamber. Twenty-seven hundred shops from the foreign concessions and from areas of Shanghai under Chinese jurisdiction forwarded their names for registration in this Commoners' Chamber. Although this movement did not get beyond the preliminary drafting of a constitution, the mobilization of petty merchants for a "commoners' chamber" was redirected into the formation of a new and powerful institutional base, a Federation of Commercial Street Unions. In the course of anti-Japanese boycott activity, Chinese merchants had organized themselves by street. Formal "commercial street unions" coalesced in protest after the Municipal Council tried to collect an increased tax levy in July 1919. The rallying cry of the Street Unions' protest was the highly effective "no taxation without representation," a slogan which at least made the British and American municipal councilors cringe, even if it did not cause them to abandon their discriminatory exclusivity.[16]

Street Union agitation reintroduced into public discussion the abiding issue of a Settlement-wide system of representation for Chinese residents.[17] Although the Shanghai Municipal Police forcibly crushed the tax strike, the Street Unions proved effective in mobilizing Chinese residents, arousing the trepidation of foreign observers. On October 26, 1919, more than twenty Street Unions joined together into a Shanghai Federation of Commercial Street Unions. The Street Unions continued to press demands for Chinese representation on the Shanghai Municipal Council. By January 1920, the Federation had doubled the number of member Street Unions and claimed a total constituency of ten thousand shops.[18]

Despite some favorable signs from the foreign consuls, the foreign Ratepayers Association (the body to which the Municipal Council was accountable) rejected the Street Unions' proposal for representation on the Municipal Council in April 1920. At the same time, in recognition of the overwhelming proportion of Settlement taxes paid by Chinese residents (70 to 80 percent), they tossed a crumb in the direction of the restive Chinese community, endorsing a committee of Chinese advisers to the Municipal Council for matters relating to Chinese residents. This half-measure, which conceded no real administrative power to Chinese, nonetheless formally posed the practical question of how to select representatives of the Chinese community. On April 17, the Municipal Council asked the Shanghai General Chamber of Commerce to develop a means of selecting "five Chinese residents . . . suitable for nomination to . . . the Chinese Advisory Committee, who should be as representative as possible of the whole of the Chinese community." Uncertain how to handle the matter in the contentious political atmosphere and less confident in its ability to represent the Chinese community than it had been before the 1919 telegram affair, the Chamber of Commerce waited more than a month before contacting the prominent Chinese commercial and native-place associations in the city. The Chamber's letter is worth citing because the careful wording suggests the authors were aware of the delicacy of the problem posed by any suggestion that the Chamber could itself presume to represent the Chinese community:

> It was decided in our . . . meeting that since the Chamber is a commercial institution we could only elect from our member organizations people who possess qualifications to serve as advisers . . .; that the other organizations whose nature is not commercial, we are not in a position to notify; that we are to write to our member organizations to effect the said election by choosing a few men out to represent them; and that we will gather all the names of the elected to send to the Council.[19]

By acknowledging that only its member commercial organizations were within its purview, the Chinese Chamber of Commerce indicated the myopia of the Municipal Council's expectation that the Chamber could superintend the assemblage of a body that would be representative of the broad Chinese community. Nonetheless, the Chamber did not reject the Council's request. Indeed, the Chinese Chamber of Commerce, together with the major native-place and commercial "guilds," had regularly served in the position of representing the Chinese community in negotiations with the Western authorities of the International Settlement in the past without criticism from the broad Chinese community.[20] At this moment, however, the oligarchic nature of these associations was under challenge. In what was undoubtedly a coordinated gesture, first the Guang-Zhao *gong-suo* and then the Ningbo *tongxianghui,* the two most prominent (and newly reconfigured) native-place associations in the city, placed themselves on the side of the "people." The two native-place associations protested the Chamber's paternalistic approach to representing the Chinese community and publicly rebuked the Chamber for presuming that associations which represented only specific sectors of the Chinese community could appropriately represent the whole. Adopting a pointedly civic, democratic, and non-particularistic stance, the two native-place associations called instead for a general election, contending that "every Chinese ratepayer, even those who are not members of organizations, should be entitled to vote."[21]

The public statements of the Guang-Zhao *gongsuo* and Ningbo *tongxianghui,* published in response to the Chamber's circular, provide a striking articulation of the themes of citizenship, civic rights, political representation, and voting procedures. Reasoning that the creation of the Chinese Advisory Committee resulted from the initiative of Chinese citizens, they argued that the rights of the full body of citizens were at stake *(guanxi quanti shimin quanli)*. Therefore, the selection of the Committee should be in accordance with the public will of the full body of citizens. At the same time as the Guang-Zhao *gongsuo* asserted its own identity as a public and representative association, it argued that a native-place association could not suitably represent the full citizenry:

> Although this *gongsuo* is a public organization representing over one hundred thousand Guangdong people, it comprises but one portion of the entirety of Shanghai residents. Numerous other groups and individuals are ratepayers and should also be entitled to vote. The Committee should be elected by the majority of the full Chinese ratepayer community. This *gongsuo* considers it improper to encroach on the voting rights of so many others by nominating a few persons as you request. . . . We consider it very important that some sort of uniform system be devised and announced for the general information of the public. . . . The [Committee] should be elected according to some regulations to be worked out . . . instead of being appointed by a few commercial organizations or unions.[22]

Even though the public nature of this statement requires that we recognize its rhetoric as self-conscious and strategic, the concerns it articulates are nonetheless remarkable.[23] In them we see the democratic vision, if not always the practice, of the Guang-Zhao reform faction. For these men, *gongsuo* reform was only the initial expression of a democratic political vision that extended beyond the native-place community.

After the public articulation of democratic principles by two leading native-place associations, the Chamber of Commerce, chastised, withdrew from the selection of Chinese advisers. The task of devising a process for electing appropriate representatives fell to the more populist Federation of Commercial Street Unions, suggesting the legitimacy and broad influence of this association in Chinese public opinion in Shanghai at the time. The Federation decided to establish a Chinese Ratepayers' Association *(Huaren nashuihui)*, with regulations modeled on the highly exclusive foreign Ratepayers' Association.[24]

In the meantime, the Federation of Commercial Street Unions itself faced democratic challenges. The context was a new domestic political movement, the campaign by Wu Peifu to establish a National Citizens' Assembly, which was popular in Shanghai commercial circles.[25] In a pattern reminiscent of the Chamber of Commerce telegram affair in 1919, a telegram was published in Shanghai newspapers on July 29, 1920, in the name of the Federation of Commercial Street Unions. The telegram stated that merchants of fifty-seven Shanghai street associations rejected the National Citizens' Assembly because such an assembly contravened the Provisional Constitution of 1912, which established the first elected parliament. (Indeed, the president and vice-president of the Federation, former parliamentarians, supported the old disbanded parliament.)

One after another, individual street associations protested this telegram. On August 7, forty-one street unions published a letter to Wu Peifu and the Jiangsu Military Governor advocating the Citizens' Assembly and repudiating the July 29 telegram. Again, questions were raised about the undemocratic and unconstitutional procedures which permitted the publication of a telegram in the name of a large public association without the consent of its constituent associations. A split between the two groups within the Federation deepened on August 21, with the establishment of a preparatory committee for the National Citizens' Assembly by a group of over one hundred industrial, commercial, and student associations. At the core of this committee were leaders of the Guang-Zhao *gongsuo* (among them Huo Shouhua and Feng Shaoshan), the Ningbo *tongxianghui,* and the group of forty-one street unions. In October, this group of street unions launched a democratization movement within the Federation demanding the impeachment of Federation President Chen Zemin and a revision of the organizational rules, including the abolition of various titles within the organization.[26]

In the next year, in an incident relating to the distribution of ballots for provincial assembly representatives, the two factions within the Federation formally parted company. On September 4, 1921, more than twenty street unions broke with the original Federation and established a New Federation of Commercial Street Unions, which elected Tang Jiezhi as President.[27] Under calls for "democracy" (translated as *pingmin zhuyi*)[28] and "egalitarianism" *(pingdeng lun),* the slogans of the 1919 Commoners' Chamber of Commerce movement, the New Federation instituted a new representative system *(daiyi zhi).* In doing so, the New Federation emphasized its departure from the board of directors' management system *(dongshihui)* of the old Federation (indeed, the New Federation's criticisms of the old Federation in this regard are reminiscent of the criticisms the old Federation had launched against the Chamber of Commerce). The New Federation also encompassed prominent labor leaders and organizations *(Zhongguo gonghui, Zhonghua laodong lianhehui).* The two federations coexisted, sharing influence in Shanghai, until their reunification in August 1923, in the context of a revitalized anti-Japanese boycott movement.[29]

Challenges to the Chinese Ratepayers' Association. The Street Unions associated with the radical "commoners'" faction that established the New Federation also clashed with the nascent Chinese Ratepayers' Association (CRA). This is not surprising, because the CRA was in the process of establishing itself as the legitimate voice of the residents of the International Settlement, the fruit of the stormy movement for citizens' rights that unfolded in these years. The principles for membership within the CRA followed the model of the foreign Ratepayers' Association and required substantial ownership of property. This meant that, in its realization, the CRA incorporated a degree of exclusivity and superiority that corresponded better to the old "aristocratic" Chamber of Commerce. This conflicted with the more inclusive "commoner" initiatives that had challenged the Chamber and mobilized the citizens' rights movement.[30]

Despite these processes of internal and external challenge and reform, this diverse group of associations provided a strong institutional network for the organization of public politics in Shanghai in the early 1920s. Subsets of these organizations provided the institutional framework for the organization of the National Affairs Conference *(Guoshi huiyi)* as well as the massive anti-Japanese boycott of 1923.[31]

Each of these movements developed within a complex institutional background and encompassed a diverse cast of characters. The institutions involved characteristically split into older and reform factions, sometimes creating new associational offshoots with which they later reunited in the face of domestic crises that demanded coordinated action for common interests. Individual movements represented specific and contingent responses to factors internal to each organization as well as to the larger political and economic context: domestic disorders and the shifting factions of government under the Republic, and growing popular concern with the transnational semicolonial frameworks governing the International Settlement and China more broadly. It is beyond the scope— or purpose—of this chapter to narrate the intricate contests of power, personnel, and rhetoric characteristic of these movements.[32] Rather, they are sketched here in order to illustrate the problematics of "free-floating" democracy, as democratic ideas and rituals became material in Chinese practice. The following discussion considers, in turn, the press; the multiplicity of institutional forms; problems with democratic procedures, elections, and legality; uniformity and dissent; issues of representation and definition of the social body; and the magnitude of technical problems in the absence of state resources.

The Role of the Press

The importance of the press in these events cannot be exaggerated.[33] Public media played a major role in all of these movements which constituted the "citizens' rights movement" in Shanghai in this period. It was by virtue of the tactical use of public media—both printed pamphlets *(chuandan)* and commercial newspapers—by all sides in these disputes that what might have been internal discussions escalated into public waves of agitation.

Different media addressed different, if overlapping, publics and enjoyed somewhat distinctive statuses within Shanghai public culture. Pamphlets were distributed within specific communities, where it was virtually assured that their contents would be read. In this respect, the public they reached was narrower than that of newspapers. Nonetheless, pamphlets—which were written in simpler language—were the medium of a more popular and less literate public sphere. In this respect they reached more deeply into society than newspapers. The persistent use of pamphlets at this time provides a reminder that newspapers were only poorly comprehended or unread by many.

An indication of the different spheres of newspaper and pamphlet readership appears in a pamphlet distributed by the Fuzhou Road and other Street Unions, which protested the mechanism of communication used by the Chinese Ratepayers' Association. The grassroots Street Unions complained of the CRA's exclusive use of newspaper announcements and its corresponding failure to circulate information in easy-to-read pamphlets:

All of the [announcements] inserted in the newspapers are merely a matter of form, [and there is no attempt to make their] meaning clear. Chinese merchants in general are well educated, but the ordinary Chinese do not know the meaning of the ads. Besides inserting ads in the newspapers, the association has never published any circulars in simple language. We have to ask the Chinese Ratepayers' Association how many persons in the International Settlement read newspapers, how many do not, how many can read, how many cannot and how many can only read simple literature. The Association [is] under the control of literary men.[34]

Despite this evidence that a level of public discussion was carried out through the circulation of pamphlets, it is also clear that—with the exception of the smaller individual Street Unions—all parties in these associational disputes regularly published paid announce-

ments in the major Shanghai papers. At high points in various movements, a series of these advertisements, placed by contending parties
in the names of their associations, could appear side-by-side in a single newspaper, forming a noticeable block of newspaper page. Such
notices not only brought the various disputes into the public eye;
they were also part of a legitimating strategy to *be* public. Being public was imperative for all public associations, because communication with the people was fundamental to concepts of social representation in the Republic. The movements sketched above were also
heavily featured in the news sections of all the leading newspapers, which printed summaries of meetings, speeches, and, on occasion, transcriptions of the ads and pamphlets being circulated (with
the result that paid ads at times appeared doubly as both ads and
news).[35]

Thus, in a manner that is familiar today, the newspapers were instrumental actors in the events that unfolded.[36] The Guang-Zhao
gongsuo crisis was fought out by contending factions on the pages of
the Shanghai dailies. In both the Chamber of Commerce and Federation of Commercial Street Unions disputes, it was the publication
of telegrams in the newspapers which exposed the political activities
of association officers to public scrutiny, setting off storms of reaction. After the telegram episode, the reform group within the Shanghai General Chamber of Commerce deftly used the vibrant May
Fourth press to gather popular support to challenge established
leaders. In a departure from past discretion, disgruntled members
openly published reprimands of the Chamber in the newspapers,
questioning the ability of the elected leaders to represent the commercial community.[37] Prior to this activist use of the commercial
press, oligarchic leaders could manipulate the constitutionally democratic procedures of their associations to their own ends. However,
in this era of rapidly proliferating public media they could no longer
control public discussion. The extraordinary media access of this period provided the opening that reformers used to expose exclusive
or corrupt practices.

These new uses of the press were volatile in an associational culture that had not customarily circulated records beyond oligarchic
circles of leadership. Once accounts of association meetings became
public, disputes arose over the newspaper reports. Parties who were

absent or not notified of "public" meetings frequently contested their validity, publishing outraged refutations. The radical ways in which new media access cut against the grain of older associational habits may be indicated by two examples. In the Guang-Zhao *gongsuo* crisis, the conservative faction responded to the publication of the reformers' proposals with paid announcements that might be described as proclamations of non-recognition. Such notices habitually ended with phrases like "our members do not recognize [them]" *(tongren bu neng chengren)*. Similarly, after one faction within the Federation of Commercial Street Unions published an account of a meeting in which an early discussion of the composition of the Chinese Advisory Committee had taken place, the other faction was incensed. The shock effect of the press in this period is indicated in the tone of their published refutation: "They have no right to publish the conversation of a minority of street delegates. Publication in the press is a serious matter."[38] Such stern assertions of control in a new media realm of public access read somewhat comically and anachronistically amidst the flood of contending accounts. They do, nonetheless, indicate the impact of the press and the awkwardness of cultural accommodation to its potential for public revelation in this period.

The reform movements outlined here not only took place largely through media discussion, but they also stimulated the creation of new newspapers as organs of particular reform factions. The Guang-Zhao *gongsuo* reformers Tang Jiezhi and Feng Shaoshan were closely linked to the publication of the *Guang-Zhao Weekly*.[39] Critics of the Shanghai General Chamber of Commerce urged the regular publication of updated commercial and political news. Feng Shaoshan, in particular, was associated with the new *Journal of the Shanghai General Chamber of Commerce (Shanghai zongshanghui yuekan)*.[40] The new Chinese Ratepayers' Association launched a monthly journal, entitled *Citizen's Gazette (Shimin gongbao)*, in January 1920.[41] The Street Union movement contained within it a number of journalistic initiatives. The Nanjing Road Commercial Street Union published a journal.[42] In the beginning of 1921, Tang Jiezhi, President of the New Federation of Commercial Street Unions, successfully launched a major new commercial daily in Shanghai, the *Journal of Commerce (Shangbao)*, which publicized all of the citizens' movements in the city.[43]

Though the press was open to manipulation by different groups who claimed to represent the public, its overall effect in this period of relative press freedom and intense press competition was radically democratic, furthering public awareness of politics as well as expectations of openness and accountability.[44] This democratic function was not necessarily a result of the quality of newspaper reportage or the objectivity of newspapers in this period. Indeed, in this period there was little actual reportage (and reportage was of poor quality), and professional notions of "objectivity" would not emerge for a number of years.[45] The democratic function resulted, rather, from the remarkable proliferation of newspapers in this period and their relative accessibility.

The Problem of Institutional Form

If the Republican-era press functioned to open and expand the realm of "the public" in this period, other vehicles of reform agitation had more ambivalent or contradictory roles in regard to practices of democracy. One arena of ambiguity involved the question of the appropriate associational form for a representative institution. Understanding the issue of associational form involves three considerations: (1) the utility of old and new associational structures; (2) the availability of divergent models; and (3) strategic considerations in the adoption of particular forms. Rather than characterizing the period as lacking an institutional basis for practices of democracy, it is more appropriate to characterize it instead through an equally problematic superabundance of forms. As the brief narrative of associational agitation provided above reflects, a variety of old and new institutional structures provided effective bases for the mobilization of democratic movements and for associational reform. These associations were relatively enduring in the flux of the times, persisting through a series of domestic regimes, international crises, and a variety of popular movements. At the same time, perhaps because of the multiplicity of institutional forms, models, and democratic ideas available, associational fluidity was characteristic of the period.

As illustrated in the case of the Guang-Zhao *gongsuo*, reformers reworked older, specifically Chinese, associational forms. Native-place *huiguan* and *gongsuo* became modern *gongsuo* and *tongxianghui*. Associations which had long "represented" their constituent sojourner communities to Chinese officials developed representative functions vis-à-vis foreign authorities in the city.[46]

At the same time that reformers reconfigured their native-place associations, they used their power bases in these reformed institutions to gain power within and transform the relatively long-standing hybrid institution of the Shanghai Chamber of Commerce. This institution was created on the basis of models drawn from observations of the interactions of Western and Japanese chambers of commerce and their consular authorities in China. Though patterned on a Western associational form, the chamber of commerce concept was reconfigured in Chinese culture, becoming something quite different. The importance of Western-inspired Chinese chambers of commerce, as not simply commercial organizations but political institutions thrust into a representative position on behalf of the Chinese community (in relation to both Chinese and foreign authorities) is striking in Chinese history.[47] The special importance of chambers of commerce in modern Chinese history resulted from the semi-official nature of their charters as established in the context of the late Qing reforms, and the availability of such chambers as an institutional form which could integrate various native-place and occupational groups in cities dense with sojourning populations. In Shanghai, because of the semicolonial structure of government in the International Settlement and the inclination of the foreign Municipal Council to deal directly with Chinese commercial circles rather than with representatives of the Chinese government, the importance of the Chamber of Commerce was heightened. For this confluence of reasons, in Shanghai in particular (as the preeminent commercial city and treaty port), the Western-modeled institution acquired a central and rather non-Western political importance in the absence of an alternative representative governing structure of the Chinese community.

The democratic potential of different associations varied with the associational form. *Huiguan* and *tongxianghui* encompassed different economic strata within their fellow-provincial rhetoric. This feature facilitated their transformation into associations that could have a modern "mass" aspect and, for that reason, an increasingly democratic appearance in the context of reform agendas. The limitation of the native-place associations, of course, was the particularistic nature of their regionally defined constituencies. In contrast, the Chamber of Commerce brought together the diverse native-place groups which constituted the broad Shanghai Chinese community. The Shanghai General Chamber of Commerce in the Republican era was, however, limited by its ties to Chinese officials in the discredited Beijing government and by its elite membership. In the context of a democratic movement, these features left the Chamber vulnerable to charges by populists of non-representative, arbitrary, exclusive, and aristocratic governance.

Although native-place associations and the Chamber of Commerce retained importance in organizing Shanghai society throughout this period, the limitations of each in terms of, respectively, interregional and multiclass principles of organization created a space for the appearance of the new institutional form of the Commercial Street Unions. As a territorial form based on local Shanghai streets, this structure both resembled late imperial neighborhood order-keeping and fire-fighting associations and was adaptable to widely accepted notions of local self-government. A federation composed of all of the settlement streets could appear to represent the full body of Chinese residents. The source for the Republican-era Street Unions was Japanese, specifically, street associations formed for self-defense in the Hongkou area by Japanese residents in the face of rising anti-Japanese agitation by Chinese residents.[48] The accidental nature of this transcultural import, and its irony, was not lost on a Western observer: "It is curious to note that the Chinese form of [Street Unions], which first appeared at the time of the anti-Japanese agitation three months ago, should be built on a Japanese model."[49] Although these Japanese mutual help, self-defense, even vigilante, groups provided the undeniable model for the Chinese Street Unions, in the leap from the sojourning Japanese to the Chinese context, the meaning of the form was opened to radical reinterpretation. In practice, the Street Unions provided the most radical instantiation of local, grassroots democratic structures. The utility of the form facilitated a citywide grassroots movement, which provided an effective institutional framework for the political organization of Shanghai urban society for several years, prior to the predominance of Guomindang and Communist party organization.[50]

The alien form of the Chinese Ratepayers' Association, in contrast, appears to have been far less adaptable, remaining instead an uncomfortable and overly exclusive institutional expression of the broadly populist citizens' rights movement that underlay its creation. In this case, however—in contrast to the accidental but opportune appearance of the Japanese Street Union structure which could be inhabited by Chinese residents to meet their needs—the specificities of form were dictated by the exigencies of semicolonial power relations. Within the Anglo-American-dominated framework of the International Settlement, not all forms were equally acceptable. The Chinese were inclined to emulate the foreigners Ratepayers' Association as a model. The creation of a Chinese Ratepayers' Association was a strategic act in two senses. It was an obvious assertion of parity with the foreigners in the city. In addition, it involved the choice of the model most likely to be acceptable to the Anglo-American-dominated Municipal Council, which claimed the right to approve or reject the Chinese advisers selected by the Chinese community.

The strategic adoption of the Anglo-American electoral model of the International Settlement Ratepayers' Association masked understandings of representation and democracy which were substantially different from those underlying the Anglo-American institution. Although the reformed native-place associations which collaborated in the formation of the Chinese Ratepayers' Association did not directly challenge the property assumptions of "ratepayer" discourse, different understandings of the mechanisms of representation are evident in differences between the Chinese texts of the *gongsuo* and *tongxianghui* statements and the English translations that were published in the *North China Herald*. The Chinese texts, despite their references to electoral procedures, nonetheless suggest a more direct notion of democracy, describing urban citizens as the political actors who themselves achieved political change *(hua guwen zhi she, wanquan wei huaren . . . shimin zhi fadong)*. Although the Chinese texts stipulate property qualifications for voting, they nonetheless suggest that the committee should be selected through the "public will of the full body of citizens" *(ying you quanti shimin gongyi tuixuan)*. Such emphases are consistent with the currents of populism and direct democracy which informed the May Fourth rhetoric of popular sovereignty.[51] The specificity of these Chinese understandings is blurred in the English translations, which not only downplayed the agency of Chinese citizens but "corrected" the Chinese text in order to emphasize Anglo-American mechanisms of political representation: "those nominated should . . . have the confidence of their electors as a whole in order that they may properly represent their constituencies."[52]

Given these differing conceptions of democracy, it is not surprising that the same Chinese groups which had fought for the Chinese Ratepayers' Association were quick to denounce its ability to function as a representative institution. In any event, deprived of any real access to political power, and shoehorned into an imitative and inappropriate format, the CRA never fulfilled the expectations that fueled its creation.[53]

The Awkwardness of Elections, Rules, and Formal Legal Procedures

All of the early Republican-era associations discussed here were constituted as representative associations, in which officers were elected through a public procedure, and in which a framework existed for participatory democracy via public meetings, discussion, and voting. General democratic frameworks had existed in Shanghai since the late Qing period, developing gradually within gentry-merchant associations like *huiguan, gongsuo,* and charitable halls *(shantang).* Formalized procedures for voting emerged in the first decade of the twentieth century, first in the General Chamber of Commerce and then in the Chinese City Council.[54] Though general democratic frameworks existed within these associations and in many *huiguan* and *gongsuo* in the late Qing period, prior to the engagement of these associations with an activist press, such bodies remained relatively closed to the public. Administrative functions were contained within a small and elite group of recognized gentry-merchant leaders. Internal conflicts were generally concealed beneath a smooth exterior of unanimity.[55]

In the early Republican era, contending factions within and on the margins of associations contested and attempted to redefine their associations' democratic procedures. The vigor of such struggles suggests both the increasing impact of the press and the difficulty of accommodating older traditions of associational life and decision-making to the new hegemonic imperatives of republican governance. In the case of the Guang-Zhao *gongsuo,* certain democratic reforms had developed as a result of the Republican Revolution. Nonetheless, there was little to ensure that the new rules were followed in practice. In regard to voting, as one of the *gongsuo* reformers recounted:

> In the election held in the second year of the Republic, only two people voted for Mr. Tang Qiaoqing. In contrast, Mr. Chen Yizhou received sufficient votes to be elected. Mr. Chen then wrote a letter to the *gongsuo,* recommending that Mr. Tang should take his [Chen's] position. Because the directors felt that Mr. Tang had served as director for years, they did not require that he receive sufficient votes. Therefore Mr. Tang was made a director together with Mr. Chen.[56]

Whereas prior to 1912 there had been twelve assemblymen within the *gongsuo,* from the first year of the Republic the number increased. The increase gestured toward inclusiveness, but the method of identifying assemblymen was not promising for the development of more open and rational governance. Selection depended on the recommendations of individual directors, and the procedures were irregular. As one reform-side director commented: "Some directors recommended more than ten [individuals]. Therefore the total number of assemblymen increased to eighty. With yearly increases the number has now reached 161."[57]

Without clear election procedures to modify the oligarchic decision-making practices, and with a far greater number of representatives than the actual relations of power within the organization reflected, most of the officers did not attend meetings.[58] In 1918, the eight senior directors were too old to leave their houses. Business was frequently conducted by only three or four individuals. There were no regulations stipulating a quorum.[59]

The reform fervor in the Shanghai General Chamber of Commerce, like that in the Guang-Zhao *gongsuo,* concentrated on organizational and procedural issues. Since its inception as an institution based on a modern Western model, the Chamber had adopted a representative structure with formal voting procedures as a means of integrating and negotiating among the different native-place and trade constituencies of the Shanghai commercial community. Nonetheless, the Chamber did not operate in a particularly open or democratic fashion prior to the May Fourth era. In the course of the inquiry that followed the infelicitous telegram sent to the Beijing government regarding Qingdao, a number of systemic lapses in procedure came to light. The Chamber was routinely lax in regard to rules for a quorum. Meetings were relatively infrequent (bimonthly), attendance was low, and urgent matters were often decided single-handedly by the chair or even the vice-chair. Moreover, the governing body of the Chamber existed in a state of regular violation of its own constitution: "According to article 24, members could serve only two terms in succession on the board of directors, but the fact is that many of the present directors have ignored this time limit by serving for many years in succession."[60] Critics claimed that a clique held control of the Chamber, electing its own men every year, in willful disregard of the regulations.

Similarly, critics of the Chinese Ratepayers' Association revealed substantial procedural malfeasance. The CRA failed to properly identify ratepayers who met the tax and property qualifications required to vote and to stand for election:

> It was the duty of the investigating committee of the Chinese Ratepayers' Association . . . to ascertain names of all qualified persons. Four months have elapsed during which no careful investigations were made. As a result, a list of about three hundred persons only was published as qualified. If this is compared with the [full] Chinese ratepayers list, . . . there are numerous names omitted, which will cause surprise—more than four hundred Chinese in the International Settlement pay an annual rate of $1,200, and there are between one and two thousand whose immovable property is valued at $500 or more. But the Association failed to make inquiries. Why were investigations not carried out properly?[61]

The frequency of such devastating critiques of procedure suggests, not surprisingly, that constitutions could be a matter of appearance. The constitutional stipulations for democratic process—easy to draft —could be alien to familiar cultural practices and also could demand onerous work for which associations were ill-equipped. Despite the *de rigueur* display of a constitution, mechanisms and resources were lacking to translate specific democratic stipulations into regularized practice. The publication of procedural lapses in the press, of course, was a useful weapon in the hands of activists. At the same time, activists were hardly more circumspect in their reverence for the democratic rules of citizenship. This seems particularly true in matters relating to precise mechanisms of representation. Formal rules for representative procedures appeared awkward in the context of the pervasive rhetoric of direct democracy.

Although democratic procedures technically in place were only inattentively followed, the ingrained habits of the elected boards of these institutions made it difficult for activists—always a numerical minority—to transform these institutions through normal electoral means. Without unprecedented use of the press to blow open institutional covers, it is unlikely that the reformers could have developed the leverage to force practices to change. Reformers also resorted to extra-procedural steps, coups, or sleights of hand in order to gain sufficient control to effect democratic reform.[62] Such rule-bending and manipulation of democratic procedure was necessitated by the exclusiveness of membership qualifications, facilitated by the impermanence of constitutions in these associations (which revised their constitutions at least as frequently as the new Republic did), and encouraged by the rhetoric of direct democracy. These practices, nonetheless, frequently made reformers as vulnerable to criticism of arbitrary behavior as the factions they opposed.

Similar obstacles to democratic citizenship existed in regard to the broad legality of the citizens' rights movement in the semicolonial context of the International Settlement. Technically, changes in the administration of the International Settlement could only be negotiated between the Chinese government and the foreign consuls. This, of course, was unlikely to happen. The lawyer Chen Zemin, President of the Federation of Commercial Street Unions, elided the problem as he urged activism on his followers in regard to the establishment of the Chinese Ratepayers' Association. Like other Chinese reformers in similar circumstances, Chen advocated a patriotic citizenship that was free from subservience to actual Chinese officials or law:

According to law, the authorities of the two nations should undertake the revision, but as they are seriously concerned, the citizens should first do their part and then the law will follow. If the [Chinese] government makes the proposal to the ratepayers, there will be doubts as to whether the people desire representation or not, but we, being ratepayers, [should nonetheless take action. This] will indicate that Chinese know not only their officials but also know what concerns themselves. The application is very proper.[63]

The Uniform Collective Citizen and the Problem of Dissent

The notion of an urban citizenry that is evoked in the documents produced by the associations and in newspaper reportage is unambiguously collective and unified. The citizens' rights movement was understood as a movement of groups, not individuals. The terms *tuanti yundong* (group movement) and *shimin yundong* (citizens' movement) were used interchangeably. Within the Chamber of Commerce, the Commoners' Chamber of Commerce, and the Street Unions, membership was by commercial concern (a firm or a shop) rather than by individuals. In a similar vein, political telegrams and letters to newspapers most commonly bore the names of groups rather than individuals.

If individuals were traditionally downplayed, this cultural tendency was reinforced in the political environment of the Republic. In the context of Chinese nationalism, in regard to both the predatory factions of Chinese militarists and a broadly recognized urgency for unity in opposition to foreign penetration of China, the individual was devalued, as representing selfish interests in regard to the public good, and as "loose sand" in regard to the urgency of national coherence. The rhetoric of nationalism, as formulated by Liang Qichao, Sun Yat-sen, and others, advocated various forms of grouping as the vehicle for citizenship in the absence of state participatory structures.[64]

This defensive emphasis on group unity in the context of modern Chinese nationalism helps to explain a prevalent feature of the democratic agitations sketched here: their pervasive intolerance of dissent. The perceived need to strengthen China and the semicolonial context of the struggle for Chinese representation on the Shanghai Municipal Council worked to reinforce the lack of a cultural framework that could easily encompass dissent. The absence of such a framework is evident in the factionalism and splitting which characterized the reform movements. Reformers, like the conservatives they criticized, manifested a habitual insistence on associational unity. In their visions of democracy, public opinion was presumed to be uniform and united.

After Guang-Zhao *gongsuo* reformers organized a public meeting to discuss the reforms they advocated, they were preoccupied with manufacturing unanimity, both in the meeting and in their records of it. After the reformers' speeches, "the whole audience raised their hands and passed [their proposal]."[65] Having demonstrated that public sentiment was on their side, the reformers exulted: "Whenever a proposal was put to a vote, all of the participants raised their hands, and no one opposed it. This shows that public opinion will decide what is right and what is wrong."[66] When, despite careful stage management, someone from the opposition unexpectedly mounted the stage and made a speech, the democratic reformers chased him away with no sense that their action violated their new democratic order: "[Su's] speech was so absurd that the audience burst into an uproar. . . . Soon the whole audience began to shout and made him stop, saying that this kind of seditious speech could not be tolerated. Su paled and fled the stage."[67]

Another striking example of the suppression of dissent by an association born of democratic aspirations may be found in a report of a meeting of the Federation of Commercial Street Unions. The Federation convened a special meeting to counteract the negative effect on public opinion of a pamphlet published by the Fuzhou Road Street Union, which opposed the Federation's organization of the Chinese Ratepayers' Association. The published protests of the Fuzhou Road Street Union were embarrassing for the establishment of the CRA and threatened its legitimacy because they detailed gross lapses of democratic procedure. Rather than reply to criticisms of procedural irregularities, the president of the Hankou Road Street Union, who presided at the Federation meeting, argued that the Chinese needed to maintain unity in the face of the Western community. Urging that "vigorous measures should be taken to stamp out anything tending to disturb that unity," he asked all representatives at the meeting, together with the residents they represented, to "treat Zhao Nangong, President of the Fuzhou Road Street Union, who was attempting to sow seeds of dissension, with contempt." The assembly resolved to take no notice of Zhao's protest. After this meeting individual street unions passed resolutions condemning Zhao Nangong, in a fashion reminiscent of practices of village ostracism.[68]

Such intolerance coexisted with the increasing evidence of dissent, and indeed, the widespread social recognition that even the most modern groups were not successfully unified. Inability to maintain unity and to successfully discipline dissent—despite the will to repress it—was what distinguished May Fourth era associations from those of either the late Qing or the imminent period of party-dominated politics. The evidence was everywhere—in the splitting of associations, in contrary accounts in the newspapers, in the increasingly revelatory reportage of differences of opinion, and, finally, in the increasingly open record-keeping practices of the associations themselves.

Defining, Representing, and Encompassing the Social Body

The miscellany of democratic ideas and forms of citizenship circulating in Shanghai fed two oscillating conceptions of the participating citizenry, one more exclusive and one more egalitarian. The democratic movements of this period are generally understood in terms of the new social elite, the bourgeoisie.[69] Certainly the category *shang* characterized the majority of participants in these movements, and certainly a significant stream of the democratic rhetoric enveloping the "citizens' rights" movement referred specifically to people in commercial and industrial circles. The social legitimacy of this commercial elite lay not in its wealth—which could not convey virtue even in the new Chinese Republic—but rather in its modernity. This is clear from the constitution of the Chinese Ratepayers' Association, which justified the uncomfortable property requirements for voting by stating that the CRA was for the self-government of the "advanced sector" (*fada jie*) of the Chinese population.[70] Nonetheless, the legitimacy of this sector, as leaders of public associations and movements for citizens' rights, depended in addition on its ability to persuasively represent, or somehow encompass, a larger "public."

Despite the fact that the associational movements described here were generally limited to the bourgeoisie and their petty bourgeois challengers, the Chinese aspirations referred to in this chapter as broadly democratic expressed a more encompassing embrace of the poor than is evoked by conventional conceptualizations of "bourgeois democracy."[71] Marie-Claire Bergère, in particular, has noted the peculiarly harmonious class vision of the radical reformers in this movement. Chen Laixin has gone further to characterize the "citizens' rights" movement as genuinely popular, noting the participation of labor leaders and labor associations.[72]

The populist social programs of the reform movements reflect ways in which the floating democratic rhetoric of equality found cultural anchors in older Chinese notions of hierarchy, community, and benevolence, and in the emerging ideas of populism these traditions engendered in the Republican era. Several of the reform movements demonstrated a real commitment to social welfare for the poor. This incorporation of social programs within new political initiatives suggests a distinctive strand of interpretation in popular Chinese implementations of democracy.

Two contending versions of populism are apparent in the materials surveyed here. In the movement for the Commoners' Chamber of Commerce, launched by 2,700 shop-keepers, the term "commoner" referred to the smaller shop-keepers and merchants who were excluded from membership in elite commercial institutions. They charged that the existing chambers of commerce in the International Settlement and in the Chinese city did not represent "the people" and did not give the commercial class in general a chance to raise its voice. They argued for inclusion as active and equal participants:

> We feel that the existing chambers of commerce have nothing to do with us . . . They assume such an important and patronizing air that we are not even fit to talk with their members. Although there are tens of thousands of merchants in Shanghai the membership of the [General] Chamber of Commerce [in the International Settlement] is limited to 200. . . . [T]here is all kinds of red tape when we common merchants desire to join the Chamber. The membership fee [is prohibitive, and] the present members do not like us, [so] we are turned down . . . It is the duty of every chamber to facilitate

communication and exchange intelligence between merchants. . . .
But has our chamber done so? In a word, we have no chamber of
commerce at Shanghai. The chambers we have at present are too
exclusive and unrepresentative. . . . We therefore consider it our
eminent duty to organize a plebiscite chamber of commerce, which
will represent the genuine sentiment of the merchants in Shanghai.[73]

This "commoners'" movement also provided for an array of social
programs, including the establishment of a school, a magazine, a
museum, and an arbitration bureau, as well as the employment of a
physician, a legal adviser, and a pharmacist. In this case these programs were envisioned as serving "commoner merchants" alone, although "commoner merchants" represented a significant addition
to the small group of institutionally represented "aristocratic merchants."

Generally, however, the individuals in commercial circles who led
democratic reform movements indicated that they represented a
constituency that extended more broadly into society. This second
approach to representing the common people is most obvious, and
perhaps least surprising, in the case of the Guang-Zhao *gongsuo* reform, because Shanghai native-place associations (despite their merchant leadership) traditionally reached across classes to theoretically
encompass the large sojourner community.

As noted earlier, a major component of the Guang-Zhao *gongsuo*
reform entailed the provision of charity. Both sides in the *gongsuo*
dispute, recognizing the modern imperative to represent the people, called attention to their side's provision of public works. One
might see this focus on welfare activities as an extension of traditional bonds of social benevolence and reciprocity that knit together
the hierarchical social order of sojourner communities.[74] Certainly it
was through such traditional practices that the conservative side understood the notion of representation. Moreover, the Confucian
classics were still sufficiently salient among educated Shanghai urbanites—despite the anti-Confucian rants of *Xin Qingnian* and other
New Culture magazines—that even reformers took care to gird their
social program with references to Mencius.[75]

Nonetheless, despite the undoubted cultural resonance of acts of benevolence, in important respects the reformers' advocacy of charity was distinctively modern. Whereas the *gongsuo* conservatives were inclined to focus their charitable energies on funerary accommodations, the reformers advocated medical services and vocational education. Not only did their benevolence take a modern direction, but also the reformers effectively challenged *gongsuo* conservatives by demonstrating their own commitment to "the people" in a more regular and substantial fashion than their opponents. This involved a major increase in the overall financial commitment of the *gongsuo* to community welfare, as well as a rationalization of the provision of welfare through regular institutionalized contributions to public works by all of the *gongsuo* directors. Whereas the older directors had been more accustomed to irregular and often symbolic acts of charity, what the reformers had in mind was something closer to institutionalized welfare programs.

In an effective bid to gain broad support within the sojourning community, the reformers presented their reforms as a plan to tax the rich in order to help the poor:

> Here in Shanghai our poor children are not in school. One thousand and several hundred of them register for the charitable school every year and cannot gain admission. We have never heard that the able and virtuous directors provided anything for them. The rent of [*gongsuo*-owned properties], if raised to market price, would provide tens of thousands of yuan each year. However . . . the directors have never promoted education for the benefit of our thousands of poor and pitiable children in Shanghai. And these children are daily driven to degradation.[76]

Advocating a broad program of taxation for social welfare programs, the reformers characterized their opponents as misers: "to get these people to open their moneybags is like cutting flesh from their cheeks . . . Don't they know that we should enable our sons and brothers to study? As for the sons and brothers of our poor fellow-provincials, can we exclude them?" The democratic vision here—in terms of ideas of access and provision for the poor—is striking. Though paternalistic, the reformers invested older notions of benevolence with a new substantiality, infusing an idea of social urgency, even basic economic and educational rights for the poor, into older notions of benevolence.[77]

The emphasis on charity within the *gongsuo* reform movement may not seem so surprising, given the traditional ties of patronage that bound sojourner communities. The presence of similar charitable concerns is more striking, perhaps, in the grassroots Street Unions, which only emerged in the context of the May Fourth movement and were not based on a preexisting type of Chinese urban association. Nonetheless, charitable provision was evidently a part of the definitions of democracy and egalitarianism (*pingmin zhuyi, pingdenglun*), the rhetorical banners under which the Federation of Commercial Street Unions coalesced in opposition to the more exclusive General Chamber of Commerce. The Street Unions in the New Federation demonstrated their commitment to egalitarianism and populism by providing a broad array of local social programs.

When they are remembered at all, the Street Unions are noted for their agitation for Chinese representation, or, secondarily, for their role in social mobilization in domestic and political affairs. That is, their democratic commitments are understood through primarily *political* notions of citizen action and representation. But it is important to note that their social mobilization abilities were based on their ability to legitimate themselves in Chinese society as associations representing not just merchants but the people. In practice, this meant an extraordinary range of social welfare activities. Street Unions were involved in rice price stabilization and the establishment of cheap rice depots for the poor, the creation of night schools (funded by the proprietors of the larger shops), the negotiation of rent reductions with landlords (even the organization of rent boycotts),[78] the formulation of mechanisms to combat the use of debased coinage,[79] and the hiring of doctors for free or nearly free medical care for poor street residents.[80] The provision of such services in Shanghai by Street Unions, even for a period of a few years, deserves notice.

It was by virtue of the provision of social welfare that the more elite leaders of associations claimed to represent the larger social body, particularly the poor. Though reform leaders took pains to encompass the poor and attend to their economic and educational rights, the reformers' social vision did not empower the poor as full citizens. When the poor were included, their inclusion did not imply a concept of equal political rights or an equal voice; rather, they were incorporated into the community through paternalistic acts of charity.

Inventing a Mechanism for Representing the Chinese Community

The welfare practices discussed above highlight the ways in which democratic notions were tied to historical practices of inclusion through benevolent provision. As such, the welfare concerns of several of the associational movements reveal ways that older Chinese notions of social cohesion infused new ideas and practices of democratic organization. This is reflected in the range of terms used for "democracy" in this period. The term *minben zhuyi*—suggesting the transformation of the hoary ideal of *minben* into a modern doctrine—was used as an equivalent to *pingmin zhuyi* and *minzhu zhuyi*, even in the rhetoric of radical iconoclasts.[81] This infusion of older meanings or concerns into the social production of new democratic meaning in Chinese society is one theme in this sketch of democratic calisthenics. Another theme is the "unmappability" or "untranslatability" of particular frameworks for citizenship in the Chinese political context. The history of the creation of the Chinese Advisory Committee and the Chinese Ratepayers' Association suggests the difficulty of an *ex nihilo* creation of either a universal community of "citizens" (which transcended both class and occupational tie, the two axes of traditional associational community in urban areas), or an elected representative body. The invention of a mechanism for representing the Chinese community was not straightforward in a context in which no such mechanism had previously existed.

The initial concept of a Chinese Advisory Committee (CAC) of five individuals was developed by the foreign Shanghai Municipal Council. The Municipal Council proposed that the CAC be formed of two nominees of the Ningbo *tongxianghui*, two nominees of the Guang-Zhao *gongsuo*, and one nominee of the Chinese Commissioner of Foreign Affairs, Yang Cheng.[82] The Municipal Council's formula both encompassed traditional Chinese associations and also gestured toward the inclusion of the Chinese government. As such, the Municipal Council did not envision the creation of a new representative body for the Chinese residents.

Nonetheless, once the proposal for a CAC moved into the Chinese community for implementation, it became clear that this formula was unacceptable, not simply because of the alienation of Shanghai residents from Chinese officials, but also because the frameworks of native-place organizations could not encompass the full body of imagined citizens. In Chinese considerations of this problem of creating an advisory committee, it is clear that Guang-Zhao *gongsuo* and Ningbo *tongxianghui* activists played a major role in behind-the-scenes organization.[83] Publicly, however, the leaders of these associations, as noted above, found it preferable to work through the apparently more encompassing representative framework of the Federation of Street Unions to develop a method of selection for representatives of the Chinese community. That is to say, it is clear that older conventions of Chinese "representation" were no longer acceptable.

At the same time, new mechanisms were not readily available. When the Federation of Street Unions began to consider the dimensions of its task, it faced the problem of identifying the qualified members of the community who might be mobilized for some sort of selection process. The Federation—the result of the unofficial and voluntary political mobilization of certain sectors of the Chinese community—had not been constructed with such an administrative purpose in mind, nor did it have the necessary information, personnel, or bureaucratic mechanisms to produce an accurate list. The Federation mobilized its constituent Street Unions to compile lists of Chinese ratepayers on their streets, together with the amount of taxes they paid. An evident—but apparently ignored—problem with this system was that there was not a Street Union for every street in the International Settlement. Moreover, the influence and personnel capacity of the Street Unions varied. Adopting the model of the foreign Ratepayers' Association, the Federation distributed forms to each Street Union containing the names of individuals qualified for election on the basis of property-holding and five years' residency in the International Settlement; they inserted notices of this action in the major Shanghai newspapers, urging qualified individuals whose names were not listed to rectify the omissions at the offices of either their Street Union or the Federation. Perhaps because of their uncertain integration in the Federation, or because of the difficulty of performing their assigned tasks, many Street Unions failed to return the forms to the Federation.[84]

The initial conception of an election for Chinese advisers was vague. No participating association on the Chinese side was certain that an election was really necessary. A preliminary meeting of the Guang-Zhao *gongsuo,* the Ningbo *tongxianghui,* and the Federation in April 1920 merely proposed that "some sort of election" could take place "should more than the required number of candidates present themselves."[85]

The Chinese Ratepayers' Association was formed on the basis of these improvised procedures. In a departure from the model of the foreign Ratepayers' Association, most likely as a mechanism through which to ensure some sort of control, an executive committee *(lishibu)* was established to nominate candidates for the Chinese Advisory Committee. Members of this executive committee were themselves to meet property and residency requirements, as well as the stipulation that they were not government officials. In the end, partly because of this innovation of an executive committee and its role in the proceedings, the Advisory Committee that was elected by the CRA was controversial. When the Municipal Council initially failed to ratify the election, Chinese critics of the CRA spoke out, exposing numerous problems, both with Chinese use of the Western model and with arbitrary behavior on the part of the CRA.

A pamphlet issued by the New Federation of Commercial Street Unions, entitled "Inside Story of the Failure of the Chinese Ratepayers' Association," describes the CRA as a "patient who is very ill." Arguing that a public airing of instances of improper conduct will "help the doctor save the patient," the authors document the CRA's failure to clarify the qualifications for office and to properly investigate the conformity of members of the executive committee to the rules for qualification. The pamphlet provides the names of individuals on the executive committee and details their political connections as well as their ineligibility to serve because of their failure to fulfill the five-year Shanghai residency requirement. Beyond this, the pamphlet exposes the inadequacy of CRA reliance on Street Unions to investigate property ownership, pointing out the absence of a

Street Union for an estimated half of Settlement roads. Finally, the authors detail the undemocratic procedures of the CRA, including failure to adhere to any notion of a quorum, the double appearance of some candidates' names on ballots, and the suppression of discussion at meetings.[86]

Although these criticisms reiterate the awkwardness of democratic procedures already discussed above, the magnitude of the problems described suggests that the root of the failure is to be found in something fundamental which more abstract approaches to the problem of democracy may underestimate—in their emphases on cultural or intellectual factors. In the absence of prior practices of citywide representation, there was no network of personnel; no bureaucratic basis; no experience in such a venture; and no overarching mechanism available to coordinate all aspects of the new task. Such empirical problems, which might look like "details" from our distant perspective, were surely fundamental. Ultimately, of course, the CRA was never effective as a representative body, because it had no real power in the governing structure of the Municipal Council.[87] The contradictions of the CRA highlight again the difficulty, if not impossibility, of engaging in a project of popular representation on the part of society in the absence of any connection to the state.

Conclusion: Questions of Culture and Power

This chapter has explored dramatic, wide-ranging, and insufficiently recognized efforts on the part of a range of social activists and associations to institutionalize democratic organizational procedures within Shanghai society during the early Republican era. The "democratic calisthenics" of the era did not lack an institutional basis. Rather, the citizens' rights movement of the years 1918–1923 was built upon a rich institutional basis for ideas and practices of citizenship as well as considerable institutional creativity. Several of the associations through which the democratic procedures and ideas of political representation were institutionalized were of considerable longevity. Even the historiographically neglected Street Unions, which were active for less than a decade, were sufficiently long-lived (and functional through a diverse series of social movements) that they should not be dismissed as ephemeral.

The documentary record of these varied institutions has permitted an examination of Chinese democracy and citizenship, not through the abstractions of Chinese political theory, but in the messier, though more tangible, realm of practice. Within the rhetoric and records of associational practice it is possible to recapture some of the political excitement of the early Republic and map, for a fleeting moment, the meanings and directions of Chinese democracy as they emerged in an extraordinary time. This exercise reveals what might be called "culture-in-motion" (or simply, culture in history, despite scholars' frequent resistance to historical understandings of culture). New elements were incorporated into Chinese culture through reference to both older and newer Chinese traditions as well as to Western concepts still freshly marked as "Western." As older Chinese concepts were brought into the new rhetoric and practices of public life, they were in turn transformed and took on new meanings.

If the concepts of democracy and citizenship with which Shanghai residents wrestled in this period were undeniably Western imports, the practices through which they became material cannot be properly understood either as purely derivative or as reflecting a poor ability to comprehend the foreign model. This chapter has noted several distinctive features of Chinese associational politics in this period: strong populism, notions of direct democracy, emphasis on the collective citizen rather than the individual, and a distinctive concern for institutionalizing social welfare along with political reform. These understandings of citizenship may be marked as "Chinese," but such marking needs to accommodate a dynamic understanding of Chinese culture.

It is difficult, even distorting, to try to clearly mark "Chinese" versus "Western" cultural habits in this hybrid time. "Chinese culture" was a moving target. Already by the early Republican era, Chinese culture in the treaty port of Shanghai reflected several generations of assimilation and indigenization of a wide variety of Western cultural imports, from newspaper technology to new notions of government. For this reason, as ideas of democracy and citizenship emerged in the context of the May Fourth movement, they were not new, but were immediately contextualized in terms of late Qing transformations of Chinese culture.

Although early Republican-era rhetoric included some gestures back toward Mencius in order to locate commensurable ideas within Chinese culture, it more frequently and explicitly connected the concepts of democracy, citizens' rights, and representative government that were at play in the associational reforms and citizens' rights movement of 1918–1923 with the history of local self-government (difang zizhi) in Shanghai (1905–1914), for which there was considerable nostalgia.[88] This modern Chinese tradition (oxymoronic as the term appears), traced in considerable detail in Mark Elvin's study of the Shanghai City Council, developed as a result of both indigenous associational transformations over three centuries and efforts to imitate and rival the foreign Municipal Council of the Shanghai International Settlement in the last years of the Qing dynasty. The result was both new and Chinese, a distinctive phenomenon which Elvin termed "gentry democracy."[89] If it is appreciated that Chinese understandings and practices of democracy and citizenship in the Republican era explicitly evoked not simply Western models, but rather, what were understood to be instantiations of democratic practices in recent Shanghai history, the ways in which Shanghai associations diverged from Western models may become more comprehensible.

Other features of the Chinese associations observed here might be easily tagged as "Chinese," for example, tendencies by association leaders to maintain exclusivity, secrecy, and unity despite aspirations toward democracy. But such a cultural explanation would neglect equally relevant factors in what must be understood as strategic choices in the political climate of Shanghai. The development of democratic conduct and openness was complicated by the delicate position of Chinese public associations in a hostile environment. Poised between the Chinese officials they mistrusted and the semicolonial institutions of Shanghai government in the foreign settlements, Chinese associations were forced to negotiate a playing field that was far from level. The political pressures resulting from the exercise of both Chinese military power and the foreign semicolonial presence inevitably influenced the practices of daily associational life.

One ever-present factor which was surely an issue for these associations was the intrusive presence of the International Settlement police, who were always eager to ferret out and neutralize social gatherings which could threaten Anglo-American interests.[90] For this reason as much as the cultural proclivities of the organizers, meetings of the Commercial Federation and other associations could not be open to the public at moments of high social tension. They restricted admission to those with tickets for the express purpose of preventing the entry of police detectives.[91] The consequences of police penetration were fully evident at the moment of the tax strike, when Settlement police engaged in violent tactics to wrest taxes from members of the most active Street Unions. Associational emphases on unity would similarly be reinforced by this climate of practical considerations.

If one were to engage in a fair comparison of practices with practices, Shanghai democracy in the early Republican period could likely hold its own with historical embodiments of U.S. democracy in this time period, say, in Chicago, or in another similar urban area. But the point here is not to rate Shanghai's Republican exercises in popular democracy. My focus, instead, has been to describe the particular patterns traced by the exercise. The paths taken by Chinese associations in the Shanghai citizens' rights movement sketched here reflect strategic choices among the many models and possibilities offered in the multinational framework of the International Settlement. Culture and power are both at play in this story. In their efforts to strengthen Chinese society, Shanghai residents encountered not only abstract, idealized Western models, but also the specific features of the semicolonial context, which produced a multiplicity of models. The Western practices on display in the International Settlement also commonly deviated from the ideal.

This chapter has traced the reconfiguring of various ideas and models to fit Chinese ideas of social benevolence and conventions of self-government, as well as modern Chinese historical referents for concepts of democracy and citizenship. But the plotline of Chinese culture is complicated by accidents of power. This is evident from the selection of particular alien structures of organization at strategic moments—not because they fit either Chinese or Western cultural ideas, but because they could win recognition and perhaps concessions from foreign authorities.

It is also crucial to recognize, not simply the accidents of particular configurations of power—which presented Chinese residents with the Street Association form of Shanghai Japanese residents, or the Anglo-American structure of a Ratepayers' Association—but, in addition, the insuperable problems posed by imbalances of power, in particular, the absence of a working government model of democracy and the absence of any legally protected power for the institutions of society. (This, rather than good social practices of democracy and citizenship, is at the heart of what distinguished Shanghai from Chicago.) Such absences, together with the resonances of Chinese culture, help to account for the contradictions, factionalism, splitting, and peculiarities of form observed here.

The diverse institutional resources that were available and deployed in the interest of developing structures of popular representation within the wildly hybrid society of early Republican Shanghai could not compensate for the most fundamental institutional problem of the citizens' rights movement as it developed. This was the problem of power, a problem that is underestimated in studies that emphasize the importance of a flourishing civil society, suggesting that vibrant associational life may in itself effect a democratic transformation of society. The citizens' movement, while capable of influencing politics to a degree through the mobilization and expression of public opinion, lacked any mechanism to force an institutionalized balance of power upon either the contending military factions that governed China or the Western authorities in Shanghai. This fundamental problem was indeed recognized by the "citizens' rights" activists at the time, who nonetheless saw no alternative to their activism:

> None of those who study Chinese politics do not believe that the fate of this nation is in the hand of the group movement *(tuanti yundong)*. In [this] situation of abnormal politics, power has run wild and political organizations have been pounded to pieces . . . thus in recent years the group movement has received Chinese and foreign attention and become the core of Chinese politics . . . To speak of proper democratic politics, only such representative bodies as parliament and provincial assemblies should serve as a forum . . . Thus we should recognize that it is not at all glorious that recently various groups organize and engage in politics indiscrimi-

nately. This is because parliament died in an early stage and politics has become abnormal. Thus those engaged in the group movement should know it is a remedy that can't be helped in a situation of abnormal politics.[92]

This recognition by social activists at the time of the crucial role of the state reinforces the recent judgments of Marie-Claire Bergère and Mary Rankin, among others, regarding the limitations of society, alone, in this period.[93]

JEFFREY N. WASSERSTROM

4 | Questioning the Modernity of the Model Settlement: Citizenship and Exclusion in Old Shanghai

This chapter brings together two seemingly disparate themes, in the hope of placing each in a novel perspective. The first is the notion that the International Settlement—the largest of Old Shanghai's two enclaves of foreign privilege—was a quintessentially "modern" place, shaped by distinctively "modern" values. This idea runs through many pre–World War II commentaries on the Settlement and also informs important late twentieth-century scholarly works, from *Shanghai: The Key to Modern China* (a 1953 book by the geographer Rhoads Murphey) to *Shanghai Modern* (a 1999 study by the literary specialist Leo Ou-fan Lee).[1] The second theme is the assumption, articulated in the 1920s by everyone from Manley O. Hudson (a specialist in international law) to Sun Yat-sen, that rules governing parks and elections together defined local citizenship in the enclave.[2]

By moving between these two topics, I attempt to add a new dimension to ongoing discussions in both Shanghai studies and Chinese studies. When it comes to Shanghai studies, my main concern is the process by which, to borrow Murphey's phrasing, modern Western "institutions" and "values" were "transplanted" to Shanghai in the late 1800s and early 1900s and became rooted in new soil.[3] My claim is that, when citizenship issues are taken seriously, this process begins to seem more complex and ambiguous than Murphey's influential account and more recent major studies such as Lee's would suggest. In terms of economic institutions (Murphey's main concern), there is nothing problematic about thinking of the International Settlement of Old Shanghai as having been, throughout much of the treaty-port century (1843–1943), the most modern section of China's most modern city. The same is true if one's focus is, like Lee's, popular culture. In this chapter I argue, however, that it is simply untenable to claim that the Settlement— or any other part of Old Shanghai—was an exemplar of *political* modernity.

This is a revisionist statement, since the impression we are given by so many writers is that the Settlement was modern through and through. The problem with this notion is that, if we accept standard accounts of the things that distinguish modern political forms from those of other periods, we find that the enclave was governed in what might best be described as a mixture of pre-modern and post-modern ways. Some aspects of local citizenship were similar to those found in the city-states that proliferated in earlier centuries; others call to mind practices associated with contemporary transnational entities such as the European Union. The one thing that the Settlement was *not* much like, where citizenship is concerned, was a nation-state—the political form that many analysts view as *the* modern imagined community par excellence.[4]

A second discussion within Shanghai studies to which this chapter contributes concerns the degree to which policies of exclusion structured local public life. Was there a clear line differentiating the position of Chinese residents (Shanghairen) as opposed to Anglophone settlers and sojourners (Shanghailanders)? And how did the status of the members of these two groups—the groups that have tended to attract the most attention from scholars—compare with that of other types of people living in the enclave (such as those belonging to the sizable local Japanese and White Russian communities)?[5] In answering questions of this sort, some influential scholars, including John K. Fairbank, have played down the importance of status distinctions between nationalities, insisting that the most noteworthy characteristic of the enclave was its fostering of international and interracial cooperation.[6] By contrast, however, historians within New Shanghai (a term sometimes used to distinguish the current unified metropolis from its predecessor) have often likened the place of Chinese in the enclave to that of blacks in Apartheid-era South Africa and African-Americans in the Jim Crow South.[7]

A detailed examination of citizenship issues in Old Shanghai of the early twentieth century shows that there are serious problems with both approaches.[8] Optimistic visions of the Settlement that emphasize Fairbank's concept of "synarchy" (joint Chinese-foreign rule) do not hold up to close scrutiny, at least for the period preceding 1928. (That was the year when three Shanghairen were added to the Shanghai Municipal Council [SMC], and when rules governing access to local parks were changed.) And yet, we will also see that lines of exclusion relating to public life (recreational and political alike) were not drawn in the same way as they were in South Africa before the 1990s or in the American South before the Civil Rights Movement. This is because the criteria used to determine who was and was not treated as a full-fledged member of the Settlement community were not rooted so clearly in racial categories per se. One sign of this is that, although many local residents of various nationalities took it for granted that Japanese and Chinese residents of the Settlement were members of a single race, the rules of public life were very different for people belonging to these two groups.[9]

Switching from Shanghai-specific to more general issues in Chinese studies, I attempt to show in this chapter that debates over local park rules and voting rights can be used to shed new light on ongoing arguments about the stunted nature of democratization in China. Some scholars have attributed the tendency of successive Chinese regimes to delay the implementation of free and open elections to the pernicious influence of a uniquely "Asian" or more specifically "Confucian" value system. This system is said to be predicated on the conviction that chaos will ensue unless control over society is exercised by educated people who know how to behave properly and who share a particular moral outlook, that is, by an elite defined by common possession of particular cultural traits. Other analysts place the blame for China's lack of democracy on the originally Leninist idea—adapted to local circumstances by theorists in both the Nationalist Party and the Communist Party—that vanguard revolutionary organizations must guide the masses until a period of political tutelage has been completed. Most commonly of all,

China specialists have claimed that a combination of Confucian culturalism and Leninist authoritarian ideas and practices lies at the root of the contemporary Chinese predicament.

Without dismissing the importance of lingering Confucian predilections or the effects of what might be called "Leninism with Chinese Characteristics," I want to bring something new into the equation: the distorted image of the Enlightenment provided to China by colonial and semi-colonial institutions and discourses. If we look closely at the rules governing the working of the International Settlement's main governing body, the SMC, we find evidence of the influence within the local *foreign community* of the same sorts of antidemocratic tendencies just described. Many leading Shanghailanders argued that Shanghairen should not be acknowledged as full members of the community until they had completed a training program in Western ways, which would bring them up to a certain cultural level. Foreign businessmen and diplomats, while generally no fans of either Confucius or Lenin, often assumed that rule by a culturally defined elite was needed to keep the forces of disorder in check. There was often a consensus among them that a period of tutelage was needed before new groups could be allowed to participate in public life, though they might differ on the question of how to decide when that educative process had been completed.[10]

Before elaborating on these ideas, it is necessary to do three things: first, to describe in more detail the conventional image of the Settlement as modern through and through; second, to provide examples of how Shanghailanders talked about public institutions such as parks and elections; and finally, to bring into the discussion the ways in which texts produced by Chinese living in or merely concerned with the fate of the International Settlement dovetailed with and diverged from those created by foreigners.[11]

Shanghai Modern?

A special thing about the enclave, according to boosters and detractors of the past and present alike, was that within its borders an unusually large number of Chinese were directly exposed to modern Western fashions, architectural styles, ideas, economic practices, methods of municipal administration, and forms of politics. It is because this equation of the Settlement with modernity is so prevalent that it has become tempting to assume that *everything* about the enclave must have been modern. Moreover, we need to keep in mind that the enclave was thought by many not just to contain modern amenities and be run in a modern fashion, but also to serve as an exemplary site of modernity for Chinese living elsewhere. This bundle of assumptions I will refer to, following the rhetoric of the time, as the "Model Settlement" mystique.

By the 1920s, virtually every guide to the metropolis was endorsing the idea that Shanghai was the "most cosmopolitan city in the world" as well as the most attractive urban center in China. The roots of the Model Settlement mystique go back even earlier, however, to Shanghailander texts of the latter half of the 1800s. From a very early point, British and American settlers and sojourners grew fond of presenting themselves as part of a sturdy band of pioneers. Together, these Shanghailanders insisted—sometimes leaving out completely the role played by Chinese in the process—Westerners had transformed a "wilderness of marshes" by the banks of the muddy Huangpu River into a metropolis that had nearly all the amenities of civilized Western urban life.[12]

Colorful early examples of this vision of the Settlement can be found in the pages of the *North China Herald (NCH)*, the leading local English-language weekly. These articles frequently presented the enclave as a bastion of enlightened values and advanced methods of governance in a backward and benighted land. The writers involved routinely hailed the Settlement as a kind of inspirational city on a hill. Already in 1881, less than four decades after the Treaty of Nanjing had forcibly opened Shanghai to foreign trade and settlement, the *NCH* was insisting that the Settlement was having a beneficial effect on not just the Shanghairen but the Chinese people as a whole. Foreign ideas, the newspaper said, were emanating from the enclave and "slowly penetrating the most carefully closed Chinese minds," and thus "doing good work in the nation."[13]

A special commemorative volume issued by the *NCH* in conjunction with the celebration of the Shanghai Jubilee (a ritual held in 1893 to mark the passage of the city's first half-century as an international port) was even more hyperbolic. Contributors spoke of the enclave as a wondrous place that had grown, as if by "enchantment," from a humble backwater to a unique example of a civilized "republic" surrounded by a benighted empire.[14] A 1915 editorial said the enclave had a "reputation" for being governed in an advanced fashion that "any city might envy." And so on.[15]

After the treaty-port era came to an end, Shanghailanders kept the Model Settlement mystique alive in nostalgic memoirs that had much to say about cosmopolitanism and little to say about discrimination. John Pal's *Shanghai Saga* is a case in point. The author recalls Old Shanghai as "a city of the world" that was "neither English, American, nor South American" but rather a "truly international melting-pot whose motto was 'Tolerance.'" Here, Pal insists, foreigners "led the Chinese, by example, into adopting things and ways of life that had advantages for them, such as personal cleanliness, domestic hygiene, civic law and order, justice, honest police administration, government by representation." He did not use the word "modern" in this 1963 book, but Pal's list includes nearly all the items typically associated with modernity.[16]

Not everyone viewed the enclave through rose-tinted glasses at the time, of course. Nor has everyone who has looked back on the period of foreign-run enclaves done so with the sense of regret that imbues Pal's memoir. Any number of references to oral histories gathered or analytical works produced by scholars affiliated with the Chinese Communist Party (CCP) could be used to illustrate this point. So, too, though, can quotes by Sun Yat-sen and other Chinese revolutionaries of his time, as well as texts by some of their compatriots with much more moderate views. This is because, for a broad array of Chinese political figures of the time, bastions of foreign privilege such as Old Shanghai's International Settlement and French Concession were a blot on China's national honor. And for many of them, election procedures and park regulations stood out as symbolic of the degraded status of the Shanghairen. The treaty-port system, the argument went, reduced Chinese to being second-class citizens in their own land and illustrated that many foreigners viewed Shanghairen as inferior beings.[17]

These themes find clear expression in a 1923 essay by the Communist leader Cai Hesen. Published thirty years after the *NCH* Jubilee volume alluded to above, it begins by noting that there is no reason for Shanghairen to celebrate the eightieth anniversary of Shanghai's transformation into an international port. After all, before the Westerners came, "every stone and every blade of grass" in the city belonged to the Chinese. Now, by contrast, Chinese who paid taxes in the Settlement could not even participate in the governance of the enclave. Nor could they use the very parks that their taxes help to maintain. By accepting such a situation, according to Cai, elite Shanghairen proved that they were content to be nothing more than *yanggou* (the lapdogs of foreigners). This rhetorical move took images of dehumanization one step further than Sun typically did (his preference was to liken the position of such Chinese to "slaves" as opposed to beasts). It was foreshadowed earlier in Cai's piece, moreover, through a reference to a popular though not quite accurate urban legend about the Public Garden, Old Shanghai's best-known park.[18]

This legend holds that a sign banning "Dogs and Chinese" from entering stood for decades by the recreation ground's main gate. In fact, there was no notice with that precise wording—or, at least, one never stood in a prominent locale. Still, it is irrefutably true that for much of the treaty-port era, a humiliating set of rules was in place that limited access to foreigners and to Chinese servants attending foreign charges. Whatever the wording of the park signs may have been, Cai's invocation of an image that paired dogs and Chinese in the foreign mind is of central importance. His goal was to encourage his readers to think of the enclave as a place where two things went hand-in-hand: park rules that equated Chinese with animals, and electoral practices that forced Chinese merchants into a position that no citizen of a community should have to accept.[19]

Turning from radical to more moderate Chinese critics of foreign privilege, we find different rhetorical moves but similar basic concerns. For example, though the official Chinese delegation to the Paris Peace Conference of 1919 was silent on the issue of the Public Garden, its members shared with Sun and Cai a feeling that voting procedures in the Settlement were immoral. It was not acceptable, this group's most famous memorandum claimed, that citizens of China were expected to pay taxes in foreign-run enclaves and yet were excluded from voting and from serving on governing boards. They singled out the composition of the SMC as an egregious example of the problem.[20]

There were also elite Shanghairen who, though conservative in their approach to other matters, periodically complained to the SMC about the fact that Chinese merchants and literati had no voice in local governance and were denied entry to the Public Garden. As early as the 1870s, some Shanghairen were suggesting that the Council should at least consult with the leaders of the local Chinese elite. And by the early 1920s, articles in the *Shen Bao* (the leading local newspaper) and the *Minguo Ribao* (a more radical periodical, at least on some points) referred to the ongoing struggle for Chinese representation on the SMC as a just effort to gain "citizenship rights" for the Shanghairen.[21] Petitions and letters to local newspapers challenging exclusionary park rules, meanwhile, began to be published in the 1880s.[22] The authors of these documents often stated that they could understand why the less cultured of their compatriots should be kept out of recreational areas, thus echoing the paternalist views of many Shanghailanders. What they could not understand was why members of the cream of local Chinese society should be excluded as well.

One thing that seemed particularly to bother these early Shanghairen critics of exclusionary rules was that even the roughest Shanghailander sailors could use parks from which elite Chinese were barred. More troubling still, at least to some, was the fact that "Japanese and Korean" residents and visitors could enter the Public Garden freely. Emphasis on one or both of these things as particular grievances would continue to show up in later texts on exclusionary policies by well-to-do Chinese.[23]

Lest it seem that the Chinese had one view of exclusionary rules, foreigners another, we should note that some comparatively liberal Shanghailanders were uncomfortable with the way public life was ordered. The American journalist J. B. Powell, editor of the *China Weekly Review,* for example, wrote frequently of the psychological harm done to Chinese, inside the Settlement and beyond, by rules that limited access to the Public Garden. He often combined references to the park with comments on the desirability of adding Chinese representatives to the SMC. A failure to provide tax-paying Shanghairen with a voice in local politics made a mockery, he insisted, of the idea that "taxation without representation" was abhorrent to Westerners.[24]

The views of Edward S. Little, a British Shanghailander, are also worth mentioning. They show it was not just American residents who criticized exclusionary rules. In 1920, Little wrote an essay—published simultaneously in several local papers, either as a guest column or a letter to the editor—that extolled the benefits to all of giving Shanghairen (fellow "citizens") a voice in enclave politics.[25] And this was an important moment for such a piece to appear, since this was just after a tax strike had been launched by native property owners dissatisfied with their lack of representation (see the preceding chapter in this volume, by Bryna Goodman, for more details). Little's essay was also written in the wake of the submission to the SMC of a petition—signed by a large group of Shanghairen—that called attention to the fact that it had been Westerners who had preached to them of the need for taxation and representation to be linked.[26]

There were, in addition, Western visitors of the day—such as Manley O. Hudson and Lewis S. Gannett, an associate editor of *The Nation*—who were critical of exclusionary practices. These visitors, like Chinese and foreign residents who took issue with the system of foreign privilege, tended to focus on voting rules, park access, or both of these things in their commentaries on the enclave.[27] And they often claimed that a Chinese Advisory Committee—of the sort first proposed in 1906 but only actually put into operation in the wake of a 1920 tax strike, in circumstances described by Goodman—was an inadequate way of giving the Shanghairen a voice in local affairs. The Chinese deserved, they claimed, to be able not just to make suggestions but to help make policy.

Some of these visiting and local foreign critics of exclusionary policies brought up a theme already alluded to above: the contradictory fact (in their eyes) that Japanese nationals had free access to the Public Garden while Chinese were banned from that space. (There was apparently a regulation in force at one point that required Japanese residents and visitors to wear Western clothing when using Jessfield Park, which was considered by many the Settlement's second nicest recreational area, but there were never limitations on their use of the waterfront grounds.) J. B. Powell, for example, noted that the best strategy open to a Chinese man who wanted to use the Public Garden was to dress in "foreign clothes" and hope the guard at the gate would assume he was Japanese.[28]

Some of these same commentators also seemed to think it odd that Japanese nationals were given political rights denied to comparable Shanghairen. Japanese males who owned enough property to have to pay rates (taxes) were allowed to vote in local elections on the same basis as Westerners, they pointed out (the fact that no woman of any nationality could vote or stand for office went unremarked). In addition, throughout the early 1900s, there were usually two slots on the SMC reserved informally for Japanese businessmen. Moreover, Japanese property owners were also allowed to participate in the Ratepayers' Association, to which the SMC had to report—a body that, despite its universal-sounding name, was one that Chinese taxpayers could not join. All of this seemed peculiar to foreigners who took for granted the racial commonality of Shanghairen and Japanese.

It is worth stressing, before saying more about exclusionary practices, that even the harshest Chinese and Western critics of the enclave tended to accept the idea that the Settlement was a distinctively modern place. They viewed it, no less than did others, as representative of many of the advanced things the West had to offer. Cai explicitly emphasized that Shanghai was a *jindai* (modern) metropolis; Manley Hudson saw it as "modernly" administered; and Powell often presented the enclave as a place where Chinese were exposed to modern Western ideas and political forms.[29]

It is also important to remember that it was by no means only boastful Shanghailanders who created and perpetuated the Model Settlement mystique. A diverse set of influential local Chinese accepted and promoted the idea that the enclave was an admirably run urban center filled with modern features that their fellow countrymen would do well to emulate. This group of Chinese included some of the journalists who worked for the *Shen Bao* and even one warlord, Marshal Sun Chuanfang. *Shen Bao* editorials from the late 1800s and early 1900s called for Chinese to try to find a place within the native-run part of the city for the modern practices on display in the Settlement.[30] And Marshal Sun argued in 1926 that making the Chinese Municipality as efficiently governed as the Settlement could be a first step toward overturning the treaty-port system. The foreigners would see that extraterritorial rights were no longer necessary, and Shanghai could be transformed into a single great modern metropolis and then incorporated into the Republic of China as a unified city that respected the rights of foreigners but was not run by them.[31]

Modernity and Citizenship

Why devote so much attention to the prevalence of the view that the Settlement was a thoroughly modern place? First, simply because this vision of the enclave continues to be casually incorporated into works by a very broad array of scholars, from literary specialists such as Lee to historians such as Ye Xiaoqing to political scientists such as Pye.[32] Second, because questioning the Settlement's purported modernity can lead us to ask new questions about the debates over citizenship that paved the way for the changes in exclusionary policies that came in 1928.

Many other scholars have looked at or dealt in passing with the debates in question. One interesting thing about them is, in fact, that they have drawn the attention of such a diverse array of analysts. This group has included diplomatic historians (Dorothy Borg and Nicholas Clifford), as well as Shanghai-based cultural historians (Li Tiangang and Tang Zhenchang) and social historians working in Taiwan or the West (Chen Sanjing and Bryna Goodman). And political scientists, such as Lynn White, have examined the topic as well.[33] I am, however, the first one, I believe, to explicitly frame discussion of the debates around the themes of modernity and citizenship.

A few words are in order concerning how previous analysts have approached the policy changes of 1928 and the discussions that preceded them. Some have focused on voting and representation only (Borg), while others have linked these issues to park access (Li and Chen), as was often done during the treaty-port era (by local historians such as A. N. Kotenev and Gang Shidong as well as by journalists and revolutionaries).[34] Some scholars have been primarily concerned with the way debates over elections and park rules affected the May 30th Movement, during which a change in voting rules and in the SMC's composition became a key demand, and the window these debates provide into the world-views of Shanghailanders (Clifford). Others have used these debates to illuminate the emerging civic consciousness or nationalist views of Shanghairen (Tang)—a theme that Goodman has taken up in earlier work and expands upon elsewhere in this volume.

Also worth noting is that some scholars have taken a short-term approach, concentrating only on the 1920s or on the period lasting from 1906 to 1928. Others have taken a more long-term view (Li and Chen, for example), beginning with nineteenth-century texts such as vague statements by Western diplomats in the 1860s that the SMC should pay attention to the needs and find out the opinions of Shanghairen. In addition, some scholars have looked at nineteenth-century challenges to exclusionary park rules, which led first to a brief experiment with monthly passes for high-status Chinese and then to the creation of a special "Chinese Park" in the 1890s.[35] There are also those favoring a long-range approach who have taken the story beyond 1928 to 1930, the year when the number of Shanghairen on the SMC was increased from three to five.

What none of the previous commentators on the debate has done is ask the following specific question—a question that, in light of the Settlement's reputation as a distinctively Western and modern place, seems especially germane. Do we find in arguments about park rules and voting rights the kinds of things that influential discussions of citizenship, such as those of T. H. Marshall and Hannah Arendt, would lead us to expect to encounter in a modern political setting?

The answer to this question is yes (but only to a small degree) and no (to a much larger one). Some features of the debates fit in well with standard accounts of the development of modern citizenship. Many aspects of them, however, fly in the face of the picture of modern citizenship bequeathed to us by Marshall and Arendt, who remain influential figures in the burgeoning interdisciplinary literature on the topic.[36] The Shanghai case also contradicts in important ways summary statements on the nature of citizenship written during the treaty-port era itself, such as Carl Brinkman's entry on the topic in the first edition of the *International Encyclopedia of the Social Sciences*. And the Shanghai debates raise questions about even some of the best recent commentaries on the topic, such as Michael Walzer's contribution to a handbook on the meanings of Western political concepts.[37]

Let us look first at the less surprising "yes" side of the yes-and-no answer—that is, at the ways in which the Shanghai debates fit into standard visions of modern citizenship. To begin with, we definitely see in the Shanghai debates a division between "activist" and "passive" forms of citizenship, a division that Walzer claims has become increasingly important in Western political history in the last few centuries. Activist citizens are those who are able to play a role in the political life of a community, while passive ones are merely entitled to a place within the "circle of the protected"—that is, they derive specific benefits from being citizens but do not participate fully in public decision-making.[38] In ancient Greek city-states, the sole important dividing line was that between citizens (who governed the republic collectively) and non-citizens (a category that included aliens and other temporary sojourners, women, slaves, and children). It was assumed by Aristotle (and many later commentators) that the only people worth thinking of as citizens were free adult males, permanently resident within a community, who were not just able to take part in public debates but routinely did so and periodically served as officials as well.[39] By the time we reached the modern period, however, according to Walzer, it had become common for many people to be considered citizens, yet either choose to steer clear of politics or be prevented from taking part in public debate because of their gender, race, or class.

The positive aspect of modernity, in Walzer's account, is that many formerly excluded groups (including the wives and children of male citizens) have been brought into the "circle of the protected," and sometimes have even been able to gain the rights of "activist" members of the community through struggle. The negative aspect is that it has become much easier for those granted the right to be "activist" citizens to abdicate their responsibility to contribute to political life. That is, it has been easy throughout modern times, and has perhaps become even more so in the present late modern period of mass media (what some, but not Walzer, call post-modern time), for even privileged members of a polity to play only "passive" citizenship roles.

In the International Settlement, the argument for overturning park rules can be interpreted, following Walzer, as a typical modern effort to establish that a large group of people (Shanghairen) should have their status as "passive" citizens symbolically confirmed. That is, their request to use the Public Garden was a demand that they be recognized as members of the enclave justified in receiving a benefit from the state. The claim that voting rights should be extended and Chinese representatives added to the SMC, meanwhile, can be seen as another sort of modern effort: a struggle by previously disenfranchised members of the community to be recognized as "activist" citizens.

Also on the "yes" side of the equation, turning from Walzer to Marshall, we see in the Shanghai debates just the sort of intertwining of demands for legal rights, political rights, and social rights that the latter argued was a hallmark of modern politics. The same people who wanted Shanghairen to be allowed to vote and stand for office (that is, to be granted political rights) also argued that the court system should be changed (a legal matter) and that the SMC should spend more on educating Chinese children (a classic social welfare issue).[40] Marshall stresses the importance of efforts by groups excluded from the category of citizen to gain the ability to do new things. He shares with Walzer, though he does not use this term, the idea that struggles to expand the "circle of the protected" are a distinctive feature of modern politics at its best. Marshall and Walzer would each, therefore, be likely to see the changes in park rules and voting practices that came in 1928 as liberal moves toward true modernity.

This extension of new rights to formerly excluded groups is, however, where the first lack of fit between the Shanghai case and the standard paradigm appears. Marshall's primary interest is in the way that barriers linked to social class were gradually eroded and sometimes forcefully challenged over time. Moreover, both he and Walzer (who combines a concern with class with an interest in barriers associated with gender and race) often seem to assume that expansions and contractions of the "circle of the protected" do not take place simultaneously. The problem is that, in the Settlement, class barriers remained firmly in place in 1928 and in one specific sense were even strengthened. The addition of three Shanghairen to the formerly all-foreign SMC, which grew from nine to twelve total members in the process, did nothing to change the class-composition of either the electorate or this governing body. Only taxpaying Chinese residents—a tiny percentage of the overall native population—were given the vote or allowed to stand for office under the new rules.

Meanwhile, the many Shanghailanders and local Japanese and White Russian residents who lacked property continued to be denied basic political rights (as did women of all classes and nationalities).[41]

In addition, when the rules that used nationality as a basis for limiting access to parks were overturned in 1928, a new economic criterion was introduced: namely, a use fee began to be charged for the first time. Though routinely described as a "modest" figure, even a small cost was enough to make the Public Garden effectively inaccessible to many of Shanghai's poorest people. In other words, while some elite male and female Shanghairen who had formerly been banned from entering could henceforth use the Public Garden and Jessfield Park, some groups now found it harder to do so than had formerly been the case. Specifically, destitute White Russian émigrés were disadvantaged by the rule change, and Chinese rickshaw pullers were still, for all intents and purposes, as excluded from these leisure grounds as they had ever been. Moreover, this was not a purely accidental development: one argument used by Chinese and Western critics of the exclusionary rules was that it was patently absurd to keep respectable Shanghairen out of a place that the "dregs" of foreign society could use. The entrance fee was introduced precisely to keep unwanted groups out of the Public Garden as well as to limit the size of crowds on its paths.[42]

Other features of the Shanghai case contradict even more directly the standard accounts of modern citizenship—and this is where the story may gain its greatest interest. Take, for example, Arendt's most frequently cited comment on citizenship: that, in the modern age, an individual is treated and should continue to be treated as a "citizen among citizens in a country among countries."[43] Brinkman, in a similar vein, describes the modern age as having witnessed the "welding of the manifold allegiances of medieval man into a single but comprehensive bond of national citizenship."[44] There is a difference between Arendt and Brinkman, however. The former argues that the idea of replacing "national citizenship" with some form of "global citizenship" is a dangerous prospect. The latter, by contrast, remains agnostic about the pros and cons of a future in which communities larger than nation-states might come to predominate. But the two share a common assumption that, in the heyday of the modern era, national forms of citizenship were the main and often the only ones that really mattered.

They are not alone, moreover, in assuming that dual citizenship was not a major issue in the first half of the twentieth century. Many analysts have noted that the pre-modern era saw cases in which municipalities and nation-states vied with one another as sources of loyalty, granters of benefits, and shapers of identity. Some have also speculated on the possibilities for a revival of divided forms of citizenship as transnational political communities become important citizenship sites. Most continue to accept the idea, however, that the early 1900s were a time when relatively unified forms of citizenship rooted in nation-states were the order of the day. This vision of high modernity has generally gone unquestioned even as the rise of the European Union and other transnational entities has led, since the 1990s, to a revised interest in whether it is possible (and desirable) to be a citizen of two or more communities at the same time.[45]

The problem here is that, in the Settlement, Shanghailanders and Shanghairen alike tended to view themselves as having *dual* allegiances. They took for granted that there were local and supralocal dimensions to their citizenship, and they also participated in (or, in the case of passive local citizens, were merely governed by) institutions with transnational dimensions. To be a citizen of Shanghai or, in Chinese terms, a local *shimin* (person of the city) was related to being some kind of a national citizen or *guomin* (person of the nation). Thus, for example, when Shanghairen worked for an extension of suffrage, they called this a struggle for *shimin quan* (citizenship rights) that would rectify an injustice that reflected badly on the Chinese *guomin* (citizenry).[46] Similarly, some of the Shanghailanders who supported letting taxpaying Shanghairen vote and stand for office said that they did so because an article of faith for truly patriotic Britons or Americans should be that "taxation without representation" is always evil.[47]

Even when they saw links between their identities as local and national citizens, however, few Shanghailanders or Shanghairen thought of the two as things that could and should be "welded" into a single "bond" of allegiance. Loyalty to the Settlement was sometimes felt intensely, but it was tellingly represented even at such moments as a secondary sort of patriotism, something that coexisted with yet did not displace love for a nearby or distant nation or empire.[48]

To make matters more complicated still, local citizenship was, as noted above, simultaneously a throwback of sorts to early modern or even pre-modern times, as theorists have presented these, and in other ways an anticipation of post-modern trends. On the one hand, with justification, some Shanghailanders likened their enclave to a mercantile city-state such as Venice, in the era when it had competed with empires and nations.[49] Yet the multinational nature of the SMC (the body in charge of domestic affairs) and the consortium of consular officials (the body responsible for the Settlement's relations with China and the outside world) made the Settlement a transnational community. That term was not yet in use, of course, but some commentators of the day referred to the enclave as a "commonwealth" or a "miniature league of nations," terms which have similar connotations.[50]

A different problem with the main models for thinking about modern citizenship and the specifics of the Shanghai case has to do with individualism. Marshall and others take for granted that citizenship, when we reach modern times, is all about a person's relationship, as an atomized unit rather than merely part of a corporate body, to a state. Tang Tsou even asserts, in his final essay on the Chinese Revolution, that the individualized nature of the liberal vision of modern politics is the major thing that differentiates Western concepts of citizenship from Mao Zedong's "mass line" approach.[51] In the Western form of politics, individuals make claims against the nation-state, but in the Chinese Communist one, it is only as members of a corporate body that they interact with the party-state.

We have already seen that, for residents of the Settlement, there were often two states involved: one local, the other not. A close look at the debate over voting shows, moreover, that even if we leave aside the two-state question, local citizenship was only partially a matter of individuals interacting with the municipal regime. The selection of members of the SMC was never a simple matter of those individuals who had the franchise voting for preferred candidates in open elections. Instead, the assumption was always that the interests of particular businesses and groups of businessmen needed to be represented on the Council, and as a result there were sometimes individuals who had more than one vote, if they were associated with more than one enterprise. Moreover, there was always an informal understanding and sometimes a formally regulated one that a certain number of places on the SMC should be reserved for people of particular nationalities. In most of the pre–World War II era, it was assumed that the foreign contingent on the SMC would be made up of two Americans, two Japanese, and five Britons. And when, in 1928, some Shanghairen were allowed to vote, they were only given the privilege of helping select the three new Chinese candidates.

An even clearer sense of the corporate dimension of local citizenship is given by earlier plans to give Shanghairen a collective voice in politics, via a Chinese Advisory Committee. As Goodman notes in Chapter 3, when members of this body were finally chosen in 1920, a newly created Chinese Ratepayers' Association, which was modeled on the foreign one that had long existed, ran the process. At first, however, the plan had been to have representatives chosen mostly by native-place guilds.[52] This, it was thought, would ensure that the interests of the Shanghairen with ties to Ningbo and the Cantonese Shanghairen were represented. The same kind of effect had always been achieved for the foreign community by informally reserving some seats on the Council for representatives of British business interests, American business interests, Japanese business interests, and so on. It was, in fact, considered a gross violation of local political etiquette when leaders within the Japanese community tried at various points to increase their number of representatives or to ensure that Shanghailanders sympathetic to Japan would be chosen for British and American slots. And fear of Japanese domination of the Settlement seems to have been a key factor in helping elite Shanghairen gain some sort of voice in local affairs.[53]

The lack of fit between standard models for conceiving of modern citizenship and the International Settlement context is not only curious but in some ways deeply ironic. This is because the most influential theoretical studies of citizenship have typically been derived from study of the political histories of Britain and the United States, and the Settlement was formed in the 1850s through a merger of originally separate British and American enclaves. The enclave may have been physically located in China, but its main political institutions, the SMC and the Annual Meeting of the Ratepayers in which the limits of the Council's jurisdiction were debated and changes in its composition decided, had distinctively Anglo-American roots. The SMC was often likened to the municipal councils found in English cities (though assumed to be considerably more powerful than those because of its larger degree of autonomy), while the annual gathering of ratepayers was frequently compared to a New England town meeting.[54]

Reinforcing this sense of the Settlement as a displaced piece of the Anglo-American political universe were the nationalities of the people who, throughout most of the treaty-port century, played the leading roles in local politics. The editors of the most widely read Western newspapers and weeklies tended to be Shanghailanders with ties to either Britain or America. The same was true of members and chairmen of the SMC. The Settlement foreign community was certainly very diverse, but until the Japanese invasions of the 1930s, Anglo-American hegemony was the rule.

If, therefore, the nature of local politics did not conform to standard Anglo-American patterns, we need to be aware that many Chinese of the 1920s got, through no fault of their own, a deeply distorted understanding of Western ideas and practices. As already indicated, some Shanghailander critics of exclusionary rules noted this distortion when they stressed that the SMC's lack of representatives of the Shanghairen violated a basic tenet of the Anglo-American citizenship tradition, and some Chinese commentators made this point as well.[55] Nevertheless, the overall impression remained that the way things were done in the Settlement was in accord not just with Western practices generally but with Anglo-American ones in particular.

Synarchy and Tutelage

I want to end by returning to a general point about China's political development, as opposed to that of Shanghai, raised at the start of this chapter: the light the debates in the Settlement can shed on the stunted development of Chinese democracy. Put bluntly, the lack of fit already discussed, and one more factor that will be mentioned below, suggest that we need to reject completely any lingering illusion that treaty-port enclaves represented a great liberal road not taken.

It is just too problematic to claim that political arrangements within that enclave offered clear lessons in enlightened thinking that the Chinese could and should have internalized.

Why is this idea, which was first popularized by Shanghailanders and Shanghairen entranced by the Model Settlement mystique, still important to debunk? Because it has gained academic prominence through the writings of two of American Sinology's most influential figures, both of whom minimize, in some of their writings, the degree to which the treaty-port system transformed local Chinese into second-class local citizens and even, at times, dehumanized the Shanghairen. The concept of "synarchy" developed by the first of these prominent Sinologists, Fairbank, has already been introduced above. What is worth stressing here is that this notion has recently been given a new lease on life by the political scientist Lucian Pye, the second influential figure I have in mind, who has written an essay on Old Shanghai as a political model. This piece, which is framed as a direct continuation of Fairbank's argument, has appeared in both Chinese- and English-language versions and has been cited on both sides of the Pacific as well as of the Atlantic. Since Pye's is the most recent and currently most influential articulation, it seems sensible to focus on it here.[56]

If only, his argument goes (and here I admit I am simplifying things), the kind of openness and spirit of experimentation that characterized life in this most cosmopolitan of enclaves had not been renounced so vociferously by the Communist Party and the Nationalist Party alike, China's path to modernization might have been less torturous. The implication is that the Chinese could have made much better use of the building blocks provided by the Settlement, and that it is misleading to assume that life there was governed by principles of exclusion and segregation.

The enclave's practices, if used as a model, could have helped the Chinese construct a vision of their nation, according to Pye—a vision that would have been free of two pernicious influences, one old and the other new. The first of these was the "culturalist" and paternalistic Confucian approach to politics, predicated on the idea that only those thoroughly familiar with particular rituals and possessing a high level of education should govern. The second was an oddly complementary Leninist vision of delayed democracy, which relegates "the people" to a passive role until they can be taught to recognize their best interests.

In contradistinction to this line of thinking, the debates on citizenship of the 1920s illustrate that the Settlement was a place where many of the ideas just described as Confucian and as Leninist were at the very heart of things. This suggests the need to rethink the complex ways in which pre-existing prejudices and new ideas of various sorts interacted in the Settlement, as well as perhaps in other colonial or semi-colonial settings.

A recent essay by Alexander Woodside provides a powerful method for framing this issue. His piece examines struggles for freedom and democracy of several generations of Vietnamese political actors, with Ho Chi-minh's experiences with colonialism playing a role for him much like that which Sun Yat-sen has had in this chapter. Efforts in Vietnam to extend liberty and defend human rights "cannot be elucidated," Woodside insists, "without an understanding, not just of local practices and traditions, but also of the compromises and even the pathologies involved in the imperfect global diffusion of Enlightenment values, by Westerners and non-Westerners alike." We need to remember the contradictory messages that colonialism could give, for example when French colonists of the early 1900s practiced "racial discrimination outside their schools while teaching Rousseau and Hugo inside them." The International Settlement, though a semi-colonial rather than a purely colonial enclave, was a place where the "compromises" and "pathologies" that Woodside has in mind were on constant display.[57]

Woodside's allusion to schools is especially germane to the Shanghai case. One version of the Model Settlement idea was that participation in the political life of the enclave should be granted very gradually to carefully selected Shanghairen as a way to educate them in Enlightenment ideals. A 1915 editorial in the *NCH* made this claim in supporting a call for the establishment of a Chinese Advisory Committee. This is a worthwhile proposal, the editorial argued, because "it will certainly be of the utmost advantage to some of [China's] leading men to be able to say that they have studied the science and art of municipal government in such a school as the Shanghai Settlements provide."[58] In political terms, therefore, we find the Settlement conceived as a school in which liberal ideas are taught; yet it was also assumed to be one where the status of students and teachers and the relations between them were defined in illiberal ways. There is always a tension, in fact, between this understanding of the enclave as a school for Shanghairen seeking or deemed ready for Enlightenment, on the one hand, and a very different one, on the other: an oasis in which foreigners could enjoy a public life free of the contamination of Chinese bodies (in the parks) and Chinese traditions (in the institutions).[59]

One implication of all this is that, while a form of synarchy may have come into being briefly after 1928, to say that the Settlement was run this way for most of the treaty-port era is to distort history. Pye's claim that exclusionary practices were a minor part of the Shanghai story simply does not wash. As Robert Bickers and I have noted elsewhere, practices that kept Shanghairen from feeling like full-fledged members of the community colored many aspects of life in the Settlement prior to 1928. Along with exclusionary rules relating to voting and park use, Chinese residents were treated as second-class members of the community during civic rituals designed to celebrate the Settlement as a political and cultural entity. Consider, for example, the Shanghai Jubilee of 1893 alluded to earlier. Shanghailanders and Shanghairen were encouraged to join in, but members of the two groups were not allowed to do quite the same things. When the Jubilee Oration that capped the event was delivered, for example, foreigners were allowed near the stage (whatever their race), while Chinese were kept outside of a police cordon (whatever their class). This may explain why, though many Shanghairen were happy to put up banners celebrating the occasion, one local newspaper ran a piece suggesting that any native resident who did this sort of thing was a *hanjian* (traitor to the Han people).[60]

Much about the Settlement situation, as my quotations from Woodside's piece suggest, can be seen as just the sort of warping of liberal values and political modernity that routinely happened in colonial settings. The specifics of each perversion of the Enlightenment project were different, though, and it is worth looking not just at the generic phenomenon but also at the details. The case of Old Shanghai shows that, even when explicitly racial criteria were not invoked, the results could be quite similar. It also shows that struggles for citizenship could be heartfelt and significant even in settings where the goal was not, as it often was in colonial as opposed to semi-colonial contexts, to be recognized as a full-fledged, rights-bearing member of a foreign empire or nation-state other than one's own. In the enclave, Shanghairen were fighting not to become "citizens among citizens of a country among countries," but rather to remove the second-class stigma from their status as *Chinese citizens* of a political community that contained citizens from many lands.

I will close with a comment on the "Clash of Civilizations" model proposed by Samuel Huntington. It is sometimes assumed that when Sun Yat-sen made democratic moves, he was showing that he had been influenced by what Huntington describes as distinctively Western values. And it is thought that the same figure's promotion of the idea of tutelage was a throwback to his Confucian roots or a bow to Soviet advisers. Could we not conclude, however, that Sun's concern with stabilizing and raising the educational level of society before implementing democratic procedures was neither of these things, but rather just a restatement of the lessons in enlightened politics offered in the school in modern ways that was the International Settlement?[61]

ELIZABETH J. PERRY

5 | From Paris to the Paris of the East— and Back: Workers as Citizens in Modern Shanghai

Workers have figured prominently in a series of political confrontations that have changed the face of modern China. From the May Fourth Movement of 1919 to the June Fourth Massacre of 1989, working-class participation has proved critical. Although these famous milestones in Chinese history are, for good reason, usually regarded as student—rather than labor—protests, the involvement of members of the working class was far from incidental. The spectacle of workers marching outside their factory gates to engage in protest not simply as laborers, but also as *citizens,* has been a notable feature of Chinese contentious politics at critical junctures throughout the twentieth century. This phenomenon, moreover, carries implications that extend beyond the borders of China itself. Worker participation in the watersheds of Chinese political history has turned out to be of some international significance as well.

This chapter addresses the vicissitudes of worker-citizen protest through a brief consideration of four movements in the city of Shanghai, beginning with the May Fourth strike of 1919 and concluding with the June Fourth Incident of 1989. Each of these events, although distinctively Chinese (or even Shanghainese), was also part of a larger transnational process. Influences from abroad (in the form of both ideas and actions) shaped the motivations and methods of Chinese participants, just as Chinese experiences exerted an impact on developments elsewhere in the world. Whereas in 1919 the flows were largely from Europe to China, by 1989 there seems to have been a turnabout in the patterns of interaction.

The movements under examination, albeit all urban and all initiated by students, were not all of a piece. Among other things, they differed considerably in the degree to which the protesters envisioned and implemented new political arrangements. Such distinctions in political ambition dovetailed with variations in the intensity of cross-class cooperation. It was only when students managed to reach out to allies among the working class that their quest for citizenship (in China as elsewhere around the world) took on exceptional political force.

The May Fourth Movement

The historic May Fourth Movement of 1919 began as a student demonstration centered in Beijing. However, not until the protest spread to China's industrial capital of Shanghai did it garner widespread social support and commensurate political influence. As Joseph Chen notes in his monograph on the subject, "The May Fourth Movement in Shanghai was an epoch-making event in modern Chinese history . . . the Shanghai movement may properly be regarded as a genuine popular movement involving *all* strata of the society. It may also be considered as the first true *total* movement ever to occur in the entire history of China."[1]

What distinguished the Shanghai wing of the May Fourth Movement was the massive participation of workers. Visiting student delegates from Beijing, in concert with student unions and other civic associations in Shanghai, proved successful in organizing a general strike in the nation's industrial capital.[2] The week-long strike in Shanghai, involving some 60,000 participants, effectively immobilized the city and forced the hand of politicians in Beijing in a way that the student protests of the preceding month had been unable to accomplish. The government offered a public apology, released student demonstrators who had been arrested, discharged three officials involved in the Paris peace talks, and refused to affix its signature to the Versailles Treaty.

This was certainly not the first time that Shanghai workers had walked off the job.[3] It was, however, the first instance of an en masse walkout that crossed industrial lines. The unprecedented cooperation went hand in hand with a newfound awareness of international developments. Japanese-owned cotton mills were the first to be affected in 1919, but soon the work stoppage spread to the shipyards, utilities, printing, tobacco, and transport industries. Significantly, the action was not limited to labor. It was part of a *general* strike—a "triple stoppage" *(san ba)*—in which students, merchants, and workers joined forces in bringing to a halt academic, commercial, and industrial activities alike.

In contrast to previous labor disputes, workers participated in the May Fourth Movement less to press workplace demands than to take their newfound place as citizens alongside other sectors of urban society. As early as 1915, a Citizens' Patriotic Society had been formed in Shanghai to oppose Japanese incursions. The group spearheaded a highly successful boycott of Japanese goods, which spread from Shanghai across much of urban China later that year.[4] It was not surprising, then, that the arrests of anti-Japanese protesters on May 4, 1919, in Beijing caused "the greatest excitement in Shanghai. The merchants, industrialists, and urban workers, stirred by this tumult, began to follow the leadership of the new intellectuals."[5]

That new ideas of citizenship spread beyond intellectual circles is seen in the utterances and proclamations of workers during the May Fourth general strike. A member of Shanghai's Copper and Iron Machinery Guild remarked: "We, the industrial workers, are also a part of the citizenry. While people from the commercial and educational circles are striving hard to save our nation, how could we, the industrial world, be left behind?"[6] Similarly, craftsmen at a Shanghai machine tool factory wrote in a letter to the editor that "all who belong to the citizenry [*fanshu guomin*] share a deep sense of indignation."[7] A handbill distributed by the chauffeurs of foreign residents in Shanghai explained their decision to strike as an act of citizenship:

A warning to our brethren:
    As a result of our diplomatic defeat our national position is in great danger, so all our *citizens* feel the greatest indignation, the students suspending their lessons and going about to enlighten our

people, while the merchants are stopping their business and praying for relief and salvation. Now, we, of the industrial world, who
have the same conscience, feel it impossible to endure and remain
inactive.

All factories on both sides of the Huangpu River have struck
work. Therefore we chauffeurs, who are also *citizens* of this country,
have decided to begin our strike on Monday next June 9, so that we
may follow the same line of action as the students, merchants and
laborers. Unless our common object is attained, we will never resume our work.

But, fellow countrymen, be careful not to do anything violent.
Preserve order by all means. Please hand this to others when read.

The Citizens[8]

China's May Fourth Movement was of course sparked by the Paris
peace talks following the First World War. The Treaty of Versailles,
the terms of which threatened to convert Shandong province into a
virtual colony of Japan, evoked a public outcry among Shanghai
workers against foreign aggression and domestic capitulation alike.
Embracing a heady new political vocabulary whose lineage could be
traced directly to the French Revolution, Chinese urbanites voiced
concerns as "citizens" of their infant Republic.

The similarities between French and Chinese protests in particular were hardly accidental. As many as 200,000 Chinese workers
had been hired by European—especially French—factories during
World War I to replace men who had left for the battlefield. In this
recruitment drive, Shanghai craftsmen were explicitly targeted by
French companies.[9] Included among these overseas workers were a
surprisingly large number (some 28,000 according to the estimate of
Chow Tse-tsung) of intellectuals. As Chow notes, the implications of
this cross-class mingling were profound:

> In the first place, it provided a chance for Chinese intellectuals to
> live together with the workers and to begin to assume leadership.
> Previously, Chinese students abroad had come mainly from rich
> families, and few of them had done any hard work. By contrast,
> these student-workers came from the poor or middle class and for
> the first time did not follow the student tradition of belonging to a
> leisure class. With their assistance, a great number of industrial and

social organizations were formed among the Chinese workers in France during the war years, such as . . . the Labor Union, the Workers' Society, the Chinese Laborers' Society . . . and "self-government" clubs.[10]

This impressive organizational activity gave rise to a good deal of labor unrest as well. Despite French industrialists' hope for a docile foreign work force, Chinese employees in France launched some twenty-five recorded strikes between November 1916 and July 1918. When the Chinese were in turn displaced by militant Frenchmen at the end of the war, they headed home well schooled in tactics of labor strife.[11] The May Fourth Movement was to some degree a product of this "education abroad" experience. It was also part of a worldwide explosion of labor unrest that occurred that year.[12]

The Three Workers' Armed Uprisings

Less than a decade later, Shanghai was again rocked by a general strike inspired in part by French exemplars. When the Northern Expeditionary forces of Chiang Kai-shek scored a series of military victories in 1926, the balance of power began to tip against Sun Chuanfang's warlord regime. Cheered by the Guomindang advance, Shanghai residents cooperated in mounting a massive resistance to Sun Chuanfang and in planning for a new form of popular governance to rule the city.

By this time the Shanghai citizenry was well accustomed to general strikes, having launched not only the May Fourth Movement of 1919 but also the May Thirtieth Movement of 1925.[13] The Three Armed Uprisings of 1926–1927, although less familiar to Western scholars than the earlier precedents, were in some respects more interesting politically. In contrast to May Fourth and May Thirtieth, the Three Uprisings were not directed primarily against imperialism (which explains, no doubt, their relative obscurity in Western-language treatments of the period). Instead, the issue that energized the latter movement was that of establishing a new political order with widespread citizen participation.

The Parisian connection proved even more influential on this occasion. Luo Yinong, then secretary of the Shanghai district commit-

tee of the Communist Party, remarked during the secret preparations for the second uprising: "First there must be a general strike.
All the masses will immediately rise up to make speeches and hold
meetings in preparation for creating a *Shanghai Paris Commune*."[14]
Luo's words proved prescient. As a recent history of the movement
notes, "Surprisingly, this rather vague and unreflective prediction
was in the end largely realized."[15]

Like the Paris Commune of 1871, the Three Armed Uprisings
were basically the product of action by factory workers. In both
cases, however, workers proved less interested in a struggle against
capitalist exploitation than in a quest for citizenship. The Paris Commune, according to a persuasive new analysis by Roger Gould, was
"much more a revolt of city dwellers against the French state than of
workers against capitalism. To be sure, the majority of the insurgents
were indeed workers . . . but it was not as workers that they took up
arms against the state."[16]

In both the Paris Commune and the Shanghai Uprisings, workers
fought alongside other citizens for the shared goal of municipal
autonomy. A popularly elected municipal council, it was believed,
would rid the community of unwelcome outside state intervention
(whether in the form of policemen or warlord soldiers) and would
offer guarantees of freedom of the press, speech, public assembly,
and association.

The movement in Shanghai was inspired not only by foreign models, but also by earlier self-governance experiments within China. In
Shanghai itself, around the time of the 1911 Revolution the Chinese
section of the city had been managed under a system that Mark Elvin
terms "gentry democracy."[17] The Zhabei Citizens' Association (*Zhabei
gongminhui*) was formed on March 1912 by residents in the Zhabei
district. At the inaugural meeting, the chair of the association pro-
claimed that "we citizens have the right to discuss and deal with all
local administrative matters."[18] Six months later a similar citizens' association was founded in Nanshi (*Nanqu gongminhui*) to handle local
affairs in that district of the city.[19]

As Xu Xiaoqun has observed, these associations—based as they
were upon residence in a particular district of the city rather than
upon native-place origin or occupation—represented a significant
departure from traditional guild forms of elite organization. Xu sur-
mises that many of the participants in these associations were local

merchants, who had a special stake in preserving social order and managing local affairs.[20] The citizens' associations took the lead in calling for fairer elections for provincial assemblymen, negotiating district boundary lines, and proposing that foreigners be made to give up residence in their sections of the city.[21] Although such initiatives were abolished in 1914, when Yuan Shikai issued an order banning local self-government organizations throughout the country, the desire for municipal autonomy did not disappear (as described in greater detail in Chapters 3 and 4 of this volume).

In the 1920s, merchants in the Zhabei district established a "Self-governance Office" *(zizhi gongsuo)* and "North-South Defense Corps" *(nanbei baoweituan)* as a prelude to "bourgeois democracy."[22] These institutions—one civil, the other military—were outlawed by the warlord Sun Chuanfang in August of 1926, but not before Communist labor organizers had also become convinced of the need for some form of municipal self-governance to supplant Sun's control of the city.

The Three Workers' Armed Uprisings, in large part the brainchild of the Shanghai district committee of the Chinese Communist Party (CCP) (a body that included a number of workers as well as intellectuals), represented a struggle to replace warlord rule with citizen participation. But what would be the roles of workers, merchants, and other urbanites in the new order? How would power be distributed? And tyranny avoided? Communists and other activists at the time engaged in heated debates over just such questions.

Simplistic Communist Party histories now instruct us, with the smug certitude of hindsight, that "right opportunist" Chen Duxiu sold out to the bourgeoisie during the first two abortive uprisings—only to be rescued by Zhou Enlai's correct proletarian line on the third, and successful, attempt. Thanks to the recent availability of detailed minutes of the secret planning meetings of the Shanghai district committee, however, we can appreciate the degree to which party leaders agonized at length over these complex issues.[23]

Ever since the May Fourth Movement, radical student activists had appreciated the importance of a mobilized labor force. Yet how much of an independent role workers could be expected to play in the revolution remained a matter of some debate. To be sure, labor organizers were making strenuous efforts to raise the consciousness of the working class. In addition to a unionization drive, young Communist cadres had been devoting considerable energy to educating workers at part-time schools.[24] Much of this educational activity was directed toward instilling a greater sense of self-respect and political efficacy among the proletariat. In literacy classes, for example, workers were taught that by vertically aligning the two characters for "worker" (*gong* and *ren*), one came up with the character for "heaven" *(tian);* thus, if the proletariat were to unite, no power on earth would be able to stop them.[25]

Despite a fundamental commitment to the working class, however, Communist organizers recognized the importance of the bourgeoisie—particularly in a place like Shanghai, where commercial interests were so highly developed. Well aware of the progressive part that merchants had played in earlier self-governance movements in the city, CCP cadres were initially inclined to grant them a leading position in any post-warlord regime. In a planning session of the district party committee prior to the first uprising, it was agreed that a "Shanghai citizens' peace preservation society" *(Shanghai shimin heping weichihui)* would be established to pave the way for a new municipal government; of the thirteen representatives to the society, all but four (two workers and two students) were to be drawn from the ranks of the bourgeoisie.[26] A central slogan for the uprising was "Return Shanghai's city government to the citizens of Shanghai!" but it was clear that merchants were to play the principal role in this "citizens' government." At the same time, the new regime was expected to guarantee freedoms of assembly, speech, and press and to permit all manner of "progressive" groups—from the women's association to the Communist Party—to operate legally and openly.[27]

After the first uprising was summarily quashed in October 1926, partisans appreciated the need to assign more weight to proletarian participation. As a prelude to the second uprising the following February, a general strike was called. Although the main force of the strike would come from factory workers—some 360,000 strong—the strike manifesto made clear that the objectives of this massive labor stoppage (which was the largest China had seen to date) were political, rather than economic:

The all-city general strike is to help the Northern Expeditionary army, to topple Sun Chuanfang, and to reclaim Shanghai . . . This general strike is completely political in nature and is not an economic struggle. Thus in the course of this movement, no economic demands will be raised. Our objective is to oppose the warlords, not to oppose the capitalists.[28]

Again, the similarity to the Paris Commune was clear. As Roger Gould explains, "Conflict during the Commune of 1871 was in many respects not about work at all . . . municipal autonomy, rather than the right to work, became the focus of political agitation."[29]

Both the Paris Commune and the Shanghai Uprisings were sparked by resentment on the part of urban residents at the occupation of their city by unwelcome intruders—whether Prussians or warlords.[30] In both cases, workers spearheaded movements aiming to give local communities political control over their own affairs. As Roger Williams writes of the Commune, "Above all else, the Commune amounted to a demand for decentralization of authority, to a demand to replace the nation-state with a federal state where small self-governing units would become the dominant feature."[31] In China, proponents of federalism saw their project as contributing ultimately to the strength of the nation-state, but they shared with the Communards a commitment to local autonomy and self-governance.[32] The parallels were far from coincidental; movements in both countries were influenced by a political discourse stressing rights of citizenship that issued directly from the French Enlightenment.[33]

Shortly after the general strike of 1926 began, a Shanghai Citizens' Provisional Revolutionary Committee *(Shanghai shimin linshi geming weiyuanhui)* was formally established. Like its namesake during the Cultural Revolution, this earlier "revolutionary committee" was composed of both party and mass representatives. The eleven-member committee included delegates from the CCP and Guomindang (GMD), as well as the Shanghai General Labor Union and the Shanghai Student Federation, who met to make plans for a new municipal order.[34]

Although the bloody defeat of the second uprising called a temporary halt to such political aspirations,[35] enthusiasm for a citizens' government was not easily dashed. In March of 1927, another general strike in conjunction with a third armed uprising elicited the participation of more than 800,000 of Shanghai's one million workers. Interestingly, the popular mobilization process that lay behind this final—and successful—insurrection bore a close resemblance to that of the Paris Commune. In the Parisian case, residentially recruited National Guard battalions allowed inhabitants of different neighborhoods to act collectively. In Shanghai, workers' pickets (*jiucha dui*)—organized by urban districts (Nanshi, Zhabei, East and West Shanghai, and so on)—served an analogous purpose. Moreover, in both instances, neighborhood mobilization was augmented by large public meetings that drew together citizens from dispersed residential settings.[36]

On November 28, 1926, some 50,000 Shanghai residents gathered at Nanshi's capacious West Gate Stadium to discuss plans for a future government, with many of those in attendance pledging to withhold taxes until Shanghai was made a special municipality under citizen self-rule.[37] Four months later, after the success of the third uprising, ten times that number—an astounding half-million people—assembled at the Nanshi Stadium to celebrate their victory. Residents marched to the stadium in parade-like fashion, led by workers' pickets. Student propaganda teams passed out handbills along the route of the march, enticing others to join the festivities. Celebratory paraphernalia such as red cloth, red paper, and firecrackers sold out across the city, and tailors stopped making clothing to sew banners emblazoned with slogans such as "Recover Shanghai's concessions!" and (somewhat more ominously) "Down with all counter-revolutionaries!"[38]

The form of government that emerged from these public deliberations was patterned on that of the Paris Commune, with provisions for direct popular election (and, if necessary, recall) of representatives. To reward the workers for their vanguard role in the uprising, it was now agreed that the proletariat would assume the dominant position in the new regime. A Citizens' Representative Congress *(shimin daibiao huiyi)* would be formed with 1,200 delegates, of whom fully 800 (two-thirds of the total) would be workers.[39]

Given that this was the first effort of the young Chinese Communists to develop a blueprint for a new governmental system, it is not surprising that they were so influenced by the exemplar of the Paris Commune. As Karl Marx had written of the Commune:

Look at the Paris Commune. That was the Dictatorship of the Proletariat . . . The Commune was formed of the municipal councillors, chosen by universal suffrage in the various wards of the town, responsible and revocable at short terms. The majority of its members were naturally working men, or acknowledged representatives of the working class.[40]

In the case of Shanghai, two levels of representative congress were specified: district and all-city. Since the councilors at both levels were to be, in Marx's words, "working men," representation was to be based upon occupational units. Thus every factory, craft union, shopkeepers' federation, peasant association, merchant guild, military barracks, school, and professional organization (for journalists, lawyers, doctors, accountants, and the like) would hold mass meetings for the direct election of both district and all-city delegates. (Academic research institutes, benevolent societies, Red Cross groups, religious organizations, native-place societies, and other "non-occupational units" were denied representation.) At the city level, every 1,000 people would have one representative; at the eight district levels, there would be one representative for every 500 residents. All delegates were to be elected for one-year terms, which, while renewable, could also be terminated for malfeasance on a recall vote by the unit that had originally elected the delegate.[41] A distinction was made between "citizens" (shimin) and "residents" (zhumin). Citizens were to enjoy complete freedom of speech, press, and assembly and held rights to suffrage and electoral eligibility. Residents, whether Chinese or foreign, were granted residential, commercial, and production freedoms and were required to obey all municipal laws and to remit local taxes.[42] In a move that departed from the Paris Commune model and foreshadowed Cultural Revolution practices, foreigners and "counter-revolutionaries" were denied voting rights in the representative congresses of Shanghai.[43]

The responsibilities of representatives at both district and city levels were specified as follows: (1) to elect an executive committee; (2) to report on the opinions of the masses whom they represent; (3) to discuss and decide on military matters, taxes, city government, wages, food supplies, rents, foreign policy, welfare, education, and so forth; and (4) to report back to the masses who elected them.[44] With the district-based workers' pickets having disarmed both the warlord troops and the municipal police forces (in the Chinese sections of the city), a unified command of the workers' pickets—under the direction of the Shanghai General Labor Union—was established in the Huzhou guild hall. This headquarters took charge of the organization and drilling of armed workers' pickets throughout the city, dispatching forces as needed to settle labor disputes and maintain social order.[45] The situation was again not unlike the Paris Commune, which had abolished the standing army and declared the sole armed force to be the National Guard—in which all workers and other citizens capable of bearing arms were to be enrolled.[46]

The victory of the Third Uprising and inauguration of a workers' government in Shanghai generated considerable excitement around the world. In Paris, the French Communist Party convened a meeting attended by more than 6,000 people to express opposition to imperialist interference in the Chinese revolution. When the Chinese representatives entered the meeting hall, they were greeted with thunderous applause. Celebratory assemblies, parades, and lectures spread from Paris to London, Berlin, and Brussels. In the Soviet Union, the official newspaper, *Pravda,* declared: "The Shanghai workers have performed the same function in the Chinese revolutionary movement as the St. Petersburg workers performed in our own revolution."[47] But the rejoicing was brief. The Shanghai Citizens' Representative Congress survived only one month (half the life-span of the Paris Commune) before it was demolished in Chiang Kai-shek's April 12 Coup. Not for another forty years would citizens in Shanghai attempt to construct a form of municipal governance inspired by the Parisian prototype.

The Cultural Revolution

The Cultural Revolution, often remembered as a period of state-sponsored terrorism, was also marked by a degree of political experimentation. The Shanghai People's Commune, inaugurated shortly after rebel forces had seized power from the municipal authorities, was perhaps the most famous—and most controversial—of these attempts at political innovation. The endeavor was short-lived and highly constrained by outside forces, yet it remains an instructive example of an effort to empower the proletariat in local government. The Shanghai Commune was self-consciously modeled on images of the Paris Commune then circulating in Chinese intellectual circles.[48]

The Cultural Revolution was introduced to Shanghai by student Red Guards from Beijing, who launched a series of "southern tours" in the summer and fall of 1966. Inspired by these missionary forays from the capital, Shanghai students were quick to found their own Red Guard organizations. However, the most important outcome of the excursion of Red Guards from Beijing was not the formation of copycat student groups, but the development of a rebel workers' movement. On November 6, the student emissaries—eager to extend their rebellion from the school yard into the workplace—convened an organizational meeting attended by several dozen worker representatives from seventeen Shanghai factories. Participants at this gathering decided to establish an all-city alliance of worker rebels known as the Workers' General Headquarters (WGH). Under the command of Wang Hongwen, the WGH became the decisive mass organization in Shanghai for the duration of the Cultural Revolution.

It was the Workers' General Headquarters that played a leading role in wresting power from the Shanghai Party Committee in January 1967 and founding the ill-fated Shanghai People's Commune the following month. On February 6, 1967, the WGH issued a handbill concerning the inauguration of the Commune (which had taken place the day before). Entitled "The country is ours; political power is ours," the proclamation makes clear that worker rebels in Shanghai saw their "new Paris Commune" as having global significance:

Under the close concern and support of the reddest, reddest red sun in our hearts, the most beloved and respected glorious leader Chairman Mao, in the raging flames of the Great Proletarian Cultural Revolution, the *new Paris Commune* of the 1960s, the Shanghai People's Commune, is established!

This is a joyous occasion for the proletarian revolutionaries, a joyous occasion for the working class, a joyous occasion for all the people of the country. We acclaim most fervently: Long live the Shanghai People's Commune! Long Live Chairman Mao! Long, long life!

The establishment of the Shanghai People's Commune is a brilliant product of the great unity, great alliance, and great power struggle by the proletarian revolutionaries. It is a milestone of the Cultural Revolution entering a new historical era, a new glorious victory of the invincible thought of Mao Zedong, *a great beginning that stirs the world!*

Chairman Mao teaches us: "The realm is our realm. The country is our country. The society is our society. If we don't speak, who will speak? If we don't act, who will act?"

Seventeen years ago, under the wise leadership of Chairman Mao, advancing wave upon wave, battling bravely, we seized political power from the hands of the imperialists and Guomindang counter-revolutionaries and established a dictatorship of the proletariat. However, in many work units we workers didn't really take charge; control of the party, government, finance, and education fell into the hands of the representatives of the bourgeoisie and the counter-revolutionary revisionist elements. Rapacious as wolves and savage as dogs, they appear as people but are backed by goblins. They persist in exercising a cruel bourgeois dictatorship over the working class. They oppose Chairman Mao, the reddest, reddest red sun in our hearts, perniciously attack the invincible thought of Mao Zedong, and are of one mind in returning our glorious motherland to a bourgeois society.

Can we watch while our country changes color? Are we happy to be enslaved again? Impossible! Impossible!!

We have arisen in revolution! Rebelled! Seized power!

We have smashed the old Shanghai Municipal Party Committee and People's Congress. We have destroyed the black *yamen* of the revisionist lords. Now we are establishing a bright red Shanghai People's Commune. We ourselves will occupy the realm and hold great power! Let us stiffen our backs, lift up our heads, and actually take command. *We gravely proclaim to the entire world: the country is ours, political power is ours, the world is ours!*

Look! The brilliant rays of a new dawn are appearing on the eastern horizon! They will vanquish the darkness and illuminate all of China, *illuminate the entire world!*

Let us again fervently proclaim: Long life to the Shanghai People's Commune![49]

Despite the exuberant calls for immortality, the Shanghai People's Commune enjoyed a very short life-span—a mere twenty days as it turned out.

Brief as the experience was, however, the debates that surrounded the constitution of the Shanghai Commune exhibited an interesting resonance with earlier experiments in citizen rule. Like the Representative Congress of 1927, the Shanghai Commune was to be based on associational units. However, in this case the units were not occupational, but political, in nature.[50] The thirty-eight rebel organizations that had supported WGH commander Wang Hongwen in his struggle against the Shanghai Party Committee would be the "constituent units" *(zucheng danwei)* of the new organization. Wang's patron, Zhang Chunqiao, later proposed that the term "constituent units" be changed to "founding units" *(faqi danwei)* in order to minimize demands for inclusion from other organizations that had not participated in the inauguration of the Commune. Nevertheless, Zhang did promise that, in the future, more rebel outfits would be permitted to join the Shanghai People's Commune; the principle of associational membership was to remain intact.[51]

The question of military involvement in the new power structure posed a particularly sensitive issue. Although Chairman Mao had insisted that any new power structure must include the military, the founders of the Commune feared that the Shanghai Garrison would prove loyal to the old party committee. As a result, the regular military participated only marginally in the power seizure and the rebels quickly began to develop their own paramilitary units. By the close of the Cultural Revolution decade, the Shanghai militia—under the direct command of the rebels—counted three million soldiers equipped with 226,000 guns, 1,900 cannon, 2,600 rocket launchers, 500 tanks, and a warship.[52] This was a force capable of challenging the regular military.

The founders of the Shanghai Commune had presumed they were acting in accord with Chairman Mao's wishes,[53] but only one week after the inaugural ceremonies Mao expressed his displeasure with the "commune" nomenclature and decreed instead that the new government in Shanghai be called the "Shanghai Revolutionary Committee." As Mao put it, "With the establishment of a commune, a series of problems arises . . . Communes are too weak when it comes to suppressing counter-revolutionaries. If everything was changed into a commune, then what about the Party? . . . There must be a party somehow! There must be a nucleus . . . be it called the Communist Party . . . or Guomindang . . . there must be a party."[54] For Mao Zedong, as for Chiang Kai-shek forty years before, a politicized labor force could be a useful ally, but it also posed a potential threat to central state control—regardless of whether the state in question was a Nationalist regime espousing support for the bourgeoisie or a socialist regime claiming to be a dictatorship of the proletariat.

The Commune was thus hastily transformed into the Shanghai Revolutionary Committee, a "triple combination" in which party and military cadres were guaranteed due influence alongside rebel representatives. Whereas the Commune had been staffed by delegates from rebel organizations who did not serve as individuals, the administration of the Shanghai Revolutionary Committee was a more formal arrangement. Among the thirty members of its first standing committee, seven were worker rebels. Subsequently an additional thirteen names were added to the standing committee, of whom four were workers.[55]

Although the "commune" appellation was dropped on orders from Chairman Mao, the precedent of the Paris Commune continued to serve as an inspiration for the worker rebels. Even after the arrest of the Gang of Four, when diehards advocated activating the Shanghai militia for armed rebellion, they continued to invoke the memory of the Paris Commune: "If we get moving, in only five days' time the whole country will be behind us. Even if we fail, we'll go down in history like the Paris Commune, having shed our blood to educate the next generation!"[56]

When the Shanghai worker rebels assumed top posts during the Cultural Revolution as members of the new municipal revolutionary committee, as bureau chiefs, or in other leading cadre positions, their salaries remained limited to their original workers' wages of only 50 to 60 yuan per month. This salary restriction was in stark contrast to the former cadres, who garnered three to four times as much for comparable assignments, and represented an explicit commitment on the part of the worker rebels to the Paris Commune exemplar.[57]

In addition to their role on revolutionary committees, workers augmented their political influence through a variety of programs launched over the course of the Cultural Revolution: worker representatives, workers' Mao Zedong Thought propaganda teams, workers' theory troops, workers' new cadres, worker ambassadors, and the like. When the Shanghai Federation of Trade Unions was reestablished in 1973 as a metamorphosis of the Workers' General Headquarters, it was a remarkably powerful organization that often usurped party prerogatives—especially in the area of personnel matters.[58]

The tendency for workers to assume new political roles during the Cultural Revolution, while most pronounced in Shanghai, was not restricted to that city. Stephen Andors concludes on the basis of his national study that "the Cultural Revolution saw a marked influx of workers and new cadres from factories into organs of local government."[59] In other parts of China as well, the Paris Commune served as an inspiration for activists seeking a new political order. Yang Xiguang, ideologist of the Shengwulian rebels in Hunan, wrote repeatedly of the need to create a "Paris Commune–style new democratic regime."[60] Despite these developments, there is little evidence that rebels in Shanghai or elsewhere used their newfound authority to advance the interests of workers *as workers*. Theirs was a quest for political inclusion, rather than a crusade to improve the lot of their fellow laborers.[61] Absent were demands for higher wages or improved working conditions. A handbill issued by the Workers' General Headquarters on January 7, 1967, underscored its explicitly political agenda:

> We are rebelling against a handful of authorities taking the capitalist road, rebelling against the reactionary line, and not primarily over "money."
>
> The worker comrades must emphasize the long-term revolutionary interest and must not rebel for the sake of a wage hike. That would be a mistake! We raise the banner of politics, not the banner of economics!
>
> Our major target is a small handful of authorities taking the capitalist road inside the Shanghai Party Committee and the East China Bureau in order to consolidate the political power of the proletariat. Political power must be controlled by the revolutionary

rebels of the proletariat; this is the core issue! Otherwise, all temporary short-sighted economic interest is empty![62]

Although the Cultural Revolution did see the emergence of a genuine labor movement during the so-called "wind of economism" that swept across China's cities in the winter of 1966–67,[63] the rebel faction *(zaofan pai)* of Wang Hongwen and company represented a very different variety of worker protest. In the tradition of the Paris Commune or the Three Armed Uprisings, the Workers' General Headquarters was seeking greater representation for workers in local government.[64] As in these other cases, workers during the Cultural Revolution were enticed out of the factories (largely at the prompting of radicalized students) to engage in wider political struggles that had little to do with workplace grievances. Despite their rhetorical embrace of "class struggle," theirs was a bid for political inclusion (or "citizenship") rather than a battle against an already moribund bourgeoisie.

The claim of the Shanghai rebels to have "stirred the world" was not empty hyperbole. The outbreak of the Cultural Revolution in China helped to trigger widespread popular protest around the world. In 1968, mass demonstrations erupted in the United States, Italy, Germany, Japan, Ireland, Czechoslovakia, and Poland. But none was more dramatic than the May Revolt in Paris.

For the first time since the Commune of 1871, Parisians in 1968 erected barricades in the center of their city as part of a massive political protest. Participants were conscious not only of their own national revolutionary heritage,[65] but also of contemporary events elsewhere around the world—especially in China.

A major wing of the student movement in Paris, known as the Union des Jeunesses Communistes, Marxistes-Leninistes (M.L.'s) was composed of self-described Maoists. As suggested by the title of their journal, *Servir le Peuple,* these young radicals saw their Maoist mission as that of ministering to other social groups. A number of them actually abandoned their studies in favor of factory jobs, where they spread the messsage of proletarian revolution. After the occupation of the Sorbonne on May 13, student activists opened the university to workers. A general strike soon swept the country, with student and worker leaders in agreement on the goal of converting neighborhood strike committees into a general workers' council that would eventually assume control of municipal governance.[66]

Global interactions seemed to have come full circle. A Chinese revolution sparked half a century earlier by European influences was now itself serving to inspire would-be revolutionaries in Europe.[67] In the end, of course, neither the Cultural Revolution in China nor the May Revolt in France would usher in the new age of proletarian rule that their proponents promised. Yet China moved into its post-Mao era, and France its post–de Gaulle period, profoundly altered by these unsettling events.[68]

The Uprising of 1989

As had been the case with the May Fourth Movement and the Cultural Revolution, the uprising of 1989 was imported to Shanghai by student militants from Beijing. Unlike these other incidents, however, the protest of 1989 did not elicit a rousing response from the workers of Shanghai. Although there was evident sympathy for the student demonstrators in Beijing, especially once the hunger strike began,[69] this did not translate into a major political initiative among the Shanghai work force.

One of the critical differences between the events of 1989 and the earlier movements was the absence in 1989 of any sustained effort by students to recruit workers to their cause. In contrast to May Fourth, the Three Armed Uprisings, or even the Cultural Revolution, the uprising of 1989 did not see concerted student forays into the factories of Shanghai.[70] Thus when workers finally did take to the streets, their actions often ran directly counter to student initiatives.

After news of the June Fourth Massacre reached the southern metropolis, students in Shanghai (in good Paris Commune fashion) began to erect barricades across the city to prepare for a general strike. Although these blockades—constructed of commandeered buses, street railings, concrete slabs, and pipes—brought traffic to a complete standstill on June 5, the city did not shut down economically. In contrast to May Fourth, the Three Armed Uprisings, or the Cultural Revolution, workers refused to lend their support to student initiatives. Threatened with sanctions if they did not show up for work, many workers walked several hours to get to their jobs. The following day, unarmed worker pickets *(gongren jiucha dui)* began to tear down the student barricades. There were even reports of fighting between worker pickets and student groups, leading to several deaths.[71] On June 8, a more systematic and effective use of worker pickets by state authorities was authorized by Mayor Zhu Rongji. Thousands of workers, organized into state-sponsored "propaganda teams" reminiscent of the Cultural Revolution, were offered a full day's wage for three to four hours of demolition work. Within twenty-four hours, all the major student barricades had been removed.

The official Shanghai labor movement gazetteer offers the following account:

> On June 8, the municipal committee decided to establish the "Shanghai Preserve Transportation Propaganda Teams." That evening, after Mayor Zhu Rongji's televised address, more than 5,000 pickets at 33 large and medium-sized enterprises throughout the city formed "propaganda teams" to converge from all directions on three command posts in the city center. By four in the morning on the 9th, more than 5,000 propaganda team members together with armed police and public security personnel, riding in trucks and holding high banners, took to the streets to clear away all obstructions. At the same time, more than 100,000 workers' pickets organized by each district sprang into action. By dawn, the 48 remaining obstructions had all been removed . . . Zhu Rongji offered praise: "The Shanghai workers' pickets took action early this morning, restoring Shanghai's transportation and ending the disorderly situation. You have performed a great service for the people of Shanghai!"[72]

As an eyewitness to the events concluded, "While the Shanghai workers sympathized with the students' concerns and silently supported many of their activities, they did not have the courage or the necessary level of commitment to take major political risks."[73]

The gulf separating workers and students in 1989 was not unique to Shanghai, and was not attributable only to workers' cowardice. The reluctance of intellectuals to reach out to a labor constituency was also a factor. A laborer in Chongqing recalled:

The workers could see that participation was being strictly restricted by the students themselves, as if the workers were not qualified to participate . . . Moreover, in Beijing the issues that the students raised had nothing to do with the workers. For example, Wuer Kaixi in his speeches only talked about the students. If he had mentioned the workers as well, appealed to the workers, appealed to them in a sincere manner, the workers might really have come out in a major way.[74]

The year 1989 was most assuredly a turning point in world history, albeit one that brought few political reforms within China. Limited as China's own uprising proved to be, in terms of both democratic ambitions and political results, the stirring spectacle in Tiananmen Square served nonetheless as an inspiration for other, more consequential protests elsewhere in the world. The demise of Communist regimes across Eastern Europe later that year was undoubtedly accelerated by the Chinese uprising, which had attracted unprecedented media coverage throughout the European continent. Most notably in Warsaw, but in other East European capitals as well, workers joined students in pressing claims for citizenship that led ultimately to revolutionary outcomes.[75] Ironically, the Tiananmen Uprising may have exerted a greater impact abroad than at home.

Conclusion

As Sidney Tarrow has noted of international protest waves in general, "the multipolarity of the interactions in these cycles makes their endings far less similar than their beginnings . . . The outcomes of protest cycles are found in political struggle."[76] Political struggles are, of course, shaped by many factors—some of which are highly idiosyncratic and contingent. Even so, variations in the political inventiveness and efficacy of modern urban protests, in China as elsewhere in the world, seem to bear a close relationship to the degree of collaboration between student activists and members of the working class.[77]

Studies of labor in pre-Communist China have emphasized the catalytic role of intellectuals—whether Communist revolutionaries or members of the left-wing GMD—in stimulating the unrest of the

Republican period.[78] While such analyses may underestimate the capacity of Chinese workers to take action on their own behalf without outside direction, they do nevertheless highlight an important fact: the milestones of Republican-period history were laid by the combined efforts of workers and students. The general strikes of May Fourth, May Thirtieth, the Three Armed Uprisings, and the civil war years all exhibited close coordination between labor and the intelligentsia.[79]

The general strikes of Republican China were watershed events. The May Fourth Movement led directly to the founding of the Chinese Communist Party and heralded a new style of populist culture and politics; the May Thirtieth Movement and the Three Workers' Armed Uprisings hastened the expulsion of warlord rule and its replacement by a new GMD regime; the civil war hunger strikes helped to unravel GMD control over the cities and usher in a new socialist order. In all of these instances, students—who saw themselves as part of a worldwide political struggle—were key allies of an emergent working class.

General strikes are unusual, albeit remarkably powerful, events. Because they entail the participation of very different—and under normal circumstances quite competitive—groups of workers, these incidents are typically fought for causes that transcend the divisive concerns of the workplace. Not wages and welfare but national humiliation, price inflation, and political oppression are the rallying points of the general strike. Working-class interest in these issues is often promoted by those who have a professional preoccupation with such problems: the intellectuals.

Under what conditions are successful cross-class alliances likely to emerge? General explanations have often focused on the wider political environment (or the "political opportunity structure," as it is referred to in the social science literature).[80] While there is no doubt that the political setting forms a central piece of the puzzle, recent scholarship also directs our attention to the social networks and collective identities of the protesters themselves.[81] How robust were the associational and normative bonds among movement participants? Were insurgents closely linked through ties of marriage, residential propinquity, and the like? Did they share a "participation identity" that defined mutual commitment to the enterprise and drew sharp lines against common enemies? As Roger Gould's meticulous analysis of the mobilization process underlying the Paris Commune clearly shows, such connections can play a key role in facilitating powerful cross-class movements that raise demands for citizenship.[82]

During the Republican period, Chinese cities witnessed a pronounced trend toward greater cross-class interaction through such channels as native-place associations, secret-society gangs, part-time schools for workers, informal gatherings at teahouses, formal national salvation associations, and the like.[83] This nascent "civil society," if one may employ that overworked term, helped give rise to popular movements in which urbanites protested not simply as workers—but as citizens.[84]

Republican-era trends were evidently reversed in Maoist China with the imposition of the household registration system, the construction of segregated places of recreation for workers and writers, the injection of class criteria into marriage choices, and so forth.[85] The limited cooperation between workers and intellectuals in the protests of the past forty years would seem to reflect this altered situation. With the exception of the Cultural Revolution, when Red Guards entered the factories on instructions from Beijing,[86] workers in post-1949 China have acted for the most part without guidance from intellectuals. Thus although intellectuals contributed greatly to the dissent of the Hundred Flowers Movement of 1956–1957, for example, there is no evidence that they attempted to join forces with the strike wave that was then sweeping the nation's factories.[87]

Under the "proletarian" People's Republic, labor unrest has elicited harsh state repression (the labor camps of 1957, the PLA takeovers of 1969, the tanks of 1989) rather than auguring a new political era. One reason for the difference lies in the success of the Communist state at isolating working-class resistance from intellectual dissent. The strike waves of the Communist era—although encouraged by concomitant student protests—developed without significant support from educated outsiders. Considering the prominent role that intellectuals have historically played in Chinese protest movements, it is hardly surprising that their absence would have such profound implications.

Under the impact of the post-Mao economic reforms, however, it appears that cross-class contacts are again on the rise—a development with profound implications for the possibility of politically explosive collective action in the future.[88] If, as has recently been suggested, the contemporary economic reforms are laying the basis for a Chinese variant of federalism,[89] then the self-governance debates of bygone days may prove of increased relevance in the near future. Brief as the experiments of the 1920s (or the 1960s) turned out to be, participants in those movements wrestled with enduring issues of political representation that are likely to regain currency in the years ahead. Political scientists are not known for their predictive perspicacity, but when the next global protest cycle gets under way, we may well find ourselves looking to the Paris of the East for yet a new chapter in worker-citizen rule.

II | The People's Republic of China

6 | The Reassertion of Political Citizenship in the Post-Mao Era: The Democracy Wall Movement

Andrew Nathan has pointed out in his book *Chinese Democracy* that since the late nineteenth century, the Chinese view of citizenship has generally meant the exercise of political rights.[1] But unlike in the West, the governments of the late Qing, Republican period, and People's Republic of China, as Nathan further explains, considered rights not as inherent natural rights, but as given by the state.[2] Governments were to grant political rights, not to recognize them. Moreover, political rights were to enable citizens to contribute to the state rather than to enable individuals to protect themselves against the state. The late Qing government, for example, allowed the establishment of county and sub-county councils as well as provincial legislatures in order to imbue the population with a concept of citizenship that tied the individual to the state in the expectation of creating a more stable political order.[3]

In the early decades of the twentieth century, there were a small number of prominent Chinese intellectuals who regarded human rights as inalienable and as a check on state power.[4] But as the ineffectiveness of China's response to Western and Japanese imperialism became more apparent and political instability accelerated, the overwhelming majority of intellectuals, like the political leadership, increasingly stressed that political rights were to enable citizens to contribute to strengthening the state rather than to limit it. China's leading intellectual of the early twentieth century, Liang Qichao, explained that granting political rights was to achieve harmony between the individual and the state.[5] Likewise, most of China's intellectuals as well as political leaders in the early decades of the century came to view political rights not so much as a means to protect the individual and group against the state, but as a means to enhance the power of the state so that China could once again become "rich and powerful." They feared that individual or group assertion of political rights would further weaken the state in its confrontation with Japan and further destabilize Chinese society.

During the Mao Zedong era (1949–1976), there was no such thing as political rights. All political activity had to be carried out under the direction of Mao and the Communist Party. In the Leninist party-state, they controlled virtually all aspects of life and demanded total compliance with their commands. Tang Tsou[6] defines the Maoist notion of the "masses" (qunzhong) as "comradeship" (tongzhi), which connotes compliance, rather than "citizenship" (gongmin or shimin), which implies assertion of rights. Participants in the Maoist polity were "comrades." At great personal risk, a handful of intellectuals criticized the party's and Mao's policies and urged the leadership to live up to its professed ideals. They were silenced, jailed, or worse. Only briefly, during the Hundred Flowers period, were intellectuals allowed to propose alternative policies or to express differing political views. And virtually all of them, as well as their colleagues, families, and friends, were targeted in the subsequent Anti-Rightist campaign of 1957–1958 in which more than 500,000 intellectuals were purged; millions more were persecuted in the Cultural Revolution.

In the post-Mao era, intellectuals once again attempted to assert the right to participate in political decision-making and express political views. They demanded the right to be treated as citizens, gongmin, not as comrades, tongzhi. In fact, the term tongzhi fell into disuse. Like their predecessors, both in the premodern and Mao periods, post-Mao intellectuals sought to bring about reform by remonstrating with the leadership. Similarly, they believed that they were acting on behalf of the people; they did not see the people as acting on their own behalf. With a Confucian sense of moral mission, they sought to reform China by reminding its leaders of their highest ideals.

Nevertheless, a small number of the Cultural Revolution generation attempted to act as "citizens" by asserting their political rights in new ways. In part, their assertion was a result of the loosening of controls and the lesser threat of harsh punishment in the post-Mao era. Although they were still unprotected by institutions or laws, usually only those involved in such acts were persecuted—in contrast to the Mao period, when millions were harshly persecuted for the acts of a few. Political activists not in the official establishment who organized their own political groups, expressed dissident views, and tried to publish political journals were imprisoned or sent into exile. Those in the official establishment were allowed to go abroad or were dismissed from their positions. Although political campaigns against dissidents continued, the campaigns did not have the crusading zeal, coerced mass participation, and forced confessions of the Mao era. Most of the targets refused to comply. Moreover, unlike during the Mao era, some of them were not completely silenced, nor were their families and colleagues persecuted.

The main difference, however, between the post-Mao advocates of political rights and their predecessors was that the later activists were imbued with a different political consciousness that reflected a growing awareness of individual rights, and they used different political strategies to achieve their aims. The first evidence of a difference was the Democracy Wall movement, which suddenly appeared in late 1978 through 1979. The participants' ideas and strategies were derived primarily from their own experiences in the Cultural Revolution, which led them to redefine their political ideas and political roles. They had little knowledge of previous efforts in China to achieve political rights. Rather than remonstrating with the leadership, they demanded the right to be heard on political issues and expressed views that differed from those of the government. Unlike most intellectuals in the early decades of the twentieth century, they did not regard rights, which they variously referred to as human, civil, and political rights, as a gift from the state or as a means of increasing state power, but as inalienable and as involving protection of individual and group rights.

The Legacy of the Cultural Revolution

An even more radical departure from previous practices in the People's Republic was the tactics that the Democracy Wall activists used to achieve their rights. They had learned these tactics in the Cultural Revolution, when Mao summoned them to "rebel against authority" by means of the "four big freedoms"—the right to speak out freely, air views fully, hold great debates, and write big-character posters. These "four bigs," as they came to be called, were added to the constitution in January 1975. Thus, in late 1978, groups of young people put up wall posters, engaged in public debates, and distributed myriads of pamphlets in front of Beijing's Xidan Wall, along Chang'an Avenue leading to Tiananmen Square, as they had done in the Cultural Revolution. The events that took place in front of this wall came to be called the Democracy Wall movement. It was a transformative event in the People's Republic. The first wall poster to appear on Xidan Wall on November 19, 1978, directly attacked Mao Zedong by name for the first time in a public space. It criticized Mao's "mistaken judgment" in carrying out class struggle during the Cultural Revolution. Shortly thereafter, posters went up almost daily until December 1979, when the wall was closed down. Some of the posters, speeches, meetings, and pamphlets not only denounced Mao and called for the return of Deng Xiaoping to power, but also called for far-reaching political and economic reforms.

It was not so much what the activists said at Xidan Wall, but what they did there that indicated that they had become "citizens." This movement was organized from below, primarily by young workers, who might have been students had it not been for the fact that the Cultural Revolution had interrupted their education. They continued the unprecedented political debates, political networking, unofficial journals, and grassroots organizing that they had participated in during the Cultural Revolution, but without permission from either Maoist or party authorities.

With these methods, the Democracy Wall activists began a public critique of the Cultural Revolution and Mao's policies, demanded a reversal of the unjust verdicts of the Mao period, and, for the first time in the People's Republic, publicly called for individual, political, and human rights in an effort to prevent another Cultural Revolution. Although the rights of freedom of expression, association, and assembly were spelled out in all of China's various constitutions from the late nineteenth century into the Deng Xiaoping/Jiang Zemin eras, they were merely conceptual and not backed up by institutions, enforcement, or laws. But like the pre-1949 political activists, the Democracy Wall participants cited these constitutional rights to justify their efforts to act like citizens rather than the subjects they had been under Mao. As one of their journals explained, "People must rely on their own struggle to get and to protect their democratic rights and not rely on any supernatural beings or emperors to bestow them. Things bestowed cannot be depended upon. If democracy is something that can be bestowed by a bestower, it can also be taken back by the bestower."[7]

During the Cultural Revolution, activists had initially employed these practices to purge party officials and the intellectual establishment in response to Mao's summons to "Rebel against Authority." But as their actions provoked increasing chaos and violence, decimated the party bureaucracy, and undermined party control, Mao sent these young people to the countryside and factories to learn from the masses. Because the Cultural Revolution undermined the party's authority, weakened family ties, and factionalized the military, by the early 1970s in some areas it had produced a relatively permissive political environment. Whereas controls remained tight in the cities, they were more relaxed in rural areas where sent-down youth (xiafang), cut off from the constraints of the party, school, and family, gathered together to exchange ideas and debate political issues. Political groups that initially had been formed and manipulated by Mao's allies and the military became increasingly autonomous. While the numbers actively involved in grassroots dissent should not be exaggerated,[8] a significant minority began to question Mao, the party leadership, and the ideology in which they had been indoctrinated. Several of these networks established during the Cultural Revolution were to play a major role not only in the Democracy Wall movement, but later in a number of other movements in the post-Mao era that sought to bring about political reform.

A precedent for the Democracy Wall movement was the April 5, 1976, demonstration in Tiananmen Square, when during the Qingming festival to honor the dead, Beijing's seemingly passive citizens suddenly marched to the square to pay their repects to Zhou Enlai, whose death in January 1976 had been barely acknowledged officially. The demonstration was at least partially premeditated; demonstrators marched to the square holding elaborate wreaths made by work units and recited poems prepared in Zhou's honor. Nevertheless, as thousands of others joined the demonstration, it quickly turned into a public outcry of ordinary citizens against the injustices of the Cultural Revolution and its instigators. Whereas Zhou was honored, Mao was implicitly denounced. Large portraits of Zhou were placed in a row directly opposite the huge picture of Mao above the entrance to the Forbidden City.[9] Criticisms of Mao were voiced in the poems, with lines such as "gone for good is Qin Shihuang's feudal society."[10] Since the 1950s and especially in the "Criticize Lin Biao and Confucius" campaign of 1974, Mao had compared himself to Qin Shihuang, the cruel, repressive first emperor of the Qin dynasty (221–202 B.C.). Clearly, Mao was the target of the participants' denunciation of the first emperor. This particular quote was recited aloud and copied down by the demonstrators. The April 5th attack on Mao, albeit indirect, broke the taboo against publicly criticizing the hitherto sacrosanct leader.

A small number of the demonstrators also called for political rights. One young worker issued a statement in which he declared: "Let the people themselves choose . . . these leaders!"[11] Another criticized the party for treating the people like children, servants, or "docile tools." Nevertheless, the overall message of the April 5 demonstration was a call to return to the pre–Cultural Revolution era, in particular the supposedly "golden age" of the early 1950s when the party apparatus was in control and leaders were believed to be upright. Only a few demonstrators talked of alternatives or of asserting their political rights. And none of the writings from this demonstration openly questioned the leading role of the party. The goal was to turn back rather than to move in a different direction.

The Cultural Revolution, therefore, left contradictory legacies. Both the post-Mao leadership and the population in general agreed on the destructive nature of the Cultural Revolution's persecutions, divisiveness, violence, chaos, and alienation. As the May Fourth writer Ba Jin explained: "Never before in the history of man nor in any other country have people had such a fearful and ridiculous, weird and tragic experience as we had in the Cultural Revolution."[12] Ba Jin criticized Mao and the political system that had given Mao the unlimited power to cause such a tragedy. Yet, despite this destructiveness, even some of its victims, including Ba Jin himself, also stressed a positive impact. Although Ba attributed his wife's death to the persecution he had suffered, he writes: "Those ten bitter years were far from being a complete waste; I gained something I cannot put into so many words, but it is something intense, shining and growing."[13]

One legacy of the Cultural Revolution was a willingness to question the Leninist political structure and the party leadership. Some of the victims among the party cadres, intellectuals, and skilled workers saw the Cultural Revolution not just as an aberration of the Leninist-Maoist political system, but as the culmination of the political campaigns that had begun in Yan'an in the early 1940s. Like Ba Jin, nearly the entire nation, including those who were persecuted and ostracized, had accepted Mao's authority. They did whatever Mao and the party had ordered them to do, even attacking their colleagues, friends, and members of their families, in the belief that they were helping to modernize and strengthen the country. They had equated service to the party-state and Mao with service to China.

It was not until the Cultural Revolution, when, as Ba Jin observes, "no one in China was spared, many narrowly escaped death, and everyone was pushed to the extremes of endurance,"[14] that some finally realized the enormity of the danger of unquestioning obedience to whatever the party leadership dictated. "To let one person or even a handful of people decide your fate and do all the thinking for you is a very dangerous thing."[15] In addition to blaming Mao and the political system, Ba Jin also blamed himself and his colleagues for what had happened. "It has taken me a long time but I am now able to admit to myself that the responsibility does not lie solely with Lin [Biao] and the Gang . . . They could not have done it, if we had not let ourselves be taken in."[16] Thus, for a segment of China's intellectuals, party officials, and youth, an indirect consequence of the Cultural Revolution was a determination no longer to let others control their fate. "Never again," many asserted, would they blindly follow orders and unquestioningly accept the authority of people whom Ba Jin called "savior officials."

For a segment of the Red Guard sent-down youth, whose education had been suspended, the Cultural Revolution was also a profoundly disillusioning experience. In the beginning, when Mao ordered them to rebel against authority, particularly against party cadres and teachers, the youths had enthusiastically participated in getting rid of "repressive" authorities in order to usher in a totally new world. But when Mao charged them with political deviation for engaging in the youthful rebellion that he had ordered, they too began to see themselves as victims who had been disinherited, betrayed, and manipulated by Mao for his own political purposes. They thought of themselves not so much as "the lost generation," as they were to be called after the Cultural Revolution, but as "the alienated generation." This sense of alienation as well as demands for political rights were expressed in the Democracy Wall movement, which quickly spread from Xidan Wall to other walls in Beijing and to other cities—Shanghai, Guangzhou, Wuhan, Hangzhou, Xi'an, and Qingdao.

The Democracy Wall Movement

For a small number, the Cultural Revolution had inadvertently been a school for citizenship. Instead of rearing a generation of revolutionary successors, the Democracy Wall movement revealed that Mao had bred a generation of questioners and political activists among a small but important segment of the Cultural Revolution generation, who sought to assert their political rights as citizens.[17] While most youths in the aftermath of the Cultural Revolution turned away from politics, a segment, particularly among the "sent-down" youth whose education had been cut short and who had become workers, emerged from that experience politically awakened, skeptical, and relatively independent. Unlike the members of the intellectual establishment, who had been purged during Mao's campaigns, but who were able to return to high positions—in government, the media, and academia—after they were rehabilitated in the late 1970s, these youth remained on the fringes of society. Because their formal educations had been interrupted, most were menial laborers.

Though some participated in the Democracy Wall movement as individuals, most participated as members of groups formed during the Cultural Revolution. And they used Cultural Revolution strategies to publicize their ideas. They became the core groups for political activism in the Democracy Wall movement and thereafter. While most of the participants focused on economic issues and Cultural Revolution grievances, a small number emphasized political issues. They coordinated their actions within a city and sometimes among cities. By mid-1979, activists were beginning to develop loose networks across regions. Although they numbered only several hundred to a few thousand at any one time, their posters, debates, ideas, and journals attracted tens of thousands of readers and listeners. Both officials and ordinary people, who shared a revulsion against Mao's use of terror and chaos and who wanted to reform the political system, were among the readers and discussants at the city walls.

They made their reappearance during the uncertainty in the months preceding and following the Third Plenum of the Eleventh Central Committee held on December 12–22, 1978, which many believed would initiate major changes in the party and its policies. At this time, the party relaxed political controls and provided few guidelines on the permissible limits of criticism and debate. Just one month before the plenum, the party officially removed the "rightist" designation from virtually all those who had been so labeled in previous campaigns. It also withdrew the "counter-revolutionary" verdict on the April 5th demonstration and released hundreds of the participants in that demonstration from prison. The poems recited during the demonstration, including the one comparing Mao to the despotic first emperor of the Qin dynasty, were officially published. In addition, Deng Xiaoping called for "socialist democracy and rule of law." He and most of his Long March revolutionary colleagues used these policies to reinforce their efforts to discredit the Maoists still in the leadership, to consolidate their power, and to reject Mao's utopian vision in favor of pragmatic economic practices. The effect of these efforts appeared to legitimize open criticism of political repression.

Unlike the brief April 5th demonstration and the later Tiananmen Square demonstration in spring 1989, which lasted about six weeks, the Democracy Wall movement continued erratically for more than a year. The movement was allowed to go on for so long because it was used in the leadership power struggle and because the leadership itself was searching for new approaches. Deng Xiaoping took advantage of the pressure of the Democracy Wall activists from below for political and economic reform to help him oust the Maoists still remaining in power. Like Mao during the Cultural Revolution, Deng used these spontaneous demonstrations in the streets as leverage against his opponents in the party and as a means of consolidating his own position. The Democracy Wall movement helped to make Deng China's paramount political leader.

When wall posters appeared on Xidan Wall denouncing Mao and other officials associated with the Gang of Four and demanding political and economic reforms, Deng, in interviews with foreign journalists in late November 1978, expressed approval of the posters.[18] As these journalists then relayed Deng's approval to the demonstrators at Xidan, their numbers swelled to thousands and wall posters spread to other walls in Beijing and to other cities. People went daily, from daybreak until late at night, to read and copy the wall posters and to listen to speeches.[19] In addition to memorializing Zhou Enlai and criticizing the Gang of Four, a number of the posters discussed the institutions necessary for a well-functioning democracy. Some proposed competitive elections from the local to national levels; others called for legal guarantees for freedom of speech, assembly, procession, and demonstration, and punishment for those who suppressed these freedoms.

Whereas purged party officials and factory managers had planned and led the April 5, 1976, demonstration, the Democracy Wall movement appears to have begun somewhat spontaneously among youth on the margins of society. Although some were sons of party cadres or professionals, in the aftermath of the Cultural Revolution they were unable to get government jobs or engage in the intellectual pursuits to which they aspired. Though a small number had passed the examinations and entered universities, because of their political pasts, after graduation most were unable to obtain positions commensurate with their skills. The author of the first wall poster put up on Xidan Wall on November 19, for example, was the son of a veteran party cadre who had become a Beijing garage mechanic.

The first unofficial journal to appear was *April 5th Forum (Siwu luntan)* in November 1978. The experiences of its editors, Xu Wenli and Liu Qing, during the Cultural Revolution as students-turned-workers were typical of other Democracy Wall activists.[20] Xu, born in 1945, was the son of a doctor, but worked as a maintenance electrician in a Beijing factory. Liu Qing finished high school, was sent to the countryside in 1965, studied at Nanjing University in 1973–1977, then worked in a factory, and later moved back to Beijing. In late November and December 1978, other influential publications appeared—*Reference News for the Masses (Qunzhong cankao xiaoxi)* and *Tribune of the People (Renmin luntan)*. In January and February 1979, *Today (Jintian)*, *Beijing Spring (Beijing zhi chun)*, *Fertile Soil (Wotu)*, *China Human Rights Journal (Zhongguo renquan bao)*, *Seek Truth Journal (Qiushi bao)*, and *Exploration (Tansuo)* came out.[21] In Beijing alone, there were several dozen unofficial journals. The editors operated out of their living quarters, and almost all of the journals were mimeographed, with print runs of just a few hundred because of the limited supplies of paper and ink. The editors of *Beijing Spring*, seeking political reform within the system and with connections to reform party officials, printed 10,000 copies of one issue. But it was an exception. The publishers of these journals wrote, edited, mimeographed, distributed, and sold their publications at the wall and elsewhere without official help.

These groups also formed coalitions among themselves to carry out shared political agendas. Although the groups that formed around particular journals advocated different viewpoints and approaches, most wanted to reform the political structure and express themselves more freely. They may not have had a clear understanding of democracy, but they knew they wanted to make the existing political system more open and democratic. While their views overlapped with those of the democratic elite in the intellectual establishment, they expressed themselves more directly and specifically.[22] Whereas the democratic elite criticized Mao indirectly through code words, the Democracy Wall activists criticized Mao openly by name. Several groups held weekly "joint conferences," where they debated and argued about politics in an intense but civil manner. They not only gathered in front of Democracy Wall to debate their ideas, but they also met in their rooms, at public parks, and at other public places to exchange ideas on a diverse range of political, economic, and cultural issues. Early on they attempted to coordinate activities in Beijing, and by mid-1979 they began to make contacts with their counterparts in other cities. Though they acted like citizens through their actions, they were limited ideologically and intellectually by little exposure to ideas other than those of Marxism-Leninism and Mao Zedong Thought. Most still expressed themselves in the idiom of these ideologies. Even the Democracy Wall activists with the most non–Marxist-Leninist view of democracy, such as Wei Jingsheng, editor of *Exploration,* and Ren Wanding, editor of *Human Rights Journal,* called themselves Marxists. Though they were aware of some Western classics, when asked what they had read, they replied that they had read only a few foreign books in translation and knew no Western languages.[23]

In an interview with a Hong Kong journal, Xu Wenli, co-editor of *April 5th Forum,* explained his motivation for setting up his journal. Despite the fact that no privately run newspaper had been allowed since 1949, Xu wanted to publish a private newspaper because he believed that it was "necessary to allow the masses to run some newspapers themselves so as to reflect the people's demands and wishes . . . to reflect the demands for democracy, rule of law and reform."[24] Thus, on November 26 he started the *April 5th Journal.* When he was joined shortly thereafter by four friends, they changed the name to *April 5th Forum.* About twenty people became associated with it, the majority of whom were factory workers and a few young teachers. Some were also Communist Youth League members. Though some of these journals may have initially been underground, they came above-ground in 1978–1979. They described their publications as "run by the people" *(minban kanwu)* and put the names and addresses of the publishers on the mastheads. Although the editors sought to register their journals officially, they were generally unsuccessful.

Most of the journals adopted a broadly Marxist-Leninist framework of analysis; their editors identified themselves as Marxists and socialists, and declared open support for party policies and leaders. They continued the April 5, 1976, critique of the Cultural Revolution, sought redress for Cultural Revolution abuses, urged economic reforms, and supported the agenda of the reformist party leaders. There were, however, several important exceptions—*Exploration, Human Rights Journal, and Enlightenment (Qimeng)*—that attacked Deng Xiaoping, criticized Leninism, and advocated alternative political ideologies. These journals had evolved from wall posters. When Wei

Jingsheng put up his famous "Fifth Modernization" wall poster—
"Without democracy, there can be no four modernizations"—on December 5, 1978, it attracted many spectators. He put his name and
address on the poster, and sympathetic readers then contacted him
directly. This marked the beginning of *Exploration,* with Wei as editor-in-chief. Even though most of its founders believed in Marxism,
one of Wei's fellow editors explained that they did not take Marxism
as the journal's underlying principle because they disagreed over
how to interpret it. They all agreed, however, on the guiding principle of freedom of speech, press, assembly, and association as prescribed in the PRC Constitution.[25] The first issue, dated January 8,
1979, carried three articles, one of which was Wei's "Fifth Modernization" essay. About 150 copies of the issue were published and sold
around Xidan Wall and Tiananmen Square.

Although they expressed different political views, most of the journals carried a broad mixture of political, social, and economic commentary and analysis and were concerned primarily with issues of
freedom of speech, publication, association, and rule of law. A few
were devoted to literary themes, short stories, and poetry that exposed the dark side of life and explored inner emotions—another
deviation from the Maoist period, which was dominated by optimistic socialist-realist literature. The literary journals, particularly *Today,*
cultivated a unique literary and artistic flowering that spread to the
artistic establishment. Poems in *Today,* for example, were published
in the official *Poetry Journal (Shikan). Today* published a host of writers and poets—Bei Dao, Mang Ke, Gu Cheng, Duo Duo, and Shu
Ting—who were to become prominent in China and abroad and
made popular a new literary genre, called "misty poetry" *(menglong
shi),* a supposedly apolitical form of poetry that expressed individual
emotions. But by rejecting politics, they too were making a political
statement in a society where virtually all aspects of life had been
politicized. They acted as citizens in asserting their right to be apolitical.

The Issue of Rights

Assertion of political rights, the pre-1949 definition of citizenship,
was revived and played an unprecedented role in the Democracy
Wall movement. Although the concept of rights *(quanli)* had been

fervently debated in intellectual circles during the early decades of the twentieth century[26] and was briefly referred to during the Hundred Flowers period, since the Communist revolution it had been denigrated as a Western bourgeois concept. Nevertheless, a small number of the journals in the Democracy Wall movement—*April 5th Forum, Exploration, Beijing Spring, Human Rights Journal, and Seek Truth Journal*—though of differing political persuasions, went beyond supporting the policies of the reform leadership to explore new avenues of political action and dialogue, specifically on the question of political, civil, and human rights, terms they used interchangeably.

As with other issues, their discussions of these rights also took place within a Marxist-Leninist ideological framework. Through their parents or associates, several editors of these papers had access to the *Reference News,* the party's internal news bulletin, which included articles on Soviet and East European dissidents, who referred to their constitutions as the basis for their actions. Likewise, the Democracy Wall activists stressed the importance of the rights of freedom of expression, association, and political participation as guaranteed in China's constitution. In addition, since Mao had inserted into the 1975 constitution the "four big freedoms"—the right to speak out freely, air views fully, hold great debates, and write big-character posters—they specifically cited the "four bigs" as the basis for their actions.

The introductory issues of a number of the journals stressed a commitment to these rights stipulated in China's constitutions. *April 5th Forum* stated that its purpose was "to exercise the right to supervise and administer the state, a right the Constitution has vested in the people, so as to turn the Constitution from provisions written on paper into a basis for the existence and development of our society." Every person, it pointed out, "has a share of responsibility for the fate of his country."[27] On January 1, 1979, *Seek Truth Journal* stated: "That which conforms to the constitution is legal and all that runs counter to the constitution is illegal. . . . In accordance with the Constitution's provisions, citizens have the right to enjoy the freedom of speech, correspondence, and press." Moreover, "the citizens' freedom of person and their homes are inviolable and the journal is resolutely committed to defending the civil rights of its staff members

[and] those who are associated with it."[28] *Beijing Spring* described itself as "a comprehensive periodical run by the masses . . . [that] fully exercises the democratic rights of speech and press as stipulated in the Constitution . . . [to] publish the appeals of the people and various kinds of articles of an exploratory nature."[29] The *China Human Rights Journal* on March 22, 1979, declared that it would "expose the various crimes of trampling on democracy and human rights and of violating the current Constitution."[30]

The editor of the *China Human Rights Journal*, Ren Wending, had earlier established the China Human Rights League and issued a "Declaration on Human Rights in China" that was hung up on Democracy Wall as an eight-page wall poster[31] on January 25, 1979, jointly signed by seven groups and unofficial journals. Calling the April 5th demonstration "a human rights movement," the declaration stated that "the significance of human rights is more far-reaching, profound and lasting than anything else. This is a new mark of the political consciousness of the Chinese people and a natural trend in contemporary history."[32] The declaration addressed the Chinese people as "citizens" *(gongmin)*, which in the context of the declaration meant participants in the political process.[33] In addition to freedom of speech and association, it demanded the release of ideological and political prisoners; the right to criticize and reassess the party's and nation's leaders; representation of many parties in the legislature because "without many parties, the party is the government and is not separated from the government." Furthermore, the declaration called for direct voting to elect national and local leaders and the legislature, which was to act as a watchdog over the government,[34] as well as the right of citizens to observe the legislature and discussions of the leadership. The declaration concluded with an appeal to "the governments of all countries in the world, to human rights organizations, and to the public for support."[35]

The actions of Soviet and East European dissidents in the late 1970s, particularly their use of human rights discourse, clearly influenced the Democracy Wall activists. Intellectuals in the People's Republic had been fascinated by events there, beginning with the Hungarian and Polish uprisings in 1956 and the writings of dissident intellectuals, particularly in the Soviet Union. On December 8, 1978, an open letter to President Carter was posted on Democracy Wall, which described Carter's concern for Soviet dissidents as "very moving." Then, addressing President Carter directly, it said: "We would like to ask you to pay attention to the state of human rights in China. The Chinese people do not want to repeat the tragic life of the Soviet people in the Gulag Archipelago."[36] Several Democracy Wall activists also cited references to Marx on human rights to substantiate their arguments. On the basis of his understanding of Marx, Xu Wenli pointed out that it was "only proper that a progressive society should protect the most fundamental rights of man."[37]

Despite Wei Jingsheng's lack of Western-language skills and knowledge of Western writings, several articles in *Exploration* revealed some understanding of Western democratic concepts. Commenting on Deng's statement to foreign reporters that China had no human rights problems, one of the editors of *Exploration* asked: "What would be the danger to the interests of Chinese citizens if they were granted the same individual rights now being enjoyed by U.S. citizens?"[38] Another article in *Exploration* asserted: "If we cannot even be ensured of the kind of civil rights long guaranteed in capitalist society, then 'rule of law and socialist democracy' will be nothing but empty talk." Paraphrasing Wei's wall poster on the "Fifth Modernization," the author asserted that "without achieving the first modernization, namely, the democratization of our politics, the 'four modernizations' we have been advocating all along can only remain a moon in the water forever."[39]

Nevertheless, the major impetus for the interest of the Democracy Wall activists in human, civil, and political rights originated in their own political awakening during their formative years in the Cultural Revolution, as revealed in interviews and articles. Though Wei Jingsheng was one of the most anti-Leninist of the editors, his experience resembled that of most of the activists. The son of a People's Liberation Army (PLA) veteran, Wei attended the elite high school attached to People's University, where the Red Guards were active early on. He was imprisoned for three months at the end of 1967 and then spent four years in the army, traveling throughout the country, where he was shocked to see such great poverty, especially in the northwest, twenty years after the revolution. After the Cultural Revolution, Wei became an electrician at the Beijing zoo. His co-editors were from similar intellectual or cadre families, who also spent time during their youth in the countryside or in factories.

Others specifically pointed to the Cultural Revolution as the source of their concern for rights. In an interview with a Hong Kong journal, Xu Wenli explained that his and his associates' call for civil rights was sparked by the Cultural Revolution, when "rights [had been] trampled upon seriously."[40] Furthermore, Xu explained, the Cultural Revolution had occurred because "the right of freedom of speech that citizens are entitled to in all of China's constitutions" is just "a principle . . . yet to be regularized institutionally and judicially."[41] When Lin Biao and the Gang of Four held power, "the people could present no legal case against them in the struggle for freedom of speech and press." This was because the Chinese people have no "legal provision to protect these things."[42]

The group that formed around *Beijing Spring* was at the opposite end of the political spectrum from *Exploration*. They sought gradual political reform within the existing political system and believed the party could reform itself under Deng's leadership. Yet its members were also concerned with rights. Two of its leaders, Chen Ziming and Wang Juntao, were university students who saw themselves as successors to the literati, carrying on the Confucian tradition of participating in politics and urging those in power to reform. Though their ideological stance was more moderate than that of most of their Democracy Wall colleagues, their experiences in the Cultural Revolution had also ignited their political activism.[43] Chen was descended from several generations that had been educated at Peking University. In 1968, at age 16, he was appointed leader of Beijing's Number 8 Middle School and was sent to a remote production brigade in Inner Mongolia. There, like Wei Jingsheng in the northwest, he and his classmates were shocked to find that most of China's peasants still lived in abject poverty and were subjected to the tyranny of local party cadres. Furthermore, the native Mongol population was discriminated against and their region was neglected. The popular image of revolutionary peasants and dedicated leaders working for the cause of the people was replaced in Chen's and his classmates' minds by a deepening sense of distrust of the party, reinforcing the distrust which already had been engendered by Mao's summons to rebel against authority and their subsequent dispersal to the countryside.

Chen formed a group among the sent-down youth in Inner Mongolia that met regularly in late-night sessions to discuss the injustices and shortcomings of the political system. On the basis of the group's readings of the Marxist classics, including *Das Kapital* and the works of Engels, the participants fervently debated a wide range of political issues. Moreover, in this less controlled political environment, Chen and his friends had more freedom to read whatever they could find. Chen read a few Western classics of the French Enlightenment, such as Montesquieu's *The Spirit of Laws,* as well as books on economics, math, and animal husbandry. He became a "barefoot doctor," and in 1970 he was appointed chair of the brigade's Revolutionary Command. In 1971 he became a member of the Communist Youth League and, through self-study, began to prepare for college; he returned to Beijing in 1974. But shortly thereafter he sent a letter to one of his friends in Inner Mongolia criticizing the Gang of Four that was intercepted by the authorities, and Chen was imprisoned in 1975. He was allowed to visit his family in Beijing before transfer to a labor reform camp just as the April 5th demonstration was getting under way. He joined the demonstrators and quickly assumed a leadership role when the crowds pushed him forward to negotiate with the authorities for the release of protestors who had been arrested.

Chen's future political partner, Wang Juntao, was the son of an official at the Military and Political Academy. He made his political debut during the April 5th demonstration when he led his high school class to the square and composed a poem in honor of Zhou Enlai. After the demonstration, Wang was imprisoned and Chen continued on to the labor reform camp. Most members of the editorial board whom Chen gathered together when he set up *Beijing Spring* had also been imprisoned for their actions during the Cultural Revolution. Such shared ordeals made its members a relatively close-knit group. Chen and several others also held seats on the Central Committee of the Communist Youth League, and Wang Juntao was an alternate member.

Despite its relatively moderate stance, *Beijing Spring* was one of the first journals to advocate such a radical strategy as the use of unofficial strikes to achieve one's rights. Its February 1979 issue applauded a student strike at the No. 1 Branch School of Beijing Teachers' College. Because this college only required three years of schooling and the students there were older, the government refused to remunerate them as they did students at four-year universities. As a result, the students went on strike to demand their rights; after a month, their demands were met. While some people referred to their strike as "ultra-democracy" and "anarchism," *Beijing Spring* supported it: "A strike with good reason serves as an impetus to institutionalizing democracy and strengthening the government." Moreover, "Going on strike is a democratic right prescribed by the Constitution." The journal hoped that when the National People's Congress formulated a civil code, specifically regulations in regard to strikes, it would be clearly stipulated that strikes are "proper democratic rights."[44]

Groups outside of Beijing also contributed to the freer political climate in Beijing. One of the most significant was an organization in Guiyang, Guizhou, called the Enlightenment Society (Qimeng she), which included over 100 ex–Red Guards who were workers or grade school teachers. Using their own money, a group of them traveled to Beijing where they distributed their journal, made speeches, and hung wall posters. The poet Huang Xiang, who was also a worker, was the most eloquent voice in this group. He had been harshly persecuted for his poems, written during the Cultural Revolution, which described the repression and expressed a profound sense of disillusionment. On November 24, members of the Enlightenment Society posted Huang Xiang's poems along seventy yards on an embankment, attracting hundreds of readers. One of Huang's colleagues, Li Jiahua, wrote an introduction to the poems, declaring that "we must free ourselves from the patriarchal rule of the past thousands of years" by insisting on the constitutional rights of citizens.[45] The Enlightenment Society also posted a newspaper-size poster at the History Museum calling for democracy and human rights. In January 1979, a Beijing branch of the society was publicly inaugurated and posted "An Open Letter to President Carter" that urged the United States and other Western countries to pay attention to the state of human rights in China.[46] They also translated the U.N. Declaration on Human Rights and other Western treatises on democracy and posted them on Xidan Wall.

Activists from other cities not only joined the Beijing groups but also made similar demands in their own cities. In late November 1978, thousands began gathering daily at People's Square in Shanghai. A significant number of wall posters in Shanghai also focused on the issues of political rights. In December 1978, one such poster re-printed the opening of the American Declaration of Independence, with its resounding phrases: "We hold these truths to be self-evident, that all men are created equal, that they are endowed by their Creator with certain unalienable Rights . . ." Unofficial journals were also published in Shanghai. One of the most famous was *Voice of Democracy (Minzhu zhi sheng)*, edited by Fu Shenqi, a repairman at the Shanghai Generator Factory. Fu's background was similar to that of his Beijing counterparts. Born in 1954 into a workers' family in Shanghai, he completed middle school, was sent to work in a Shanghai factory, and in 1977 entered Shanghai No. 4 Normal College; he returned to the factory the following year and became a member of the Communist Youth League.[47] Another form of grassroots movement coalesced in Shanghai: demonstrations by families demanding the return of sent-down urban youth, who had been transferred to remote rural areas and had not yet been legally allowed to return to the cities.

The experience of He Qiu, also known as He Fang, one of the editors of the Guangdong journal *Voice of the People (Renmin zhi sheng)*, similarly resonated with that of the Democracy Wall activists. He was born in 1948. His father, a dentist, was a member of the Democracy Party of Farmers and Workers and a local party representative. He graduated in 1965 from junior high school and entered the Canton Shipbuilding Academy. During the Cultural Revolution, he became a worker at a shipbuilding factory. Citing Marxist views, he criticized the Cultural Revolution and Mao's policies in a letter to his brother and was sent to a prison camp. After the reversal of his case, He Qiu joined the *Voice of the People,* where he declared that China "must first realize the 'four great freedoms' granted in our constitution."[48] Thus, members of the Cultural Revolution generation acted as citizens by demanding political rights and publishing unofficial journals and wall posters in China's major cities in the late 1970s.

Repression Evokes Coordinated Action

As Deng solidified his political position in the months following the Third Plenum, he no longer needed the grassroots support of the Democracy Wall movement. Moreover, as the leadership became

aware of the anti-Leninist views and actions of some of the participants, they began to move against the more radical Democracy Wall
leaders. In response, various Democracy Wall groups joined together
to defend their associates. Despite their wide range of views and internal factionalism, the party's repression impelled these disparate
groups to form a united front to defend those under attack. Such a
coordinated defense was unprecedented in the People's Republic.
Few people during the Mao era dared to defend even members of
their own family, let alone their associates, for fear of endangering
themselves and other family members. Yet, though they may have
disagreed with the views or tactics of those under attack, the leaders
of the Democracy Wall movement came to the defense of their colleagues. While the coalition building and organized resistance may
be attributed to a loosening of party controls, the activists' Cultural
Revolution experiences of joining together to challenge authority
may have also contributed to their willingness to stand up for their
colleagues.

The first event to galvanize these disparate groups into coordinated action was the arrest of Fu Yuehua, one of the few woman activists in the movement. As petitioners from all over the country
gathered in Beijing in early January 1979 to seek redress of their personal grievances against local officials during the Cultural Revolution, they marched with placards calling for an end to oppression
and demanding human rights. Fu took the lead in helping the petitioners and organizing collective action.[49] When she was detained
for her activities on January 18, 1979, her family contacted the Democracy Wall groups, which then sent a delegation to the police demanding to know what had happened to her.[50]

The unofficial journals, led by *Exploration* and *April 5th Forum,* ral-
lied to Fu's defense and gathered weekly to plan coordinated action.
Seven groups issued a "Joint Statement" on January 25, 1979, declaring that "if the various mass organizations, civilian publications and
their affiliated citizens are victimized because of their involvement
in activities stipulated in the Constitution, the mass organizations
and publications have the responsibility to publicize the news at
home and abroad in order to rally support of public opinion." They
"should carry on sustained efforts to rescue citizens subjected to persecution and demand to visit the prisoners."[51]

As the various groups forged a sense of organizational solidarity among themselves, they jointly staged rallies and demonstrations, put up a series of posters, published articles protesting Fu's detention, and demanded her release. On January 29, 1979, they held a forum in front of Xidan Wall, calling for an appeal to the higher courts against the detention of human-rights activists. On February 8, another delegation of unofficial editors, led by Wei Jingsheng, went to the police station to inquire about Fu. Moreover, the *Tribune of the People* made the cause of the petitioners, which Fu had championed, its battle cry. On March 11, 1979, *Exploration*'s third issue published an article by Wei, entitled "The 20th-Century Bastille—Qincheng No. 1 Prison," exposing the brutal methods and torture used in the prison in which Fu was imprisoned. While Soviet dissidents had been writing about conditions in the gulag in their samizdat for years, this was the first time such an exposé had been published in the People's Republic.

The coalition to defend those under attack held together even when Deng Xiaoping personally moved against Wei Jingsheng in late March 1979. Wei had denounced China's invasion of Vietnam in February 1979, and in the March issue of *Exploration* he published an article entitled "Do We Want Democracy or a New Dictatorship?" in which he warned that Deng would turn into a new dictator if the existing political system continued. Such boldness infuriated Deng, who ordered Wei arrested on March 29. Six months later, at a show trial from which his family and friends were excluded, Wei was sentenced to fifteen years in prison and placed in solitary confinement in Qincheng No. 1 Prison, whose terrible conditions he had just written about.

Party leaders were undoubtedly worried that the activities of the Democracy Wall participants and their allies would lead to spreading social unrest and threaten the party, as revealed in Deng's speech to the Theory Conference on March 30, 1979. Deng charged that a small number of persons "instead of accepting guidance . . . of leading officials of the party . . . have raised sundry demands . . . [that] are altogether unreasonable. They have provoked or tricked some of the masses . . . holding sitdowns and hunger strikes, and obstructing traffic." He was particularly infuriated about their demands for human rights. "They have raised some sensational slogans . . . as 'give us human rights.' . . . There is a 'China Human Rights Group' which has gone so far as to . . . requesting the President of United States to 'show concern' for human rights in China. Can we permit such an open call for intervention in China's internal affairs? . . . Can we tolerate this kind of freedom of speech which flagrantly contravenes the principles of our Constitution?" He also criticized "trouble makers" who "speak in the name of democracy, a claim by which people are easily misled . . . have begun to form all kinds of secret . . . organizations which seek to establish contact with each other on a nationwide scale. . . . We must . . . [endeavor] to clear up the ideological confusion among a small section of the people, especially young people."[52] He then enunciated the four cardinal principles—uphold the socialist road, the dictatorship of the proletariat, party leadership, and Marxism-Leninism and Mao Zedong Thought—which came to mean upholding the Leninist party-state. He concluded: "We practice democratic centralism . . . not bourgeois, individual democracy."[53]

Despite Deng's attack, Wei's *Exploration* colleagues came to his defense. On March 31, they drafted a leaflet, "*Exploration*'s Declaration to Citizens of the World," protesting Wei's arrest. Although they tried to continue publishing their journal after Wei was sentenced, their printing devices were confiscated and other editors were arrested.[54]

Although Liu Qing and Xu Wenli, the editors of *April 5th Forum*, did not agree with Wei's rejection of the socialist system and his tactics, they put up a wall poster on October 20, 1979, stating that Wei may have been mistaken in his ideology, but that did not mean that he had broken the law, nor was he guilty of being a "counter-revolutionary," as charged. The *April 5th Forum* then pieced together secret recordings from Wei's defense at his trial and sold the transcript at Xidan Wall on November 11, 1979. When the police detained those selling the transcript, Liu Qing and several others went to the police station to find out on what legal grounds their colleagues had been detained. Liu Qing was then arrested. In December 1979, Democracy Wall at Xidan Wall was closed down.

Liu Qing's family defended him by citing the constitution's stipulation of freedom of speech, publication, association, demonstration, and strike. "This is a most basic civil right. . . . It also guarantees the right of every citizen to supervise and address inquiries to the state, government, and officials at all levels. . . . Nothing Liu Qing did went beyond the limits set by the Constitution. He was merely exercising his constitutional right to propagate the need for democracy and legality. Law . . . should place the same constraints on the heads of state as on ordinary citizens. . . . By collaborating with Fu Yuehua and publishing the transcript of Wei's trial, Liu Qing did not violate Article 45 of the Constitution."[55] In October 1980, a "National Committee to Save Liu Qing" was established by sixteen unofficial journals from all over the country. In an account of his detention smuggled out of a labor reform camp, Liu compared his case to the Dreyfus case and reminded his colleagues that "our democratic system cannot develop from the benevolence of an emperor but depends on the efforts of society itself."[56]

What made the resistance to the party's crackdown on the Democracy Wall activists into a citizens' movement was that it was not just the activists' families and like-minded colleagues who came to their defense. Democracy Wall participants with opposing views and strategies united together. Even the most moderate and officially connected of the unofficial magazine groups—the *Beijing Spring* group—eventually joined the coordinated efforts to defend their colleagues. Initially, the editors of *Beijing Spring* refused to join the coordinated protest against Fu Yuehua's arrest or to sign an agreement calling on all unofficial groups to defend their comrades. But as the party intensified its efforts to suppress the movement, the April and May issues of *Beijing Spring* expressed some concern, and in its June issue, the journal protested for the first time against the arrests and repression, but without mentioning the names of those who had been arrested. Its August 10th issue reprinted Wei Jingsheng's "The 20th-Century Bastille—Qincheng No. 1 Prison," as did other unofficial magazines all over the country. The September issue openly defended Wei Jingsheng and Fu Yuehua. Paraphrasing Patrick Henry, *Beijing Spring* declared that it did not agree with Wei, but defended his right to express his ideas.[57] After Wei was sentenced, Wang Juntao was summoned to the Communist Youth League offices and ordered to cease publication. But just enough time was allowed for a final issue of the journal to appear with a plea on Wei's behalf. "What had Wei been guilty of opposing?" the editors asked.

"Certainly not public ownership, but privilege, injustice and dictatorship."[58] In November 1979, *Beijing Spring* was also closed down.

The End of Democracy Wall

Even though Deng was briefly interested in political reform in the late 1970s, the Democracy Wall activists' demands for political rights went much further than Deng intended to go. Limited terms of office for government officials, more regularized party procedures, an increase in younger party members, and the introduction of some rules of law were in accord with Deng's political goals, but the assertion of civil, political, and human rights and demands for freedom of the press and association challenged the Leninist one-party state, a basic tenet of Deng's thinking. Moreover, events in Eastern Europe—the 1977 Charter Movement, led by Václav Havel in Czechoslovakia, and the emergence of the Solidarity movement in Poland—influenced both the demands of the Democracy Wall activists and the party's repression. Perhaps, even more than Democracy Wall and the protests of petitioners in Beijing, Shanghai, and other cities, China's leaders were worried about the impact of East European dissident movements and an independent labor movement on the Cultural Revolution generation, which was ready, in terms of both outlook and actions, to challenge the political system from below. For a leadership already worried about its legitimacy, the Democracy Wall's grassroots coalition of workers and intellectuals appeared to be a burgeoning Solidarity movement, even though these two movements were actually quite different.

There is evidence that the Democracy Wall activists were well aware of the Solidarity movement. Although Liu Qing was arrested in October 1979, his co-editor, Xu Wenli, was not arrested until 1981 and continued to publish several more issues of *April 5th Forum*. In its September 1980 issue, Xu Wenli published an open letter to Lech Wałęsa which said: "My friends and I learned with great joy that your independent and autonomous trade union Solidarity has successfully accomplished the legal formalities for registration." Xu heralded Solidarity as "a shining model for working classes in socialist countries the world over." The editorial board of the *April 5th Forum* also called attention to Solidarity's worldwide impact. It "breaks through national boundaries and achieves a wide international significance."[59] The Shanghai journal *Voice of Democracy* likewise declared its support for the "strikes of Polish workers fighting for democracy and against bureaucratic tyranny."[60]

When in the winter of 1980 three thousand Taiyuan steel workers united to protest against their poor living conditions and were supported by the local unofficial journal *Wind against the Waves,* the leaders of the protest were arrested. In 1981, the party moved against the leaders of the remaining unofficial publications and groups. Liu Qing's co-editor, Xu Wenli of *April 5th Forum,* was sentenced to fifteen years in prison. Though *Beijing Spring* had spoken in moderate tones, it still had engaged in political activities similar to those of *April 5th Forum.* Nevertheless, whereas the editors of *April 5th Forum,* who were mostly workers, received long prison terms, *Beijing Spring*'s editors continued with their university educations—Chen Ziming at the Chinese Academy of Sciences and Wang Juntao in the Physics Department at Peking University.

The party repudiated some of the laws that the Democracy Wall activists had cited to support their activities. On February 29, 1980, the Fifth Plenum of the Eleventh Central Committee proposed the elimination of the "four big freedoms" that Mao had inserted into the 1975 Constitution. On July 26, 1980, the editorial boards of the remaining sixteen underground journals in twelve cities issued a joint statement that protested the party's proposed abrogation of the four big freedoms and called for a publication law. But the Third Plenum of the Fifth NPC in September 1980 decreed that because "the four bigs" had never played a "positive" role, they should be eliminated. Thus, they were omitted from the 1982 Constitution.

Significance of the Democracy Wall Movement

Although the Democracy Wall activists employed the same methods of wall posters, pamphlets, open debates, and networking that they had used when Mao summoned them to rebel against authority during the Cultural Revolution, their goals were quite different. A substantial minority were searching not so much for new leaders as for new political institutions and new ideas. Most continued to use the Marxist terminology in which they had been indoctrinated, but because of the suffering which they and their families, friends, and colleagues had experienced during the Cultural Revolution, they called for political, civil, and human rights, protected by institutional and legal procedures, to prevent such repression and arbitrary treatment in the future.

Despite the suppression of the Democracy Wall movement and its leaders, some of the proposals the activists had advocated, such as the need to revise Marxism and to carry out political reforms, continued to be echoed in the official media in the 1980s by establishment intellectuals connected to the reform party leaders Hu Yaobang and Zhao Ziyang. Several of these intellectuals had personally observed the activities at Democracy Wall, and a few, such as the political scientist Yan Jiaqi, had published in the unofficial journals under pseudonyms. Most, however, stayed away, fearing that any connection to the Democracy Wall movement would deprive them of the status and the public forum they had just recently been granted in the post-Mao era. A few protested the closure of Democracy Wall, such as Guo Luoji, a professor of philosophy at Peking University, who spoke out against the arrest of Wei Jingsheng. For this he was sent to Nanjing University, where he was no longer allowed to teach. Most establishment intellectuals, however, chose not to become associated with the Democracy Wall activists. Nevertheless, some of the demands of the Democracy Wall activists—for political, civil, and human rights and freedom of speech guaranteed by law—were heard in the revival of discussion on political reform in 1986 and again during the 1989 Tiananmen Square demonstrations.

It was not so much what the Democracy Wall activists said, however, as what they did that defined them as citizens in the People's Republic. They sought to assert their political rights without seeking permission from the party and to establish their own groups and publications without party approval. By the late 1990s, most of the Democracy Wall activists had been silenced, rearrested, or sent into exile. Nevertheless, the unprecedented movement in 1978–1979 of ordinary individuals and groups acting like citizens, by asserting their right to speak out on political issues, resonates with widespread protests in China's countryside and cities in the 1990s, whether by workers, pensioners, or villagers demanding their rightful share.

The Cultural Revolution not only imbued a segment of China's youth with a desire for political rights; it also provided training in organizing networks, making speeches, writing wall posters, printing pamphlets, and garnering support of others that continues today. Most important, it created a generation which, if and when it achieves power, may help lead China toward a political system that allows the assertion of human, individual, and political rights as a protection against the abuse of political authority. Although people have more freedom in their personal, economic, cultural, and academic life in post-Mao China, they still risk imprisonment, persecution, labor reform, or exile if they challenge the leadership and party publicly and in an organized fashion. They will not be able to act as citizens in their own country until they achieve political rights that can restrain as well as strengthen the power of the state.

7 | Personality, Biography, and History: How Hu Jiwei Strayed from the Party Path on the Road to Good Citizenship

Let every man make known what kind of government would command his respect, and that will be one step toward obtaining it.
—Henry David Thoreau, "Civil Disobedience"

In his study of the evolution of citizenship in Western philosophy and polity, Peter Riesenberg speaks of "passions . . . directed to a higher purpose, the public good."[1] Citizenship, in his definition, is a moral concept linking the choices and actions of individuals with the interests of the group. Tracing the concept from the Greek city-states through medieval and Renaissance Europe to the French Revolution, he portrays citizenship as a spiritual commitment as much as a question of political practice and organization. It is also a kind of barter with secular leaders: in return for political enfranchisement enabling them to participate in ruling, citizens also fulfill obligations that come with being ruled. In Riesenberg's interpretation, citizenship is not a creature of modern democracy; on the contrary, it originally took root and flourished as an exclusionary institution within authoritarian political systems.

From this perspective, one might argue that China has long had an analogous notion of limited citizenship in the figure of the "establishment intellectual," whose history and contemporary configurations have been so well explored by Hamrin, Cheek, Goldman, and others.[2] The scholar-bureaucrats of imperial China struck a Faustian bargain, to be sure, in accepting the duties and perquisites of official position along with the idealized obligation to remonstrate against greater wrongs and the retribution that could result; and the intellectual-functionaries in the service of the People's Republic of China are heirs to this quandary. Yet in return for their loyalties and services, they could claim a modicum of moral involvement in governance. One also might argue that China's brand of communism, at least in Mao Zedong's emphasis on voluntarism, mass participation, and fierce devotion to the collective, provides another adaptation of the concept of citizenship in an era when government legitimacy rested at least in part on a popular mandate rather than the mandate of heaven.

Yet crucial aspects of citizenship as it evolved in Europe and later in America do not find parallels in the Chinese setting. The inexorable trends in the Western tradition seem to have been expansion, extension, enhancement, and elaboration: expansion of the scope of citizenry, extension of citizenship to increasingly diverse constituencies, enhancement of legal and civil status across a range of class and political interests, and the emergence of increasingly complex institutions to channel the activities of citizens. This inexorable and increasingly undifferentiated application does not describe the Chinese pattern.

Furthermore, and perhaps more important, underlying these developments in the West were increasingly universalistic notions of civil and political rights adhering to all those deemed citizens of sovereign nations.[3] Although some have argued that nascent concepts of inherent human rights, including civil and political rights, may be found far back in Chinese political philosophy,[4] more persuasive scholarship suggests that even the most enlightened of Chinese political thought well into the twentieth century has conceived of rights as concessions rather than entitlements.[5] The latter analysis suggests a more restricted view of rights as grants tentatively accompanying membership in the nation rather than inborn claims automatically attendant to citizenship.

China's post-Mao reforms have brought these sorts of comparisons and contrasts to the fore, with plentiful and often furious discussion of human rights over the past two decades. Questions of dissent and dissidence, the interactions between political and economic reform, the prospects for development of independent voices, "civil society," and a "public sphere"—such topics are now common preoccupations among scholars of China even as they become materially lived as well as intellectually disputed issues within China.

This volume's emphasis on citizenship brings together many strands of these larger debates concerning rights and entitlements, duties and obligations, freedom of expression and political participation. In this chapter I endeavor to focus the discussion further by illuminating the case of one political actor who, over the last several decades of political ferment, made a transition from establishment intellectual to member of the loyal opposition to breaking ranks. In essence, this is a story about an individual growing into what could be construed as a novel conception of citizenship—novel for him personally, and novel for China.

The protagonist is the journalist, former legislator, and political and legal theorist Hu Jiwei, who in the past was very much the establishment intellectual, with a personal stake in the Chinese Communist system and a propensity to accept its fundamental legitimacy even when criticizing mishaps or perceived flaws. As a party newspaper editor during the formative decades of China's revolutionary new order, Hu helped build up the very institutions he later would seek to rattle and rearrange as stodgy and paternalistic, and ultimately would come to condemn as fossilized and undemocratic. Along with this shift in perspective has come a shift in behavior, from compliance to defiance.

Hu's changes in thinking, as with others in his cohort of revolutionary intellectuals, developed gradually from middle age onward, but accelerated dramatically in the reform period, ultimately producing what even some of his friends and colleagues would deem rash talk and precipitous action. He is best known, both in China and abroad, for the culminating years of his career with the Chinese Communist Party's flagship newspaper, *Renmin Ribao (People's Daily)*, where he served as editor-in-chief in the late 1970s and early 1980s; for his calls for meaningful press freedom and democratic reforms in the 1980s; and for his efforts to convene an emergency meeting of the Standing Committee of the National People's Congress (NPC), on which he sat, to discuss the 1989 student demonstrations. This last move ultimately earned him ejection from his legislative posts and suspension from the Chinese Communist Party.

The route Hu has taken, from enthusiastic party hack to imaginative party innovator to thorn in the party's side, is neither unique nor unexamined.[6] Indeed, it may be said that principled insubordination as a form of civic virtue enjoys a long and illustrious history in Chinese political thought and behavior. Nevertheless, Hu's story has much to offer as a contemporary example, not least for the historic moment at which his most public ideological transgressions occurred. Hu's posture in China's post-1989 political landscape reverberates beyond individual remonstrance; rather, it is part of a general social quest to redefine the individual's place in the political process. Meanwhile, from a sociological perspective, the trajectory of Hu's life and thought provides a vivid illustration of the dynamic relationship between self and society—for our purposes, the interaction between broadly shared and evolving social conceptions of citizenship and changing self-concepts of citizenship.

Having come to his views as a tenacious advocate of political reform and having jousted with the system "from the inside out," Hu cannot properly be called a "dissident." Instead, we might regard him as both proponent and example of a new brand of civic virtue that prizes individual conscience and independent action over prescribed wisdom and deference to authority. At the same time, we should not idealize Hu Jiwei, nor the model he represents. Civic virtue is not necessarily synonymous with personal virtue—in fact, a paragon of propriety would not have gone where Hu has gone. Perhaps it is no coincidence that among the vanguard in China's march toward democratization we find a stubborn and obstreperous old man.

The account that follows, based largely on conversations with Hu Jiwei conducted intermittently during the 1990s,[7] should help illustrate the interaction of biography and history in the emergence of new notions of citizenship in China. Hu's presence at key places and moments of China's revolutionary and reform history provided context and impetus for his ideological transformation; at the same time, his willful, sometimes impetuous, generally ebullient character has been no small factor in his responses to those settings and stimuli. Personal background, beliefs, idiosyncrasies, and inclinations alone cannot account for the path this individual has taken; likewise, social movements and historical developments have not strictly dictated the course of his life. Rather, the personal and the social have intertwined to produce this particular story and define its significance within a larger historical tapestry.

Hu Jiwei pre-1949

A native of Sichuan province, Hu Jiwei became involved with the movement for revolution and national liberation as a 20-year-old college student in 1936, joined the Chinese Communist Party a year later, and soon abandoned studies in math and economics to become an editor for the Communist press. By the time of the founding of the People's Republic in 1949, the young Hu already had proven his commitment through his years with the underground revolutionary press in southwest China and his work as a reporter and editor in the Communist base area of Yan'an.[8]

As a child, Hu was conscious of belonging to the poor wing of a wealthy family, and was constantly struggling to wrest school fees out of his better-off relatives. Recalling his youth, he cites this poor-relation status as one of three factors in his political inclinations:

> I lived a hard life at school. My second uncle's son was going to the same school with me. My uncle paid for his son, but did not pay for me. For example, he took his son to the movies in Zigong City on Sundays, and to restaurants. He did not want me to go. I was under heavy family oppression. It was the material basis for my desire to join the revolution. I was economically oppressed in the family.
>
> Another reason was that I was gradually exposed to the revolutionary history of my family, including the story of my granduncle [dabofu]. My granduncle was still alive at that time. I often visited him when school was out. He liked us very much. He told us stories about the 1911 Revolution, about the ten failed attempts by Dr. Sun Yat-sen before that. I was deeply impressed.
>
> The third reason was that when I was in junior high, the September 18th Incident occurred. It promoted nationalist ideas in us. We were dissatisfied with the Guomindang. They surrendered to the

Japanese, but fought hard in the civil war. Ordinary people had a hard life. I was educated to resist the Japanese and help China. I was for fighting the Japanese, for having democracy in domestic affairs, and for improving the people's lives.

Hu's early education was at missionary schools. Leaving home for high school, he discovered the Communist Party when he heard some older students talking about people getting arrested for subversive activities. He remembers that the first impetus for him to explore revolutionary ideas was mere curiosity:

At that time, novels by Guo Moruo and Jiang Guangci were banned. The newly published banned books were called ragged-edge books . . . They had a red cover, with red characters and red designs, this sort of thing. These were revolutionary books. They were made in such a way that as soon as they were published, they caught people's attention. Or a red flag was printed on the cover. When we were young, we thought those things were strange and looked interesting. We liked to check them out.

At that time I did not know the Communist Party well. But I felt that the Communist Party and the Guomindang should not fight civil war. Chinese should not fight Chinese.

Hu's substantive interest in revolution developed when he entered college in Chengdu and began reading voraciously. He admits to considerable limitations in his intellectual grasp of the material at the time:

I read a lot about Marxism, but did not really understand it. For example, I read *Das Kapital*. I was determined to finish it. I spent two to three months on it. But I did not understand it. I was not able to understand it, given the education I had at that time. What was relatively comprehensible was Mao Zedong's works. I could understand a little of Stalin's and Lenin's works. Many things I could not understand . . . But my desire to learn was very strong.

I still do not know how I could have that much energy and could do so many things each day. It seems that I hardly slept, working from morning till night. I hardly went to any classes. I opened my book, opened my pencil-box, and uncapped my pen. Then I said to the classmate sitting nearby, if the teacher asks about me, just say I went to the bathroom. When class was over, my classmates would take my things to my room. I did not go to any of the classes. But strangely, I did well in examinations.

Hu's revolutionary sensibilities grew, encouraged by mentors in the Communist underground. He thus decided to leave school to become a journalist, which he felt was a more useful occupation for changing the world. As a young editor working for the revolutionary cause under an inhospitable government, he put out a succession of dissenting publications in Chengdu, gleefully reopening under a new name each time the authorities shut one down.[9]

Hu went to Yan'an in late 1939, riding a military lorry along the Sichuan-Shaanxi highway and proudly wearing the uniform of an Eighth Route Army military clerk, his introduction letter from the Sichuan Party Committee sewn into his cloth belt. He immediately took a liking to Yan'an and the Communist regime of the Shaanxi-Gansu-Ningxia Border Region. He found the atmosphere egalitarian, free, and full of hope. And for the first time, he did not have to worry about food or clothing, as these necessities were distributed.

Everybody wore the same clothes, the same big old cotton-padded coats. We all got along. When we met at a meeting, we would chat freely with each other. It didn't matter if you were a member of the Central Committee or the Politburo. I was very young at that time, only twenty-something. But it didn't matter. Everybody got along just fine. From "big" writers to "small" common cadres, all were equal and free. The government of the border region was indeed democratically elected. We participated in the elections ourselves. I think our elections today are not as good as our elections then.

In Yan'an, Hu Jiwei took charge of the border region newspaper, holding this responsibility through the 1940s. His first supervisor in Yan'an was Hu Qiaomu, head of the Propaganda Division of the Youth Work Committee. The degree to which, decades later, these two Hu's would be at loggerheads over the philosophy and practices of party propaganda was of course unimaginable then. Hu Jiwei had nothing but the highest regard for the party leaders in Yan'an.

What did I think of Mao Zedong? I supported him and admired him at that time . . . I thought he was a wonderful individual. I supported his ideas. At that time, he often came out and walked around to see how things were going. When we were doing production work, he also came to the fields and hoed the weeds, spread manure in the fields, and so on. We felt that this leader was not at all like leaders in the Guomindang. We supported him with all our hearts.

Throughout this period, Hu also was greatly influenced by his first cousin Hu Dehui, an assertively independent woman four years his senior, whom he addressed as "elder sister" (*jiejie*). Married with two children but separated from her husband, Hu Dehui took the unusual step of getting a divorce. In fact, she and Hu Jiwei had long been in love, and they continued to see each other intermittently during the Yan'an period.

In the first volume of his memoirs, Hu Jiwei unflinchingly describes their problematic courtship.[10] With a daughter born out of wedlock, they requested party permission to marry in early 1949. It was granted despite customary prohibitions against marriage between first cousins—and particularly between children of brothers, which they had convinced themselves was worth defying as a reflection of reactionary patriarchal attitudes. In fact, in just one more year, with the passage of the new marriage law in 1950, a marriage such as theirs would have been banned.

Clearly, Hu's youthful outlook on life, love, work, and politics was shaped in large part by personal background and idiosyncratic experience. At the same time, his political convictions emerged from the particular revolutionary crucible of underground Communist Party proselytizing and the organizational and ideological environment of Yan'an. Tang Tsou's astute analysis of the foundations of state power in contemporary China is especially helpful to understanding this context.[11] In Yan'an, Tsou observes, the party both achieved hegemony and enjoyed popular support through its exercise of persuasion, direct leadership, and effective use of the "mass line" policy. Under these auspices, Hu assumed what would grow into a lifelong role in the mediating apparatus between party and masses. Party journalism pivoted on Mao's strategies for mobilizing social groups to recognize their own interests and take part in decisions and policies. These pragmatic, instrumental ideas about political participation within a particular class formation, in marked contrast to liberal, universalistic notions of civic rights and responsibilities, were carried over into the construction of the People's Republic.

Hu Jiwei and the New China

On the eve of the Communist victory, Hu Jiwei was sent to Xi'an to work as an editor for *Qunzhong Ribao (Masses Daily)*, the party's organ for the northwest region. In early 1953, he became one of several dozen party editors reassigned to Beijing to bolster the editorial staff of the party's premier newspaper, *Renmin Ribao*, successor to the pre-1949 *Jiefang Ribao (Liberation Daily)*. With the move to Beijing, Hu and his wife finally were able to live together. She was 40, he 36.

If Hu's youth contains glimmers of rambunctious tendencies, his comportment into middle age was characterized by compliance—a result, he now says, of his own inability to perceive problems. From the first hints of hierarchy and arbitrary decision-making during the Yan'an days through the series of increasingly tumultuous political movements that marked the first quarter-century of the People's Republic, Hu set aside intermittent doubts and continued to serve the party machinery. "Going along to get along" was quite likely part of the impetus, but not the only one, for Hu maintained an essential faith in the party and confidence in the journalist's role as an instrument of party policy. His retrospective criticism entails no assertion that he realized then what he realized later; he readily admits to "hindsight" rather than foresight.

Upon his transfer, Hu became first deputy chief editor of *Renmin Ribao*, a position he held into the mid-1960s. In his written reminiscences of the period, he criticizes the succession of political campaigns that took place during those years but makes no claim to prescience about their flaws at the time, while crediting others with greater perceptiveness and personal rectitude.[12] In conversation, he expands on this theme, contrasting his own lack of understanding with the fortitude and vision of those who spoke out during the Hundred Flowers movement, only to be labeled "rightists" afterwards, or the intellectuals felled in the first salvos of the Cultural

Revolution. Foremost among those he esteems is Deng Tuo, his chief editor at *Renmin Ribao* into the late 1950s and one of the first casualties of the Cultural Revolution.[13]

> Deng Tuo was very educated. His morality and his writing were both excellent . . . He was respected by everybody in the office, high and low, old and young. Looking back, his ideas were really ahead of his time. He had foresight. He recognized the mistakes in policy and Chairman Mao's mistakes in the 1950s. I was low in consciousness at that time. I was just a handy assistant under him, helping him with the daily routines of the editorial office, and with the layout of the newspaper. That was my job . . . I was not on the same level with him in thinking.
>
> He had a lot of experience and knew that to be frank and straightforward in China at that time was not allowed. So he kept his mouth shut about many things. But it can be seen in the articles he wrote before he died, especially his "Evening Chats at Yanshan [Swallow Mountain]." It is clear he was talking about the mistakes in the Communist Party's policies, and mistakes of Comrade Mao Zedong in his working style. Thus, he was able to use his knowledge of history, his rich knowledge about other things, to express himself. Ordinary people would not be able to get his point. Those who had knowledge would know what he referred to. Others could not understand the difficulties he had.

Again emphasizing his own political naïveté, Hu says that Deng Tuo protected him and others at *Renmin Ribao* during the Hundred Flowers movement.

> He told me earlier about the Central Committee's plan of "luring the snakes out of the hole." He warned me to hide and not to say anything. He did not let me go to the criticism meetings. He told me not to go to those free and open expression meetings . . .
>
> Other newspapers, such as *Guangming Ribao (Guangming Daily)* and *Wenhui Ribao (Wenhui Daily)*, were beginning to freely and loudly assert their opinions. They were happy. They thought Chairman Mao's speech "On the correct handling of contradictions among the people" was well done and that he was encouraging letting a hundred flowers blossom and a hundred schools of thought

contend. So they started to criticize the party freely. But Deng Tuo was taking it with a heavy heart . . .

Since Deng Tuo did not launch open forums like *Guangming Ribao,* there were not as many [people labeled] rightists within *Renmin Ribao.* Deng Tuo later told me that he was actually able to protect a large number of people this way. Otherwise, there surely would have been more rightists within *Renmin Ribao.*

Hu Jiwei also vividly recalls the moment his own reservations about Mao Zedong began to germinate. It was the summer of 1957, when Mao had summoned the top editorial staff of *Renmin Ribao* to a meeting at his home.

He criticized Deng Tuo severely, calling him not only "a bookish scholar running a newspaper" but "a corpse running a newspaper." He cursed hard. We were shocked . . .

Nobody dared say anything. Then Chairman Mao asked me: "What do you think?" I started to talk. I said, "It is hard to run *Renmin Ribao* because it cannot make decisions itself. It dares not offend anybody." I then proposed that as long as we were learning from *Pravda,* we should really learn from *Pravda*'s practice of having a Politburo member as its editor-in-chief. I said a Politburo member should be sent to *Renmin Ribao.*

Hu's comments may come across now as tantamount to a betrayal of Deng Tuo, whom he claims to so admire. Hu says that in fact he was trying to find a way to ameliorate Deng's untenable position of lacking the authority to run the paper he was charged with running. Hu now sees his suggestion as ridiculously naïve, but he says he meant it in all earnestness at the time.

Following that meeting, in a move that Hu characterizes as "apparent promotion but actual demotion," Chairman Mao dismissed Deng Tuo as chief editor of *Renmin Ribao,* and the much more pliant Wu Lengxi was appointed in his stead. Deng became director *(shizhang)* of the paper, a largely ceremonial position which he soon left in frustration to return to work for Beijing's Municipal Party Committee. Little did Hu imagine that some twenty-five years later, he would be kicked upstairs in precisely the same way.

In Hu's view, Deng's departure put an end to editorial caution and

precipitated a drastic decline in journalistic standards at the party
paper, which proceeded to celebrate the purported achievements of
the Great Leap Forward.

> *Renmin Ribao* went to the other extreme, that is, it became an obe-
> dient tool of the party. No matter what nonsense Chairman Mao
> spoke, the newspaper spoke the same. During the period of the
> Great Leap Forward, the propaganda of the newspaper had a very
> bad effect. That's why Liu Shaoqi, while pointing out the mistakes
> *Renmin Ribao* had made during the Great Leap Forward, said half
> the blame should go to the Central Committee's leadership and
> the other half to *Renmin Ribao*. The Central Committee exercised
> its power of leadership through the newspaper. Liu said it was
> worse to have a newspaper than not to have one . . .
>
> At least before the Great Leap Forward, it was very rare that
> *Renmin Ribao* published lies. It was emphasized in the old days that,
> say, when we were fighting the Guomindang on the battlefield, we
> should not report one gun more than what was actually captured.
> We could not report carelessly. We had to count the guns and bul-
> lets and report accordingly . . . But later on it was simply openly tell-
> ing lies. They were obviously false but you had to report them.
> Those above you wanted you to tell lies . . .
>
> At first we did not really know. We were just suspicious. For exam-
> ple, how many tens of thousands of *jin* of grain could a *mu* yield?
> You thought it was not possible. Later on when this place said yes,
> that place said yes, and they all competed in reporting the num-
> bers, you thought it could not be possible . . .
>
> The numbers were reported by the local party committees. You
> dared not but to publish them. At that time even Mao Zedong him-
> self was dizzy with the false news, thinking it was real.

The rhetoric and exaggeration cooled in the early 1960s as China
endeavored to recover from difficulties caused by widespread famine
and the withdrawal of Soviet experts, along with the excesses of the
Great Leap. Even then, however, Hu Jiwei was not prepared to question the party leadership or contemplate its fallibility. His conviction
remained that "the party's newspaper should listen to the party."

> I thought at that time that of course the party represents the peo-
> ple, that it serves the people wholeheartedly. I did not expect that

Chairman Mao could make mistakes, that the party Central Committee could make mistakes.

Hu's ideas at the time reflect both individual status and societal consensus. On the one hand, his continued stable position within the party propaganda bureaucracy made questioning ideological fundamentals inappropriate. On the other hand, despite political turmoil and economic crisis, what Tang Tsou calls an "uneasy synthesis" between revolutionary tendencies and prudence endured into the period of recovery; party-state legitimacy remained intact.[14] It would take the Cultural Revolution, and the experience of mass movements taken to extremes, to undermine that legitimacy and, as Tsou notes, open the way for a new quest to develop rule by law and a system of civil rights.[15]

Hu Jiwei and the Cultural Revolution

Hu Jiwei says he "began to wake up" during the Cultural Revolution, but even then the process was gradual.

When the Cultural Revolution first started, I was for it. Chairman Mao said at that time that we were to expose the dark side of our party from the bottom up and to smash the whole structure of bureaucracy. I thought he was for real. I supported him sincerely. I realized that I too had bureaucratic practices. For example, I was not in touch with the masses. I seldom went to the countryside or to the factory. I stayed inside the office, buried in piles of articles, working on getting the paper published. I realized that I was part of the bureaucracy too. So I believed in him.

But later on I felt it was not right. Especially when Liu Shaoqi and the like were labeled as revisionists, I thought something was wrong.

Hu's misgivings grew as he worked under Wu Lengxi at the start of the Cultural Revolution, understanding but also unsettled by Wu's docile adherence to Mao Zedong's will. Wu would telephone Hu every night to convey instructions coming out of Central Committee meetings. "Basically if we received a phone call at night, then within the next two days the articles would be published. Or there would be a news report reflecting Chairman Mao's thinking."

Hu was acting as "an out-and-out obedient tool," he acknowledges. But he was not happy with the results. "I was very depressed. It would not do if you wanted to have some ideas of your own. But it would not do if you tried to be totally obedient. There was no way out for this newspaper."

Yet, despite growing doubts about Mao Zedong's judgment, Hu continued to cling to his basic faith in the party and the system. "At that time I still believed that the party was basically good. I just thought that Mao's policy was incorrect. He was wrong. For example, he wanted to 'fix' Liu Shaoqi, he wanted to 'fix' Zhou Enlai, he wanted to 'fix' these [good] people. This was his mistake. But the party as a whole was good."

Wu Lengxi's tenure came to an early end when Cultural Revolution rebels took control of the paper; and Hu Jiwei's removal came soon after. He was sent to "reform through labor," first cleaning toilets, and then working at the newspaper's printing house. "I thought it was a joke," he recalls. "It could not last long. It would soon be over."

Instead, the movement accelerated, and former top editors were sent to live and work at a May 7th Cadre School outside Beijing. Hu was charged with being a ringleader of a "reactionary gang" of about a hundred *Renmin Ribao* people, and was put in charge of building housing at the site. "I led the group to buy lime, to bake the bricks and tiles, to prepare the wood. We laid the bricks, put the tiles on the roof, did everything all by ourselves." When the housing was ready, everyone except Hu and a few others moved in. "We were called the arch-reactionary gang members. We were not allowed to live in the new house. We stayed in a small shed. In winter, when I got up, icicles had formed on my beard." Then Hu and others were sent even farther away, to rural Henan, where he again led people to build housing, and again had to live in a shack.

In the meantime, a military official, Lu Ying, had been put in charge of *Renmin Ribao*. In Hu's assessment, "He was a straw bag [i.e., an idiot] who knew nothing and was very incompetent."

In the early 1970s, at the instigation of Premier Zhou Enlai, Hu and several other former editors were recalled to work at the paper, but the assignment was short-lived.

It was 1972 when I was liberated the first time. I was made party branch secretary of the theory and propaganda department of

Renmin Ribao—a demotion of several levels. When I returned to Beijing, we began to have activities underground. That is, several comrades would contact each other and exchange information. We did some studying of problems.

Premier Zhou, who was in charge of actually running the country, felt the country had no future going this way. So he proposed opposing the extreme leftist trend of thought and anarchism. It was not enough just to produce revolutionary slogans and talk revolution and revolution alone. It would not do to abandon production and study altogether. The Premier nominated a few individuals to form a proof-review group. This group's task was to offer advice before putting together the pages and to read the proof to see if there were any problems.

This group did not last long; within months, Hu Jiwei was again demoted and returned to Beijing's rural suburbs, where he remained until Spring Festival of 1975, when Premier Zhou again began bringing veterans back to the workplace.

In the meantime, as Hu describes it, he and old friends had reestablished contact, and their network of communication remained active.

For us [old cadres] to come back and rise again, we owe mostly to Deng Xiaoping's support. But we did not see Deng Xiaoping much. It was Hu Yaobang who was in touch with us . . . We had gotten to know each other well during the Cultural Revolution because we were both labeled reactionary gang members. Thanks to Premier Zhou, who preserved the good system of medical care for us, we high-level cadres had a special medical relationship with the hospital. Premier Zhou would not let them get rid of this system. So we were criticized and condemned in every other respect, but when we became ill, we still could go to that "imperialist hospital" to see the doctor.

In fact, the hospital became an underground station for our reactionary gang. We often made arrangements to go there at the same time and used the opportunity to exchange information and organize some activities. The most important topic of our conversation was about how to get rid of Jiang Qing and her group . . . Other people were not allowed to go there. Only our reactionary

gang could go. When we met there, we found a place to sit together
and started talking.

Such anecdotes illustrate the sort of activities that helped many
through the vicissitudes of the Cultural Revolution. Resilience and
pragmatism, as well as luck, are certainly among the factors that got
Hu through. He cheerfully relates, for instance, figuring out how to
obtain relief from the agony of the "airplane position," the bent-over
stance, arms swooped back behind the head, in which individuals
were forced to endure during criticism meetings. "Every time people
shouted 'Down with Hu Jiwei!' I'd straighten up and thrust my fist
into the air like this"—at this point he demonstrates—"and yell
'Down with Hu Jiwei!' too. Then they'd push me back down." He
also describes how, laboring in the countryside, he would walk far
out into the fields where nobody could hear him, and curse his per-
secutors at the top of his lungs.

Again, Tang Tsou's discerning analysis reveals the broader political canvas behind individual adjustments in political thinking and
action. "The Cultural Revolution," Tsou writes, "pushed to the extreme Mao's idea of mass movements as an instrument for waging
class struggle, flagrantly violated almost all laws and rules, and seriously infringed the civil rights of a large majority of politically powerful or politically relevant individuals, not to say their customary privileges."[16] The result was a reexamination of party tenets and practices
along with, and as justification for, the launching of political and
economic reforms. However, as Tsou also notes, the party did not
abandon the imperative of "ideological uniformity," which would
continue to constrain any tendencies toward more liberal concepts
of citizenship.

Hu Jiwei and the Post-Mao Reforms

After the death of Mao Zedong, the arrest of the "gang of four," the
rise of Deng Xiaoping, and the adoption of a new strategy for economic development, Hu Jiwei returned to *Renmin Ribao* as editor-in-
chief, assuming a key role among what Goldman calls China's "democratic elite" of the reform period.[17]

Hu says it was only with great reluctance that he returned to journalism. When veterans were starting to be recalled to work in 1975, he felt depressed and disinterested; moreover, he had hepatitis. So he asked for sick leave and stayed at the home of an old friend in Chengdu. "I was idle for eight months. I went sightseeing and toured scenic spots all day long."

In 1976, Hu accepted an assignment to help edit volume 5 of Mao's *Selected Works*. By this point, he says, he had made up his mind that he would never return to *Renmin Ribao*. After the fall of the "gang of four," however, former colleagues began urging him to go back to the newspaper, and Mao's successor as party chairman, Hua Guofeng, called him in for a talk.

> He said that I must go back. I did not want to, and very firmly said so. I said I was not up to standards to run a party newspaper for the Central Committee, I was not good enough to be in charge of this work. He then said, so you are not even as good as Lu Ying, that foolish editor-in-chief? . . . I said of course I was better than him. He said, okay, then, you take the job. I accepted the job.
>
> It was not long after I returned to *Renmin Ribao* that Hua Guofeng realized he had made a mistake in asking me to come back. He thought I was still the same old obedient editor-in-chief. Actually I was beginning to be disobedient.

Not surprisingly, the Cultural Revolution had a profound impact on Hu's political thinking and commitments. He drew lessons more explicitly than many of his colleagues. To him, the Cultural Revolution had been not merely a "mistake," but proof that party policy and public interest could diverge. This view led him to an emphatic conviction that the party itself had to be subject to the constitution and the rule of law.[18] In the realm of journalism, he emphasized that newspapers must reflect popular sentiment while promoting party policy, and where public interest diverged from party policy, papers should have the autonomy to side with the former.

> I raised the issue of the relationship between the party newspaper and the party then and there. The party newspaper should listen to the people besides listening to the party. If what the party says contradicts what the people say, it should be able to think carefully. When what the people say is wrong and what the party says is right,

then the newspaper should follow the party's opinion and persuade and educate the people; but if the situation reverses, when
the people's opinion is right and the party is in the wrong, then the
newspaper should represent the people's opinion and try to persuade the Central Committee to change its policy. Of course they
[party leaders] were not happy about this opinion of mine.

Even so, Hu asserts, he failed to recognize fully the enduring problems of China's political system. "Otherwise, how come I survived?"
he asks rhetorically. This, of course, is a critical issue. Some of his
contemporaries in the propaganda apparatus who suffered earlier
and longer than Hu still contend that at key moments Hu made
opportunistic choices. Hu is not quite that hard on himself, but
he does admit to lack of acumen. "I was at *Renmin Ribao* nearly
twenty years, from deputy editor-in-chief to editor-in-chief to director. I worked in [leadership positions] the longest; no other person
worked as long as I did. There was one important reason, that is, I
had a lower level of consciousness."

In one example of a position taken during the early years of the
reforms that he probably would not have taken later, Hu gladly supported Deng Xiaoping's initiative to remove the "four bigs" from the
Chinese constitution (usually translated as the right to "speak out
freely, air views fully, hold great debates, and write big-character
posters," written into the 1975 constitution and retained in the
1978 revision). Hu thought that *dazibao* (big-character posters) had
played a glorious role in 1976 when used to criticize the "gang of
four," but that this was a transitory exception. "They were used by
the gang of four to attack anyone they disliked while the victim was
not allowed to defend himself," he was quoted as saying. He supported deleting the phrase as a means of "improving and strengthening socialist democracy" and the legal system—adding, however,
that people should be free to write posters against bureaucratic leaders at their workplaces as long as they are factual and signed.[19]

Just a few years later, stymied in his efforts to advance formal
protections for the press and becoming increasingly insistent on the
need for public airing of problems, Hu might not have seen any
harm in retaining the provision guaranteeing the "four bigs."

Goldman states that the evolution of political beliefs among the network of democratically inclined advisers to Hu Yaobang during the reform period "was shaped principally by their Cultural Revolution experiences and their continuing persecution by the reformist Deng regime."[20] In Hu Jiwei's case, the Cultural Revolution certainly sowed misgivings; but the process was accentuated by the frustrations he encountered once change seemed possible again.

Nevertheless, as chief editor of *Renmin Ribao,* Hu was able to direct significant changes. He oversaw broadened coverage of political and social issues, greater transparency in reporting of governmental affairs, more attention to grassroots problems and complaints, a boost for investigative reporting, and marked expansion of international coverage. Under his leadership, the central party paper was viewed as a pacesetter for journalism, and much of its contents—from readers' letters to works of reportage to provocative theoretical treatises—aroused great excitement.

Meanwhile, Hu Jiwei was moving toward positions on matters of politics, governance, journalism, and law that were increasingly at odds with official orthodoxy. In addition to his editorial post, he had numerous other platforms from which to make his evolving views known: he was founding president of the Beijing Journalism Studies Society, set up in early 1980; one of six vice-chairmen of the All-China Journalists Association when it resumed activities later that same year; deputy director as well as lecturer and adviser to graduate students at the Institute of Journalism under the Chinese Academy of Social Sciences; and a deputy to the National People's Congress as well as a member of Sichuan's provincial congress.

Along with colleagues such as Yu Guangyuan and Wang Ruoshui, Hu Jiwei came to be seen as a key figure among "the progressive intellectuals of Hu Yaobang's network."[21] *Renmin Ribao* resisted the campaign against "spiritual pollution" in the early 1980s and supported Hu Yaobang's calls for restraint.[22] And as Hu Yaobang's political fortunes fluctuated, so did Hu Jiwei's. Thus, in the spring of 1982, Hu Jiwei was moved to the post of *Renmin Ribao* director—not really a "promotion," as *The New York Times* called it,[23] nor merely a "ceremonial post," as *The Washington Post* would have it,[24] but certainly a removal from day-to-day authority over news. Then, when Deng Xiaoping intervened to halt a renewed political campaign against "bourgeois liberalization" in late 1983, part of the trade-off reportedly was Hu Yaobang's acceptance of the "reassignment"—in fact, the dismissal—of Hu Jiwei as well as deputy editor Wang Ruoshui.[25]

Renmin Ribao reached its peak circulation during Hu's tenure as chief editor—some eight million copies a day, with actual readership presumably many times higher. By the late 1990s, the paper's circulation had fallen to just over two million. Numerous factors account for this drop, including the proliferation of competing newspapers as well as much more competition from other types of media; a decline in mandatory organizational subscriptions to party papers; and an overall lessening of the compulsion for close readings of the "mouthpiece" of the Central Committee. Another explanation, of course, is that no one quite as nervy as Hu Jiwei ever replaced him. In some respects, *Renmin Ribao* has become more professional in the years since Hu ran it; but in others, especially in contrast to enterprising tabloids and specialty publications, it has become more predictable.

Hu Jiwei Sidelined

In a paradoxical way, Hu's forced distancing from his traditional bureaucratic affiliations gave him the freedom to think more innovatively about journalism, law, civil and political rights, and the meaning of citizenship. Stripped of his influence at *Renmin Ribao,* Hu Jiwei drifted even farther from institutions of party power as he became a vocal advocate of both individual conscience and structural change. He remained active in journalism education and research, and also as a legislator and member of the Standing Committee of the National People's Congress, and his views on freedom of expression and political reform became increasingly audacious and broadly circulated.

Having labored long and faithfully at the pinnacle of the Communist Party propaganda apparatus, in the post-Mao era Hu became a thorn in the side of orthodox propagandists. He continued to challenge the prescribed view that serving the party and serving the public in journalism were synonymous, saying history already had shown that party interests could run counter to the public interest. Well before Chinese students took demands for freedom of the press to the streets in 1986 and again in 1989, he was a vigorous advocate for greater press freedom and an outspoken proponent of a national press law to bolster the vague guarantees for freedom of expression contained in the Chinese constitution.[26]

Hu's pronouncements at academic and professional gatherings were even more pointed. He criticized the party and government establishment for paying insufficient attention to reform of the political structure, and called repeatedly for greater democracy, by which he meant assurance that ordinary people could exercise actual—not merely nominal—rights to information, free discussion, political participation, and supervision of their leaders. Only criticism and exposure, he said, could prevent the party and government from making errors in policy, legislation, and enforcement of laws.

At one meeting in the fall of 1988, Hu lamented that certain of China's leaders had backtracked on earlier endorsements of journalism reform, noting that the previous year's slogans about press supervision of public officials and greater openness in reporting no longer were being bandied about. But it didn't matter, he went on, because where there was a will, there was a way. The keys were determination and ingenuity. "Boldness is very important," he said. "The atmosphere now is not so ideal. Why, under difficult conditions, do some newspapers achieve success and others not? Journalists must be active and be willing to take initiative . . . Why can't we develop some methods of struggle? You have to think up methods—it's not that there's no way."[27]

Hu's last major commentary before the Tiananmen crackdown of June 3–4, 1989, appeared in the semi-official newspaper *Shijie Jingji Daobao (World Economic Herald)* of Shanghai, which subsequently would be closed for its sympathetic stance toward the protesters. Presenting what might be called a "steam valve" theory of political protest, Hu argued that permitting robust expression of opinion, far from encouraging social turmoil, would minimize unrest. Press freedom would increase communication and information flows between the grassroots and decision-makers and compel leaders to handle work with care and correct mistakes, while providing a "safe" channel for people to vent dissatisfactions and a means to help clear up misunderstandings. The right to expression could provide manageable outlets for anger and other "extreme sentiments." Hu also said that only authorities who were wise enough to permit press freedom could enjoy genuine political support.[28] The timing of publication suggested a rebuke to leaders who equated the protests with social disorder. This may have been the editors' intent, though in fact Hu's article was based on remarks he had delivered at a meeting months earlier.

After the imposition of martial law in Beijing in mid-May 1989, Hu was involved in attempts to convene an emergency meeting of the NPC Standing Committee with the stated objective of discussing the student movement—an effort which opened him up to the charge of encouraging the protestors.[29] As a consequence, following the crackdown, Hu was "recalled" from his post as a Sichuan deputy, suspended from the Communist Party for two years, and consigned to a mild form of house arrest in Beijing. From mid-1989 on, propaganda authorities launched a new criticism campaign against Hu's views on journalism and press freedom. He stubbornly refused to admit to any wrong thinking or conduct.

Even during his period of suspension from the party, Hu was cheerful and unrepentant. Friends and colleagues, ignoring his status as an outcast, often came by his home near the old Beijing railway station and kept him informed. He jokes that being deprived of his posts, along with his office and personal secretary, was not all bad, since it enabled him to stay home and write instead of constantly attending meetings. He is derisive of those who orchestrated the campaign to dismiss and discredit him without even giving him a chance to reply. He regards his accusers as cowards: "They stifle you and then criticize you. They tie your hands and then hit you." Even during the Cultural Revolution, he remarks bemusedly, the accused got to face their accusers.

He does say, though, that the criticism he endured after June 4th was "much more civil" than in previous movements.

My home was not searched . . . My wages are still the same. I still have access to a car. But I no longer have an office or a secretary. Also, they took away my special secret-code telephone [a phone directly connected to Zhongnanhai party headquarters].

For quite a long time I was allowed to attend the meetings of the Central Committee. But now I can't. I joked with them [my critics] and said, you do not let me attend the meetings of the association of journalists; I was not even allowed to attend meetings held by the association of senior journalists. My more than 50 years of a journalism career didn't count. I could not attend!

Indeed, from all appearances, Hu has a devil-may-care attitude. His feistiness and irreverence seem to have increased with age—and a new partner cheers him on. His first wife, Hu Dehui, died in 1992 after a decade-long battle with breast cancer; the following year he married Di Sha, a fellow writer and editor, who encourages and edits his writing.

Hu has continued to write on political reform, including articles in two books that were published and promptly banned as politically unacceptable just a few years after the Tiananmen debacle.[30] He sees books like these as part of an unrelenting campaign to expand freedom of the press and publication, saying, "They didn't let us put out a book, but we put it out. Then we'll do another. Then we'll put out a magazine. Then a newspaper!" He does not see this sort of struggle as having a life of its own; rather, he believes that China's prospects for political reform hinge on continued economic reform. Yet he is increasingly impatient with the notion that economic reform alone can bring political reform.

At the same time, the ideals that shaped the mind of Hu Jiwei as a young Communist have endured, and Hu retrieves them in their simplest, purest rendering without the least trace of cynicism or bitterness. The problems stem not from motivation, he believes, but from men's fallible applications of their dreams:

> I would say that Stalin and Lenin's style of Marxism is useless now. But I think the basic principle of Marxism is to build a society where there is no exploitation or oppression and where everybody is free and equal. I still believe in this Marxist ideal. I can say that I am still a Marxist. I call myself a Marxist.
>
> But I can also say that I am not a Marxist because Marx said that we must acknowledge not only class struggle but also the proletarian dictatorship. Lenin once said that one is not a Marxist if he does not acknowledge the proletarian dictatorship. But I am not for this proletarian dictatorship . . .
>
> I agreed with Mao that we should use military and armed means

to encircle the city and take power. But I do not believe that after
we have obtained power we still need to use military means. It is
feasible to use armed force to take power. But it is not feasible to
use it to build and consolidate power. To use the old Chinese saying, one can take the world on horseback, but one cannot rule the
world on horseback.

Reviewing the lessons of his political life, Hu reaches even farther
back, to some of the humanitarian principles he learned in missionary schools:

Our Communist Party in fact became a religion, not a polity. It
turned a political belief into a religion. One of my "crimes" during
the Cultural Revolution was saying we should not treat Chairman
Mao's quotations as the Gospel. I went to religious school. In religious school, everything was done as Jesus Christ said this and that.
I was criticized and condemned because I said not to take Chairman Mao's quotations as the Bible.

I am for the religious teaching of love, love among and of all people, freedom, tolerance . . . Chairman Mao said that love has a class
distinction: We have to make it clear that we love our comrades and
not the enemy. In fact we messed it up. We turned those people
who were not enemies into enemies.

Was revolution first based on humanitarianism? Yes, some humanitarianism. Marx said that each person's freedom is a necessary
condition of freedom for all. The *Communist Manifesto* says that all
people are equal. People should love each other. This is humanitarian stuff. This part is right. So I am not for abandoning everything
Marxist. But I think it was wrong to practice the stuff taken from
Lenin and Stalin.

The transformation of Hu Jiwei's thinking reflects a larger shift in
the party intellectuals' understandings of democracy. That concept
is no longer merely an expediency, as in "the people's democratic
dictatorship"; nor is it simply a "style of work"; rather, it is a fundamental objective, attainable only through the development of a comprehensive legal system and a system of civil and political rights.[31] Yet
the events and repercussions of 1989 pushed Hu even farther along

the path toward new conceptions of citizenship, grounded in a political culture of open expression and independent thought.

In the new millennium, Hu, in his mid-80s, seems all the more adamant in his criticism of the Communist Party and its leaders. At times, the distractions of daily life—including a painful case of shingles and the disruption of moving to a new apartment in the *Renmin Ribao* compound—can be more consuming than politics. But Hu always returns, in his writings and conversations, to thoughts of bettering China's political system.

Hu Jiwei and countless compatriots have left the circumstances that fostered ideological conformity, psychic denial, and voluntary self-suppression far behind. In Hu's case, the will to resist that emerged in one form in his youth has resurfaced in another guise with age, and does not appear to be flagging. Granted, Hu Jiwei may be a fairly extreme example of headstrong confrontation with a system of authority he once accepted, if not totally, at least in large part; but he also represents a larger trend of independent thought and action which, increasingly, is a defining element of the personal evolution of many of China's citizens.

My idea is to use peaceful and democratic methods to win democracy. Then this democracy should be maintained through peace, only through peace. And how? It will be through the legal system, through the people's power. Besides, this is a gradual process worldwide.

It cannot be a sudden change. It cannot be that today it is Jiang Zemin's government, tomorrow he is overthrown and somebody else has a government, like what our Communist Party did in the past, founding the People's Republic of China, overthrowing everything established before, and regarding everybody as reactionary. This road should not be taken any more. This is not a through lane.

8 | Villagers, Elections, and Citizenship

More than five months had passed, but the oversized characters scrawled on a storefront on Wangjiacun's main street were still legible: "We're citizens. Return us our citizenship rights. We're not rural labor power, even less are we slaves. Former village cadres must confess their corruption." The village leadership had little doubt who was behind this infuriating graffiti, namely one of the twenty complainants who had accused Wangjiacun's party secretary and his predecessor of engaging in graft, but they felt it was unwise to take any action. The corrupt cadres were said to be afraid that whitewashing the wall would only add fuel to the complaint and confirm their guilt. Instead, they would tough it out: refuse to turn over the accounts, stick with their story that the books had been destroyed in a fire, and wait for the summer rains to wash the charges away. But in the meantime, the allegations would stand unrebutted, there for all to see.[1]

Claims to citizenship have been a rallying cry for the excluded in many times and many places. In this one north China village, an enterprising farmer framed his critique of power in terms of citizenship rights, and in so doing hamstrung a group of extremely hard-nosed cadres.[2] Couching a long-standing grievance in the language of community membership, his claim to inclusion became unassailable. By reworking official "rights talk," he had turned a controversial demand for accountability into a simple plea for respect. Decollectivization had freed him. New political reforms had promised financial openness. As a citizen, he had a right to inspect the village accounts, and as a citizen, he had the right not to be treated as a slave.

In Wangjiacun, claims to citizenship have begun to affect how villagers and cadres interact. But this is only one village. Is the language of citizenship alive in the Chinese countryside today? Are Chinese villagers citizens in anything other than the narrowest juridical sense?

Citizenship in Rural China?

At first glance, searching for citizenship in rural China promises to be an excursion into the world of make-believe. Since at least Weber's time, the development of citizenship has been associated with cities—cities mainly in the West.[3] Moreover, citizenship is often linked with notions such as political equality, civil society, democracy, and national integration that apply badly (if at all) in Chinese villages.[4] It is also obvious that many of the institutions that support citizenship are missing in rural China. Villagers play no meaningful part in choosing national leaders. Country folk are weakly represented in people's congresses, and congresses have a limited role in policy-making and checking executive authority.[5]

Still, the subject of citizenship in the Chinese countryside cannot be dismissed. For one thing, recent studies have shown that the early history of citizenship was often local and parochial as much as it was national and universal. Although citizenship first appeared in the cities of ancient Greece and medieval Europe, it did so in autonomous, relatively small-scale towns (sometimes populated by as few as a thousand people) that were more rural than urban.[6] Even in England, the origins of citizenship can be traced to pastoral regions in the fourteenth century rather than the industrializing cities of the nineteenth century. Long before the Industrial Revolution, certain rural dwellers had translated community autonomy and solidarity into a capacity for association and participation. It was in distant woodlands, not urban areas, where English peasants first appropriated labor laws and interpreted them as conferring citizenship rights.[7]

Citizenship, it would seem, can emerge deep in "the local node of a national legal structure": in small communities where power is unfragmented and manageable size encourages participation and makes it easy to observe one's rulers in action.[8]

Linking citizenship with civil society, democracy, and equality also has a whiff of the ahistorical about it. Charles Tilly has noted that the authoritarian regimes of Mussolini, Hitler, and Franco all emphasized bonds of citizenship, and Michael Mann has identified five varieties of citizenship, only one of which is associated with free association, strong legislatures, and liberal democracy.[9] A cursory review of world history also shows that citizenship has long been an organizing principle for regimes riven by class, ethnic, and gender distinctions, and feminist scholars have been quick to point out that the idea of citizenship has always implied exclusion and discrimination as well as inclusion and political equality.[10]

Inasmuch as it is clear that citizenship, cities, democracy, and equality cannot be tied up in one neat bundle, it becomes reasonable to ask whether villagers in contemporary China are becoming citizens. Toiling far from urban centers, living under authoritarian rule, and being subject to institutionalized discrimination do not, in other words, rule out the first stirrings of citizenship. But if citizenship is not invariably associated with a specific location, regime type, or even equality, what does it entail?

Being a Citizen

In its most general sense, citizenship refers to a privileged legal status. A citizen is a full member of a community. As citizens, categorically defined persons perform duties and possess rights, the most basic of which is the right to have rights.[11] In nearly all communities, some residents are complete citizens and others fall short. Citizenship, in other words, excludes at the same time that it includes; it draws boundaries and ranks the populace.[12] Some people, such as children, the insane, and criminals are excluded (at least temporarily) owing to an incapacity to exercise their rights and fulfill their obligations. Others, such as foreigners, refugees, and guest workers, are excluded because they are aliens.[13] Citizens are in a privileged position vis-à-vis other community members because they possess rights that non-citizens and incomplete citizens lack.

Citizenship rights have evolved over time and have little fixed content. In today's world, however, citizenship is usually understood to have three components. *Civil citizenship* involves rights required for personal liberty, such as freedom of speech, the right to make contracts, and the right to a fair trial. *Social citizenship* entails the right to a decent and secure standard of living, as well as education, health, and welfare entitlements according to a society's standards. *Political citizenship,* our main concern in this volume, is associated with the right to participate in the exercise of power. It promises an individual a place in the polity. In modern times, the sine qua non of political citizenship has become the right to elect state leaders—in the executive, in national parliaments, and in local councils.[14]

The Opportunity to Participate: Electing Top Leaders

It goes without saying that ordinary Chinese do not enjoy the right to elect their president or other officials near the apex of power. In 1997 President Jiang Zemin ruled out national and provincial elections, and a year later Premier Zhu Rongji professed support for democratic elections but pointedly excluded the posts of president and premier. Such an important reform, Zhu said, needed more study, and it was hard to predict when the election of officials of the first rank could take place.[15]

Although villagers (and city dwellers) have no direct means to determine who rules China, they are entitled to some say over a number of appointments through their deputies in the National People's Congress (NPC) and local congresses. In Mao Zedong's era this meant little more than a right to hear that one's representative had "voted" for whomever the party Organization Department had nominated, but over the last two decades the process for picking high-ranking members of the executive and judiciary has been revamped. Although the NPC has yet to remove an official on its own accord or reject a nominee placed before it,[16] competition has been introduced for many positions, and the number of dissenting votes has grown. At the 1995 plenary session, for instance, nearly 37 percent of the NPC's deputies abstained or voted against a party-nominated candidate for vice-premier.[17] Local congresses have shown even more mettle when challenging name lists put forward by the party's Organization Department. Among notable instances of assertiveness, provincial assemblies alone have impeached a vice-governor in Hunan, rejected party-sponsored nominees for governor in Guizhou and Zhejiang, and elected a deputy-nominated chief judge over a party-designated candidate in Jiangsu.[18]

It is wrong, however, to interpret this newfound feistiness as a sign of significant growth in citizenship rights. For one thing, placing and removing persons from high office has long been the weakest link in legislative performance, and a smattering of newsworthy examples to the contrary does not mean that business-as-usual has changed. The party still manipulates nominations, and procedures surrounding senior appointments remain "extremely vague and ill-formed."[19] Legislators, as in the past, are provided scant information about candidates, and campaigning is frowned upon. Competition typically entails having one more nominee than the number of positions (for example, six candidates for five spots); and for top posts (for example, president, vice-president, governor), deputies are usually presented with a single nominee, who is then voted up or down.[20]

Competition at the rank of chief executive remains limited even in the lowest reaches of the state hierarchy. In a 1999 election observed by a delegation from the Carter Center, town deputies were presented with five candidates for four deputy magistrate positions, but only with the incumbents for people's congress chair and magistrate. To delegation members it was "very obvious" that once the nominee for a top position was put forward, "all deputies understood the message and refrained from nominating any new candidates."[21]

Ordinary Chinese of course have even less say over high-level party positions. Members of the Politburo and its Standing Committee, as well as provincial first secretaries, are all selected at party conclaves with no pretense of mass participation. At the very top, the situation is much as it has been since 1949: there are few constraints on the ruling elite, and formal means of accountability count for little in a system that is innately elitist and (at times) intentionally unresponsive. Opportunities to participate in the exercise of political power are closely held. China's top leaders respond to popular opinion as a matter of choice or tactics, not out of obligation or because they fear removal in a democratic election.

Electing People's Congresses

The structure of people's congresses also impedes popular participation. Of particular importance to villagers is the fact that Chinese electoral laws favor urban over rural districts. Deputies from the countryside represent four times as many constituents in county people's congresses, five times as many people in provincial congresses, and eight times as many people in the NPC. This discrimination is said to be called for because cities are the nation's political, economic, and cultural centers and because working-class leadership is desirable as industrialization proceeds. Equal weighting of urban and rural residents, it is claimed, would produce large majorities of low "quality" (suzhi) rural deputies, which might diminish the vitality of representative assemblies. In recent years, some scholars and deputies have suggested righting this imbalance somewhat, perhaps reducing the disparity to two-to-one, but calls to end malapportionment have seldom been heard.[22]

Even many advocates of stronger legislatures have doubts about institutionalizing political equality. Despite constitutional provisions guaranteeing equal protection to all Chinese, they feel that undereducated peasants cannot take part in politics and that congresses should be "galaxies of talent" stocked with the nation's best and brightest. Such self-proclaimed reformers are hesitant to grant too much power to "backward" country people. Instead, they would replace deputies who cannot read complex legal documents or understand budget proposals with highly qualified officials and professionals. To do this, they would gerrymander election precincts so that cadres and intellectuals were elected in disproportionate numbers. Supporters of tinkering with legislative composition argue that the interests of the least educated can be upheld by others, and they have little sympathy for farmer (or worker) deputies who weigh down congresses and dilute the influence of people (like themselves!) deemed more able. Although this view is usually expressed in hushed tones and elliptical language, recent election results suggest that it has made considerable headway. If education and professional abilities continue to be valued highly, the under-representation of rural people in people's congresses will only increase.[23]

How legislators are chosen also affects the extent to which villagers are included in the polity. People's congresses may be symbols of popular sovereignty, but deputies are elected in a popular vote only up to the county level. Above that, members are "produced" *(chansheng)* by deputies who serve in the congress immediately below. Regulations call for a measure of competition, with 20 to 50 percent more candidates than positions, but by all accounts these "indirect" *(jianjie)* elections are strongly influenced by quotas and party-provided name lists. The selection process is generally secretive, and nominations from the floor are unusual and fare poorly. A lack of campaigning leads to much "blind" *(mangmu)* voting, and party luminaries are often assigned to represent a region in which they grew up or worked, but where they no longer live.[24] Proposals to begin direct voting for provincial congresses and the NPC spring up every few years, and since the mid-1990s NPC research staff have been exploring what would be needed to expand popular elections. "But given the undermining of other Leninist states by even modestly competitive legislative electoral reforms, such reforms are unlikely in the immediate future."[25] Thus, there is little reason to think that deputies produced through indirect elections would be chosen in a popular vote.

Direct elections to county and township congresses offer greater opportunities for political participation. In the 1980s, the first several rounds of contested county elections took place with much fanfare. Early reports suggested that new provisions requiring more candidates than positions were generally observed and that some nominees put forth by voters had reached the final ballot. At the same time, it was also clear that manipulation of the nomination process was rife; unapproved nominees were frequently crossed out or replaced. Election officials sometimes offered flattering introductions and a preferred place on the ballot for candidates they favored, and voters had few chances to meet their representatives or find out what they thought. Groups of constituents "very rarely" proposed their own nominees, and secret balloting was the exception, especially in rural districts. According to Chinese commentators, many voters simply "went through the motions," and villagers, in particular, often felt elections were "meaningless."[26]

More recently, a team of observers who witnessed a town election expressed concern with ballot secrecy and distribution, voter identification, and limited candidate responsiveness to voters' concerns, but was impressed by the large turnout and the eagerness of deputies to criticize the performance of town officials.[27] Tianjian Shi's surveys have also shown increased interest in choosing local congress deputies. Although the authorities still work hard to hand-pick nominees, many voters have apparently decided to take part in imperfect, semi-competitive elections to punish corrupt leaders or promote political change. Private, informal campaigning is on the rise, and better educated, more informed voters are less inclined to boycott elections as a means of showing displeasure with the candidates presented to them. Instead, they sometimes use elections to get rid of or humiliate leaders they dislike. Insofar as defeat at the polls always causes a loss of face, usually leads to a transfer, and often triggers an investigation, casting a ballot has become a way to exercise a dollop of influence. Small procedural reforms, in sum, have changed voting behavior, and some Chinese have become adept at turning a reformist authoritarian system to their advantage. In the cities, this means making the most of limited-choice people's congress elections. In the countryside, these contests draw less interest. The most promising avenue of inclusion lies with village-level voting.[28]

Electing Villagers' Committees

Villagers' committee (VC) elections have attracted much notice in China and abroad. This is not surprising. As a breeding ground for citizenship rights, VCs have two decisive advantages over people's congresses: they are more autonomous, and they control things people care about. Legislators may remonstrate for groups or individuals to whom they feel an attachment. But congress deputies have few resources and less power, and they must rely on others to carry out their decisions.[29]

Members of villagers' committees work with fewer constraints. Under the Organic Law of Villagers' Committees (1987, revised 1998), VCs are not part of the state apparatus; rather, they are "autonomous mass organizations" through which villagers manage their own affairs, educate themselves, and meet their own needs (Art. 2). VCs are composed of three to seven members, each of whom is elected for a term of three years. Committees have broad powers and limited but real autonomy from township governments that sit above them. While the committees, for instance, must "help" townships in their work, they are not subject to top-down "leadership relations" *(lingdao guanxi)*, and townships are prohibited from meddling in affairs that fall within a VC's purview (Art. 4).

Villagers' committees also control resources. In eight villages that I visited in Fujian, VCs managed on average 15 percent of the yearly income earned by villagers.[30] Although party secretaries usually dominate enterprise management in richer areas, even weak VCs own a village's land and usually have "veto power to decide the general use of village resources—what might be called macro-economic control."[31]

Whether Chinese villagers are currently political citizens in more than a formal sense rests in large part on the quality of VC elections. What rights does the Organic Law guarantee? Have rural people been enfranchised, and are village elections free and fair?

The Organic Law details an impressive array of citizenship rights. To begin with, all registered, adult villagers are entitled to vote and stand for office (Art. 12). With the exception of "those deprived of political rights by law," there is no notion of being "among the people" or of the class-based identities of the Maoist era. These provisions repeat standard Chinese eligibility rules, except that in some places restrictions have been added that exclude the mentally ill.[32]

Special efforts have also been made to protect the rights of women. In the years after the Organic Law was first passed, balloting on a family basis was common. This often placed a household's vote in the hands of a family patriarch. More recently, reportedly as a result of foreign prodding, household voting was banned in Fujian and a number of other provinces.[33] Both the original Organic Law and its 1998 revision also accord women "appropriate" *(shidang)* representation on VCs (Art. 9).

Recent amendments also strengthen voter privacy and freedom of choice. For the first time, secret voting, semi-competitive elections (that is, more candidates than the number of positions), and open counts are required (Art. 14). Some provinces have also taken the lead in prohibiting proxy voting, experimenting with absentee ballots, and making primaries mandatory. Since the mid-1990s, the Ministry of Civil Affairs has promoted "sea elections" (open nominations), and Fujian, a pacesetter in carrying out villagers' autonomy, now requires more than one candidate for each VC post.[34]

Perhaps most important, villagers have been empowered to fight misimplementation of the Organic Law. For many years civil affairs officials have been receptive to complaints about election irregularities,[35] but now voters are expressly authorized to combat dishonest elections ("threats, bribes, forged ballots, and other improper methods") by lodging "reports" *(jubao)* with local governments, people's congresses, and other concerned departments—for example, civil affairs offices (Art. 15). At the same time, the Organic Law clearly states that no organization or individual is allowed to "appoint, designate, remove or replace" members of a VC (Art. 11).

By all accounts, the quality of village elections has improved since the early 1990s and voter interest is on the rise. In the words of two observers, "local elections appear to be acquiring high salience in the political life of the countryside," and "peasants have shown great enthusiasm for this grassroots political reform."[36] Early on, many villagers had scoffed at their voting rights, and in some places they shunned VC elections.[37] But this seems to be changing. According to an official in the Ministry of Civil Affairs, "most villagers did not pay attention to the first round of elections, but some became interested the second time, and by the third time many actively participated." After seeing that elections could dislodge incompetent, corrupt, and high-handed cadres, some villagers now take them so seriously that a nationwide survey showed that 15 percent of villagers have nominated a VC candidate.[38]

There is good reason to pay attention, because elections have given rural people a way to unseat some horribly unpopular cadres. In balloting between 1995 and 1997, VC turnover in seven provinces ranged from 2 to 30 percent, averaging just under 19 percent.[39] In some villages, particularly where economic growth has been disappointing, elections have sidelined a team of village cadres en masse. Freshly installed leaders are said to be younger and more entrepreneurial than the people they replaced.[40] In some locations, write-in campaigns waged by maverick businessmen have been successful,[41] and as Bruce Dickson shows in Chapter 10 of this volume, 15.5 percent of 524 private entrepreneurs surveyed in eight rural counties had been candidates for village chief.

Cadres chosen in popular elections may also be more responsive to their constituents. Jean Oi and Scott Rozelle found that "in some villages where there have been elections, there is more open accounting of village spending." Amy Epstein has argued that elections give villagers more control over how taxes are spent. A four-county survey designed by political scientists at the University of Michigan and Peking University showed that cadres in villages with competitive elections were closer to their constituents' positions on the state's role in the economy than cadres in villages that had not held competitive elections. Interviews in the countryside also suggest that where voting is the norm, village leaders live in a different world than the officials above them. As one VC director explained to Lianjiang Li: "We village cadres depend on the 'ground line' *(dixian)* (that is, villagers' votes); those at higher levels depend on the antenna *(tianxian)* (that is, appointment by higher levels). If we wish to be cadres, we must win the masses' support."[42]

Limits on Participation

Although VC elections offer villagers entry into the local polity, the inclusion they confer is incomplete. The state has yet to recognize certain citizenship rights, and it has not taken the steps needed to ensure that all the rights it recognizes are honored.

Under the Organic Law, non-residents cannot take part in village elections (Art. 20). This would be of small concern if rural-to-rural migration were not accelerating. In a sprawling industrial complex in the Tianjin suburbs, I was surprised to hear that the population topped out at 1,100 villagers. Only later did the party secretary mention that the village was also home to more than 2,000 guest workers and their families. The secretary acknowledged that in many places outsiders were treated like "slaves" *(nuli),* and that it was a struggle to guarantee their labor and welfare rights, let alone to imagine enfranchising them. In a Shandong village that relies on non-residents to work its gold mine and to perform other back-breaking labor, the exclusion and condescension directed at guest workers were evident.[43]

Women are also under-represented on VCs. Quotas may exist,

but even in provinces that have embraced grassroots elections, few women are nominated to committees and even fewer serve as VC directors.[44] In the twenty-odd villages in which I have done interviews, the VC usually includes one woman, and it is easy to guess her task— the thankless job of enforcing family planning. Male domination may grow further if plans to streamline the government and lighten "peasant burdens" come to fruition. Since the mid-1990s, female representation has begun to drop in some villages as the size of VCs is pared to cut costs.[45]

There are also a number of areas in which election practices and rules are wanting. Practices and institutions that impede political participation include the following.

Election committees. Election steering groups, often led by the village party secretary or a representative of the township, play a murky role in selecting nominees and final candidates.[46] Sometimes VC candidates even serve on these committees, despite regulations to the contrary.[47] Although the revised Organic Law (Art. 13) empowers villagers' assemblies or small groups to "select" *(tuixuan chansheng)* the village steering group, it is unclear how this provision will be implemented and how much control it will provide.

Nomination procedures. VC candidates are chosen in a bewildering number of ways. While formal and informal primaries are becoming more common, procedures for whittling down the number of nominees are far from transparent and leave considerable room for manipulation. Much still goes on behind closed doors, and townships and village party branches have numerous opportunities to prevent unapproved candidates from reaching the final ballot.[48]

Competition. Village elections are short of being fully competitive; in many provinces, only one more candidate than the number of seats is required. This makes curbing voter choice extremely easy and encourages ruses such as placing an obviously unqualified candidate on the ballot alongside the incumbents, or putting up a husband and wife (when only one woman is running and couples are not permitted to serve).[49] In some villages, no VC races were contested as recently as 1998.[50]

Campaigning. Candidates ordinarily make a brief statement on election day. Spirited speeches brimming with promises appear here and there, as does door-to-door campaigning,[51] but lobbying for votes is not encouraged. Many VC members liken campaigning to self-promotion and regard "pulling votes" *(lapiao)* to be unfair, even corrupt.[52] Running against the Communist Party or organizing a new party are, of course, forbidden.

Secret balloting. Before the Organic Law was revised in 1998, comparatively little attention was paid to secret balloting. In some locations, polling booths were provided but not used; in others, voters filled out their ballots in public while milling about and chatting with neighbors.[53] Attention to voter privacy may be growing, however. A survey of 2,906 villages in three provinces (largely in demonstration areas) showed that 65 percent of the villages had employed a secret ballot. Still, outside of democratically advanced provinces like Fujian and Jilin, it is unclear if the importance of casting a vote privately is fully appreciated by election officials or most voters.[54]

Proxy voting. Proxy voting is used to boost turnout and protect the rights of the aged, the sick, and those away from home. But, as the Carter Center and International Republican Institute have pointed out,[55] allowing one person to vote for up to three others can compromise voter privacy and freedom of choice. Anne Thurston discovered that the dominance of a family's senior male was so ingrained in Lishu County, the nationwide model for village elections (!), "that few women or younger men would even think of casting an independent vote."[56] So far, only Fujian has banned proxy voting, and in some villages one-fifth or more of the ballots are cast by proxy.[57]

Roving ballot boxes. Roving ballot boxes are used in remote areas and to help the sick and elderly vote. Like proxy voting, this practice attests to a desire to be inclusive, but it also poses a threat to ballot secrecy and is open to abuse. In some places, mobile boxes are used mainly for the convenience of busy villagers. In one Liaoning village, for example, more than 90 percent of the votes were cast in mobile boxes rather than at polling stations. Many election observers advise that proxy voting and roving ballot boxes should be replaced by absentee voting in order to protect the integrity of voting, to promote the civic awareness that comes with going to a polling station, and to reinforce the principle of voting by and for oneself.[58]

Certification. Township governments have also been known to annul elections if the "wrong" candidate wins or to dispense with voting and appoint "acting" VC members.[59] Sometimes sitting cadres go so far as to bribe township officials to subvert the Organic Law. They may, for instance, coax township officials to cancel or rig an election by offering expensive gifts, hosting lavish banquets, or purposely losing at mah-jongg.[60] In some counties, semi-competitive village elections have never been held.

VC-party relations. VCs seldom have final say over village political life. In many areas, the influence of the village party branch exceeds that of the VC, and "real power remains in the hands of the party secretary who makes the key economic decisions regarding industry."[61] Concurrent membership on villagers' committees and party branches is common, as is convening joint or consecutive meetings. The revised Organic Law (Art. 3) has further muddied relations between VCs and party branches, and increased the temptation to meddle, by stipulating that the party branch is a village's "leadership core" *(lingdao hexin).*

Chinese villagers have certain rights, but theirs is a partial, local citizenship. Rural dwellers have few opportunities to participate outside the village, and their inclusion in the wider polity is not well established. While villagers have a foothold in grassroots politics, and some resources, their ability to rein in state sovereignty is slight. The inclusion that rural people have been offered is piecemeal and incomplete.

Citizenship from Below

If citizenship were solely a status awarded by the state, our story would end here. But citizenship is more than a collection of rights bestowed on passive recipients.[62] It is also an outcome of historical processes that emerges as members of the popular classes seek to improve their lot by confronting the powers-that-be. Citizenship, in other words, arises out of negotiation between representatives of the state and social groups, and all initiative does not lie with the state. In fact, in many places, enlarging the scope of citizenship requires prolonged struggle,[63] and new rights are acquired only through bottom-up pressure and the painstaking extraction of concessions. Citizenship, in this sense, is less granted than won, less accorded than made.

Understood this way, citizenship is a "way of life growing within"[64] that reflects new aspirations and demands. Its spread depends on changes in people's hearts and minds, and it leads to changes in behavior. As with the farmer from Wangjiacun, who denounced corruption using the soothing language of community membership, the rise of citizenship signals new identities and a growing fluency in "rights talk." To understand how citizenship develops, tallying up what the state recognizes is important, but tracing changes in popular consciousness and claims-making is just as important.

When the spotlight shifts to how citizenship rights emerge, popular dissatisfaction with incomplete inclusion takes on a new meaning. It becomes a sign that ordinary people are learning to speak the language of power with skill, to make officials prisoners of their own rhetoric by advancing claims in a particularly effective way. Consider the following incidents:

- Two men in Hunan, when facing an illegal snap election, organized their neighbors to plaster seventy-four posters around their village, recommending rejection of hand-picked candidates and opposition to "dictatorial elections."[65]
- Hundreds of Shanxi farmers besieged a county government building, demanding that a VC election be nullified after a cadre seeking reelection escorted a mobile ballot box on its rounds.[66]
- Residents of two Shanxi villages occupied a township office and refused to end their sit-in unless officials agreed to make their villages "special zones" where free and fair elections would be conducted.[67]
- Nearly a hundred Hebei villagers lodged complaints with the Central Discipline Inspection Commission concerning a township party committee that insisted a village party branch had the right to nominate VC candidates.[68]

- Over twenty Liaoning complainants, indignant over "minor" technical infractions, traveled to the county seat, the provincial capital, and finally Beijing, at each stop reciting chapters of the Organic Law while appealing for new elections.[69]

In each of these cases, villagers cited specific clauses or the spirit of the Organic Law to back up their charges. By pointing to procedural irregularities that peasants are usually thought to ignore, these strict constructionists turned the gap between rights promised and rights delivered into a political resource. They challenged official misconduct using state-sanctioned symbols, and deployed rights claims to protest illegal or undemocratic practices. To protect themselves and increase the likelihood of success, they shrewdly couched their demands in the language of loyal intentions while professing little more than a desire to make the system live up to what it was supposed to be. The regime had promised them a place in the polity, and they expected the system to live up to its billing.[70]

These are not isolated incidents. Villagers in many locations in China shower officials with complaints when their electoral rights are abridged. One study reported that two-fifths of the occasions on which rural residents contacted officials concerned elections; another survey showed that as many as 5 percent of villagers nationwide have lodged complaints about election fraud.[71]

Chinese villagers are increasingly identifying, interpreting, and challenging improper elections using the vocabulary of rights.[72] Aware that the Organic Law and local regulations have granted them certain protections, they appropriate rights discourses and press to unclog channels of participation. These well-informed, exacting critics exploit the "discursive trappings of democracy"[73] to trip up local officials who refuse to acknowledge rights that the Center has ostensibly recognized. They often invoke a contractual logic borrowed from their economic life to demand that protections they have been guaranteed are respected. When local cadres dare to manipulate elections, these villagers are quick to step in and charge them with prohibited behavior. Venturing forth in the name of unimpeachable ideals, they say they are simply seeking faithful implementation of the Organic Law.[74]

When villagers come to view state promises as a source of entitlement and inclusion, they are acting like citizens before they are citizens. Certain citizenship practices have preceded the appearance of citizenship as a secure, universally recognized status. In fact, practice may be creating status, as local struggles begin in enclaves of tolerance, spread when conditions are auspicious, and evolve into inclusion in the broader polity.[75]

For now, however, the claims that villagers put forward mainly demand entry into local politics. Villagers seldom press for wider civil and political rights to association, expression, and unlicensed participation; nor do they often question the legitimacy of existing laws and policies, not to mention the right of unaccountable leaders at higher levels to promulgate laws and policies. Although it is possible that rights-oriented contention may find elite patrons (or generate political entrepreneurs) who organize regionally or even nationally significant pressure groups, this is not apparent. The intervillage organization and national aspirations of most villagers appear to be rather limited. Even the most assertive among them rarely demand provincial or national elections, wisely avoiding an issue that might alienate the allies they need to enforce their claims against local officials.[76]

Rural complainants know that they exist at the sufferance of higher levels and that the "rights" they act on are conditional. Unlike the rights discourse employed by some of the intellectuals discussed by Merle Goldman in Chapter 6, there is little evidence that villagers consider rights to be inherent, natural, or inalienable; nor do most claimants break with the common Chinese practice of viewing rights as granted by the state mainly for societal purposes rather than to protect an individual's autonomous being. Demanding citizenship is therefore more a claim to community membership than a claim to negative freedoms vis-à-vis the state. Villagers seldom argue that rights flow from human personhood, but rather that the government's right to loyalty depends on ensuring that its officials fulfill their obligations. The duties of those below must be reciprocated by the duties of those above.[77]

Chinese villagers, accordingly, are best thought of as occupying an intermediate position between subjects and citizens. When they use unenforced citizenship rights as a weapon, they are demanding that the representatives of state power treat them equitably, respect their claims, and deliver on promises made by officials at higher levels.

They are exploiting the spread of participatory ideologies and patterns of rule rooted in notions of equality, rights, and the rule of law. By tendering impeccably respectable demands, they have found a persuasive way to agitate for the accountability the Organic Law calls for and to challenge those who would usurp their electoral rights. Ultimately, their efforts may help make various still-contested rights real. Though villagers are only partial citizens in the local polity, we may be witnessing the beginnings of how a more complete citizenship comes about.

Some Historical Perspective

Although this chapter has highlighted the upsurge in rights-based contention in recent years, rules consciousness and a sensitivity to the power of government discourse are not new in China. Members of the popular classes have always been adept at taking advantage of government commitments, professed ideals, and legitimating myths.[78] Chinese villagers, in particular, have long seized on official rhetoric, whether framed in terms of Confucianism, class struggle, or citizenship rights, to press claims against malfeasant power holders.[79]

In late imperial China, the Qing government tried "to establish a direct rapport with tenants," and tenants sometimes used official rulings as a pretext to delay or refuse payment of rent.[80] Rural people also objected to taxes when they felt that local authorities had ignored proper collection procedures and would back off when faced with popular complaints. Such challenges typically rested on appeals to equity and fairness, focusing on how the tax burden was apportioned, adjustments for harvest conditions, and the use of biased measures and conversion ratios. Local officials understood the protesters' logic and, provided fiscal concerns were not overly pressing, sometimes gave in.[81] Villagers, for their part, often submitted to all sanctioned impositions and used their fidelity to established values to launch attacks in a rhetoric that even unresponsive elites had to recognize. In the Laiyang tax revolt of 1910, for example, peasants considered the regular rates to be fair enough and employed them to fend off irregular levies. Like the rural complainants of a later era, their resistance was not only a reactive effort to restore what they had. Beyond demanding the removal of exploitative tax farmers, the Laiyang protesters "also proposed a system to help ensure that corrupt power was not regenerated—namely, the public election of new functionaries to administer reform programs."[82] This defiance thus transcended run-of-the-mill rules consciousness. As with contemporary villagers who press for free and fair elections, the Laiyang resistance was both loyal and proactive: it was simultaneously a means to advance group interests within existing limits and a way to assert new rights and pry open new channels of participation.

Other elements of today's "rightful resistance" were also apparent in Republican China, particularly in clashes surrounding taxation. Studies of the Nanjing Decade depict a state that was already too fragmented to treat as a unified actor, and villagers who did not experience the state as a single entity with a single face. According to Patricia Thornton's account, provincial leaders, circuit court judges, and the Administrative Yuan regularly received letters of complaint from peasants and "citizen representatives" *(gongmin daibiao)* criticizing official misconduct. But as incidents of tax and rent resistance rose, it was local administrators who bore the brunt of popular ire. "Rural residents seeking redress from fiscal predation of county officials and their minions tended to see central authorities not as culprits or co-conspirators in the fiscal battle being waged against them, but as potential protectors" against their real antagonists—local bureaucratic capitalists. Thornton goes so far as to argue that portrayals of the central state in popular sources were more positive and optimistic in the Republican era than they are now. Still, she acknowledges that while Republican taxpayers generally did not perceive the central government to be accountable to the citizenry, "rural residents in the reform era expect more from central authorities in Beijing."[83]

Contemporary protesters, one might add, sometimes find the intercessors they need. State power is divided against itself, and pressure points exist where elite unity crumbles. Resourceful villagers nowadays can often ferret out supporters in various bureaucracies (such as the Ministry of Civil Affairs) who have a stake in seeing their appeals addressed and in upholding the policies they invoke. Villagers may be pessimistic, but they are also surprisingly successful in locating advocates to champion their claims.

The Maoist era offers an ambiguous legacy to villagers pursuing citizenship from below. On the one hand, rights discourses were not in vogue, and late Cultural Revolution–era protests, for instance, were "almost exclusively of a defensive and reactive character. The participants defied political despotism, but only a few went so far as to demand an expansion of participatory rights."[84] On the other hand, using the regime's own words as a weapon clearly did not begin in the 1990s. Adopting slogans from the official discourse to express heterodox views was a common tactic throughout the Cultural Revolution and the Hundred Flowers Movement.[85] By instilling in the popular consciousness the idea that there is a right to rebel in the name of symbols embraced by those in power, Maoist practices set the stage for the partly institutionalized, partly legitimate resistance we see today. A generation of mass mobilization reinforced existing resistance routines and inspired innovation at the edge of the repertoire of contention. It altered popular expectations and very likely made people more willing to act up when faced with official misconduct.[86]

It is hardly novel to say that new identities are built on the shoulders of old ones. Contemporary Chinese villagers are the inheritors of a repertoire of contention that has been honed over decades, even centuries. In one sense our Wangjiacun graffiti artist was using a familiar tactic (writing a wall poster) and seeking a "return" (*huan*) of his rights. In another sense he was cloaking a daring proactive claim in reactive terms, demanding citizenship rights he had never enjoyed, while making it appear he had just been deprived of them.[87]

9 | Ethnic Economy of Citizenship in China: Four Approaches to Identity Formation

The Rise of Civic Discourses in China

China's experiments in village autonomy and democracy have spread quickly since the 1980s, becoming a favorite subject among China scholars since the mid-1990s.[1] Elections for village directors, village council members, and even village party division secretaries are common. Closed-door experiments with direct or quasi-direct (public or *gong*) elections for county directors also occurred frequently toward the end of 1998. State policies have benefited greatly from the bettering of cadre–mass relations, as villagers themselves assumed charge of grain procurement, birth control, social welfare, and other administrative requests previously enforced by the county government and village party divisions uninterested in the fairness or legitimacy of their methods. Many villages have also reportedly witnessed an economic upsurge as popularly elected cadres manage local resources much more efficiently than before.

In contrast to the widespread praise of democratization inside China, assessments by outside scholars vary. Some foresee the whole of China moving gradually toward village democracy,[2] while others either question the stress on formality over substance in village democracy,[3] spotlight the non-liberal perspectives of autonomous villagers,[4] or caution against an over-reading of individualism into China's democracy.[5] Most would agree, however, that the complexity of China's topography, with the vast differences between coastal and inland areas, cities and mountains, high and low altitudes, and agrarian and pastoral sectors, renders talk of any universal response to the new experiment of autonomy at the village level premature at best.

We are used to the notion of democratization as a progression from the traditional to the modern, and of elections as an indicator of democratization. This quick jump from elections to democracy provides a cognitive link between China's village elections and a liberal democracy with which we feel familiar. We are reluctant to recognize alternatives to our own routes to democracy. At the same time, the exposure of local cadres to global acclaim heralding the arrival of democracy in China creates pressure for uniformity in appearance. What is overlooked is that inside each village there are all kinds of responses hidden behind ballot-casting on election day. After all, the idea of the autonomous citizen has never been a central part of Chinese political culture.

According to classical Chinese political theory, the state should be an extended family, and there should be only a single principle, or Dao, to which "all under heaven" subscribe. There would be no individual self if there were no great state self. Similarly, elections for local cadres today are not necessarily understood as promoting individual villagers' rights of participation. Rather, they bestow public trust on the person who represents everyone, not just those who voted for him or her. The concept of individual political rights has not yet become salient in any of the more than thirty sites I visited over the past six years.[6]

It is difficult to describe what I call "collective democracy" in the academic discourses available today.[7] One indirect solution to this discursive incapacity to express the realities of human relations, rather than to posit an autonomous subjectivity, is to visit places where ordinary civic practices impose less pressure to conform. These places include the mountains in which minority peoples reside. My study of village politics and citizenship in these mountain areas differs from conventional approaches to Chinese local citizenship in three ways. First, my research does not center around elections, but around what people want to talk about in their lives. Second, the interviewees are not of Han descent, and thus they may be freer to reveal their motivations in language other than the official. Third, my research highlights the difficulty of substituting democratic individualism for collectivist identities. The following discussion will concentrate on the third point, and will examine the extent to which such a substitution occurs.

Civic Discourses Regarding Minorities

The creation of a modern civic culture in China involves an effort to "individualize" peasants. Only when peasants are liberated from total absorption in local parochial relations can they express loyalty to an abstract "state." Peasants used to pay loyalty to the ruler of "all-under-heaven" *(tianxia)*, a concept that encompassed all parochial relationships. There was no contradiction between loyalty to emperors and loyalty to local leaders. Even after revolutionary leaders replaced emperors, a parallel continued to hold between central party leadership and local party cadres.[8] The new revolutionary ethos and the extant human relations formed hybrid characters.[9] Dealing with minorities is a different matter, however, for it involves more than an issue of political loyalty. In the past, emperors were never natural recipients of loyalty from minorities (who were seen as aliens). The revolutionary party was therefore not a natural substitute for the imperial court.

In fact, "minority" as a political and legal concept did not exist outside of the contemporary sovereign state discourse. "China" meant the central plain, or the capital of the court. China could have frontiers, but not borders. Aliens who subscribed to the emperors' reign were Chinese; otherwise they were aliens. When the central plain was taken over by various barbarian intruders espousing one harmonious spirit, Chinese themselves became aliens. When they united, aliens became Chinese. "Aliens" and "Chinese" were discursive, intellectual, historicist, context-driven, and "nested" or "leveled" notions.[10] Aliens were aliens because they had a different mind or spirit. In any case, aliens were not minorities. The political and legal minorities today, fifty-five in total, share, by definition, one spirit with all others residing inside of sovereign China.

Racism, or Han chauvinism, was popular among intellectuals toward the end of the Qing dynasty. Anti-Manchu sentiment was triggered by widespread anti-imperialism, which the Qing court failed to co-opt. Few thinkers really explored what Han actually represented, however,[11] for the confrontation with imperialism ("the hairy") and the Manchus ("the furry") helped avoid self-examination. This egocentric image of China ostracized all aliens inside the borders until it was obvious to revolutionary leaders that Han was not, and could not be, the same as China. Calls for patriotism replaced racism.[12] Once patriotism and the associated sovereignty discourse prevailed, racism among intellectuals, while still high,[13] lacked a discursive means of dissemination.

Constitutional drafts one after another shared one thing in common: all stated specifically that discrimination based on ethnic background was not allowed.[14] From this time, minorities have been legal in China. The remaining task was to determine who belonged to which minority. Aliens were no longer compatible with the notion of China. If aliens continued to reside in China, there could be no united China to resist imperialism.[15] Their becoming minorities presupposed assimilation. It was thus imperative not only to promote, but also to prove to Han leaders themselves, that Han–minority relations were harmonious.

Minority policy literally means ethnic policy, without which there could be no Han policy. One's minority status must be supported by some birth document, which no person claiming Han status is required to supply. A practical consequence is that a Han can have a minority brother. The implication is nonetheless that Han is a permanent base, an unquestionable and essential identity, from which a Han grants minorities their minority status.

The difficulties of classification may be underestimated if one overlooks the procedures undertaken to determine whether the language, history, customs, means of production, or religion of a people identify them as a minority.[16] Arbitrarily drawn minority boundaries are inevitable, for the Han cannot afford ambiguity. Ambiguity in minority-identification would mean two things. First, the Han themselves would be unclear. Second, since not all are Han, if they were not minorities, they would revert to being aliens, who are not supposed to reside inside of China. This clear demarcation of minorities allows the execution of citizenship projects. Minority identity is a basis of minority policy; minority policy is a basis of patriotism; patriotism is a basis of a sovereign China; and a sovereign China is a (reluctant) response to imperialism.

To prove that former aliens are no longer aliens is more important than the accuracy of identifying minorities. There cannot be any scientific test of one's blood mix without having the "original" blood type of each minority (or Han), and it is impossible to know these blood types. Scientific truth, however, does not deter the official claim that all minority categories are the result of scientific investigation. In short, while it is acknowledged that an individual's identity may be mistakenly represented, the category to which he or she is assigned must not be questioned. Many external studies have suggested otherwise—for example, minority identities such as Yi,[17] Miao,[18] and Qiang[19] involve more artificial construction than authenticity. This artificiality is camouflaged by ethnic policy, which treats minority identities as authentic, and for various reasons people acquiring minority status cooperate with this policy. In general, minority policy has four legs: shifting resources into minority areas, promoting minority cadres to rule the areas, recruiting minority cadres to staff central government agencies, and providing exemptions or privileges.[20]

Minority policy easily validates minority identities.[21] Classification of former aliens as minorities for the sake of patriotism has had the effect of consolidating minority identities. New minorities either see periodic mobilization as a kind of unwanted distraction, or else they are willing to exchange their consent for material benefits provided by the policy.[22] In the case of the latter, it may be accurate to say that minorities do not choose their identities, but it would be wrong to regard them as totally passive in the process. The research literature on state and society often overlooks minority experiences, assuming that they follow in step with modernization. How minorities actually respond is a rich topic yet to be explored. Moreover, their responses have implications for the meaning of village autonomy and democracy among average Han people. This is the focus of an ethnic economy of citizenship.

The ethnic economy of citizenship does not look at how state organization mobilizes and allocates resources on current issues; rather, it adopts a historical perspective to assess how the construction of minority identity affects resource allocation in the long run. Four questions will be explored here. First, how has minority status incorporated civilizing projects? Second, how has minority status facilitated identity formation? Third, how has minority status affected resource allocation? And fourth, how has minority status given new meanings to local resources? For the first question, Yunnan's education programs permit us to explore the hybrid meaning of modernization; for the second, Wuzhong Muslims illustrate a creative reconciliation of state and religious identities; for the third, Yongshun Tujia and Miao show how policy exemption and privileges have sustained a feeble ethnic identity; and for the fourth question, the Zou of Ali Mountain County indicate how minority status can prove useful to identity formation.

Xishuangbanna, Dali, and Lijiang[23]

Civilizing projects are presented as emancipating; they purport to transform people into individual citizens for the sake of their participation in modern state operations. However, minorities must first recognize their minority status in order to regard citizenship projects with a positive attitude. Minority identities and civilizing projects are thus two sides of the same coin: neither can persist without the other. The notion of minority suggests a cognitive distinction between the autonomous subject and a mobilized other. Civilizing projects reproduce the distinction between the advanced and the primitive who, once enrolled in the projects, will have no perspective to problematize their minority identities. Citizenship projects thus essentialize minority identities to the extent that people with these identities willingly engage in self-civilizing exercises. In the process, Han civilization avoids self-examination, which may go a long way to explain the failure of civilizing projects. Yunnan provides a clue.

Yunnan is the most complicated administrative jurisdiction in China in terms of ethnicity. Intermarriage among ethnic groups is common. An outsider finds it difficult to discern the differences among ethnic identities. These differences may be manifested in language, religion, and customs, as well as in clothing style, yet none of these distinctions applies universally. Moreover, such traits are not necessarily correlated with the strength of identity. For example, despite their stylish clothing and distinctive language, Bai in the Dali area are relatively weak in terms of ethnic consciousness.[24] Most people in Yunnan know their ethnic allegiance. Those who come from hybrid families can choose their identity. The artificiality and arbitrariness of ethnic identification bother very few. With various nationalities living together, inferiority stereotyping has little audience and ethnic conflicts are rare.[25] However, one encounters more stereotyping the farther away from the cities one goes. The Han officials' superiority mentality is strongest at the lowest levels.

In an autonomous ethnic district, only cadres of the majority ethnic status can serve as heads, yet the deputies are typically Han. Many of these Han cadres are borrowed from large cities. For a number of years, they go on leave from their work unit, which may be a university, a people's congress, or an administration outside of Yunnan. Wholeheartedly in support of civilizing projects, Han cadres portray their subjects in lethargic, barbarian, closed, timid, and foolish images.[26] Reflected in policy, these images encourage all kinds of bans—for example, there are bans on fire cultivating, hunting, land-grabbing, road-grabbing, woodcutting, and unauthorized construction.[27] In contrast, the large-scale, and much more serious, deforestation and land grabs carried out by collective national farms and the People's Liberation Army in the same region are by definition not included in the scope of civilizing projects.[28] Hunting continues, not so much to feed minority villages in the remote mountains as to sustain Han tourists passing through the base of the mountains.

Minorities who succeed in the cities are those who assimilate themselves better to Han culture. Their "success" signifies to Han officials in charge of mountainous areas that minorities in their jurisdiction, by contrast, are inferior people. The closer a school is to the city, the higher the level of assimilation. Children who perform well have the opportunity to enroll in ethnic schools supported by the autonomous district government. In Xishuangbanna, these schools reach the level of senior high school. The rationale is to prepare future cadres for service in their home counties. The district education commission as well as its lower prefectures take special pride in the classes for girls in these schools. The graduates carry the expectation that one day they will fill the lacuna of female cadres.

Similar expectations do not fare well in Dali, where the Bai people also prepare their girls for higher education. One Bai scholar who specializes in gender relations pointed out the following dilemma facing the Bai women. Unlike Sichuanese and Hunanese girls, who leave their homes for good after school, Bai girls return to their home counties with high school diplomas, only to find that the men there cannot match their education. They still have to marry, however, and many live in depression *(kumen)* as a result.[29] In other words, assimilation does not necessarily mean higher social status, for everything depends on one's willingness to immigrate to the cities. From the perspective of the government, this is not a good reason to question assimilation; for most minority cadres, assimilation is the end goal. All interviewed cadres agreed on the necessity of greater assimilation. The major rationale is economic: assimilation, it is believed, prepares minorities to enter the market. This concern with the economy naturally leads to a stress on Mandarin, which is the common language used in the marketplace.

Mandarin education is supposed to start as early as possible, and primary schools are under considerable pressure. On the whole, minority schools in the mountains receive more attention than Han schools. This is especially true in Yunnan, because Yunnan schools have all the traits that the Beijing authorities look for in determining eligibility for privileges: mountainous, peripheral, and populated by minorities. In Menghai Prefecture, for example, the majority of the people are Dai, who have the tradition of boys studying Buddhism in a temple. Many boys leave for the temples when they turn ten, thus demoralizing the rest of the class, with their friends (often girls) all quitting. Village security patrols in the area sometimes are ordered to catch "little Buddhas" on their way to school.[30] The rate of enrollment is a critical indicator of underdevelopment throughout China, while in Menghai it is additionally an indicator of assimilation. Education and identity are closely related.

On the one hand, education has a futurist orientation, with the goal of luring minorities out of the mountains toward modernity. Bilingual education in Xishuangbanna must be viewed in this perspective. The Dai language is used in the first two years of education, but not for the sake of preserving native culture; on the contrary, the function of the Dai language is to smooth the assimilation process until classes can be conducted entirely in Mandarin. This practice is in sharp contrast to the situation of Korean nationals in Manchuria, where all schools up to the senior high level use the Korean language. In short, the goal of bilingual programs is to promote Mandarin.[31] However, complicating the state's civilizing project is the fact that several minorities mingle in the Menghai mountains. The four major minorities are Dai, Aini, Lahu, and Bulang. The policy in this area is that only Mandarin be used. The autonomous Dai district holds language tests regularly for teachers of elementary schools. Responsible also for promoting government policy among the villagers, teachers go to the county government to attend policy-learning sessions. In these mountains, moreover, a village school often has only one teacher, who must help the villagers with bookkeeping, game-refereeing, and so on. The teacher's Mandarin capacity is a bridge between the state and minorities.

On the other hand, education has an orientation toward the past, encouraging a permanent obsession with historical origins. There is concern that minorities will lose their identities. Although in Xishuangbanna people want to leave behind their native language, the story is the opposite in Lijiang where Naxi is the majority nationality. The state, on its own initiative, organizes local minority scholars to preserve Naxi's written Dongba language, which is in serious jeopardy because of the rapid marketization of the region in the past two decades. Their work is to translate the Dongba Bible under the sponsorship of the Yunnan Social Science Academy, a work the government calls "rescue" (qiangjiu). They have even located the two remaining Dongba priests (who were not real priests themselves but grandsons of past priests) to recall Dongba rituals. The academy has no check on the validity of their recollections. Nonetheless, the recollection satisfies the requirements of nostalgia and, above all, establishes a distinctive Naxi identity. Alongside the Naxi nationality is also a Mosuo nation. Its fame has to do with the preservation of many matrilineal traits of an earlier society. The Mosuo try hard to retain their matrilineal family style, partly to win tourist attention— no state-affiliated tourist guide could fail to mention the "exotically feminine" Mosuo people.[32]

One's constructed past lingers in one's present life, because this is what the state and the Han want to see. The state wants to make sure that minorities remain minorities, while Han tourists look for an "exotic" encounter. The fact is that no one reads Dongba in the Naxi villages now. The sense of loss is clear, as one Naxi scholar observes that fewer and fewer Naxi people speak the Naxi colloquial language. This is in dramatic contrast with the way things "used to be," when Naxi friends would completely ignore all outsiders within earshot and speak in Naxi. Nowadays, Naxi people do not know who their Naxi fellows are in the anonymous market.[33] One Bai scholar is suspicious of all this nostalgia, however, since the Bai tradition is always fluid, and talk of "preserving the national tradition" can have no point of reference.[34] Indeed, for the contemporary, all can be tradition. I myself witnessed a Naxi funeral with both Mao's photo and the five-star red flag alongside the Daoist gods, following the body wrapped in rugs. Mao has become a god—and thus a Naxi tradition!

Anthropologists long ago pointed out the impossibility of defining the concept of nation;[35] nonetheless, the objective existence of a minority nation is the premise of minority policy. A state, busy supplying minorities and transforming them from their underdevelopment, is a critical element in China's self-image. In reality, however, the Han's state farms (and the People's Liberation Army) contribute more to barbarism in Menghai than the locals; Han tourists stimulate more hunting than minorities need; bilingual education brings both emigration and depression (in addition to potential future cadres), and it also faces difficulty in cohabitant regions. Little Buddhas wander around as their Han teachers are constantly on the lookout for opportunities to leave the mountains. The incomplete projects of assimilation provide a sense of progress as well as a challenge to the Han state. "Minority" thus becomes a process. Being involved in civilizing projects and being a minority mean the same thing, except that those undergoing the process do not determine its end.

Wuzhong Muslims[36]

As citizens, minorities perform two functions: they participate in market activities to accumulate wealth, and they participate in politics to protect their own interests. Regarding the latter, the civic participatory spirit is at best lukewarm in Muslim Wuzhong. Despite the promotion of village democracy by the Ministry of Civil Affairs, most Wuzhong villagers have yet to appreciate their political rights. Competition exists in a limited number of villages during some elections, but overall the party continues to control village politics. Village democracy operates in a collectivistic setting, where a few "wisemen" typically enjoy popular support, unchallenged. This is not very different from the situation of most other places in China.[37] However, in terms of market activities, the collectivistic culture in enterprises does not inhibit Wuzhong villagers from taking advantage of the policy of "reform and opening" to the outside world. In fact, Wuzhong is a model of reform precisely because of the capacity of its suburban villages for profit-making in the past decade.

Few touring Wuzhong would doubt that Islam is conducive to business operations. Wholesaling, tourism, food processing, small-scale manufacturing, and animal husbandry (among others) are the most popular trades. Village cadres appear unanimously satisfied with economic growth.[38] To ensure political stability, the county government intervenes in local personnel arrangements much earlier than the end of a term.[39] When the economy is slack, the party seeks replacement without any hesitation.[40]

Although economics is in command, it cannot explain why Muslims continue to identify themselves as Muslims. Furthermore, marketization may dampen Muslim identity. People leaving home for business cannot always find nearby mosques to perform rituals five times a day. Even in the Wuzhong area, where mosques are always within a short distance, one cannot afford to participate in the rituals because of time pressures of the business world. Many villagers who make a living in construction work cannot sustain themselves physically if they take Muslim dietary regulations seriously. The Bureau of Education promotes occupational education, providing an alternative self-designation for those acquiring special skills. The atmosphere seems particularly inhospitable to Muslims when village cadres brag about their profit-generating capacity and the size of their dividend package.[41]

The market provides a common language between Muslims and Han people, obscuring the difference in their ultimate identification. I visited Han villages in which people often spoke of "local uniqueness" in addition to "economic achievement"—pointing to social welfare, elementary schooling, homes for the elderly, and so on. Many of these "unique" features are really rather ordinary, but

Han villagers understandably want to see themselves in a special light. In Wuzhong, by contrast, no differences are articulated, while in reality the local distinctions are quite obvious in terms of dress, food, and religious surroundings.

Out of curiosity, I inquired about mosques. These reappeared right after the Cultural Revolution, before reform, and well before people became rich. As the economy took off, every village built at least one, even though the majority of villagers are Han. Some villages have four mosques. None was sponsored by the government, whose only role was to issue a permit. Considering the suppression of religious activities after 1949, particularly during the Cultural Revolution, the recent revival has been rapid and widespread.

The seeming contradiction between market and religious activities—in terms of time, energy, and resources—is likely to be true only in the short run. It costs a lot to build a mosque, and once one is erected, it costs more to hire priests (or Ahhongs). Moreover, every year, more and more people vie for a place on a pilgrimage to Mecca. Each trip costs over 200,000 renminbi. In this regard, economic growth contributes to Islam. Villagers do not simply reinvest in production. If there is a trade-off between religion and economics, at some point the choice shifts to religion. This turning point is determined not simply by how much money one has made, but also by age. Young people go to mosques because their parents take them there. Once they reach the age of fifty, however, an ever-growing number of people attend rituals five times a day.[42] Those who have visited Mecca stop working completely upon their return, spending virtually all their time praying and preparing rituals. Marketization delays (rather than diverts) religious identity. The delay may even have a reinforcing impact upon people at an older age. Wuzhong city-dwellers (as well as villagers) avoid marrying their girls to Han people, but they can accept Han girls in a Muslim home. This is to make sure that when conversion occurs, it is from Han to Muslim— not vice versa.[43]

Muslim identity and symbols are politically sensitive. The official line is that politics and religion must be kept separate. On the one hand, party secretaries should not go to the mosques to promote politics; on the other hand, Ahhongs should not work in the government, and in accordance with the Koran it is anathema to rule.

Nonetheless, in people's congresses as well as political consultative conferences at all levels, seats must be reserved specifically for Ahhongs. Ahhongs of village mosques report to the municipal Bureau of Religion once a month to learn about government and party policies. When they give lessons every Friday in mosque sessions, they are supposed to propagate these policies. Ahhongs' speeches are much more influential than those of officials.[44]

Ahhongs adapt to the state by helping disseminate its policies, reporting to the government periodically, and otherwise avoiding politics. Business certainly attracts young Wuzhong villagers' attention, but it also provides resources for religious projects. And the religious motivation behind business becomes clearer as one matures. The Wuzhong case suggests that creative adaptation to the state's citizenship projects can actually enrich one's ethnic identity. While the state is happy at seeing more active market producers and policy advocates, Wuzhong villagers are left alone with their Muslim identity and practices.

Yongshun Tujia and Miao[45]

Since civilizing projects put emphasis on economic development, the level of development is also a critical factor in categorizing ethnic groups.[46] Drawing on Marx's theory of historical materialism, the government identifies the historical stage of each ethnic group to determine if it deserves a separate label. Some minorities are considered slave societies; others are deemed feudal societies, basically in reference to their major means of production at the time of investigation. Nonetheless, for most Chinese, "nationality" and "minority" are primarily cultural or lineage concepts. This explains a seemingly racist component of Chinese nationalism.[47] On the other hand, anyone claiming to be a Han today is likely to be of hybrid descent in actuality. In the past, what distinguished an alien from a Chinese was whether or not one was under the reign of the Son of Heaven, while today it is whether or not one holds citizenship in the People's Republic of China. However, the intrusion of Marxism into the definition of "nation" introduces the new element of production, explaining differences in culture in terms of historical stages; it also transforms the subjective into the objective. As a result, ethnicity connotes the primitive and the inferior in a "scientific" tone, and intermarriage does not automatically change one's ethnic identity.

After the state completed its categorizing, some people acquired a new identity. This was the case in western Hunan, where some had thought they were Han before the government let them know otherwise.[48] Whether those who become Miao through this means can develop a different feeling about themselves is doubtful, for their identity does not come from their parents' words or deeds. Most important is that their life-style hardly distinguishes them from Han. How they differ from Tujia or Han is not very clear or important to them.

Yongshun is basically a Tujia Prefecture whose cadres are largely Tujia, with a few Miao and Han. Both Tujia and Miao speak Hunan dialects; few Tujia still speak Tujia dialects, and attempts to do so may elicit giggling from a bystander.[49] What distinguish Tujia from Han or Miao are their high-stilted houses, which reflect the Tujia people's custom of living along rivers. They are otherwise indistinguishable, especially with regard to religion, because all worship the same complex of gods. Both the local museum and Yunnan's grander Ethnic Museum display unique Tujia clothing and utensils, which are no longer used in the daily life of Yongshun Tujia. Tujia characterize themselves as having a "sincere" personality (which, however, is the same self-stereotype of most other minorities in China). Their self-characterization smacks more of Confucianism than ethnicity: sincerity, hospitality, concern for others, and modesty.[50]

Evidence suggests that local ethnic identities in this area have long been weak. Yongshun villagers respect heaven, earth, and national leaders just as they once worshipped emperors.[51] The nostalgia for traditional norms is stronger here than in coastal Han villages I have visited, and it is not the result of top-down mobilization. The implications are both that local villagers conceive of imperial rulers as consistent with their ethnic identity, and that the substitution of the Communist state for the emperor poses no cognitive hurdle for them. Modern history is filled with famous battles between bandits and government in this area, yet these confrontations are never portrayed in terms of ethnicity. In brief, Tujia and Miao identities are not consciously emphasized by the local residents, and there are few symbols by which they can present themselves as unique to outsiders. Consequently, citizenship projects as potential threats to alternative identities pose little problem to Yongshun dwellers, who have less need to find room for a different identification than the Wuzhong Muslims. In addition, neither Tujia nor Miao have a historical, written language such as Dongba of the Lijiang Naxi; and since they and the Hunan Han share the same language, there is no bilingual issue. Traditions in the locality do not have a strong ethnic orientation. The living standard of the minority groups is also at the same level as that of the Han. The problem of feminine depression that Bai women encounter has no parallel here. No Han cadres can reasonably feel superior, as do their counterparts in Menghai. Even intermarriage between Tujia and Miao is common. Yongshun thus represents an archetype of the state-sustained nationality.

As an ethnic autonomous district, Yongshun also enjoys economic privileges in addition to the priority the locals have in regard to personnel decisions. One example is Yongshun Tobacco, which is run primarily by Tujia managers and workers. Government policy discourages the manufacture of tobacco but grants exemptions to minorities, including the Tujia. Tobacco manufacturing is a highly profitable business, contributing to the economy of mountainous Yongshun. Tujia managers do not understand the exemption in ethnic terms, however. The general manager discounts the usefulness of national character in the age of reform.

Another privilege for minorities is birth control exemptions. Yongshun villagers are allowed a second child, but the birth must follow a four-year interlude. However, if the second child is a girl, many go ahead and have a third child immediately, anticipating no further exemption.[52] They give birth in a neighboring village or outside of the region and simply pay a fine upon return.[53] The Wuzhong case, where birth control is completely in line with state policy, suggests that economic development is a more pertinent factor than ethnicity in villagers' compliance.[54] Similarly, the economically developed Dali region has no difficulty in carrying out its birth control policy.[55] In Yongshun, however, even cadres have more than three children. Older generations often average six or seven. Young grandmothers encourage their daughters-in-law to break the regulation.[56]

The last element of policy privilege has to do with education. The autonomous district is too poor to adequately support Yongshun schools, but there is a university in Jishou, the capital of the district. Yongshun schools are better off compared with the one-teacher schools found in the Menghai mountains. All teachers are employees of the government. Educational resources depend heavily on Project Hope, which delegates the responsibility of developing local schools to work units in better-off regions.[57] Yongshun First High School is well known despite its unpromising environment. With some extra credits allowed to all minority examinees, Yongshun alone sends several dozen students to national universities each year. Local teachers are proud of the literary tradition in Yongshun and love to name famous scholars of literature and novelists who are of Yongshun origin. The identification with Confucian Chinese culture is obvious.

It is tempting to conclude that Tujia and Miao identities would have become irrelevant had it not been for all the policy privileges and exemptions Yongshun has received. The scope and content of these ethnic identities are confined within the scope and content of state-conferred privileges and exemptions. Yongshun Tujia and Miao have shown little interest in developing their own language or religion. This is not to say that the Tujia are not Tujia or the Miao are not Miao; both exemplify historical backgrounds that warrant a distinctive label. However, this historical experience is of little relevance today in Yongshun. The meaning of being Tujia or Miao is not as salient as the identity of being Muslim in Wuzhong or Naxi in Lijiang. Nonetheless, it is unlikely that ethnic borders could be redrawn today in Yongshun, for the political repercussions outside of Yongshun would be too complicated to measure—and probably too drastic to accept.

Shanmei Village, Ali Mountain County[58]

Aboriginal politics erupted in Taiwan suddenly in the 1990s. The nine aboriginal peoples, once lumped together under the category of "mountain people," have acquired a new label: "Original Residents." Original Residents, along with the Southern Fujianese, the Hakkas, and the Mainlanders, form the "four great ethnic groups" (FGEG), as they are called, in Taiwan today. There was no concept of

FGEG before 1990. As an element of the prevailing political jargon, FGEG is actually a discursive tool of new national leaders for creating a new civic culture in Taiwan. Ideally, this new civic culture testifies to the emergence of a new national identity vis-à-vis the supposedly old feudal culture of Chinese origin. On the basis of the new civic culture, the government in Taiwan can acquire an autonomous subjectivity—in accord with its own sovereign status, which is politically independent from the People's Republic of China.[59] This explains the rationale for launching civilizing projects in Taiwan: to emancipate people from their old Chinese identity and to accept a Taiwanese identity.[60] Aboriginal identity politics is useful in this regard.

The differences among the nine aboriginal groups (some would prefer to say ten) are greater and more significant than those among the three Han groups of Southern Fujianese, Hakkas, and Mainlanders. A reason to lump aboriginal groups together may have to do with the limited size of their populations, but calling them "Original Residents" connotes a definite discursive strategy. "Original" reveals the importance of time: "Original Residents" are those who arrived in Taiwan first, and in this sense they are all in one ethnic category, despite an enormously wide variety of traits. As a result, the notion of ethnicity here becomes a matter of timing. Only when ethnicity is defined by the timing of arrival in Taiwan can one legitimately differentiate Southern Fujianese and Hakkas from Mainlanders, who arrived along with their children after 1949. By cultural or blood standards, Southern Fujianese who came before the Japanese colonial occupation beginning in 1895 and those who arrived after 1949 share the same ethnicity, and the same is true of earlier-arriving Hakkas and post-1949 Hakkas. In addition, one could say that the Manchu, Mongol, Muslim, Tibetan, Miao, and Yao (and so on) share an ethnicity with the Han, simply because they all arrived after 1949—not to mention the fact that intermarriage among FGEGs is widespread. The politics of FGEG, seemingly unreasonable on all counts, is nonetheless discursively rational to the extent that it tells how far removed in time one's group is from residence in present-day mainland China. This reason alone suffices for the government to promote the FGEG discourse in full gear.

The Zou, one of the nine Original Residents, were in a passive position when granted their new ethnic identity. Considered to be Cao by the Han until 1998, the Zou were not the focus of the FGEG discourse. Their situation parallels that of American Indians over two centuries ago. Upon arriving in America and encountering Indians, white settlers viewed the strangers from a European perspective. To some of the American colonists, Indians were animals; to others, they had human potential to be converted.[61] At the Boston Tea Party, however, leaders of an incipient war of independence wore Indian dress to assume an indigenous position against the old European powers. The Zou were once also stereotyped with a barbarian image, and yet today, Zou people represent the indigenous spirit which the government measures favorably against China's alien and aged character.[62] The Original Resident status of the Zou is further fixed by the creation of a cabinet-level commission specializing in Original Resident affairs. Through this manipulation of the temporal discourse, differences among the nine are reduced; in contrast, differences with Mainlanders are strengthened, as are differences between Mainlanders and Chinese.

As an ethnic identity, Zou must be Zou, not Original Residents. After repeated efforts and promotion for a few years, the Zou finally succeeded in getting the government to change their name from Cao to Zou.[63] That the Zou refuse to be considered Cao is purely a symbolic matter. This was not an issue in the past, before China policy sensitized ethnicity in the 1990s. Their name rectification was one of the first few initiatives that the Zou took in responding to the government's civilizing projects. For the government, the FGEG discourse purports to create a new Taiwanese identity for all—although some are purer than others, with the Zou in a passive, receiving position. The responses from Zou people seem to indicate a higher sensitivity toward symbols related to Zou, not Taiwan. The Zou are not alone in this enhanced sensitivity toward one's own ethnic identity. The Saixia, for example, went to the Philippines only to find one aboriginal group there speaking almost the same language.[64] Such identity formation across national borders goes against the whole idea of a new Taiwan identity. But because of the very limited size of all nine aboriginal groups, the government perceives no threat in these activities that involve searching for roots. On the contrary (and fortunately for the Zou as well as the Saixia), these activities are considered conducive to the temporal sensitivity the government wants to heighten.

Many Zou people have left Ali Mountain, where they had resided for generations, for good. The sense of community has always been weak in Ali Mountain County, and people are lukewarm toward public affairs.[65] Although Shanmei villagers themselves do not make money, economic incentives have become increasingly important. Mobilization through human networking no longer suffices, as it did during the previous hunting generation. Elders have no long-term plan for the village, and school graduates have nothing to do in the mountains. For Shanmei villagers, tourism does not serve local development in any way. Having seen what happened to neighboring Zou villages, Shanmei villagers concluded that profits from tourism always fall into the hands of Han developers.

The market economy nonetheless attracts the attention of Shanmei villagers. They have formed the Association of Shanmei Community Development for the sake of protecting Shanmei resources from being abused by Han developers. One example concerns the tradition of honey cultivation, which had recently been ruined. According to custom, once a tree was marked by the person who had spotted honey bees, others would not cultivate it. The tradition was resumed during the late 1980s. In the beginning, the priority of the association's leaders was not money making, but conservation. River resources later proved to be the key to the rise of community consciousness in Shanmei. The worry that Han developers might abuse the rivers and leave Shanmei permanently backward has motivated the previously docile villagers to action. Their slogans do not emphasize a competitive and participatory spirit in the commercial market, but rather one of unity, harmony, and progress.[66] Villagers nonetheless used elections to form the first board of the association. It turned out that all major families in the village have either family members or in-laws elected to serve on the board.

The most significant river resource in Shanmei is a fish that villagers call gu-fish, which is one of a kind. In the past, Zou people, while skillful mountain hunters, were not used to considering gu-fish a resource. The elderly were typically uninterested in protecting the river. When the association began to regulate river resources, the first few people who were caught stealing gu-fish were invariably Zou villagers, even staff members themselves. Finally, the elderly intervened to ensure that a heavy penalty was imposed on all thieves. As Zou people all became protectors of resources, only Han people could possibly be thieves. Shanmei villagers would not send Han thieves to the police, however. The issue of how to treat them led to some intense discussion when the first case appeared. The villagers decided to fine them (over one hundred thousand New Taiwan Dollars) in private, and they kept the fine for village development.[67] Catching Han thieves was a thrill. Younger villagers all participated with excitement in night patrols, and they came to see gu-fish as a symbol of Shanmei. A new culture began right in the Danuoyi Valley, where there were gu-fish and where villagers patrolled at night. Off-duty villagers in their twenties escorted their friends on shifts in the valley, and were themselves escorted on their own shifts, drinking, singing, and dancing through the dark night until morning. Nights in the Danuoyi Valley changed completely. Gu-fish and the valley symbolized the unity of the villagers. When the first gu-fish festival took place, Shanmei was still incapable of receiving the thousands of tourists brought by unexpected media coverage in advance. It was at this late stage that the market entered villagers' calculations. Fortunately, tourism validated the significance of Shanmei's new symbol of identity. Shanmei's economy grew quickly in the early 1990s.

A crisis struck in 1997. Typhoon Herbert wiped out valley construction completely, eliminating as well the gu-fish in the valley river. The Shanmei villagers were shocked and speechless, until a message sent back from a team deep in the valley reported signs of gu-fish. Suddenly, desperate villagers showed an unprecedented and spontaneous spirit of unity. Even the elderly joined in the rescue. In three days, a temporary trail leading to the valley was opened. In two weeks, the road construction was completed. Shanmei, gu-fish, and the Danuoyi Valley now form a trinity in the villagers' minds. One particular lesson for the leaders of Shanmei is that, from now on, all large-scale activity must be undertaken by voluntary workers, for only if people do not get paid will they be devoted and united. The perceived relationship between lack of pay and devotion may be disputable, but there is no doubt that there is a full supply of voluntary workers. In comparison with an earlier period when villagers feared that their determination to protect gu-fish might exacerbate theft of the fish, the self-confidence seen ten years later is truly impressive.

The growing sense of community ensures that the role of the association surpasses that of the village office. Elections for the board of the association are intense. Multi-seat elections do not exclude any major family; in fact, records indicate that the board composition has always been balanced. When elections for village director or county director occur, the villagers get together to make a decision. This does not mean that everyone complies with the collective choice, but it does mean that Shanmei has a collective position. Zou people are a minority; a public position is deemed essential to showing unity. Other villages complain that Shanmei villagers have too strong a sense of unity during elections. Their reply is that unity is the only appropriate solution to counter Han people's various electoral tricks.

The development of Shanmei has an origin outside of Shanmei. The government enlisted identity politics in its China policy, sparking a series of civilizing projects that led to a new civic discourse and a sense of Zou identity. This identity did not follow the government's discourse, however; Zou people's self-identification evolved against a backdrop of Han developers' intrusions in the neighboring mountains. Environmental consciousness led villagers to resume past norms, and the intervention of the elderly at an opportune moment led to a Zou–Han separation in gu-fish politics. The FGEG discourse, aimed at mobilizing all island dwellers to jettison their Chinese identity, created a new Zou identity, which is neither just "Original Resident" nor even new Taiwanese. Resistance entered citizenship discourse without any participant consciously wanting to resist.[68]

Responses Outside of Civic Discourses

The examples discussed in this chapter illustrate four different responses that minorities have had to the civilizing projects of the state. For the state, there does not seem to be any great distinction between civic discourses in general and those involving minorities in particular. The emphasis is always fourfold: economic growth, harmony with Han people, respect for minority cultures, and recruitment of minority cadres. The responses are never unanimous, however. They carry complicated meanings and are open to various interpretations. Resistance has been evident beneath all these responses, even when it is not intended.

In Xishuangbanna, Dali, and Lijiang, the state has actively assisted in rebuilding ethnic-oriented identities such as the Dongba language, or the Mosuos' matrilineal trait, on the one hand; on the other hand, the state engages in assimilation through bilingual programs to smooth the introduction of a market economy. The result is ambivalence. People get lost between modernity and tradition—some in depression, others in images of barbarians, still others in exotic stereotypes to make a living. In Wuzhong, quickly adapting villagers and Ahhongs have preserved niches outside of the state to keep their Muslim identity, making citizenship projects a means to a higher spiritual activity. The state finds them compliant and cooperative as they accumulate resources for an ultimate return to Allah later in their lives. In Yongshun, innocent villagers who take advantage of the policy privileges or exemptions granted to minorities remain interested in their Tujia and Miao status only in a very pragmatic manner. Maintenance of ethnicity, as well as the implications of civilizing, becomes exclusively the responsibility of the state. In Shanmei Village, Ali Mountain County, for the sake of mobilizing a new Taiwan identity to resist China, the Han government in Taipei coincidentally sensitizes the Zou people's self-identity—which, however, evolves in opposition to the Han. The Han become a symbol of exploitation, in opposition to the truly indigenous Zou.

The problem with citizenship projects in China and the discourses associated with them is that they are top-down mobilizations of a presumed traditional, underdeveloped, and previously conceived alien target. The major rationale is anti-imperialism (or, in the case of Taiwan's Zou, anti-China). "Minority" is a discursively and psychologically necessary category to embody China's pursuit of a strong, unified country. Citizenship projects presuppose a national goal and targets of assimilation, the execution of which provides a feeling of historical progress. The wish is that imperialists should regard minorities in China as their enemy. The unfortunate fact, however, is that minorities are often in friendly touch with missionaries—cross-border, foreign-based teams who are themselves in close cooperation with imperialism. Such contacts fuel a perception that minority identity politics, unless initiated by the state, are a form of subversion. Ironically, the state itself, for its citizenship projects to continue, needs to preserve minority identities. Different identities are treated according to an identical policy. The politics of new citizenship ensures that the relationship among minorities, Han, Chinese, and sovereign China must be the same for all. As a result, minority identities lose their usefulness in guiding relationships with the Han.

Prevailing citizenship discourses do not acknowledge the distinction between minority identities (each of which has its own characteristics) and the state-permitted minority identities. The resolution is left for minorities themselves to handle. The strongest and most remote, such as the Muslims in Xinjiang, may appeal to physical resistance; the weaker and closer must adapt to the state and make adjustments. Some, such as the Wuzhong Muslims, do this well. Inadequate adaptation can incur anxiety (as in the marketization and bilingual programs in Xishuangbanna) or depression (as with the educated Bai women), depending on the situation. Those with weaker identities may simply accept citizenship projects and benefit, as in Yongshun. When opportunities permit, identities may acquire new meanings, as has been observed among the Shanmei Zou.

10 | Do Good Businessmen Make Good Citizens? An Emerging Collective Identity Among China's Private Entrepreneurs

The emergence of private entrepreneurs in China over the past decade or so has been one of the most striking and intriguing features of the reform era. Originally limited to very small-scale operations by state policy and met with suspicion by society, the private sector in China now encompasses the *getihu* (individual business households) at one end, and large-scale industrial and commercial enterprises with hundreds of workers and a scope of operations that cover the whole country and even the international market, at the other. Not only are private entrepreneurs responsible for most economic growth and job creation, and therefore essential to the local economy and the careers of local officials; they are also increasingly well organized and politically active.

The state has created a variety of business associations to which most businessmen belong. Previous research has indicated that some associations are effective advocates for their members' interests, while others remain agents of the state. Entrepreneurs are also beginning to convert their economic influence into political power, for instance by competing in village elections. These trends have generated a great deal of interest among observers, who understand the important role that entrepreneurs have played in fomenting political change in other countries.

How should we make sense of this emerging trend, and what changes should we anticipate as a result? China's private entrepreneurs are increasingly organized and active, but are they *citizens* in the sense of holding civil, political, and social rights as described by Marshall and others? In the sense of having autonomy from the state, the answer is no; entrepreneurs are closely embedded in the state, and are partners with local officials in particular. In the sense of enjoying rights, either normatively based or legally enforced, the answer is again no, although new laws are being put into place to protect the rights and property of the private sector. In the sense of having shared beliefs and interests, the answer is more promising. China's entrepreneurs exhibit a set of beliefs regarding the efficacy of their business associations, the legitimacy of their interests, and basic political values that are distinctly different from the beliefs of the local officials with whom they most closely interact.

From survey data and interviews with private entrepreneurs, several key tendencies are apparent. Entrepreneurs have a greater corporate identity, facilitated by the state's corporatist strategy of creating business associations and co-opting successful businessmen into the Chinese Communist Party (CCP). They have a greater self-awareness and belief that their social status is rising. Moreover, they believe that their interests are communal interests, that what is good for business is also good for the community as a whole. They share a belief that entrepreneurs and their associations can engage in collective action, and that the legal system is an effective means of solving problems. They have confidence in the ability of institutional mechanisms to deal with their concerns, and they downplay the importance of personal relations as a factor in business success. They share beliefs regarding current policies, future preferences, and basic political values that are significantly different from those of incumbent officials in their communities. Although they cooperate with local party and government officials and are willing to be co-opted by them, they do not share the beliefs of those officials. More surprising is that the beliefs of former officials who have joined the private sector have more in common with other entrepreneurs than they do with incumbent officials. Of course, these views are not uniform among all businessmen. One of the tasks of this chapter is to explain variations in the beliefs of China's private entrepreneurs.

While it is premature to say these businessmen believe in their rights as entrepreneurs or as citizens, they clearly believe in their importance and efficacy. As the legal status of private entrepreneurs in China becomes better institutionalized, and the laws protecting the private sector become better implemented and enforced, their appreciation of the opportunities available to them may evolve into expectations of rights enjoyed by citizens. At present, however, China's entrepreneurs are not yet ready to make demands on the state to protect or expand their rights or even to change policy.

The Concept of Citizenship in Comparative Perspective

The concept of citizenship, as outlined by T. H. Marshall on the basis of England's experience, is an evolutionary concept beginning with demands for civil rights and later expanding into political and social rights. This basic sequence may not be a proper guide for understanding the evolution of citizenship in China. As R. Bin Wong has recently described, the idea of social rights emerged first in China, not last as it did in England and elsewhere in Europe. Whereas state-making in Europe emphasized the expansion of citizenship claims, China's imperial state evolved quite differently with the creation of large-scale bureaucracies, coercive efforts to maximize tax revenues, and an emphasis on war efforts.[1]

> Those features absent in European cases—deep concern with elite and popular education and morality, active promotion of material welfare especially of the poor and peasants, invasive curiosity about and anxiety over potentially subversive behavior—did not emerge for several centuries after they first appeared in China. . . . Ideas and institutions that are specifically "modern" in the West are simply not "modern" in China.[2]

However, the concept of political representation, a key development in Europe, was not as well developed in China. Although this seemed to be the precursor of "modern" social welfare values in Europe, those same values were present in China even in the absence of civil and political rights.

The "authoritarian socialist" model of citizenship described by Michael Mann more closely approximates China's situation. Like the fascist alternative, the authoritarian socialist model did not provide civil or political rights, but it did emphasize social rights—the basic subsistence of all. Unlike the British path outlined by Marshall (civil, political, then social rights, roughly one hundred years apart), it offered only social rights without the foundation of full civil and political rights provided by traditional liberal regimes. Writing in 1987, Mann said that this alternative "appears no less stable than other enduring types of regimes." Unlike the other alternatives (authoritarian monarchy and fascism, which were "assassinated" in the world wars), the authoritarian socialist model died a natural death in Eastern Europe (the "velvet revolution" from within) and the former Soviet Union.[3] Even in China it is less stable and its survival less certain than in the past. The Chinese state is slowly expanding the parameters of political participation, but selectively allowing certain voices into the process while continuing to exclude others. Is the concept of citizenship in China now expanding beyond that of basic subsistence?

From a comparative perspective, it may seem unusual to look at private entrepreneurs as a test case for an emerging notion of citizenship in China. It should come as no surprise that China's entrepreneurs live better and enjoy opportunities for access and influence not available to other groups. This is not unexpected for economic elites. But China's entrepreneurs had previously been labeled class enemies and nearly persecuted into extinction. Their reemergence as a significant and increasingly coherent economic and political force has generated much interest among policy-makers and scholars inside and outside China.

Some see entrepreneurs as the vanguard of an emerging (or reemerging) civil society, which is seen by many as a necessary prerequisite for political development and democratization in particular. Barrington Moore's succinct prediction, "no bourgeoisie, no democracy," conveys their important historical role. Others go even further, using a vulgarized version of modernization theory, to predict that the same people who are promoting and benefiting from economic liberalization will also advocate political democratization. But just as Przeworski and Limongi show that there is no correspondence between economic change and democratization, the existing evidence suggests that China's entrepreneurs are not proto-democrats and are not willing to play the role that others have predicted for them.[4]

In the current political context in China, it is unrealistic to find explicit evidence of determined efforts on the part of private entrepreneurs to change the political system. That is probably too much to expect from an entrepreneurial class that is barely a decade old, with a precarious legal identity and poorly protected property rights. Private entrepreneurs are more likely to be partners with the state, rather than adversaries of it, and are more likely to focus on local and procedural issues rather than abstract notions of civil, political, and social rights. Nevertheless, they are changing China's political system in gradual, incremental, and perhaps even unintended ways.

China's Entrepreneurs and Their Organizations

The gradual and limited liberalization of China's political system in the post-Mao era created renewed interest in notions of civil society. A vibrant debate began among scholars about whether a civil society was emerging as a consequence of the *gaige kaifang* (reform and opening) policies, whether these trends had antecedents in the late imperial and Republican eras, and even about the usefulness of the concept for understanding state-society relations in contemporary China.[5] The potential for civil society in the 1980s looked quite fragile after appearing to be snuffed out at the time of the Tiananmen massacre in 1989. But the gradual and limited liberalization of China's political system has been accompanied by an increase in organizational activities. Associations of all kinds, from professional groups to hobby clubs, have blossomed all over the country.[6] Business associations have received particular attention because they have the resources—the means to create economic growth—that the state requires, and because of the special contributions that entrepreneurs have made to political change in other countries.

Private entrepreneurs and their associations in the pre-1949 era have also received a great deal of attention from historians and political scientists. Businessmen became increasingly well organized from the late Qing period forward, sometimes as extensions of the state, other times as autonomous bodies representing local interests to the state. In contrast to the traditional assessment of the Qing state as anti-business, more recent scholarship has shown a cooperative relationship between progressive officials and businessmen, especially at the local level. Government policy toward business from the late Qing period onward has been complex and often contradictory, providing ample evidence for competing claims that the state repressed, neglected, colluded with, or promoted commerce.[7]

Local guilds, trade associations, and chambers of commerce had several main functions: regulatory, such as setting standards and weights, regulating new entrants into a given trade, establishing contractual obligations, and providing credit; social, such as local worship and philanthropy; and representative, conveying not only the views of their own members but also a wider array of local opinion to local and higher-level officials.[8] These guilds and associations were primarily local in nature, but over time they began to create inter-guild linkages to better assert their interests and influence. The Qing government, believing chambers of commerce to be "cost-effective instruments for extending administrative reach," built an empire-wide network of chambers of commerce to encourage merchants' identity with the state and allow greater influence over economic affairs.[9] As the guilds and chambers of commerce became better organized and more closely embedded in the state, they got involved in all aspects of municipal affairs, from road construction to establishing police forces and local courts.

The representative function of guilds and chambers of commerce proved to be the most controversial, creating conflict between merchants and the state and also within the merchant groups themselves. Many merchants were politically progressive and sought a more influential role in public affairs. Most chambers of commerce actively supported the 1911 revolution, the May 4th movement, and the May 30th movement, but there were sharp disagreements within local chambers about whether they should play a confrontational or a more conciliatory role. The political influence of chambers of commerce rose and fell with the stability of the government: in times of instability, chambers of commerce played an active role in providing government services and mediating between contending political elites (as in the late Qing and warlord eras). But once the stability of the state was restored, the new leaders restricted the political activities and influence of merchants.

The Nationalist government tried to organize local merchants for its own purposes, as had the Qing government. Their goal was to create "a politically conscious merchant community that could be mobilized for the goals of the party-state."[10] But once Chiang Kai-shek and other government leaders were able to gain dominance over those in the party bureaucracy, this effort was abandoned. Chiang and his supporters sided with the conservative economic elites over the more militant merchants. This ushered in a more coercive, less cooperative relationship between government and business. In the latter years of the Nanking decade (1927–1937), the government "gained control of business and banking organizations, seized the banking industry, and usurped the leadership of the commercial and industrial sectors."[11] Government policy exploited capitalists, especially in Shanghai, to squeeze out additional revenue for military operations, rather than collaboration between government and business to promote national development. The Nationalist government in Nanking sharply restricted the autonomy and scope of activities of business elites and their organizations.

When the CCP came to power in 1949, they followed a United Front strategy of cooperating with a wide range of non-communist groups. Private entrepreneurs were designated the "national bourgeoisie" to distinguish them from the "bureaucratic capitalists," who had links to the old Nationalist government and whose property was confiscated by the new regime. In the early years of the PRC, these national bourgeoisie were treated with respect and given positions in the coalition government. But this policy of collaboration was short-lived. In 1952, the CCP launched the Five Anti campaign against alleged economic crimes and tax evasion by large-scale entrepreneurs. In 1953, the government announced a new "general line for the transition to socialism" that called for the eventual socialization of industry and commerce. By 1956, the private sector was eliminated and all significant industrial and commercial assets were taken over by the state, with some compensation given to their former owners.[12] Small-scale private trade in the rural areas was also abolished during the mid-1950s.[13] For the remainder of the Maoist era (1949–1976), the state controlled all significant aspects of industry and commerce in China.

As the post-Mao reform era unfolded, the private sector began to reemerge, initially consisting of street vendors and very small-scale enterprises, and later expanding to include much larger industrial and commercial operations.[14] With the expansion in the size and scope of the private sector came business associations established and staffed by state officials. These associations were designed to allow state influence over the growing private sector through direct organizational links with private enterprises.

Scholars have noted two particular features about business associations and individual entrepreneurs in contemporary China. First, different associations have varying degrees of influence, based largely on the types and amount of resources they control. Associations made up of large-scale manufacturing enterprises have more clout than those made up of individual vendors. Consequently, the more influential associations may be developing an identity of their own that will lead them to represent the interests of their members rather than being loyal agents of the state.[15] Second, although businessmen have a keen awareness of their business interests, interviews with individual businessmen indicate that they are reluctant to get involved in politics, either by supporting other societal groups who are pushing for political reform or by using their associations for collective political action.[16] At best, they may be part of what Yanqi Tong calls the "non-critical" sphere of civil society, which is organized to regulate the supply of goods and services but does not pose a direct challenge to the regime, and may even be welcomed by it. The emergence of this realm as an autonomous element of civil society may have important implications for subsequent political change, but it will not lead directly to democratization without the cooperation of the "critical" realm of dissidents and political activists.[17] Taken together, these two insights suggest that China's entrepreneurs are developing a clearer notion of their individual and group interests, but they are unwilling—at least at present—to be advocates of political change.

Most of these studies are based on intensive work in one location, and sometimes in one economic sector.[18] To assess the generalizability of the findings discussed above, I conducted a survey and interview project targeting the owners and operators of large- and medium-scale private enterprises (those with reported annual sales of over 1 million renminbi [RMB]) and the local party and government officials with whom they interact. Separate questionnaires were used for these two groups, but most questions were asked of both. In all, eight counties were selected as survey sites: two each in Zhejiang, Shandong, Hebei, and Hunan. The sites were selected to include a mix of areas with varying levels of economic development and privatization. The survey was conducted in three counties in the fall of 1997, and the other five counties in the spring of 1999.

Entrepreneurs were selected from three townships and towns where the private economy was relatively developed for that particular county. The name lists of relatively large-scale enterprises provided by the Industry and Commerce Bureau were used to create a sampling pool, with the first 100 names from the lists of two townships/towns and the first 150 names from the list of a third township/town. Using a random start, fixed interval system, a sample of 20 enterprises was chosen from the first two townships/towns, and a sample of 30 from the other. In each county, specific officials were targeted: 17 county-level party and government cadres, including the party and government leaders and those in charge of the relevant political, economic, and united front departments; 6 township and town *(xiangzhen)* cadres from the places of the enterprises in the sample; and 6 village-level cadres. This is not a random sample of China's population, and was not intended to be. The respondents represent the economic and political elites in their communities. In all, 524 private entrepreneurs and 230 local party and government officials participated in the survey, a response rate of 78 and 99 percent, respectively. The following analysis is based on data collected from this survey.

The Role of Business Associations

Most of the private entrepreneurs in this study belonged to one or more business associations, and the distribution of membership varied significantly among the eight counties studied (see Table 1). When private entrepreneurs belonged to more than one business association, they were asked which one they most closely identified with, and the analysis given below is based on this distinction.

A brief word about each of the main associations will set the stage. Although there has been an explosion of industry-specific business

Table 1   Membership in Business Associations (percent)

Self-Employed Laborers' Association	22.6
Private Entrepreneurs' Association	21.4
Industrial and Commercial Federation	20.6
Other	4.4
None	31.1

groups, the main ones are the catch-all associations that are organized by the scale of the enterprise rather than the industrial sector. In a classic state corporatist arrangement, they were organized by the state to provide a means to integrate the state with these organizations, and their heads generally serve simultaneously as government officials.[19] The Self-Employed Laborers' Association (SELA) is aimed at small-scale operations with small numbers of workers and low sales volumes. As a consequence of this, previous research has found SELA to have the least amount of prestige and influence.[20] The Private Entrepreneurs' Association (PEA) encompasses slightly larger enterprises. The Industrial and Commercial Federation (ICF) includes the largest and most prestigious enterprises, and is therefore found to have the greatest clout. Although the SELA and PEA are products of the post-Mao era, the ICF has its origins in the 1950s United Front strategy of including capitalists in the policy deliberations of the state. Its status is equivalent to one of the eight so-called democratic parties. Each of the business associations is headquartered in Beijing, with local branches throughout China.

Members of all business associations show a strong identification with their associations (see Table 2). The vast majority of businessmen believe that business associations represent the interests of their members. Similar proportions of business association members believe that their business association shares their personal views. Cadres have similar views on these two questions, and a difference of means test shows no significant difference between the two groups. One surprising finding is that even entrepreneurs who do not belong to any business association believe that the associations represent their members, and even share their own views. This may allow for increased opportunities for collective action in the future.

As seen in Table 2, a slight majority of businessmen believe the associations represent the government's position. Given findings by previous studies, we would expect to find that private entrepreneurs belonging to the SELA would be more likely to agree that their business association represented the interests of the government over their own, and that private entrepreneurs in less developed areas would have the same viewpoint. Yet neither of these predictions is supported by the survey data. Only 48 percent of SELA members believed that their business association represented the government; in contrast, over 76 percent believed that the SELA represented the interests of its members and the personal views of the respondent. A bare majority of the ICF members believed that the ICF—the largest, and generally regarded as the most influential, business associa-

Table 2   Views toward Business Associations (percent)

1. Business associations are able to represent the interests of their members.

	Strongly Agree	Agree	Disagree	Strongly Disagree
SELA	24.3	56.8	15.3	6.1
PEA	33.7	55.5	10.9	0.0
ICF	31.0	55.0	12.0	2.0
Other	40.0	50.0	5.0	5.0
None	21.9	53.5	18.4	6.1
All Entrepreneurs	28.3	54.2	14.1	3.4
Officials	27.0	50.1	17.6	4.5

2. Under most circumstances, the business association and I share the same viewpoint on the affairs of enterprises.

	Strongly Agree	Agree	Disagree	Strongly Disagree
SELA	22.9	56.0	17.4	3.7
PEA	25.5	61.8	11.8	1.0
ICF	24.5	61.2	14.3	0.0
Other	30.0	65.0	5.0	0.0
None	13.6	61.8	19.1	5.5
All Entrepreneurs	21.9	60.4	15.9	2.5

tion—represented the government. The PEA and other local business associations had the highest percentage of members who believed that their associations represented the government's perspective. In short, there was no simple linear relationship between the reputation for independence and influence of a business association and the views of its members regarding whether it represented the views of the government.

The level of economic development and privatization strongly influenced the beliefs of respondents. Entrepreneurs in the four counties with prosperous economies and high levels of privatization were much more likely to agree that their business association represented the government's viewpoint: 71.9 percent as opposed to only 41.6 percent in the four less prosperous counties. A difference of means test was highly significant ($t = 6.55$, $p(t) = .0000$). This apparently paradoxical finding fits the findings of other studies from China, and elsewhere in East Asia, showing a close partnership between government and business, rather than the adversarial relationship more familiar in the United States.[21] In the areas where the economy as a whole and the private economy in particular is more prosperous, the government-business relationship in China may also be more developed and the belief in shared interests more pronounced.

Surprisingly, as shown in Table 3, the views of local party and gov-

Table 3 Business Associations and the Government's Views (percent)

On most matters, the business association represents the government's views.

	Strongly Agree	Agree	Disagree	Strongly Disagree
SELA	24.1	24.1	34.3	17.6
PEA	30.0	32.0	35.4	3.0
ICF	15.6	35.4	39.6	9.4
Other	30.0	30.0	40.0	0.0
None	9.2	46.8	33.0	11.0
All Entrepreneurs	20.9	34.4	34.6	10.9
Officials	11.0	51.4	29.4	8.3

ernment officials did not vary according to the level of economic development. On average, 62.4 percent of officials agreed that business associations represented the government. Whether through better socialization, better knowledge, or a different perspective on the roles of government and businessmen, officials consistently shared similar views on whether business associations represented the government's perspective.

Although business associations may not be merely agents of the state, neither are they completely autonomous. This delicate balance between autonomy and embeddedness is the key to government-business relations and successful economic development in a variety of developing countries, and is similar to the way other studies have found individuals in China view their relationship with the state.[22] Changes in that balance may indicate the changing potential for political change. However, the evidence here suggests that the perceived harmony of interests between the state and business associations *rises* with economic development. If private entrepreneurs are expected to be agents of political change, we would expect the views of private entrepreneurs and officials to be diverging in the most prosperous areas. That is not what these survey data reveal, however. Instead, we may find that economic development accentuates the convergence of views between government and business, at least in the short run.

Most businessmen reported that they have used their business association to try to resolve their problems (see Table 4). These problems most commonly had to do with economic and financial matters (such as getting loans on time and payment of taxes), disputes between businesses, or general problems, such as getting permits or having goods inspected for export. In previous studies, Unger and Nevitt report that the SELA is the weakest of the associations in this regard. Although a majority of the SELA members interviewed in my project reported that they had sought help from this association, the percentage was smaller than for the PEA (59.4 versus 69.3). However, only 44.2 percent of the ICF members had sought their association's help. There appears to be no direct correlation between the perceived clout of a business association and the willingness of its members to seek its help.

Table 4   The Helpfulness of Business Associations to Their Members
(percent)

1. When you encounter problems, have you ever gone through your
business association to solve them?

	Yes	No
SELA	59.4	40.6
PEA	69.3	30.7
ICF	44.2	55.8
Other	57.9	42.1
None	NA	NA
All Entrepreneurs	51.2	48.8

2. How helpful was the business association in solving your problem?

	Very Helpful	A Little Helpful	Not Very Helpful	Not Helpful At All
SELA	30.2	57.1	9.5	3.2
PEA	34.9	54.6	10.6	0.0
ICF	27.5	67.5	2.5	2.5
Other	20.0	80.0	0.0	0.0
None	NA	NA	NA	NA
All Entrepreneurs	26.8	60.9	9.6	2.7

3. If you encounter a problem again, will you ask the business association
to help you solve it?

	Yes	No
SELA	85.7	14.3
PEA	85.7	14.3
ICF	79.6	20.4
Other	87.5	12.5
None	NA	NA
All Entrepreneurs	79.9	20.1

In the most developed areas, however, a different picture emerges.
In these counties, 70.8 percent of the SELA members sought its help
(compared with 56.1 percent in the less developed counties), but
only 42.5 percent of the ICF members did likewise. There seem to be
two stories running in parallel here. First, the ICF members have
other resources to draw upon to solve their problems and do not

need to rely on their business association. The fact that roughly the same percentage sought ICF help in prosperous and in poor areas supports this claim. Second, SELA members have fewer resources to draw upon than ICF members, and in particular the former do not have close ties with influential officials, so relying on their association may be their only option. In areas with developed economies, SELA may have a greater role to play because the private sector as a whole is more developed and officials are more inclined to lend their help.[23] This claim is supported by responses to a follow-up question. In the developed areas, 41.2 percent said SELA had been very helpful in solving their problems, but in poorer areas only 26.1 percent said it had been very helpful. Thus SELA's reputation for effectiveness seems to be higher in the more developed areas. In fact, the percentage of members who felt the association had been helpful or very helpful was virtually identical for all three business associations; in less developed areas, however, SELA scored lower than the other two associations. The effectiveness of SELA in developed areas likely encourages its members to seek its help, but this finding is not consistent with previous scholarship, based largely on Beijing and Tianjin. Further work is needed in other locations with varying degrees of development and privatization to clarify this contradictory finding.

While noting the variations in the data, it is important not to lose sight of a more fundamental point. The members of these business associations are learning to turn to them to solve their problems, and the overwhelming majority of businessmen have found the associations to be effective. This indicates strong confidence that the business associations can act on behalf of their members, specifically by intervening to resolve their business problems. This experience will make them more likely to turn to the business associations again in the future and will encourage others to do likewise. Although business associations will not totally replace clientelism as a means for getting things done (as seen in the small numbers of ICF members who sought its help), this does add another option to their repertoire of problem-solving techniques. Developing a reputation for "delivering the goods" is the best way for business associations to demonstrate their value to private entrepreneurs, and to elicit greater support from them.

Can business associations influence the local implementation of policy? This is a more important measure of their potential for act-ing as agents of change, and therefore a potentially more conten-tious matter in a political system that has limited interaction between the state and organized groups outside the state. On this crucial issue, businessmen and officials express markedly different views: over two-thirds—68.4 percent—of businessmen believe that the asso-ciations *can* influence policy implementation (interestingly, SELA members are the most optimistic), but three-quarters—74.9 per-cent—of officials believe that business associations *cannot* influence policy (see Table 5). On this issue, the difference between the busi-nessmen and officials is a difference of kind, not of degree, and shows the potential for future conflict. If the associations and their members believe they can influence policy, they are more inclined to try; and if they believe they can influence the implementation of pol-icy, it is a small step to try to influence the making of policy.

Do all private entrepreneurs believe their business associations can influence the implementation of policy? In the less developed areas, roughly three-quarters of private entrepreneurs believe they can, and this optimism holds across all business associations, and even among those who do not belong to one. In the more developed counties, however, private entrepreneurs have a less optimistic—and one might say more realistic—perception of business association in-fluence over policy. Nevertheless, a clear majority—61.2 percent—of

Table 5   The Policy Influence of Business Associations (percent)

The business association can influence the local implementation of policies.

	Strongly Agree	Agree	Disagree	Strongly Disagree
SELA	26.4	43.6	21.8	8.2
PEA	25.3	40.4	25.3	9.1
ICF	17.9	48.4	23.2	10.5
Other	25.0	35.0	35.0	5.0
None	15.6	55.1	22.0	7.3
All Entrepreneurs	21.5	46.4	23.6	8.6
Officials	5.5	19.6	48.0	26.9

private entrepreneurs believe that business associations can influence policy, and there is a positive relationship between the perceived clout of a business association and the degree to which its members believe it can influence policy implementation, with the SELA lowest and the ICF highest (ironically, those who do not belong to any association are the most optimistic on this point).

Taken together, these data indicate that businessmen view business associations as appropriate means for representing their views, solving their problems, and influencing the local implementation of policy. These three factors, especially the last, are positive indicators of an emerging sense of collective identity among entrepreneurs, and this shared identity may in fact lead to a concept of citizenship. The organization of interests is seen as legitimate by both businessmen and officials, and therefore creates the potential for those organizations to engage in collective action on behalf of those shared interests. These business associations may have been created by the state as part of its strategy of adaptation and incorporation of new elites, but if they serve the interests of its members as much as—if not more than—the interests of the state, the foundation of a civil society will be enhanced.

The analysis, however, also points out a cautionary note: in the more developed areas, the views of private entrepreneurs and officials regarding the roles of business associations are converging, and the expectation of business associations' influence over policy implementation is also lower than elsewhere. These findings suggest increased embeddedness, not greater autonomy; but it is the latter which the literature on citizenship and civil society identifies as a necessary factor for progress.

The CCP and Private Entrepreneurs

The CCP has a close relationship with the private sector, forged in several different ways reminiscent of Jowitt's concept of "inclusion" for post-revolutionary Leninist regimes and for the way complex organizations more generally adapt to their changing external environment.[24] First, as described above, the party has created organizations to link the state with the private sector, with the intention of thereby being able to control it, but also setting up the potential for having influence run in both directions between the state and society. Second, many party and government officials have left their positions and plunged into the sea of private enterprise. Third, the party has tried to co-opt successful and potentially influential businessmen by recruiting them into the party.

According to earlier reports, roughly one-fifth of private entrepreneurs are party members.[25] Of the entrepreneurs surveyed in this project, 40.4 percent admitted to being party members, which is much higher than the national average (see Table 6). The business association with the largest share of party members is the ICF, which is to be expected, since it is the oldest, most established of the associations, and the one that encompasses large-scale enterprises (relative to other private-sector firms). Of these entrepreneurs in the party, roughly two-thirds were already party members before going into business and one-third were co-opted into the party after they went into business. Following the logic of co-optation, we would expect that the CCP would target the largest, most successful entrepreneurs for recruitment, and in fact, a large percentage of the ICF members (32.7 percent) were co-opted into the CCP. But the survey data indicate that even larger shares of co-opted entrepreneurs belong to the PEA and SELA, 39 and 36.7 percent respectively. This finding may be a quirk of the sampling technique used in this project: focusing on the medium- and large-scale enterprises, rather than using a random sample of all private enterprises. Similarly, the CCP targets the most successful entrepreneurs for recruitment into the party. Still, this unexpected finding merits additional research.

Although the CCP has targeted successful entrepreneurs with some success, it has been less successful recruiting workers from private enterprises or building party organizations in them. Only 25.3 percent of private entrepreneurs included in my survey reported that workers in their enterprises had been recruited into the party in recent years, and only 27.6 percent said there was a party organiza-

Table 6   Private Entrepreneurs in the CCP (percent)

	Total	SELA	PEA	ICF	Other	None
CCP	40.4	29.1	39.1	57.0	73.7	35.1
Non-CCP	59.6	70.9	60.9	43.0	26.3	64.9

tion in their enterprise. This is indicative of a larger trend: as the private sector has expanded, the CCP has been unable to extend its organization into most private enterprises, and in particular has had difficulty recruiting from among their workers. This is the flip side of its co-optation strategy—the CCP is now targeting elites instead of its traditional focus on workers and peasants—but the absence of party life inside the private sector presents a challenge to the party's ability to monitor what goes on there. As the disintegration thesis suggests, the transition from socialism is weakening the party's traditional means of monitoring trends in society.[26] The co-optation strategy is a partial substitute for the deeper penetration of the state into society that characterized the Mao era, but whether it will suffice is not yet clear.

Despite the logic that underlies this strategy of co-optation, officials and private entrepreneurs disagree on some of the implications of private entrepreneurs in the party. A majority of private entrepreneurs strongly disagree that private entrepreneurs should be banned from the party, whereas almost one-quarter of officials agree they should be banned, and the difference of means test is statistically significant ($t = 3.68$, $p(t) = .0003$; see Table 7). On July 1, 2001, President Jiang Zemin called for allowing entrepreneurs in the

Table 7   Do Private Entrepreneurs Belong in the CCP? (percent)

1. Private entrepreneurs should not join the CCP.

	Strongly Agree	Agree	Disagree	Strongly Disagree
Entrepreneurs	5.8	6.2	30.9	57.2
Officials	12.3	10.1	32.0	45.6

2. Private entrepreneurs provide the skills the party currently needs.

	Strongly Agree	Agree	Disagree	Strongly Disagree
Entrepreneurs: Developed counties	35.5	47.1	14.2	3.2
Less developed counties	9.4	15.8	44.3	30.5
Officials	12.0	46.2	35.6	6.2

party. On this issue, there is also a difference among private entrepreneurs, with the average party member strongly disagreeing with the ban on private entrepreneurs in the party and non-members simply disagreeing ($t = 2.27$, $p(t) = .02$). In addition, there is a sharp difference on *why* they should be allowed into the party. Although both officials and private entrepreneurs agree in roughly equal proportions that party members have advantages when it comes to business, private entrepreneurs also believe that the party benefits from what they have to offer. Private entrepreneurs are more likely to agree that they have the types of skills and experiences the party needs—a nice example of self-aggrandizement—and the difference of means test is again significant ($t = 3.68$, $p(t) = .0003$; see Table 7). Indeed, whether an entrepreneur is a party member or not is of no significance on this issue: virtually the same percentage of both groups agreed with the statement. While the entrepreneurs recognize that they derive benefits from their party membership, they also believe that the party stands to gain from their skills, and therefore view their relationship with the party as symbiotic. Under these circumstances, they are unlikely to be simply loyal agents of the party.

Civic Roles of China's Private Entrepreneurs

Previous reports show that China's private entrepreneurs commonly make donations to the local community, but the motivations for these donations are not clear. Some view this behavior as a result of official pressure, especially in those areas where the local government does not have the financial means to build new schools, better roads, or other similar projects. Others argue that it is a "payback" to the local community for the sudden prosperity of the new entrepreneurial class: businessman give back to the community to preempt societal dissatisfaction with them and their businesses. This would follow the historical pattern in China and in other countries: civic contributions and charitable donations have been used to enhance the status and prestige of the donor. A third possibility is that private entrepreneurs feel a genuine sense of civic responsibility, separate from tacit or overt pressure from state or society.

According to the respondents in my survey, private entrepreneurs have contributed to a variety of community projects, the most common being schools and transportation projects (see Table 8). A comparison of the business associations reveals that members of the ICF—the oldest association and the one with the largest entrepreneurs—donate at a slightly higher rate than the other business associations, and that entrepreneurs who do not belong to any business association donate at a lower than average rate on many issues. There is no discernible pattern in the regional variation of civic contributions; although donations for roads and temples are more common in poorer counties and those for parks more common in more developed counties, the overall rate of contributions is generally consistent.

Why do entrepreneurs make contributions to community projects? On this issue, entrepreneurs and officials show marked differences of opinion (see Table 9). The vast majority of entrepreneurs said their donations were entirely voluntary, whereas less than half of officials agreed. Of those who said pressure played a part, the smallest proportion of both officials and private entrepreneurs said it was due to state pressure alone, more said it was due to societal pressures alone, and the largest proportion of both groups said it was a combination of societal and state pressures. The proportions are noticeably different, but the rank order is the same for both groups.

The large proportion of private entrepreneurs who said their contributions were entirely voluntary—80.6 percent of the total—deserves more attention. Previous reports have suggested that one motivation for charitable donations is to enhance the local reputations

Table 8   Community Contributions by Private Entrepreneurs (percent)

Type of Project	Total
Schools	54.6
Roads, bridges, dams, wharfs, etc.	42.6
Social welfare projects	42.4
Helping students with financial hardships	29.8
Local holidays or other celebrations	26.5
Hospitals and medical facilities	4.6
Parks	3.5
Temples	9.9
None	10.1

Table 9 Reasons for Community Contributions (percent)

1. Did you provide contributions to these public welfare projects voluntarily or were you under pressure? (Officials were asked a similar question regarding private entrepreneurs' motivations.)

	Entrepreneurs	Officials
Voluntarily	80.6	46.4
Under pressure	1.7	1.8
Both	17.8	51.8

2. If you were under pressure, what kind of pressure was it? (Officials were asked a similar question regarding private entrepreneurs' motivations.)

	Entrepreneurs	Officials
Source of Pressure:		
Social	30.4	32.7
State	27.9	9.6
Both	41.8	57.7

of entrepreneurs and protect them from backlashes motivated by envy, called the "red eye disease." The data from my survey indirectly support that finding, especially since many of the local projects to which entrepreneurs most commonly contribute—schools, social welfare, providing financial aid to needy students—do not directly benefit business operations. About 85 percent of entrepreneurs agreed that private entrepreneurs had an obligation to help local poor families and to contribute to local public welfare projects. In contrast, only a little more than 70 percent of officials agreed. Thus private entrepreneurs felt they had a greater obligation than officials, although for both groups the numbers were quite large.

If private entrepreneurs give local donations to enhance their social standing, then by their own estimates they have been successful. Over 80 percent said that their social status had improved in the past year, and slightly more said it had improved since they went into business. As might be expected, SELA members were the least likely to agree with this question, ICF members the most likely, and private entrepreneurs in developed counties more likely to strongly agree with this statement than those in poorer counties. Local officials may not be the most neutral observers on this question, but 56.5 percent of them said that the social status of private entrepreneurs had clearly improved in recent years, and another 42.6 percent said it had improved somewhat—in other words, over 99 percent of officials felt that the social status of private entrepreneurs was getting better. In contrast, only 41.7 percent of officials felt that their own social status had improved in recent years.[27]

These data indicate that private entrepreneurs are involved in their communities, not just by providing jobs and tax revenue, but also by helping provide collective goods. In return, their contributions may benefit their own reputations as good citizens. This combination—increasing wealth coupled with increasing social status—confirms the party's logic in co-opting and organizing these new elites in order to cooperate with them, rather than compete with them.

Political Participation by Private Entrepreneurs

In addition to their membership and participation in business associations and the CCP, private entrepreneurs are also beginning to assume official positions. A few private entrepreneurs serve, or have served, as members of local people's congresses and political consultative congresses. Of the 524 private entrepreneurs in this sample, 52 (11.2 percent) either have served or are serving in local people's congresses, and 21 (4.6 percent) in local political consultative congresses. The vast majority of them are party members (77.8 percent of private entrepreneurs in people's congresses and 60.9 percent of those in consultative congresses). The CCP carefully screens those who are able to participate in these congresses; for all those, including private entrepreneurs, who want to be politically active in formal institutions, party membership has definite advantages. Only six private entrepreneurs (1.4 percent) belong to one of the eight democratic parties. Some have speculated that one avenue for private entrepreneurs to become more active in the political arena—aside from their involvement in the CCP—may be through the democratic parties, which have shown renewed signs of life over the past decade. Judging by the data from these eight counties, however, there is little evidence of that.

Of greater importance is the participation of private entrepreneurs in village-level elections. Anecdotal evidence from around China indicates that private entrepreneurs in some areas have begun running for village head, ostensibly in an attempt to combine their economic power with some measure of political power, even though village head is not a particularly powerful position. In my sample, 81 private entrepreneurs (15.5 percent) had been candidates for village head, and there was no difference between counties attributable to level of development. Only 28.7 percent of these candidates were party members, a percentage that is lower than the share of party members among private entrepreneurs in general, and much lower than that for those serving in people's or consultative congresses. Moreover, almost half of them were *co-opted* party members who had joined the party after going into private business, not former officials. This again vindicates the party's strategy in co-opting private entrepreneurs: as always, the party wants to keep all political participation under its control, so if private entrepreneurs are going to run for local office, the party would prefer that they also be party members. Otherwise, having large numbers of non-CCP entrepreneurs successfully run for village head could present a challenge to the party's control over political positions.

Private entrepreneurs and officials show very similar attitudes toward this trend (see Table 10). Both groups are—in principle, at least—in favor of having private entrepreneurs run for village head, and although officials are more likely to prefer that private entrepreneurs have proper qualifications, very few from either category advocate restrictions on private entrepreneurs running for local office. If a private entrepreneur is elected who is not already a party member, both private entrepreneurs and officials agree—in large proportions—that he should join the party. But a surprisingly large number of officials responded that private entrepreneurs should not join the CCP, even if they are elected as village head. This is a reflection of the fact that most of these officials believed that private entrepreneurs did not belong in the CCP at all.

If the trend of private entrepreneurs running and winning elections for village head continues, and furthermore if competitive elections move up to higher levels of the political system, the CCP may be faced with an awkward dilemma. If private entrepreneurs demonstrate that they have the local popular support needed to win

Table 10   Participation by Private Entrepreneurs in Local Elections
(percent)

1. In some areas, successful businessmen have run as candidates in
elections for village head and village council. What do you think of this
trend?

	Entrepreneurs	Officials
Should be encouraged	37.7	25.7
Only if qualified	58.6	73.0
Should be restricted	3.7	1.4

2. If a private entrepreneur is elected as a village official, but he is not a
CCP member, should he join the CCP?

	Entrepreneurs	Officials
Yes	67.9	59.0
Does not matter	28.4	27.5
No	3.7	13.5

elections, the CCP may not be able to refuse their candidacy or dis-
avow their election, especially if they are already party members. Are
the beliefs of private entrepreneurs sufficiently different from those
of the local officials with whom they interact that their incorporation
into the political system will necessitate change in that system? To as-
certain the likelihood of this scenario, in the next section I will compare the political beliefs of private entrepreneurs and officials.

Comparing the Political Beliefs of Private Entrepreneurs and Local Officials

When one compares the views of private entrepreneurs with those of
local officials, a pattern is apparent: although private entrepreneurs
and officials have significantly different outlooks on most basic political beliefs, they have similar outlooks on policy-specific issues, such
as the pace of reform. While basic beliefs may differ, this difference
alone, however, may not lead to political action by private entrepreneurs so long as their issue-specific opinions conform to those of officials.

A list of questions designed to tap basic political beliefs is shown in Table 11. The first group of questions concerns the causes and consequences of personal prosperity. According to Doug Guthrie, *guanxi* (personal connections) is declining in importance for Chinese firms.[28] Personal relationships and connections continue to be important to business in China, but in the same way that relationships are important to business in any country. Relying exclusively on *guanxi* to get things done increasingly is seen as inappropriate and even illegal, because it is often tied to corruption. The practice of *guanxi* is being replaced by reliance on laws and regulations and on competitive pressures within the market. Guthrie's research was based on Shanghai. The data from my survey support his finding. Private entrepreneurs are more likely than officials to agree that personal success is based on ambition and skill, although the vast majority of both groups agree. The vast majority of both entrepreneurs and officials also do not agree that *guanxi* is the most important thing in business, but here the level of development is significant: private entrepreneurs and officials in the more developed counties are much more likely than their colleagues in less developed areas to disagree that *guanxi* is the most important. Moreover, officials are more likely to deny the importance of *guanxi,* especially in the more developed areas. This may be a result of their desire not to be tainted by the increased attention given to China's rampant corruption. Both entrepreneurs and officials also overwhelmingly agree that relying on the legal system is an effective way of solving business disputes. This suggests that economic development, and privatization in particular, is changing one of the most fundamental aspects of traditional values and behavior in China, with important implications for both the commercial culture and potentially the political culture more generally. This is a controversial assertion, of course, but it fits with Guthrie's findings in Shanghai.

While it is understandable that private entrepreneurs would believe that their wealth is due to their hard work and talent, perhaps as a consequence of this they are more likely than officials to agree that rich people should have more influence over policy matters. The logic may be that people with ambition and skill should be influential, and if those same attributes are responsible for wealth, then wealthy people should have more influence. This goes directly against the political rights of citizenship, by arguing that the privi-

Table 11   Basic Political Beliefs of Private Entrepreneurs and Local
Officials (percent)

	Strongly Agree	Agree	Disagree	Strongly Disagree
Because of *gaige kaifang* policies, anyone with ambition and skill is able to succeed in business.				
Private Entrepreneurs	44.8	39.2	14.0	2.1
Officials	33.5	38.3	22.0	6.2
Enterprise success mainly depends on relationships *(guanxi)* and connections *(menhu)*.				
Private Entrepreneurs	11.3	17.7	43.7	27.2
Officials	4.8	15.4	47.4	32.5
Rich people should have more influence in policy-making than poor people.				
Private Entrepreneurs	13.3	35.9	38.9	11.9
Officials	8.4	26.9	41.0	23.8
What is good for business is good for the local community.				
Private Entrepreneurs	39.2	42.8	15.5	2.5
Officials	15.7	44.4	35.9	4.0
Competition between firms and individuals is harmful to social stability.				
Private Entrepreneurs	27.9	40.8	21.3	10.0
Officials	3.1	8.8	54.6	33.5
If everybody does not share the same thinking, society can be chaotic.				
Private Entrepreneurs	15.5	22.8	42.8	19.6
Officials	6.2	15.9	51.5	26.4
Locally, if there are many groups with different opinions, that can influence local stability.				
Private Entrepreneurs	15.4	27.9	40.1	16.6
Officials	11.4	22.4	50.0	16.2

leged should enjoy greater rights of representation than others. This viewpoint is not unique to China, however. Many democratic countries began by first enfranchising property owners and other elites with socioeconomic privileges, and only later expanding citizenship rights to a wider range of society. The belief that talents, rather than personal connections or birthright, deserve the reward of greater influence also leaves open the door to others who become successful through merit. Many Chinese entrepreneurs may have an elitist attitude on this question, but it is a fluid notion. Furthermore, they are more likely to agree with the "GM theory": what is good for business is also good for the local community. On all of these questions, a difference of means test shows that private entrepreneurs and officials are distinct groups, although the differences are ones of degree, not of kind. In other words, where private entrepreneurs strongly agree with a proposition, officials will simply agree. It is the intensity of views that distinguishes the two groups, not the nature of those views, but that difference of degree can be significant, substantively as well statistically, during public policy debates.

A second group of questions on basic political beliefs has to do with issues of maintaining stability, widely viewed as a core feature of Chinese political culture. One of the concerns expressed by those who oppose privatization is that market competition is a threat to stability. This viewpoint finds little support among the officials surveyed here, but entrepreneurs are divided on the basis of the level of development of their counties. The vast majority of officials oppose the notion that "competition between firms and individuals is harmful to social stability," but entrepreneurs are less certain. However, 44.7 percent of private entrepreneurs in the more developed counties and almost 88.4 percent—almost twice as many—in less developed counties believe that competition *is* harmful. This is a good indication that increased experience with competition among firms reduces concern over potential risks of instability. For now, though, the concern is still quite strong, at least among private entrepreneurs in less developed areas.

Two related questions were also asked: whether diversity of individual thinking and groups with different opinions can lead to chaos. There is a subtle but important difference between these two questions: one concerns individuals, the other organized interests. And the results are also subtly, but significantly (at least in a statistical sense), different. Officials were more likely to oppose the question concerning individual differences of opinion, but slightly less opposed to the question concerning threats to stability posed by organized interests. The difference between private entrepreneurs and officials was statistically significant on the first question, but not on the second. One inference that can be drawn from these data is that local officials feel the strongest threats to stability are, first, organized groups, second, diverse individual viewpoints, and least, economic competition. This would also fit with observations of the types of threats that local officials are quick to suppress.

Other questions on political beliefs concern more concrete policy and political issues (see Table 12). On the issue of the pace of reform, a clear majority of both groups believe that the pace is about right, and a sizable minority would prefer the pace to be even faster; the difference between the groups is not statistically significant. But on the issue of economic opportunity, there is again a statistically significant difference of degree: officials were most likely to disagree strongly with the notion that "*gaige kaifang* has not given the vast majority of people the opportunity to get rich," whereas entrepreneurs were most likely simply to disagree. This of course is a politically explosive issue at a time when regional variations in levels of development and the gap between rich and poor have been growing.

Entrepreneurs and officials express different preferences when asked to make trade-offs between growth and some of its consequences. Officials are willing to emphasize policies of growth even if they result in inflation or—surprisingly enough—instability. Private entrepreneurs, on the other hand, are willing to put up with inflation in order to achieve growth, but they are not willing to sacrifice stability. This is one of the few issues where the differences between the officials and the entrepreneurs are differences of *kind*. This identifies one potential area of discord between entrepreneurs and local officials, who have been selected and promoted on the basis of support for growth-oriented policies. But if those policies begin to undermine stability—as anecdotal evidence of recent years indicates they are—it may lead entrepreneurs to question their support for these policies, even though they have until now benefited greatly from them.

On the fundamental issue of political reform, however, the ma-

Table 12   Policy Views of Private Entrepreneurs and Local Officials (percent)

	Private Entrepreneurs	Officials
Do you think the pace of economic reform is:		
Too fast	9.7	8.9
About right	58.9	60.6
Too slow	31.4	30.5
Gaige kaifang has not given the vast majority of people the opportunity to get rich.		
Strongly agree	11.6	3.6
Agree	13.8	8.0
Disagree	39.8	33.3
Strongly disagree	34.8	55.1
Currently, some people believe the government should slow down the pace of economic development in order to control inflation; others believe inflation is a regular phenomenon of economic development. What do you think the government's current top priority should be?		
Speed up the pace of economic development	70.1	75.3
Control inflation	29.9	24.7
Some people are afraid that rapid economic development may be harmful to social stability; others believe the best way to preserve stability is to promote further economic development. What do you believe the government's top priority should be?		
Maintain social stability	58.3	39.4
Promote economic development	41.7	60.6
Measures to improve the political structure should be initiated by the party and government, not by society (*laobaixing*).		
Strongly agree	21.9	24.5
Agree	28.2	23.6
Disagree	34.5	40.6
Strongly disagree	15.4	11.4

jority of private entrepreneurs surveyed for this project show the conservative view that other scholars have found:[29] nearly equal percentages of private entrepreneurs and officials agree that political reform should be initiated by the party and government, rather than by society (the difference of means is not statistically significant). These survey data, however, do not support the view that businessmen are universally, or even overwhelmingly, opposed to societal pressure on the state for political reform: in fact, they are evenly divided between those who feel society should have a role and those who feel the state alone should initiate political reform. The level of development is a significant factor on this issue: private entrepreneurs in less developed areas are more supportive of a societal role than those in developed areas, and the difference is statistically significant ($t = 2.95$, $p(t) = .003$). This reinforces the point that economic development is not yet leading to demands for greater autonomy by entrepreneurs, as the literature on citizenship and civil society would lead one to expect. There is another noticeable difference among private entrepreneurs: 57.9 percent of party members agree that the state alone should initiate political reform, but only 43.7 percent of non-members agree. By belonging to the party, either before going into business or after, those entrepreneurs *are* part of the state. What types of political reform—if any—might be desired by entrepreneurs remains to be seen. Moreover, what part they will play in bringing about political change may be determined by how they view their role: as members of the state or as a societal force.

Questions about political beliefs expose discernible, and in most cases statistically significant, differences between private entrepreneurs and officials. It is worth emphasizing again that these differences are primarily ones of degree, however; only on the trade-off between growth and stability are the two groups diametrically opposed. This is an important finding.

Conclusion

This survey of Chinese private entrepreneurs and local officials reveals several trends in their beliefs and behaviors. First, there are clear differences between entrepreneurs and officials on most of the issues identified above, but these are differences of degree, not of kind. Only rarely do the two groups take opposing views. Second, entrepreneurs show an evolving concept of organized interests and are willing to use the business associations for collective and individual purposes to address business concerns. In contrast to the expectations of concepts of citizenship and civil society, however, they believe that the associations represent both their interests and the viewpoint of the government. And on the key issue of political reform, entrepreneurs and officials have a similar range of views: both groups are roughly evenly divided between those who believe the party and government should initiate political reform and those who believe society should have some (albeit unspecified) involvement. While the entrepreneurs are not demanding civil, political, or social rights that would clearly mark them as citizens, they do exhibit an awareness of their shared interests and potential for collective action that may set the stage for the emergence of a more explicit concept of citizenship. This is an important trend, even if it does not have immediate and direct implications for China's potential democratization.

China's entrepreneurs are not yet seeking an autonomous status with which they can challenge the state. In fact, in the areas that are most economically developed and where privatization has advanced the furthest, the convergence of views between entrepreneurs and local officials is most pronounced. This is in sharp contrast to theories of citizenship and civil society based on the Western experience, even though it is in keeping with the experience of other East Asian countries and China's own past. Instead of seeking an officially recognized and protected autonomy, entrepreneurs seek to be embedded in the state, and the state in turn has created the institutional means for linking itself with private business interests. For those who expect entrepreneurs to be agents of political change in China, the evidence so far—based upon the data presented here and in previous research by other scholars—does not lend much support. However, entrepreneurs already exhibit a strong belief in the efficacy of their business associations and their ability to influence policy that may one day lead them to play a more assertive role.

China's private entrepreneurs are therefore receiving increased attention—by scholars and the state alike—because they are potential "kingmakers" between the state and the "critical realm" of civil society. Although their views are essentially compatible with those of local officials, the question arises of what could make that situation change. To avoid having to answer that question, the state has adopted a two-pronged strategy of creating new institutions to integrate the state with the business sector, and co-opting individual entrepreneurs into the CCP. This strategy has been successful so far in preempting demands for autonomy or citizenship rights. Whether it will continue to be successful in the future may determine whether private entrepreneurs remain in the "non-critical realm" of civil society or use their organizations to promote collective action on political issues.

YU XINGZHONG

11 | Citizenship, Ideology,
and the PRC Constitution

The question of whether citizenship can be employed as
an effective conceptual tool to understand and analyze social and political life in contemporary China is debatable.
In contrast to the concepts of "party," "state," "people,"
"working class," "cadres," and even "villagers," there is
little understanding of the concept of citizenship as being relevant to China's political, legal, and economic life,
partly because of cultural and ideological confusion in-
herited from China's past, and partly because of the serious disparity among citizens resulting from the post-Mao
economic reforms. In terms of theory, little has been written about citizenship in Chinese political and legal literature. The revival of citizenship debates in the United
States and Europe and new Western theories of citizenship put forth in the late 1990s have not yet caught the attention of China's observers of international intellectual
trends. In practice, it is unclear whether some recent
events in China, such as village elections, the emergence
of government-organized non-governmental organizations, and even citizens' suits against government personnel, can be seen as the manifestation of a growing
consciousness of citizenship participation. Are the people
who participate in these activities actually aware of the
concept of citizenship, and do they understand its meaning? For instance, when villagers are asked to attend a

village election meeting, do they consider the meeting to be different from other gatherings they attend, such as a village fair?

It is said that in ancient Greece, citizens who neglected their civic duties in the *polis* by not attending assemblies, voting, serving on juries, or performing military service were labeled *idions,* the term from which the modern word "idiot" is derived. Aristotle indicated that a good citizen "must possess the knowledge and the capacity requisite for ruling as well as being ruled."[1]

By any yardstick, Chinese citizenship consciousness fails this test substantially, if not completely. Throughout China's long history, managing the country has always been the business of a few people. The populace was never encouraged or permitted to become involved in decision-making on political and other major issues that concerned the state. In fact, they were required *not* to be interested in affairs such as politics and adjudication, except when they were coerced to perform military service. Since the state was regarded as the private property of the imperial families and running the country the task of men chosen by the emperors, anyone who showed a slight interest in state affairs was described as "casting his covetous eyes on the divine power" *(kuiqie shenqi).* Political participation by commoners was only possible through violent rebellion and the overthrow of an existing dynasty. The capacity for ruling was completely separate from that of being ruled, and the issue of who would rule the ruler was never broached.

The modern concept of citizenship in the West, following the work of T. H. Marshall, is generally understood to have three elements: civil, political, and social. The civil element is composed of the rights necessary for individual freedom: liberty of the person; freedom of speech, thought, and faith; the right to own property and conclude valid contracts; and the right to justice. The political element refers to the right to participate in the exercise of political power, as a member of a body invested with political authority or as an elector of such a body. The social element refers to a range of rights, from the right to a modicum of economic welfare and security to the right to live as a civilized being according to the prevailing social standards.[2]

These elements have been codified in international human rights law, including the Universal Declaration of Human Rights, the International Covenant on Civil and Political Rights, and the International Covenant on Economic, Social, and Cultural Rights. They have also been incorporated into the domestic constitutions of many countries and have become yardsticks for judging whether and to what extent a country is democratic, follows the rule of law, or provides social welfare for its citizens.

The current Chinese constitution, following this general trend, also has these elements of citizenship in place. However, because the concept of citizenship is essentially a Western product, there is still a large gap between the constitutional provisions and reality. Even the meaning of citizenship as incorporating all three of these elements has not been entirely clear in much of the history of the People's Republic of China (PRC), and the constitution contains provisions that are detrimental to the enforcement of citizenship rights. In fact, the meaning of citizenship has changed over the course of PRC history. In the mid-1970s, for instance, the most important aspect of citizenship in China was to obey and support the Chinese Communist Party (CCP) and socialism; in the 1980s and 1990s, Chinese citizens were not allowed to engage in strikes.[3]

The PRC has had four formal constitutions (1954, 1975, 1978, and 1982) as well as a provisional constitutional document called the Common Program of the Political Consultative Conference of the PRC (Common Program) in 1949. The 1982 constitution has been amended three times, as recently as March 1999, to reflect changing circumstances since the introduction of the economic reforms in the post-Mao era.[4] These constitutions, unlike their counterparts in liberal societies, serve as the party-state's programs for ideological guidance and as political documents that reflect government policies. The development of these constitutions provides a good opportunity to understand how the concept of citizenship and the government's attitude toward it have changed over the years. In this chapter I will analyze the changing meanings of citizenship in the People's Republic of China by examining the provisions for citizenship in the various versions of its constitution. I will focus specifically on the concept of citizenship as succinctly summarized by Earl Warren: citizenship is the right to have rights.[5]

The most important quality of the concept of citizenship as the right to have rights is the equal enjoyment of such a right by all the members of a given society. In Section I, I will examine the differences between the concepts of "people" and "citizens" as determined by the constitution and how these differences sabotage the notion of citizenship. In Section II, I will explore the changing scope of citizens' rights, the rise and demise of the "four great freedoms," and the relative importance of citizens' rights with regard to the state. In Section III, I will discuss the constitutional sanctification of the leading ideology which discourages the equal enjoyment of citizenship. In Section IV, I will outline the difficulties in enforcing the constitutional provisions for citizenship. In Section V, I will examine the reality of the stratification of citizenship since the reforms.

I. The Changing Subject of Citizens' Rights in the Constitution

Since Chinese constitutions reflect ideological changes in the CCP, it is useful to say a few words about these changes before discussing the constitutional provisions. The concept of citizenship was borrowed from the West, and thus when it was introduced into China, different Chinese terms were used as its equivalent. The preferred Chinese term for "citizens" prior to 1949 was *guomin* (nationals). After the founding of the PRC, however, especially since 1953, the term *gongmin* (citizens) came into use.[6]

Citizens: Guomin *or* Gongmin

Although consciousness of citizenship failed to develop in traditional China, the Chinese did have a very strong sense of belonging, whether to a family, clan, alliance of clans, community, or dynasty. That sense of belonging, however, consisted more of passive association than of active participation in the affairs of the community or the dynasty, which were taken care of by the officials and/or the gentry class.

"Folksmanship" rather than citizenship was what brought scattered commoners together. Even in recent times, relationships between fellow-townsmen or fellow-villagers are closer than those with people from other places. The sense of belonging to a people, a culture, and the nation, though not based on citizenship, produces patriotism and nationalism. Just the fact that they are Chinese is sufficient for people to become patriotic and nationalistic.

Bowing to domestic and Western pressure, the Qing government reluctantly undertook a series of reforms during the first decade of the twentieth century. Increasing interest in what would now be termed citizenship accompanied these reforms.[7] The term used then was *guomin*,[8] signifying both "state/nation" and "citizens/people"; this was later adopted by the Nationalist Party as part of its name, Guomindang (Kuomintang).

The term *guomin* is occasionally found in China's classical literature.[9] It often refers to subjects under the jurisdiction of feudal states or vassal estates during pre-imperial China. The status of the people belonging to the feudal states was always clear: they were *chenmin* (subjects), rather than *guomin* (nationals) in the modern sense.

The modern use of *guomin*—identifying independent individuals enjoying equality, liberty, and other civic rights, as well as fulfilling their required responsibilities—was occasionally seen before the 1898 reforms, probably as a translation of the Western concept of citizens obtained via Japan. Liang Qichao was the first to provide a clear definition of *guomin*. In an article published in October 1899, Liang stated that "*guomin* means treating the country as the public property of the people . . . the people of the country are to run the affairs of the country, make laws for it, think in the interest of it, and defend it in times of disaster. The people must not be insulted and the country must not perish. That is the meaning of citizenship."[10]

The Ideological Difference Between People and Citizens

In the early years of the PRC, the term *guomin* was still used in formal legal and political documents—for instance, in the Common Program. After 1953, *guomin* was replaced by *gongmin* (citizens), and this term has been used ever since, referring to all PRC nationals.

The Common Program, as well as the four formal constitutions, also used another, more preferred term: *renmin* (people). Zhou Enlai clarified the difference between *renmin* and *guomin* in his 1953 speech explaining the Common Program. As Zhou explained it, *renmin* includes only the working class, peasant class, petty bourgeois class, national bourgeois class, and some patriotic democratic elements who have consciously separated themselves from the old reactionary classes, while *guomin* includes not only the above-mentioned classes, but also reactionary classes such as the bureaucratic class and the landlord class who need to be transformed following the confiscation and reallocation of their property. The latter categories of citizens do not enjoy the rights of the people, but have to perform the duties of citizens.[11]

This difference was further consolidated by Mao's theory of contradictions. In his 1957 speech entitled "On the Correct Handling of Contradictions Among the People," Mao Zedong expounded the thesis that all the contradictions in Chinese society could be categorized either as hostile contradictions between the people and their enemies or as non-hostile differences among the people. The former kind, antagonistic contradictions of a political nature, were to be solved by the dictatorship; the latter kind, contradictions among the people whose basic interests are identical, in practice were to be solved by persuasion and education.[12] This distinction between the people and their enemies virtually invalidated the concept of citizen and citizenship, even if the concept was written into the constitution and national laws.

Consequently, the classification of the citizens of the PRC into "the people" and "the enemies" and the simultaneous use of the terms "people" and "citizens" to refer to those with PRC nationality confused the idea of citizenship and prevented the development of citizenship consciousness in China. To be a citizen would not necessarily be as good as being a member of the people—a citizen could be a criminal or a bad element, whereas it would always be safe to be one of the people. In the Mao years when people were frequently forced to identify their stances on important issues, this difference was of great significance. Most people, for the sake of survival, would identify themselves as members of the people rather than as citizens because failure to enlist as a member of the people would by default result in their aligning with the enemies.

Furthermore, the distinction between the people and the enemies also provided support for the theory behind the people's democratic dictatorship. If there were no enemies, the role of the people's democratic dictatorship would be lost. Since enemies are also citizens, some citizens will inevitably rule over other citizens. That is, "people citizens" would rule over "enemy citizens."

Constitutional Provisions

The ideological difference between the people and citizens is reflected in the PRC constitutions. All four PRC constitutions as well as the Common Program used the concepts of both "people" and "citizen," with the former referring to the good elements of society and the latter, both the good and bad elements. In the 1949 Common Program the terms "people" and "citizen" were both used, with the definition of people being much more narrowly defined than in subsequent constitutions.[13] Article 7 of the Common Program did not regard the following groups as belonging to the camp of the people: Nationalist war criminals, major counter-revolutionaries, ordinary reactionaries, feudal landlords, and bureaucratic capitalists. The 1954 constitution also made use of the concepts of "people" and "citizen." Article 19 of that constitution listed traitors and counter-revolutionaries as the targets for suppression, while feudal landlords and bureaucratic capitalists were targets for deprivation of political rights.[14] The 1975 constitution during the Cultural Revolution emphasized the need for further class struggle and revolution in China after it had entered into a new socialist era. It also utilized the concepts of "people" and "citizen," with more categories of individuals becoming ineligible for inclusion in the camp of the people. Article 14 of the 1975 constitution listed traitors and counter-revolutionaries as the targets for suppression, and specified landlords, rich peasants, reactionary capitalists, and other bad elements as targets for deprivation of political rights.[15] The 1978 constitution did not make many changes to the provisions of the 1975 constitution regarding the enemies of the people. Article 18 of the 1978 constitution added one new category of enemy, the so-called "new bourgeois elements," who were also to be punished.[16] The 1982 constitution continued using the concepts of "people" and "citizen," even though the definition of the people was extended to include all Chinese, except those who had been in trouble with the law or had difficulty in accepting the official ideology.[17]

II. The Leading–Led Mentality in the Constitutions and the Principle of Equality Before the Law

The 1949 revolution had as its ideal that the party would lead the Chinese people toward a society where neither classes nor exploitation would exist, and where every Chinese person would equally be able to enjoy a happy life and freedom. Before long, however, the party-state realized that it would be difficult for China to move immediately into the Communist stage. A pre-Communist stage, that is, a socialist stage, was needed, in which people could be treated differently—some as leaders, others as followers, and a few as enemies. Constant and continuing campaigns led by the vanguard were needed to construct a new society and transform the bad elements of the citizenry.

The idea that a group of people would serve as a vanguard leading the whole country toward a better life necessarily resulted in the division of people into the leaders and the led, similar to the traditional pattern of the rulers and the ruled. This leading–led mentality prevented the modern concept of citizen participation from taking hold in China. It also served to justify the supervision or regulation of citizens' activities by the state to the extent that the government considered appropriate.

While this leading–led mentality is apparent in all the PRC constitutions, some degree of change has occurred. In the Common Program, it was explicitly stipulated in Article 1 that the PRC would carry out the people's dictatorship led by the working class, based on an alliance of workers and peasants. No provision for the CCP leadership was made. The 1954 constitution repeated and clarified this provision of Article 1 of the Common Program with concise language. In its preamble, the 1954 constitution, for the first time, recorded the leading role of the CCP in the victory won by the PRC, but it did not explicitly stipulate the role of the CCP in future endeavors. The 1975 constitution stipulated the subjection of the Chinese people to the absolute leadership of the CCP and the state. Its preamble deified the CCP and its then paramount leader, Mao Zedong, making them supreme. Although the working class was still regarded as the leading force in the country, the CCP was poised to take over direct control. Article 26 of the 1975 constitution stated that the basic rights and duties of PRC citizens were to support the Communist Party and socialism and to obey the constitution and laws. The 1982 constitution, in contrast, was less direct in confirming the leading–led mentality. It had no provision for the role of the CCP in the main body of the constitution. Rather, it maintained in its preamble that the Chinese people under the leadership of the CCP had attained the victories and achievements of the PRC, and that the Chinese people would continue to be led by the CCP in future endeavors to build socialism. Subsequent amendments to the 1982 constitution have maintained the basic tone, adding one more eternal leader, Deng Xiaoping, as a source of ideology.

At the same time, PRC constitutions have also endorsed the idea of equality before the law. The 1954 constitution introduced the principle of equality before the law into the Chinese constitutional system. Article 85 of the 1954 constitution states that all citizens of the PRC are equal before the law. The 1954 Organic Law of the People's Courts also stipulated that in applying the law the people's courts should treat all citizens as equals, regardless of differences in their minority group, race, gender, profession, social status of origin, religious belief, education, property ownership, or years of residence. This principle, however, was discarded from the 1975 and 1978 constitutions. In the 1975 constitution the equal enjoyment of citizens' rights was not considered appropriate for the socialist period, and the existence of classes and class struggle was seen as being necessary. The 1978 constitution retained much of the radical thinking that had marked previous constitutions, with emphasis still on classes and class struggle.

The 1982 constitution revived the principle of equality before the law and made it more precise in three clauses stating that all persons holding the nationality of the PRC are citizens of the PRC, are equal before the law, and enjoy rights. Yet at the same time they are expected to perform duties prescribed by the constitution and the law.

The provision in the constitution for the leading–led mentality in conjunction with the principle of equality before the law poses a structural dilemma for citizenship consciousness and practice, which has undermined the constitution's function to protect citizens' rights and promote citizenship.

III. The Changing Substance of Citizens' Rights in the Constitutions

The 1954 constitution stipulated broadly the rights and obligations of citizens. It specified first the citizens' rights, followed by their obligations, reflecting the philosophy that rights precede duties. The section on citizens' rights followed the sequence of provisions on political rights, civil rights, and economic, cultural, and social rights. The scope of the rights stipulated is similar to that of the 1982 constitution. In contrast, the 1975 constitution narrowed the scope of citizens' rights considerably. It eliminated the principles of equality before the law, freedom of movement, the right to engage in scientific and cultural research, and other important rights. It also abandoned the sequence of placing political freedom first, followed by economic, cultural, and social rights. It did introduce some new rights, however, such as freedom of correspondence, the right to strike, freedom to have or not to have religious beliefs, freedom to propagate atheism, and, most important, the "four great freedoms." The 1978 constitution restored most of the provisions of the 1954 constitution on citizens' rights, with the major exception of the principle of equality before the law. It also affirmed the "four great freedoms" introduced in the 1975 constitution.

The 1982 PRC constitution, which is currently in force, stipulates an extensive list of citizens' rights. These include the right to equality before the law; political rights and freedoms, such as electoral rights and the freedom of speech, publication, assembly, association, procession, and demonstration; the right to lodge complaints and charges against state organs or functionaries and the right to compensation for infringement of their citizens' rights by state organs or functionaries; religious freedom; personal freedom; social and economic rights, such as the right to work and rest; cultural and educational rights, such as the right to receive an education and engage in scientific research and literary, artistic, and cultural pursuits; rights relating to women and the family; and finally, rights of Chinese people living abroad or returned from overseas.[18] It is apparent that Marshall's three types of citizenship rights are all incorporated in this list.[19]

The Rise and Demise of the "Four Great Freedoms"

The "four great freedoms," namely the freedom to speak out, air views freely, hold great debates, and write big-character posters, were first introduced as part of the Anti-rightist movement of 1957, and they became important forms of civil struggle in the Cultural Revolution. They were written into the 1975 constitution and became special home-grown rights for the Chinese people until they were abolished in 1980 during constitutional revision. A brief discussion of these special rights will serve to illustrate how strongly ideological changes have influenced changes in the conception of citizenship in China.

As political instruments, the "four great freedoms" were first systematically summarized and promoted by Mao Zedong. In his speech at the Third Plenary Session of the CCP Eighth Central Committee in 1957, Mao commented that the "four great freedoms" were a product of cooperation between the CCP and the Rightists. He held that these freedoms had three merits: first, they were most suitable for mobilizing the masses and raising their consciousness of responsibility; second, they were conducive to overcoming subjectivism, bureaucratism, and arbitrary command, and to enabling the cadres to mingle with the masses; third, they brought socialist democracy into full play and hence were a great development in the democratic tradition of the CCP. He concluded that the "four great freedoms" were the solution to questions of all types, great or small, concerning revolution or construction, class struggle or disputes among the people.[20]

In subsequent years the "four great freedoms" became widely practiced political institutions and extra-legal rights conferred by the CCP. In the CCP Central Committee's Decision on the Great Proletarian Cultural Revolution, passed at the Eleventh Plenary Session of the Eighth Congress of the CCP on August 8, 1966, the "four great freedoms" were reiterated as forms for mass struggle. This decision ultimately found its way into the 1975 constitution. If the 1975 constitution sanctified the "four great freedoms" by pronouncing them "new forms of socialist revolution created by the masses of the people," then the 1978 constitution made them home-grown rights to be enjoyed by the people of the PRC.

Of course, not all CCP leaders were equally enthusiastic about these special rights. Deng Xiaoping, for one, disliked them from the start. He and Liu Shaoqi, who were at that time in charge of the daily work of the Central Committee of the CCP, attempted to constrain the spread of the "four great freedoms." They tried to discourage the practice of posting big-character posters on the streets, arguing that it was detrimental to keeping the work of the CCP confidential. However, having encountered strong opposition from Mao and his followers, they abandoned their efforts.

When Deng Xiaoping returned to power in late 1978, he was resolute on the fate of the "four great freedoms." In 1979, unconstitutionality was not an issue or even yet a concept in China. So despite the fact that the 1978 constitution was still in effect, the 1979 PRC Criminal Law in its Article 145 criminalized the use of big-character or small-character posters to publicly inflict insults or defamation. This was the beginning of the process of making the "four great freedoms" illegal. In a speech given on January 6, 1980, entitled "Current Situation and Tasks," Deng Xiaoping completely rejected the "four great freedoms":

It is the firm policy of our party to persistently expand democracy and develop the legal system. But as with China's modernization, democracy and the legal system cannot be put into practice by the method of the Great Leap Forward or the method of "speaking out freely and airing one's views fully" . . . The "four great freedoms"— that is, speaking out freely, airing one's views fully, writing big-character posters, and holding great debates—have been written into the constitution. But when we sum up our historical experience, we have to recognize that, taken as a whole, these practices have never played a positive role. The masses should have the full right and opportunity to express responsible criticisms to their leaders and to make constructive suggestions, but "speaking out freely and airing one's views fully" is evidently not the proper way to do that. Therefore, in the light of long practice and in accordance with the opinion of the great majority of the cadres and masses, the Central Committee is going to submit to the Standing Committee of the National People's Congress and the coming session of the National

People's Congress a proposal that the "four great freedoms" provision be deleted from the constitution.[21]

Following Deng Xiaoping's speech, in February 1980 the "four great freedoms" were formally abolished by the Decision on Revising Article 45 of the Constitution of the People's Republic of China passed by the Third Plenary Session of the Fifth National People's Congress of the PRC. The 1982 constitution further affirmed the elimination of the "four great freedoms" from the Chinese political and legal lexicon.

The Relative Importance of Citizens and the State

The comparative importance of the state in relation to its citizens has also changed over the years. As reflected in China's consitutions, there has been at least a partial liberation of the citizens from absolute subjugation to the state. The 1954, 1975, and 1978 constitutions placed the provisions for citizens' rights after the chapter on state organization or near the end of the document; the 1982 constitution, however, placed them before the chapter on the state. This symbolic shift may reflect the changing attitude of the government toward the relationship between the state and its citizens. Some scholars have even suggested that this change may have been more significant than it appears—it is not a mere structural change, but reflects changes in the value and conception of citizens' rights and obligations. Placing the provisions for state structure before the provisions for citizens' rights indicates that the state is more important than its citizens, while the reverse arrangement indicates the opposite view.[22] In the context of the Chinese mentality, where sequence and ordering are important, this argument may be justified.

IV. Enforcement of the Constitutional Provisions for Citizens' Rights

The constitutional guarantees for citizens' rights provided by the 1982 constitution are difficult to implement not only because of restrictive provisions in the same constitution,[23] but also because of the lack of a constitutional enforcement apparatus. China at the end of the twentieth century still did not have a constitutional court, nor a single filed case having to do with the constitution. Although each year on December 4 China commemorates the promulgation of the 1982 constitution, and in Shanghai, a Constitution Week is devoted to the study of the constitution,[24] without constitutional litigation, the constitution is only a piece of paper. Interviews have revealed that ordinary people still do not identify with the constitution.[25] Another reason for the populace's indifference to the constitution is the fact that the constitution is not the ultimate authority in the Chinese political and legal system. Even though the CCP has not been granted such a power or function in the constitution, it frequently revises and amends the constitution to suit its own political goals. All proposals for amending the 1982 constitution since its promulgation have been made by the CCP.

Under these circumstances where constitutional litigation is lacking, the enforcement of citizens' rights provided for in the constitution has to be performed by ordinary laws and by the workings of the general legal system. Over the past two decades China has established a number of laws and regulations that directly or indirectly address issues concerning citizens' rights.[26] The judiciary, which includes both courts and prosecutors, has also grown in size and substance.[27]

Since 1978, China has restored the people's courts, the people's procuratorates, and the arbitration system, all of which were demolished during the Cultural Revolution. The legal profession and legal education have developed rapidly. A number of reforms were also initiated, such as open trials (except in political cases), popularization of legal knowledge, and provision of legal aid services, which have led to members of the public being more aware of their rights and of legal procedures. At least in theory, China has established a preliminary legal system, which is indispensable for citizenship formation and participation.

In addition, the post-Mao government has enacted a number of administrative laws, including the Administrative Litigation Law of the PRC (1989), the Administrative Penalty Law of the PRC (1996), and the Administrative Supervision Law of the PRC (1997), and has also established administrative tribunals. These provide access to the law and allow citizens to obtain redress if their rights are encroached upon. People have reportedly used these laws to sue government personnel who have encroached on their citizens' rights.[28] The Law of the PRC on State Compensation, promulgated in May 1994, requires that if state agencies or members of their personnel infringe on the lawful rights or interests of a citizen, they should compensate him or her. Since the implementation of this law, people's courts at the intermediate and national levels have set up compensation committees, which have settled hundreds of cases claiming state compensation. A considerable number resulted in decisions that compensation should be paid by state organizations.[29] Effective since October 1, 1999, the Administrative Reconsideration Law of the PRC allows citizens to bring lawsuits against various policy documents issued by government agencies at different administrative levels, if they feel that such documents have encroached on their rights.[30] This can be considered an important step toward letting the law take precedence over policy. In addition, televised public trials and the monitoring of sessions of the local people's congresses in certain regions are also signs of the state's positive attitude toward active participation by citizens.

These changes in the legal system show the state's increased willingness to protect the rights of citizens. The state seems to have accepted some legal limits on its power, as well as the fact that citizens should be able to sue its working personnel. Such developments have created some space for the promotion of citizenship consciousness and awareness of rights. Nevertheless, the legal framework that would enable citizens to participate in the management of their political and social life still remains largely on paper.

The reforms of the legal and constitutional system, therefore, should not create the misleading impression that the effort to achieve citizenship rights in China has reached a new stage, or that there are unlimited opportunities for promoting citizenship in China. Despite the new and potentially transformative legal developments discussed above, deep-rooted problems in China's political psyche and reality continue to hinder the growth of citizenship consciousness and the practice of citizens' rights.

V. Economic Reform and Citizenship

Ideally, all citizens of a given country should enjoy citizenship, as the right to have rights, equally. History has shown, however, that this has not been the case. The opportunity to participate in the Greek *polis,* for example, did not extend to everyone. Women, children, resident foreigners, some laborers, and slaves were excluded from the "privileges of rule" and were not citizens. Some critics say that even in a democratic society, citizenship cannot be equally enjoyed because of social and economic stratification.[31]

Although egalitarianism accompanied China's Communist revolution, all PRC citizens were not placed on an equal footing. Under the proletarian dictatorship and later the people's democratic dictatorship, PRC citizens were clearly divided into different categories according to political, economic, regional, and educational status. The notorious household registration system had the effect of institutionalizing the unequal enjoyment of citizenship in China. On one hand, the reforms since 1978 have created more space and the legal framework needed for the promotion of citizenship; on the other hand, instead of eliminating the existing stratification of citizenship, they have extended and deepened the existing gaps between different layers of society. One could argue that despite the stratification of social and economic rights, citizenship could still be meaningful if political rights are guaranteed. It is true that political participation helps to advance social and economic rights and eventually the equal enjoyment of citizenship, but it is also true that unequal social and economic rights hinder political participation. This is a difficult dilemma to reconcile in any society.

Chinese economic and legal reforms have in general followed a pragmatic approach in which government policy precedes and sometimes conflicts with the law. These conflicts between policy and law exist in the realm of citizenship, where they play a negative role. Although the formal legal framework is intended to provide for citizenship to be enjoyed equally, some of the policies implemented before and since the economic reforms often point in the opposite direction.

The economic reforms, which began in 1978, are discriminatory in nature. They were tried first at the local level and then practiced at the national level, which allowed selected regions, industries, and persons to enjoy special privileges at the expense of other regions, industries, and persons. The creation of the Special Economic Zones and open cities, along with the preferential economic and political policies accorded them, led to regional and income inequalities and discrimination among citizens residing in different regions of the PRC. The economic policies designed to encourage the investment of foreign capital, the establishment of foreign enterprises, and their employment of Chinese citizens have widened the disparity between low-wage earners working for Chinese state companies and the better-paid employees of foreign enterprises. The conflict between politically stringent policies and economically relaxed policies has also led to polarization between the politically loyal but economically poor and the politically indifferent but economically well off. This increasing economic polarization of Chinese society has turned the politically loyal into rent seekers, directly contributing to rampant official corruption.

As a result, PRC citizens have been divided into de facto classes, categories, or groups, enjoying or not enjoying different rights and duties.[32] Stratification of citizenship may also be found elsewhere, but in China this phenomenon has its own unique characteristics. There are privileged Chinese citizens, for example, who not only enjoy the rights prescribed and allowed by law and policy, but also receive various types of special treatment beyond these rights. Communist Party members are among the politically privileged with access to the inner circles of political power. The economically privileged through their relational networks also are able to deploy the economic resources of the country, administered in the name of the state and the people. The geographically privileged who happen to be residents of special areas such as Shenzhen also have access to state-sanctioned resources. Their privileges hinge on good fortune bestowed on them by state fiat.

At the other extreme, there are people who not only lack access to resources but also are not aware of what it means to be citizens. These are mainly peasants who live in the vast countryside of China and are tied to their small portion of land. Even Mao's radical campaigns aimed at transforming them did little to change their citizenship consciousness and sense of identity, although the campaigns did make them obedient to Mao's will. These people represent the majority of Chinese citizens.

Even though the household registration system was eliminated in 2001, the divide between urban and rural citizenship will remain for some time. Because of that system, citizenship means completely different things to urban citizens and rural citizens, with the former usually in a more advantageous position. While the rights of rural citizens to move and choose where to reside had been limited for several decades,[33] the reforms and the move to the market loosened government control over freedom of movement to urban areas.

Yet, in urban areas, workers in bankrupt state enterprises are losing their jobs. Once considered "masters of the country," as the PRC constitution refers to workers and peasants,[34] in the post-Mao era they are humiliated citizens. The economic reforms in the last two decades of the twentieth century have in various ways humbled the masters of the country, with massive layoffs of workers from state-owned enterprises.

There are alienated citizens in all nations who receive whatever protection the state provides and are uninterested in political participation. They regard the state as alien and choose not to participate politically.[35] Alienated citizens in China are typically those who have lost confidence in the political ideals they used to embrace. After experiencing all kinds of political and personal crises during successive political campaigns, including the Cultural Revolution, they feel betrayed by the government.

Other groups of differentiated citizens are women, who are considered weaker than men, and minority groups which are given varying degrees of protection by the state, provided they forgo certain political rights such as the right to self-determination. There are also unwanted citizens who are political dissidents, not willingly receptive to the leadership of the CCP or ready to identify themselves with the existing political and social order. These citizens are jailed, restricted from leaving China, or prohibited from returning to China if they go overseas. There are even "bargaining chip" citizens—a few well-known dissidents whom the government uses as bargaining chips in its relationships with foreign governments, human rights groups, and international non-governmental organizations.

Conclusion

The concept of citizenship reached China almost a century ago.[36] Because there was no concept of citizenship or of individual rights in China's historical heritage[37] and because the Communist political system enforces a strong state presence, citizenship, whether as a legal status or as voluntary participation in political and social life, mainly entails fostering citizenship consciousness, the advancement of individual rights, and the growth of civil associations against state control. To the extent that the public realm in China has been monopolized by the state, every gesture of withdrawal of the state from the public realm can be interpreted as providing a possibility for citizenship to grow.

While acknowledging that the state as an omnipotent, abstract, ultimate authority still controls China's social and political life, the Chinese government today is more accommodating toward citizens' rights than at any other time in PRC history. The government's changing attitude toward citizens' rights has been reflected by the changing meaning of citizenship as expressed in China's various constitutions. Recent events in China, such as village elections and the emergence of quasi–non-governmental organizations, also reflect progress toward citizenship consciousness and practice. Nevertheless, there are still conceptual, ideological, economic, and policy obstacles that are likely to prevent broader understanding of the concept of citizenship and hence discourage more active participation.

If the concept of citizenship is to be effectively incorporated into Chinese political life and discourse, conceptual difficulties such as the confusion between the terms "people" and "citizens" and the leading–led mentality must be resolved. The perception that the concept of "people" is superior to the concept of "citizens" is detrimental to the equal exercise of citizens' rights. Moreover, citizenship, the right to have rights, could be more easily attained if the leading–led mentality gave way to equal and voluntary participation. Instead of being constantly reminded of the correct leadership of the party-state, PRC citizens could be defined as autonomous, independent, and responsible individuals in political and social life, acting on their own decisions.

Citizenship entails much more than the government's moves toward a market economy and well-administered laws. It requires a strong sense of individual rights, well-established community values, and a stable and rational social framework. All of these take time and effort to develop. A universalistic and transcendental civil enlightenment may be the prerequisite for true citizenship to take hold on Chinese soil.

12 | Law and the Gendered Citizen

The film *The Story of Qiu Ju* traces the journey of a young village woman through the tiers of the Chinese legal system in her quest for justice against an arbitrary village chief. Like most Chinese stories, this film is subtle and ambiguous in its messages—in this instance, about the efficacy of legal formalism and the meaning of justice. Yet, not the least of the film's multiple messages is the fact that Qiu Ju is an ordinary village woman determined to assert her rights, and the target of her legal complaint is a male village chief. Selling her pepper crop on several occasions to finance her trips, Qiu Ju seeks redress not only within the traditional informal and extrajudicial dispute resolution mechanisms of the village and clan, but also beyond, to the formal and judicial authority of the nascent Chinese legal system.

That a member of one of the most vulnerable groups in Chinese society would seek legal redress against this symbol of traditional power highlights the role that law plays in the complicated relationships among individuals, civil organizations, and the state, and in particular, the shifting hierarchy of gender politics in the post-Mao era. That Qiu Ju is able to finance her efforts to assert her rights through the selling of her farm products, as allowed by the newly reformed market economy, suggests the undeniable link between economy and law. As such, then, Qiu

Ju's journey may also be the journey of economic and legal reforms in China, and of the way that reforms may be changing traditional values of the personal and duties to the market-economy values of the impersonal and rights. What rights Qiu Ju may have, how she asserts those rights, and how she may be transformed by the process are questions relating not only to dispute resolution, but also to identity formation and the changing concepts of citizenship in China.

This chapter explores the interrelation between gender, law, and citizenship in the context of China in the midst of its reconstruction and transition to a market economy. What are the contested rights and the attending identity of a Chinese citizen? What is the "instituted process" within which we must understand the development of citizenship rights in China? Are Chinese citizens exercising their rights through law and defining their own citizenship rights not from the top down but rather from the bottom up?

An important issue is how women's rights as citizens are being implemented through the legal system in China. This is significant because the test of a legal system is its ability to protect the most vulnerable; women arguably make up the subgroup of the Chinese population with the most ambiguous relationship to the Chinese state. How women have used the legal process to assert their rights is informative about citizenship formation generally as well as the role of legal reforms in this construction.

The picture that emerges at the end of the twentieth century is complex. Market development in China has led to a decrease in some spheres in rights for women, but also, at times, to an increase in autonomy. The attendant changes in the legal system have not only created opportunities for the assertion of legal rights but have increasingly placed responsibility for the assertion of those rights on individuals, and thus fostered a sense of "rights consciousness." Women who are financially independent appear to be taking advantage of this opportunity.

At the same time, however, the assertion of rights by Chinese women citizens appears to be more for social than political rights, more to seek freedom from local abuses than from national control, more by financially independent women than by financially dependent women, and more among urban citizens than among rural citizens. To the extent that the assertion of legal rights remains dependent on the development of greater institutional support, even this nascent rights consciousness is in jeopardy. The guarantee of some rights requires continuing involvement of the state in some areas because the free market does not always ensure total protection of rights.[1]

Law and Citizenship

With a global economy and proliferating internal migration, the boundaries of community membership, individual identity, and justice are in flux in China. T. H. Marshall defines citizenship as "a personal status consisting of a body of universal rights and duties held equally by all legal members of a nation state."[2] As a personal status, citizenship equalizes by according its members increasing rights, in the form of political, civil, and social rights. In classical republican thought, the status of citizen implies a measure of independence from governmental powers. Most citizenship theorists assume a symbiotic relationship between capitalism and the birth of modern citizenship rights. The idea is that "the right to private property, as guaranteed by the rule of law, can create a sphere of private autonomy in which citizens can operate without fear of public intervention."[3]

To understand the concept of citizenship, one must understand not only the rights associated with the status, but also the practices associated with those rights. As argued by Margaret Somers, citizenship is an "instituted process," that is, a set of institutionally embedded social practices.[4] As such, citizenship rights are not "ready made" rights granted by the state, but rather are contested membership rules transmitted via national laws and institutions. But whether or not these laws are converted into actual universal rights depends on the local contexts—the social and political places in which they are activated.[5] In looking at rights protection in China, then, one needs to examine the substantive formal legal provisions establishing such rights, and also the institutions, practices, and procedures provided for the assertion of such rights and interests.

One possible site for the assertion of rights is through law and the formal legal process. Even as law produces and identifies cultural meanings as an aspect of its powers, courts can be "a site for performances in which problems are named and solutions determined."[6] Adjudication can be a form of social ordering, a way in which the relations of people to one another are governed and regulated.[7] This approach emphasizes the centrality of law as a symbolic and cultural system, one that is constitutive of the larger social order and, at the same time, suffused by that order. Law occasionally provides opportunities to challenge the power of the ruling class.[8]

These theories of law and citizenship pose several questions in the context of Chinese women. Does the legal system imply for women in China "a measure of independence from government powers"? Are women's rights not only "transmitted via national laws," but activated as an "instituted process," that is, a set of institutionally embedded social practices? Are the Chinese courts a place "in which problems are named and solutions determined" for and by Chinese women or for and by any Chinese citizen? The emerging picture is complex and challenges some of the assumptions underlying T. H. Marshall's historical definition of citizenship.

Areas of Concern to Chinese Women

Just as we cannot generalize about women as a "category," we cannot generalize about all third-world women or all Chinese women. There is the particular danger of Western feminists over-essentializing the "Other"—usually poor, nonwhite, third world—while holding out the West as a norm with which to criticize the Other as wanting.[9] Chinese women have a multiplicity of identities and voices, leading to a range of responses to the state and its demands. Older women, for example, after experiencing pre-revolutionary feudal patriarchy, will hesitate to break from the state in their strategies for equality, while younger women will push beyond the state's definition of them as women. Despite these differences, however, all Chinese women must face the common challenge of gender inequality. Chinese women share with one another "a history of human oppression based on gender and treatment as the homogeneous and subhuman object of a dominant patriarchal ideology and its institutions of power."[10] Thus the term "Chinese women" may still be useful as an analytical category.

Since the start of China's economic reforms and reentry into the global economy, a variety of social problems have emerged or re-emerged, posing a threat to Chinese women's status and well-being, including their rights as equal citizens in the Chinese state. The problems may be traced to what might be called the "commodification of the feminine" and take form in two contrasting trends: (1) the migration of women out of their native localities for labor and for marriage, which has forced women to transcend the local to the regional and national; and (2) the inverse migration of women from the public workplace to the private space of home and hearth. Both these trends have tended to result in greater isolation for women, a higher incidence of poor health and suicide, greater threats of violence against women both in the family and in the workplace, and greater family instability with higher rates of divorce.

The first of these trends, the outward migration of Chinese women from local to regional to national, is a recent phenomenon. One can imagine China as one huge nation in migration. Chinese sources report that 50 million women have given up farming for industrial-sector labor. Among these millions are the women, collectively known as *dagongmei* (laboring sisters), who have migrated to cities to work in the exploding numbers of foreign-invested, township, and private enterprises. Women workers constitute the majority of migrant workers in the factories that have been the focus of the economic reforms. In some factories in the special economic zones, they constitute 90 percent of the labor force.[11]

This outward labor migration renders women especially vulnerable to male exploitation because it places young uneducated rural women under the authority of urban male factory supervisors. Moreover, since these migrating women often take non-contractual, less desirable temporary jobs without urban residence registration, they work without the social benefits normally guaranteed for state workers.[12] While it may be argued that such jobs are better than no jobs at all, what is problematic is the societal stratification created by these jobs, with women workers consistently at the bottom rung. The combination of abusive bosses and limited state benefits thus subjects women to poor working conditions, discrimination, sexual abuse, and harassment.

Rural women are also migrating outward from rural to other regions for marriage. About 30 percent of migrating women in China do so to marry, and this migration is generally from poor areas.[13]

This migration is further fueled by the resurgent practice of buying and selling rural women as brides, a practice that the government disapproves but is unable to halt.[14] At the border, where many young women congregate, a young woman is worth from $250 to $800.[15] Even in the best circumstances, out-migrating women cannot significantly draw on the support of their natal families, which results in greater isolation and possible abuse. At its worst, the buying and selling of rural women represents a literal example of the "commodification" of women.

The second form of migration taking place in China is the inverse migration of women from the public to the private sphere. This has meant a decline of women's participation not only in the formal political sphere, but also significantly in the public workplace.[16] China's economic reforms have led to redundancies in the work force, with women workers bearing the brunt of this change. They are often the last to be hired and the first to be laid off.[17] By the end of 1997, about 53 percent of the 5.768 million jobless people who had registered with their local governments were women.[18] While constituting only 39 percent of China's work force, women constituted nearly 61 percent of its 10 million laid-off workers. Moreover, 75 percent of the women laid off were still unemployed after one year, in contrast to 50 percent of their male counterparts.[19]

In the early 1990s there was even an official "return home policy," as women were called to serve the state by returning to the home and hearth. The growing commodification of women as "beauty objects" encouraged this inverse migration. As beauty objects, women are both consumers and products, but are relegated to the roles of wives and mistresses rather than equal workers "holding up half the sky," as they supposedly did during the Mao era. This view has led to women being valued simply for their youth and beauty and serves as a justification for denying them employment: women at age 40 have been termed "too old" or "too fat" to be hired.[20]

The relocation of women to the private sphere of home may be adding to women's vulnerability to violence and loss of financial autonomy. There have been growing reports of family violence.[21] According to a 1994 survey by the Beijing Society for Research on Marriage and the Family, one-fifth of the wives in 2,100 families surveyed had been abused by their spouses. Extramarital affairs have increased, as has the number of divorces.[22] In a divorce, women can suffer both financial and emotional setbacks because they often receive the short end of property and housing divisions.

The status of Chinese women today challenges the assumption that markets will inevitably lead to greater citizenship rights. Dorothy Solinger has pointed out that market reforms and the migration of workers generally have led to the formation of a "virtual layering of types of citizens in cities," with peasants in the city in the position of second-class citizens.[23] This "virtual layering" is even more complicated when examined through a gender lens. Intermixed with the secondary status faced by peasants in the cities are peasant women who face the double bind of being both women and peasants.

Migrant women workers face the added obstacle of gender discrimination in the workplace. They are likely to experience the greatest deprivations of rights and occupy the lowest position in the hierarchy of citizens. In contrast to the equalizing term *gongren* or worker, the term *dagongmei* given to migrating rural women workers implies a lesser status: *dagong* means the "selling of labor" and *mei* refers to a single, unmarried, and young sister.[24] At times, even the Chinese government's hiring preference reflects the pyramid of "citizen" status. On one Beijing campus, for example, government hiring first solicits male workers with urban residence, then male workers from out of town, followed by female workers with residency, and last, female workers from out of town.[25]

In sum, Chinese women face an increase in reported violence (including domestic violence), a higher rate of divorce, and discrimination in hiring, firing, reemployment, and pay. This is in addition to the continuing problems of education and health. For example, Chinese women still constitute 70 percent of the nation's illiterate population (since rural girls are often kept at home to help with the farms), and experience a high suicide rate.[26] The Chinese government has acted to remedy some of the dilemmas created by the market reforms, as described below. Nevertheless, the market reforms in collusion with the Chinese government have unintentionally opened up new spaces for women even as they are closing off others.

Citizenship as a Set of Formal Legal Rights

The Chinese government has adopted a number of formal, though arguably incomplete, substantive legal protections for women. These rights are more in the nature of "affirmative" social, civil, and economic rights than "negative" political rights to be enforced against the government. To begin with, women's equality and civil rights are guaranteed both by the Constitution and the civil code.[27] Several pieces of national legislation enacted in the 1980s also contain specific protection for women: these include the Marriage Law (revised in 2001), the Inheritance Law, the Labor Law, and the Law of the PRC on Maternal and Infant Health Care. In addition, in 1995 the Chinese state enacted the *Funü Quanli Baozhang Fa* (Law of the PRC on the Protection of the Rights and Interests of Women), known colloquially as the Women's Rights Law. This law, enacted in anticipation of the 1995 U.N. World Conference on Women, serves as what might be called "posterboard" legislation, as a public statement of the Chinese government's commitment to women's equality.

It is in the area of the family and marriage that women have received the most formal legal protection. Both the Women's Rights Law and the Marriage Law set forth protections for women's freedom in marriage. The laws also provide for equality between men and women in property ownership in marriage[28] and inheritance.[29] This protection is especially defined for rural women, who face great threats of discrimination in the distribution of village land. On divorce, Chinese laws also provide that special protection be given to women and children in the division of property[30] and housing in divorce.[31] These laws even prohibit "the husband from filing for divorce within a year of the wife's pregnancy or delivery."[32] Despite these protections, rising divorce rates in the reform years, compounded by the shortage of housing, have left many divorced women without housing. This prompted the Supreme People's Court to issue further interpretations such as "Concerning the People's Court Adjudication of Property Divisions in a Divorce," which reaffirmed women's rights in housing division in a divorce.[33]

In the area of labor, in addition to the Labor Law applicable to both sexes,[34] the government has promulgated regulations specifically addressing problems faced by Chinese women in the reform years. These include prohibitions on discrimination in hiring, promotions, and layoffs, provisions for maternity leave, and protection for women's health.[35] The National People's Congress is even considering legislation that will punish sexual harassment in the workplace.[36]

With reference to bodily harm, the PRC Constitution prohibits the abuse of women, the elderly, and children.[37] Chinese laws and regulations also prohibit the abduction, sale, and kidnapping of women and children, and ban "organizing, forcing, inducing, accommodating and introducing women to prostitution."[38] The Revised Criminal Code specifically punishes traffickers, as well as buyers and officials who fail to rescue trafficking victims.[39] The newly amended Marriage Law, promulgated on April 28, 2001, specifically details available administrative remedies for victims of domestic violence ranging from mediation to administrative sanctions for perpetrators.

On the statute books, then, Chinese women seem to have substantial rights. Yet the danger exists that formal legal rights, along with the rhetoric of the powerful, are used to pay homage to human rights and dignity but, at the same time, to maintain an oppressive regime. Gender-differentiated laws can be criticized as stereotyping and defining the treatment of women along biological lines. Furthermore, Chinese legal reform efforts are not without their critics, and there are limits to the law as a route for achieving gender equality.

Specifically, Chinese legal reforms can be viewed as instrumentalist, serving more to implement state and party priorities than to preserve the rights of individuals. Consistent with socialist legality, which views law as a tool for social engineering, socialist law runs the risk of subordinating the protection of individual rights as secondary to the rights of the collective and state. This is particularly true in regard to gender equality, which has consistently been relegated to a lower priority than more pressing state goals—first the socialist revolution in the Mao era and then economic development in the post-Mao period. Implementation of women's rights provisions has thus been uneven and dependent on whether the protection is perceived as contrary to or consistent with present state goals. The goal of gender equality, for example, can be subordinated to the higher national goal of the one-child family. A woman worker who has a second child outside the mandates of the population control policy is not accorded the benefits provided by the labor and health regulations.

Law as reflective of institutional, cultural, and political values also retains patriarchal traditions. Under the guise of protecting women, law runs the danger of reinforcing the "natural" and traditional roles of women. This is particularly problematic in "protective" legislation for women, such as those in the labor area, which can work to reinforce the biology of women as mothers and wives rather than enhancing the choices for women as workers. Indeed, the Women's Rights Law itself asserts that there are "certain work categories or positions that are unfit for women."[40]

Finally, some question the efficacy of these laws on the grounds that they are nothing more than a set of normative principles to be inculcated through education rather than through strict rules of conduct backed by sanctions. For example, Chinese scholars have criticized the Women's Rights Law as being too broad and insufficiently detailed to be useful.[41] The law itself does not provide for any new private causes of action or any new penalties or remedies for violations of the law. Any lawsuit that seeks to vindicate the rights that the law enumerates must be based on another law. In practical terms, then, most women's groups and individuals are more likely to look to the Civil Code, the Marriage Law, the Labor Law, or the Inheritance Law rather than to the Women's Rights Law as the basis for asserting their rights.

These laws, however, do signal a change in the discussion of rights. Rhetorically, "rights and interests" are superseding "class," and terms like "rights and obligations" are making inroads into Chinese law and jurisprudence.[42] Thus, while some Chinese activists have viewed the Women's Rights Law as of limited use, others believe that the symbolic importance of a law affirming the rights of women should not be underestimated. The Women's Rights Law, as a piece of national legislation, and in the language of rights that it uses, helps to heighten the importance of women's rights in the minds of the general populace.

Citizenship as an Instituted Process

Although "rights talk" appears to be making inroads in Chinese legislation, the question still to be addressed is to what degree the language of rights has been translated into practice for average Chinese women. What do rights mean for them? Have these legal provisions been implemented, or have they remained only on paper? In what ways are Chinese women invoking the protection of these laws?

Answering these questions requires not simply a reiteration of the substantive provisions but also a discussion of the Chinese legal system in operation. It requires a consideration of the legal actors involved as well as the procedural changes that may affect the process of Chinese women seeking legal protection. Encouragingly, Chinese women are litigating in the courts, often against the odds, which suggests complex calculations on the part of women litigants and an interesting and changing role for the courts in China.

In an interesting blend of creative strategies, women are using law inside and outside the formal legal system to pursue their rights and interests. Chinese women bring lawsuits in the courts, petition administrative and supervisory organs, and appeal to the press. These blended strategies are in part a residue of traditional Maoist-Leninist ideology that relied on mass organizations (such as the residence or mediation committees) to resolve disputes. They are also a response to the reality that Chinese laws are sometimes unclear and Chinese courts unpredictable, requiring women litigants to resort to other arenas in addition to the courts.

Similarly, the laws themselves direct litigants to both informal and formal routes for redress. According to the Women's Rights Law, women whose rights have been violated can petition to the relevant administrative unit, or to women's organizations, or can file a complaint with the courts.[43] In seeking a divorce, a party may seek mediation through the "relevant administrative units" (residence committee, work unit, or marriage registration office of the Ministry of Civil Affairs) or may proceed directly to the courts.[44] In the area of labor disputes, a woman may apply to the dispute arbitration committee; if not satisfied with the result, she may file a lawsuit in court. This mix of options is illusory, however, because some sites for dispute resolution are withdrawing even as others are not yet in place. I visited several residence committees in 1999 in Guangzhou, for example, where committee workers could not even recall the last dispute they had mediated.

Increasingly, however, the Chinese state is encouraging the use of courts, which it sees as integral to a stable society and consistent with its goal of reining in local bureaucrats. In 1996, the Supreme People's Court decreed that Chinese courts should "further improve the work of trying civil cases, protect the civil rights and interests of citizens and legal persons according to the law, and promote the just, safe, civilized and healthy development of society."[45] This is certainly a far cry from the sentiments of the 1950s, when disputes were directed away from the formal legal system and handled informally.

To improve the working of courts, China is shifting from its traditional priority of substance first and procedure second to a more concrete focus on court process. Thus, while the first ten years (1979–1989) of China's legal reforms saw the enactment of primarily substantive legislation, the subsequent ten years saw greater attention being paid to the improvement of the legal process itself. Numerous legislative as well as experimental changes were put in place. These included an elaborate civil procedure law in 1991 to replace the provisional one; an administrative litigation act in 1990, which for the first time gave citizens a limited right to challenge illegal administrative decisions; and a revised criminal procedure law in 1997 which more clearly delineated the respective authorities of judges, prosecutors, and lawyers.

There has also been an effort to professionalize the legal profession, which has included increased training of lawyers and judges and the enactment of the first Law on Judges[46] (revised in 2001) and the Law on Lawyers in 1996.[47] Both laws attempted to move the qualifications for the legal profession away from political correctness to solid legal knowledge. A Legislation Law was enacted in 2000—detailing the process of formulating and promulgating legislation—and under discussion is a revision to the Organic Law of the People's Courts, which will restructure the court system.[48] These legislative activities suggest a growing recognition that law on paper alone cannot protect people's rights. The major issue at hand is the implementation of these laws and the institutional and procedural reforms needed to ensure proper implementation.

What is equally significant, China has been experimenting with aspects of the adversarial system with its focus on individual party autonomy to supplement its inquisitorial, civil-law-based legal system. The contemporary Chinese legal system is a blend of the continental civil-law legal system and traditional Chinese legal philosophy with an overlay of Marxist-Leninist-Maoist legal thought. This has meant that in the past, courts (and judges) have taken an active role in the investigation and adjudication of cases. In recent years, however, law enforcement has taken on a more individualistic tone with a reduction in state intervention and an increased reliance on the market in the provision of legal services and individual responsibility for the assertion of rights. Revised court procedures place increasing responsibility on individual litigants for bringing and proving a case.[49] Moving away from the civil-law inquisitorial tradition, Chinese law reforms specifically place the burden of presenting a case on individual litigants, rather than on the judge (and, hence, the state). The policy slogan in the Chinese courts is now *dangshiren zhuyi* (litigant's choice). Judges serve less as educators or counselors to resolve a "contradiction," and increasingly as arbiters in the resolution of a dispute brought before them. By placing greater responsibilities on individual litigants, the Chinese legal system is relying more on the market to provide justice and less on the state to step in to alleviate power differentials between litigants.[50]

With these changes, Chinese litigants are increasingly turning to the courts as a final arbiter of rights and interests. An indication of this phenomenon is the rate of civil litigation, which almost doubled from 1,455,130 cases filed in 1988 to 2,718,533 filed in 1995.[51] It is important to look at civil cases, as opposed to economic cases, because civil cases by and large are brought by individual ordinary citizens.

In 1995, civil cases filed in the Chinese courts rose by 14.04 percent from the year before. On the civil docket, marriage and family cases constituted close to 50 percent of the case load, and divorces constituted the majority of cases in this category.[52] In 1992, divorce cases constituted 86.01 percent of marriage and family cases, or 46.01 percent of the civil cases, nationwide.[53]

While civil cases rose by 70 percent between 1989 and 1996, cases brought to the People's Mediation Committee dropped by 21 percent in the same period.[54] Moreover, cases completed by internal mediation in the courts dropped from 71 percent in 1988 to 56 percent in 1995.[55] In divorce cases, for example, the proportion of judgments to dismissals was greater in 1996 than in 1988 (3.42:1 in 1996 as opposed to 2.85:1 in 1988), reflecting judges' growing willingness to decide cases.[56]

Certainly, one could draw a number of differing conclusions from these statistics. Both the rise in lawsuits and the resort to adjudication to settle disputes reflect the fast-changing economic and social order in China. This may also demonstrate self-interested promotion on the part of the courts. Undeniably, however, it could also represent the fact that, despite continuing problems in the courts, litigants sometimes receive justice.[57]

When we delve beneath the overall statistics, and focus on what kinds of cases women are bringing to the courts, they tend to coalesce around the civil and criminal realm and not the economic arena. Interviews with Chinese lawyers suggest that litigation involving women as plaintiffs (that is, as initiators of lawsuits rather than as defendants, as in criminal cases) usually concerns matters of marriage, family, and bodily injury. A recently published anthology of civil cases, selected for use in the training of Chinese judges, also bears this out.[58] In that anthology, women are the plaintiffs in only 17 of the 140 published civil cases. These cases involved marriage and family (5), property (4), torts (4), contract (2), labor (1), and land-use (1) disputes. As co-plaintiffs with men, women participated in 15 additional cases of the 140.[59]

There were notably few labor cases in which an individual woman worker challenged either state or company policies detrimental to her. The anthology includes only one case brought to court by a woman worker seeking relief from inappropriate withholding of her wages. While labor disputes must first be submitted for administrative resolution, this exhaustion requirement does not explain the paucity of litigated cases, since administrative decisions can be appealed to the courts. Either all labor bureaus are correctly deciding cases, or, more likely, women themselves understand the calculation involved in bringing cases that are less likely to be successful in the courts.[60]

Which women are bringing cases to the courts? One might expect intellectuals to be more likely to be aware of their rights and thus to be most active in bringing suits, but a study of divorce cases suggests the contrary. Professor Li Weisha's study in 1983 showed that women acted as plaintiffs in 69.74 percent of the 760 divorce cases filed in the Wuchang District Court. Among these, 74.16 percent had an educational level of junior high school or lower, and those who were workers or service providers made up 78.46 percent.[61] This trend was consistent with more recent interviews of women litigants, lawyers, and judges in Shanghai and Guangdong in 1998 and 1999.[62] The interviews revealed that intellectuals continue to view going to court as an unseemly process, whereas women workers are more likely to utilize lawyers and the formal court system.

Financial independence, rather than educational level, may be more significant to women's decisions in bringing suit. According to Professor Li, litigants tend to be those who "have their own income and are able to lead an independent life . . . These women are imperceptibly influenced every day by traditional culture, including traditional ideas on marriage . . . [and] they show a strong and non-traditional inclination for self-determination." Thus, scholars have noted that migration for some women has led to a limited measure of financial autonomy, such that these women are able to "buy out" of unhappy marriages.[63] To the extent that market reforms will increase women's financial independence, they will also likely increase women's assertion of rights and resort to the courts. A corollary of this is that urban women, who are more likely to be financially independent, will be more likely to assert their rights than rural women.

Litigating at the Borders of Social Change

The availability of the formal legal procedure of courts "can provide opportunities for participation and control in a political system" and make individuals fuller members of society.[64] Adjudication represents moments of conflict and the institutional and social content of those moments. As such, adjudication is not only a source of private dispute resolution, but also a process by which public rights are determined and articulated.[65]

However, the full implications of these adjudicative processes for citizenship rights are much more complex. Although the Chinese government maintains that it upholds the rule of law rather than the rule of man, Communist Party policy can still affect the outcomes of given cases. Constitutionally, it is the CCP that leads legal work, and hence court decisions should never conflict with party policy. Theoretically, the CCP cannot single out individual cases, but in practice, it does not have to since most judges are party members and are habitually sensitive to changing party policies.[66] Thus, individual cases are brought and adjudicated in the context of central state policy.

It is not surprising, then, that far fewer labor cases than family law matters are being brought by women plaintiffs to court. Labor cases more directly challenge the state goals of economic reforms and market efficiency, and thus are more likely to be relegated to administrative resolution. For many women, there may be a tacit understanding that social policies such as gender equality must yield to overriding economic goals. In recognizing this reality, women litigants are more likely to assert their rights as plaintiffs in private litigation involving marriage, divorce, or bodily harm, than in cases touching on more pressing public issues such as labor policies, where the defendant tends to be a powerful company or the state.

Even in the case of divorce, state policy may affect the availability of relief. In the early years of the People's Republic, official state policy discouraged divorces, and there were accounts of petitioners waiting over twenty years for a divorce petition to be granted. The 1980 Marriage Law ushered in an era of liberalization for divorces, with the result that divorce petitions could be obtained in as little as three months. Today, escalating divorce rates have once again alarmed the state, which views divorces as an unfortunate by-product of economic reforms and a threat to a stable society. This concern with rising divorce rates gave force to another round of revisions to the Marriage Law in 2001. It may also have affected the outcome of some divorce petitions.

In a case brought by a woman named Chen in Shanxi province, for example, the reversal of a grant of divorce was discussed in the context of the undesirable trend of rising divorces.[67] In 1994, Chen filed a divorce petition against her husband in the courts, on the grounds of domestic abuse. The husband had, at times, beaten her so severely that she required hospitalization. Although the court of first instance granted her a divorce, the court of second instance reversed the lower-court judgment. Commentators on the casebook praised the latter decision, saying that the court of second instance acted correctly in denying the divorce, given the unfortunate tendency of lower courts to grant divorces too easily. Citing an investigation of the court of first instance in September 1995, the commentators noted that the lower court had granted a divorce to 83 of 175 divorce petitioners. Of the 83 couples granted divorces, five had reconciled, suggesting to the commentators that there had been "incorrect" decisions by that court. Hence, despite the finding of domestic violence in Chen's case, the commentators maintained that the court of second instance acted correctly in denying her divorce petition.

Such cases reinforce the view that the use of courts is more an avenue in the area of social rights than political rights, and more an avenue to contest local abuses than to oppose national policy. This conclusion in part affirms but also challenges the historical determinism predicted by citizenship theorists such as T. H. Marshall, who see a natural progression of political, civil, and finally social rights development with markets and capitalism.

Law and the Collective Gendered Citizen

Another aspect of the increased use of courts is the courts' growing inclination to place responsibility for the development of proof on individual litigants. This responsibility of individual litigants to assert their rights may lead to the development of greater rights consciousness, but it can present special problems for those without power. Without independent lawyers, the adversarial process may not be conducive to litigation by the powerless against more powerful defendants. Indeed, without financial resources or legal knowledge, it is difficult for litigants to navigate the judicial system to understand how to obtain proof, or even to know what proof is necessary. Such problems have already surfaced in the area of divorce, where one spouse, usually the husband, can hide the family assets from a divorcing wife. Whether Chinese women can truly assert their legal rights in the courts may depend in large part on the growing body of lawyers trained in recent years, and on the market that provides for their services.

As of 1996, China boasted some 102,000 lawyers, an increase from 3,000 lawyers in 1982. But that number is still small by comparison to a population of 1.22 billion.[68] Women constitute a fast-growing percentage in the profession, but as of 1992, there were only 21,012 women in the judiciary and 4,512 women lawyers.[69] According to scholars such as William Alford, Chinese lawyers are moving from being simply state workers to being capitalist entrepreneurs, which means greater autonomy but questionable professionalism. Since marriage and family cases are not as profitable as commercial cases, the marketplace of legal services has left women litigants in need. Thus, allowing the market to determine the distribution of legal services may mean a maldistribution of justice.

This disparity in the availability of legal services may be felt especially by women in the rural areas. Although there are plans to establish a nationwide legal aid system, such programs have so far primarily been in economically developed areas, leaving the rural poor still in need.[70] At least one Women's Legal Services Center in Qianxi County was opened precisely in order to address the needs of rural women. Although cases can be litigated without the assistance of counsel,[71] the limited legal services in rural areas may simply mean that rural citizens will be less likely to bring formal claims to court.

The maldistribution of legal services presents clear obstacles to the assertion of rights. The opportunity to assert rights should be determined not by markets but rather by concepts of justice. Indeed, the market will not provide any greater protection for women unless old social institutions adopt new practices, or newly established social institutions become more conducive to rights assertion.

The answer may lie in the balance of asserting individual responsibility and rights in a collective sense. Litigation could take more collective forms, gathering around interests rather than class or party. This "collective" litigation could appeal to residual Confucian and Maoist ideologies, with their focus on the group and community. The 1991 Civil Procedure Code provides for such a mechanism and has been used with some success in China. This code allows for cases to be brought jointly where "the litigants of one or both parties involve two or more people with common litigant objects or objects of the same type,"[72] in other words, a form of "class action." Women litigants may be more comfortable in using such collective mechanisms to bring more public litigation like labor cases, where the defendant is a corporation or collective, or even the state itself, that is more powerful than individuals.[73] This mechanism of collective litigation has been used in labor disputes with some success.

The Center for Women's Law Studies and Legal Services in Beijing,[74] for example, brought a collective action for twenty-five peasant women to enforce their demand for back pay.[75] This Center, founded in December 1995 by the Law Department of Peking University, is a unique example of a legal organization bringing collective actions.[76] The Center primarily handles cases that are considered representative of serious social problems. These cases include those relating to domestic violence, injuries to women due to implementation of the family planning policy, unprofitable state enterprises laying off more female than male workers, divorcees losing housing, and unfaithful husbands concealing family property.

Of the twenty cases viewed by the Center as particularly complicated, several involved collective action suits seeking enforcement of labor rights. Among these was a group litigation case in which eighty female workers sued their employer for being two years behind in wage payments. Other cases include one where several senior technical and professional female employees sued their employer for forcing female employees to take early retirement, and another where seven female workers sought to enforce their right to work.

Rural women may also find this collective action appealing. One recent case demonstrates both the potential and the limits of such litigation. In this case, six rural women brought suit against their village for violating their right to an allocation of land-use fees.[77] The defendant argued that three of the plaintiffs were not entitled to a land-use fee since they were not farming the land, and the other three plaintiffs were not entitled to such fees because they had lost their residence status *(hukou)* in the village after marriage. Demonstrating a deference to administrative units in a case involving economic policy matters, the court declined to hear this claim on the grounds that it lacked jurisdiction until the appropriate administrative agency first considered the case. The court pointed out that it would be appropriate for the plaintiffs to appeal to the court if they were dissatisfied with the administrative decision.

This group litigation suggests the appeal of strength in numbers. It also shows the procedural obstacles faced by litigants, even those who obtain legal assistance. Here, the court deferred to administrative organs, reflecting negotiation as to the respective spheres of authority of courts and administrative units. Moreover, when confronted with an issue of economic and social policy—the possible conflict between changing land-use policies and gender relations—

the courts declined to take action. In that sense, then, Chinese courts are not yet at the stage at which public issues are articulated and determined.

Interestingly, the concept of collective litigation may also involve a changing role for traditional mass organizations such as the Women's Federation. As the party weakens, there may be greater opportunities "to struggle autonomously for group defined interests."[78] While the traditional role of the Women's Federation is to serve as a conduit for state policy and as an arbiter of disputes, there is a potential new role for it as a group representing pluralistic interests. The extent to which mass organizations serve as representatives of individual rights in many ways signals a change in the balance among mass organizations, individuals, and the state.

At present the Women's Federation has a staff of lawyers, but the staff primarily disseminates legal information and provides legal consultation, rather than representing individual clients. However, members of the Women's Federation sometimes enter the courts as expert witnesses and can even sit as adjudicators along with judges. When the Women's Federation becomes involved in a case, the woman litigant has a better chance of winning. If the Women's Federation continues in this area—serving as an expert on women's issues in public policy cases—it may begin to transform itself into a true civil-society organization, mediating between the state and individuals.

There is support for such a role for the Women's Federation in the laws themselves. Chinese legislation has expanded the legal responsibilities of mass associations and formally enlisted them in the cause of "social protection."[79] The Women's Federation, however, has so far remained largely outside the legal arena. Although the Federation has expanded its functions, experimented with new types of activities, and created new departments, it continues to view its role of education and social activism as part of a system of social protection *and* control. To serve as a representative of litigants and provide information to the courts would be a far cry from its traditional role. This emerging concept of mass organizations providing representation in court may lead to new relationships between such organizations and the state. At present, however, their presence in individual litigation is still limited, even as the state seeks to balance social policy with individual rights and interests and to reinsert a collective voice in an otherwise individual action.

Conclusion

Groups of Chinese women today are journeying from their natal villages to townships and cities. Removed from the workplace, they are migrating from the public back to the private. From public to private, from rural to regional to national—these are migrations of the mind as well as the body. When more and more people live in what Edward Said has called "a generalized condition of homelessness," our identities become de-territorialized, at least differently territorialized.[80] This may be a time for Chinese women to adopt practices and institutions that will fully assert their status as citizens.

At the beginning of the twenty-first century, the assertion of private rights by ordinary Chinese citizens is rising. Women litigants have not shied away from civil litigation. The bulk of the civil cases have to do with marriage and family, and women are often the plaintiffs and initiators of such litigation.

Where the courts can be a site in which problems are named and solutions determined, women's litigation presents a potentially important "bottom up" route by which public rights are determined and articulated. Each time a citizen participates in the legal process, whether to "applaud or to criticize, whether to appropriate or to resist," the participation sustains "legality as an organizing structure of social relations."[81] The fact that women are participating in litigation should therefore itself be applauded.

The increased use of courts can point in the direction of rights assertion, as each litigation represents a moment of rights contestation. Chinese citizens are exercising their rights through law and defining their own citizenship rights. But the "instituted process" of rights assertion, in this instance court litigation, suggests variation in the kinds of rights being asserted. The institution, practices, and procedures for court litigation are such that Chinese women are more likely to assert personal rights in marriage or personal injury than to assert social and economic rights such as labor protection and land use. This suggests that citizenship as contested membership rules is still evolving in China.

The fact that women are turning to the courts, even in the context of the more contentious employment claims, also suggests that there may be a more complex calculus in which the women weigh both the potential of government retribution against perceived challenges to its policies, and employer retribution. As alternative normative systems are weakening, the legal system may gain greater strength as one of several overlapping systems of governance.

Finally, the rise in court litigation by itself might not necessarily suggest a "measure of independence from governmental powers." In fact, the closer court cases get to national economic and social policy issues, the less it appears that courts will afford avenues for redress. Collective action might be an avenue through which courts could play a greater role. Until then, Chinese courts in this era of social transformation are still limited in their ability to present themselves as an arena for the determination and articulation of public values.

13 | Constructing Citizenship: The NPC as Catalyst for Political Participation

Since the mid-1980s, the National People's Congress (NPC) has played a key role in catalyzing the development of normative notions of political citizenship in China. Examples of this include the development of political norms of private-interest (non-state) participation in legislative drafting and of private-interest representation by parliamentary delegates. The NPC's catalytic activity in this area is due to at least three factors. First, the strength of the NPC's political influence, and by extension its individual leaders, within China's political environment depends in significant part on its ability to appear "democratic" to other political actors in China. Second, the NPC structure is particularly accessible to private interests and actively encourages private-interest input, particularly in its legislative drafting activities.

The third factor is that the NPC's institutional structure promotes a special kind of organizational decision-making that encourages new norm formation within China's constitutional and political environments. This kind of decision-making, which I will call discursive benchmarking, emphasizes innovation by lower-level bureaucratic entities (as opposed to centralized innovators) and by consensual institutional decision-making (as opposed to decision-making via monocratic decree or majoritarian vote). A discursive benchmarking process is plainly evi-

dent in the developmental histories of the political citizenship innovations discussed above. The NPC promotes this process by incorporating a wide range of political and social actors in its institutional
processes, and by delegating significant decision-making responsibilities to lower-level bureaucratic entities.

Examples of New Norms of Political Citizenship

Since its rebirth in 1978, the NPC has helped catalyze a number of
significant new norms of public participation in China's political
environment. One such norm is public participation in legislative
drafting. In the mid-1980s, the NPC's Committee on Legislative
Affairs (CLA) began soliciting input from a relatively wide range
of social institutions—academics, trade groups, corporatist interest
groups—in the process of drafting legislative instruments.[1] This procedure was probably developed more out of utilitarian rather than
ideological concerns: the CLA is somewhat unique among China's
legislative drafting organs in that it cannot claim distinctive institutional expertise in many of the areas of regulation into which its
legislative drafting takes it,[2] and must therefore look to resources
outside its own organizational confines, that is, civil society, for substantive competence.

In the early 1990s, the NPC began identifying normative implications in the CLA's participatory practices. At that time, the NPC's
General Office Research Department began documenting formal
and informal parliamentary practices of the NPC and of local people's congresses, and identifying normative, democratic implications
in these practices. Since the 1980s, the NPC has been appealing
for greater authority within China's political environment, and has
founded this appeal in part on its unique status as principal reposi-
tory for the democratic legitimacy of China's constitutional and, by
extension, political systems. Identifying and promoting the democratic implications of the CLA's legislative drafting practices thus
promoted the strength of these appeals to democratic legitimacy,
and derivatively, strengthened the NPC's political authority.[3]

This articulation was not merely strategic: the NPC also internalized the political citizenship norms that it uncovered in the CLA's
particular procedures. Within the NPC, the CLA was able to extend

its own authority vis-à-vis other NPC departments by exporting its public-input procedures to other aspects of its own operations. For example, in addition to drafting its own legislation, the CLA is also responsible for reviewing draft statutory legislation developed by other departments in the NPC and by other constitutional organs. In the early 1990s, the CLA adapted its public-input procedures to this aspect of its operations and began exhibiting greater aggressiveness in this review, arguing that such aggressiveness was necessary to ensure that a fuller range of relevant societal concerns sufficiently informed these drafts. The success of these efforts suggests that these appeals to emerging norms of political citizenship had an effect within the NPC. (It might also be noted that even actors who complained about this aggressiveness, both in the NPC and in the State Council, have acknowledged that the CLA is indeed channeling outside social concerns, not simply those of the NPC leadership.)[4]

After the NPC began publicizing its receptiveness to public input in its legislative drafting processes, other political actors in China began employing and publicizing similar procedural devices in attempts to overcome their own legitimacy problems. In 1994 the Beijing Municipal Government, confronted by overwhelming public interest in a proposed pet dog regulation, held and publicized three days of open-access legislative hearings to give Beijing residents an opportunity to articulate their concerns. More than one thousand Beijing citizens participated in these hearings.[5] In late 1995, after the electoral performance of its nominees embarrassed the CCP in several provincial legislatures, the CCP publicly amended its nomination procedures to allow wider input from both inside and outside the party.[6] In the late 1990s, Shanghai Municipality implemented informal open-access hearing procedures for both administrative and legislative regulations.[7] And in 1999, the Guangdong People's Congress developed and publicly heralded what it claims are China's first formally codified procedures for open-access public hearings.[8]

The NPC's and CLA's participatory drafting practices have also become embedded in, and are now promoting the development of, an emergent civil society in China. Definitions of civil society vary. As used in this chapter, civil society refers to "a crucial space between a changing state and society, in which individuals interact and define themselves in relationship to the political."[9] Numerous scholars have noted that, particularly in corporatist regimes such as that of China, the formation of this kind of space can lay an important foundation for the subsequent development of a social autonomy that catalyzes political citizenship.[10]

The NPC's participatory drafting procedures have provided a unique opportunity and incentive for many state-corporatist institutions to begin disaggregating themselves from the state and to promote constituent interests more aggressively in political decision-making processes. Although these organizations are still subject to strong state oversight in many areas of their operation, they have been able to enjoy relative autonomy in this particular aspect of their institutional operations. This budding autonomy could represent a significant step toward a "neo-corporatist" model of liberal civil and political society.[11]

A good example of this can be seen in the institutional evolution of the All-China Federation of Trade Unions (ACFTU). Since the mid-1980s, the ACFTU had been trying to institutionalize within China's political system a praxis in which state policies affecting labor interests would be developed through a tripartite labor-management-state dialogue similar to that used by the International Labour Organization to develop international labor norms, in which the ACFTU would represent labor.[12] The ACFTU's ability to participate in NPC legislative drafting was a crucial catalyst in the eventual success of these efforts. The tripartite arrangement sought by the ACFTU first manifested itself, albeit tentatively, in the NPC's consideration of the draft State-Owned Industrial Enterprise Law in 1987.[13] In the early 1990s, the NPC effectively codified this new norm when it entrusted the final development of the Labor Law, enacted in 1995, to an intentionally-structured tripartite drafting group consisting of the ACFTU, representing labor, the Chinese Enterprise Directors Association, representing management, and the Ministry of Labor, representing the state.[14] Since that time, this tripartite arrangement has become the standard mechanism used to address labor-management policy issues.[15] It is interesting to note that participation in legislative drafting is the principal area of the ACFTU's political autonomy that the state/CCP did not significantly curtail in the aftermath of the 1989 Tiananmen demonstrations.[16]

Another example of how normalized access to NPC legislative drafting has catalyzed more autonomous authority in China's corporatist institutions is seen in the All-China Lawyers Federation (ACLA). Since 1995, the ACLA has been gradually extricating itself from the Ministry of Justice (MOJ) and the state.[17] One of the earliest concrete manifestations of this extrication occurred in 1994, when the ACLA used the CLA's participatory processes to oppose the MOJ's efforts to include particular legal aid provisions in the draft Lawyers Law.[18] Since then, the ACLA has stated that legislative lobbying is to be a key aspect of its efforts to develop an independent institutional presence within China's political and legal systems.[19] A similar dynamic can be seen in the institutional development of the All-China Women's Federation, whose participation in the drafting of the Women's Rights Law in the early 1990s was one if its first significant displays of independent institutional force.[20]

The opportunity to participate in the legislative drafting processes of the NPC and lower people's congresses has also encouraged the formation of new kinds of interest groups. For example, the Wuhan University Center for the Protection of the Rights of Disadvantaged Citizens, which opened in 1996, seeks to promote the unique interests of disadvantaged groups within the NPC and other legislative bodies.[21]

A second example of how the NPC has catalyzed the emergence of new norms of public participation in China's political environment can be found in the development of new norms of political representation of non-state interests (what we might call "pluralist representation"). Modern China's Communist/Maoist ideology did not recognize pluralist conceptualizations of the public good. For this reason, the state has historically expected political representatives to pursue a *common* vision of the public good, as opposed to individual social interests.[22] The transition to a more pluralist conceptualization of political representation began in the mid-1980s, when the NPC began professionalizing its delegate body and improving the quality of participation in decision-making.[23] The fruits of these efforts became apparent by the late 1980s, when delegates provoked significant changes in a draft Intellectual Property Law, the Enterprise Bankruptcy Law, the State-owned Industrial Enterprise Law, and—to a lesser extent—the Three Gorges Dam project.[24]

As the delegates professionalized, they became better able to achieve political compromise in the service of distinct social interests. Various aspects of the NPC's representational scheme also facilitated this development. China's economic reforms and the corresponding governmental decentralization have caused increasing divergences in regional interests, divergences that centralized authorities in the CCP are unable to suppress.[25] The NPC, like all parliaments, organizes its delegates along regional lines, and this allows representatives more easily to promote regional interests.[26] Regional representation was one of the first forms of delegate pluralism to appear in the NPC. In the late 1980s, for example, delegates from Hubei province cooperated in forcing considerable delay and compromise regarding issues of resettlement in the passage of an NPC resolution approving the Three Gorges Dam project. A few years later, delegates from China's economically depressed inner provinces cooperated in lobbying Zhu Rongji to loosen his anti-inflationary, tight-money policy.[27]

Another way in which the NPC's representational nature facilitated delegate pluralism was through its long-standing practice of reserving, sub rosa, delegate slots in the NPC and on the NPC Standing Committee for persons from state-corporatist social-interest institutions, such as the All-China Women's Federation and the All-China Federation of Trade Unions.[28] As noted earlier, many of these organizations began disaggregating themselves from the state in the 1980s, and one of the ways they did so was by promoting their unique constituent interests in the NPC. Although the state has sought to rein in at least some of these organizations in the wake of the 1989 Tiananmen demonstrations, it has not impeded the new constituent-oriented mentality of their representatives. By the early 1990s, many of these organizations had come to value their NPC representatives quite highly.[29]

As the most prominent forum for pluralist interest competition in China, the NPC also gained de facto authority to articulate how this new kind of competition fit intellectually within China's political framework. As part of the NPC's effort to identify unique, democratic aspects in its institutional architecture (as discussed above), its research staffers began exploring the proper role of NPC delegates in parliamentary and constitutional decision-making processes. Collecting information about the procedures and experiences of the NPC, China's provincial people's congresses, and foreign legislatures, these researchers articulated a much more activist and plural-ist norm of delegate participation in political and parliamentary decision-making, one which, like that of public participation in legis-lative drafting, sought to promote the NPC's institutional authority by highlighting the NPC's unique ability to accommodate the con-tentious aspects of democratic deliberation.[30]

This normative articulation caused the delegates themselves to be-gin viewing their own roles in increasingly pluralistic and assertive terms. In 1995, over one-quarter of the delegate body failed to sup-port a proposed Education Law and a proposed Banking Law; over one-third also refused to endorse work reports tendered by the Supreme People's Court and the Supreme People's Procuratorate; and almost one-third refused to confirm a CCP nominee for vice-premier. Delegates also forcefully criticized the NPC leadership for failing to develop the NPC's supervisory authorities.[31] Moreover, po-litical actors and departments have generally responded to this criti-cism, which suggests that it can have a significant disciplining effect in China's political environment.[32]

Largely favorable coverage in the domestic press has tended to confirm this new, pluralist conception of political representation,[33] and pluralist delegate assertiveness is now a normative feature of China's political landscape.[34] At the 1997 Plenary Session, for exam-ple, the delegates were able to force the removal of a controversial provision in the draft amendments to the Criminal Law that gave blanket immunity to police officers who injured or killed others while on duty, in spite of the fact that the NPC leadership itself sup-ported this provision.[35] This norm has also spread to other political institutions in China which, like the NPC, base their authority in part on their representative character. In 1996, the political emergence of the NPC caused many political leaders to begin questioning the institutional relevance of the Chinese People's Political Consultative Conference (CPPCC), the CCP's parallel to the NPC. In response, the CPPCC began publicly emulating the greater delegate assertive-ness and more contentious delegate deliberation found in the NPC, suggesting that the CPPCC's leadership believed such norms could promote its own authority as well.[36]

Growing acceptance of this new norm of political representation can even be seen in the behavior of the CCP. Through the 1980s, the CCP leadership had sought to suppress expressions of delegate pluralism in the NPC, arguing that such expressions were not appropriate for "socialist" parliamentary systems. But the party largely abandoned such efforts by the early 1990s, despite significant NPC delegate support for the Tiananmen protestors in 1989.[37] In 1995, the CCP and the State Council effectively capitulated to the delegates' new norms of activism by issuing new rules requiring CCP and State Council officials to be more available to NPC delegates and more receptive to their particular concerns. Delegate assertiveness in provincial parliaments also caused the CCP to adopt new nomination procedures that gave parliaments greater say in the selection of CCP nominations.[38]

The emergence of this new norm has also encouraged an ever-widening range of pluralist interests to seek to articulate their views within the delegate bodies of the NPC, provincial parliaments, and the CPPCC. In the NPC these include, for example, factions promoting educational spending and reform, labor issues, environmental protection, and women's empowerment. More recently, private-business owners, state-owned enterprise managers, and medical professionals have also begun to assert their particular interests at NPC and CPPCC plenary sessions.[39]

Catalytic Factors

The NPC's ability to catalyze new norms of political citizenship is due to at least two factors. First, as we have seen, the strength of the NPC's political influence, and by extension that of its individual leaders, depends in significant part on its ability to appear relatively "democratic" within China's constitutional and political environments. As a result, the NPC structure is relatively accessible to private interests, and this in turn encourages private interests to make use of, expect, and gradually legitimize greater access to political decision-making.

Internal Incentives

The NPC's incentive to promote stronger norms of citizen participation in China's political decision-making comes from its unique constitutional pedigree. Unlike other major political actors at the national level, the NPC cannot appeal to any unique technocratic expertise in seeking to assert intellectual authority within China's political decision-making environment. Whatever special authority it does enjoy must stem primarily from its formal status as the principal source of the democratic legitimacy of China's constitutional system.[40] The utility of that status depends, in turn, both on the degree to which China's larger political environment recognizes democracy and public political participation as important concerns in political decision-making, and on the degree to which the NPC is seen as truly reifying these norms in its institutional operations.

The "democracy" from which China's political structure in general and the NPC (and lower-level congresses) in particular claim legitimacy is rather inchoate at present, and does not include many of the formal institutional attributes that in the United States are considered to be core elements of a democratic regime, such as open elections for national office and secure rights to free expression and association. But here we are concerned with developmental potential, not developmental status.[41] Thus, a commitment even to an inchoate notion of democratic legitimacy can provide significant incentives to develop, implement, and promote new norms of political citizenship within China's political environment.

As shown in the examples above, the NPC has not been shy about acknowledging this link between its own political authority and the degree to which norms of democracy and political citizenship become embedded in China's political environment.[42] This linkage is very evident in the NPC's long-standing support for rural village election reforms. At the start of these reforms in the mid-1980s, Peng Zhen, then the chairman of the NPC Standing Committee, publicly noted that one of the major benefits of these reforms is that they would promote the NPC's own unique authority within China's national political environment.[43] Since that time, the NPC leadership has consistently pushed for more aggressive expansion of these reforms. The strength of the institutional linkage between the NPC's authority and these reforms is particularly evident in the case of Li Peng. When he was premier of the State Council, he consistently resisted NPC calls for faster rural electoral reforms. Since becoming chairman of the NPC Standing Committee, however, Li Peng has supported their expansion.[44]

The NPC's ongoing efforts to improve the quality of political citizenship in its own institutional decision-making, despite the fact that this obviously impedes the NPC leadership's own control over NPC decision-making, further confirm the presence of a symbiotic linkage between the NPC's institutional authority and political citizenship norms in China. Even as public participation and delegate assertiveness began intruding on NPC leadership interests in the 1980s, the NPC leadership support for these developments remained steadfast.

Many argue that in China, the CCP's continued hegemonic dominance of the political environment effectively prevents any opportunity for meaningful development of a political citizenship praxis. The relationship between the CCP's own institutional incentives and emergent norms of political citizenship, however, is much more complex than such arguments assume. The CCP may oppose some recognized aspects of political citizenship, namely those that threaten its hegemonic status within China's political environment. Yet, there is little evidence that the party opposes the notion of political citizenship per se. The CCP has readily accepted increased public political participation when and to the extent that it does not threaten the CCP's hegemony in areas such as labor relations and local governance, and in the formation of the CCP's internal nomenklatura determinations.[45]

Indeed, in China's present environment, the CCP's continued hegemony may well depend on its ability to continue promoting or accommodating greater political citizenship. In patronage institutions like the CCP, organizational discipline is maintained primarily by reciprocal patterns of loyalty between patrons and clients.[46] But the growing fragmentation of China's civil environment is causing increasing fragmentation and disputes to arise among the CCP's core clients.[47] Resolving such disputes internally within the CCP threatens to rupture the bonds of personal loyalty (since at least one of the clients to the dispute is bound to be disappointed by the patron-imposed outcome) on which client cooperation depends. One solution to this dilemma is to supply clients with independent forums, visibly outside the patron's control, in which clients can settle those pluralist disputes that do not significantly affect the patron's own political interests. By devolving responsibility for political decision-making onto affected clients in this way, such forums represent new institutions of political citizenship.[48]

In other words, social and political fragmentation effectively compels the CCP to "sell" power in order to maintain its hegemonic status, and institutions of political citizenship are crucial to effectuating this kind of trade. Such a dynamic is readily observable behind the development of the NPC. For example, the CCP has been largely unable to adjudicate between the competing social interests of economic privatization and unemployment, because the proponents of rapid privatization and the proponents of labor interests are both integral clients in the CCP's power structure. The CCP appears to have allowed this dispute to be debated primarily in the NPC. In contrast to the scripted avoidance of any discussion of this issue exhibited by CCP forums, open and contentious discussion of the employment-privatization issue has dominated recent plenary sessions of the NPC.[49]

This dynamic can also be seen in the CCP's changed attitude toward assertiveness by NPC delegates. Up until the 1990s, the CCP invariably sought to suppress delegate assertiveness in the NPC. By the mid-1990s, however, the party merely sought to limit domestic knowledge of this growing assertiveness. This new arrangement suggests an institutional compromise in which the CCP has ceded some degree of actual power over delegate (and hence NPC) behavior in exchange for being able to maintain the appearance of power, and thus its hegemonic status, within China's larger political environment.[50]

Finally, we also see this dynamic at work in the CCP's decision to open up its internal nomenklatura system to greater congressional and public input. During the mid-1990s, the CCP suffered a number of embarrassing defeats and near-defeats in regional parliamentary confirmations of candidates for regional and national public office. Unable or unwilling to discipline congressional delegates effectively in such voting, the CCP subsequently revised its internal nomination procedures to give congressional and other non-party interests greater input into the selection of CCP nominees.[51] On the one hand, this allows the party to maintain institutional hegemony over political placement, by ensuring that meaningful discussion on public placement decisions occurs primarily within CCP forums. On the other hand, extending greater involvement of non-CCP institutional interests obviously weakens the CCP's power over its own nominating procedures.

Institutional Attributes

The NPC's institutional posture in China's constitutional and political environments makes it an especially attractive forum for this kind of pluralist contestation, from the viewpoint of both China's political elite and its emerging civil society. Under the standard constitutional paradigm, administrative and judicial institutions generally base their political authority on claims of special, technocratic expertise—that is, on their ability to promote effectively particular administrative and regulatory goals. This same general framework also informs Chinese constitutionalism.[52] Pluralist contestation, however, does not involve disputes over how best to effectuate particular goals; rather it involves disputes over what those goals should be. Thus, pluralist contestation lies outside the traditional scope of technocratic authority. Since a parliament, like the NPC, does not base its authority exclusively on technocratic expertise, it is better able to address the particular issues of preference ordering that underlie pluralist contestations.[53]

Moreover, the NPC's institutional structure is inherently more fragmented than that of other Chinese political institutions, in the sense that it embodies a wider range of conflicting institutional preferences. For this reason, it is particularly attractive to newer social interests seeking forums in which to assert themselves initially in political decision-making. The NPC's fragmentation derives from at least two unique institutional features. First, as we saw earlier, NPC representatives serve different constituencies with a wide range of frequently conflicting preferences. Second, while the NPC does not stake its authority on its technocratic competence, it must exhibit some degree of technocratic understanding in its decision-making. For example, a parliament that wishes to encourage national policies that promote full employment rather than economic privatization will need to show at least some understanding of how such policies would affect economic growth if it expects others to take its deliberations seriously. Thus, parliamentary decision-making must answer to two distinct intellectual masters (pluralism and technocracy), and this further enhances conflict between institutional preferences.[54]

This fragmentation of the NPC's institutional structure provides emergent social interests with a greater variety of potential points-of-entry into the NPC political decision-making process. The greater the number of distinct concerns that are involved in a particular political decision, the easier it is for any particular social interest to find a particular set of actors with compatible concerns who might support that interest in political decision-making.[55] This makes the NPC particularly attractive to newer political entrepreneurs who do not enjoy ready access to more traditional patronage networks. Thus, during the mid-1990s liberal law reformers, for example, were able to use delegates' concerns over high crime and police corruption as a lever for introducing significant restrictions on police authority into draft amendments of the Criminal Procedure Law. At the 1999 NPC Plenary Session, a group of state-owned enterprise managers used delegates' concerns about corruption to lobby for pay increases for their managers.[56]

Discursive Benchmarking

The social dynamic of political development. Obviously, the development of new norms of political citizenship in China faces many institutional obstacles. The basic shape of China's current centralized political and constitutional environments was framed during a time when public demand, and by extension state legitimacy, focused primarily on economic growth and social stability.[57] The architecture, vocabularies, and ideologies of these environmental frameworks are thus focused primarily on these goals, and in the process they reinforce, within their respective institutions, the political "truths" regarding the role of the state and the foundation of political legitimacy that inform these goals. But, as we have seen, both state and society in China are exhibiting growing demand for political-citizenship-like devices. This demand is not easily captured, or expressed, by the particular vocabularies that give meaning to the centralized state's institutional apparatus.[58]

For this reason, discoveries of new practices of political citizenship are most likely to occur in institutions whose particular goals are different from those that inform China's centralized state apparatus. The institutional goals of China's centralized state/party apparatus as a whole are not reflected in each of its individual component organizations and institutions. Organization involves bureaucratic specialization, and the latter causes different subordinate institutions within the centralized apparatus to adopt somewhat different institutional goals, and hence develop different institutional architectures, ideologies, and vocabularies.[59] In China, some of these subordinate configurations are much more sensitive to emerging demands for political citizenship. Local grassroots institutions, for example, are much more vulnerable to the kinds of "collective inaction" through which ordinary Chinese citizens most commonly express dissent. At the central level, some bureaus find their political mandates irreparably fractured as a result of growing divergences among China's political interests.[60] Such problems can encourage subordinate institutions to evolve new internal architectures, vocabularies, and ideologies that are more receptive to issues of inclusive political participation, and derivatively, to discoveries of devices that promote political citizenship.

What this means is that initial discoveries of political citizenship in China are most likely to arise, not as already theorized components of China's existing political ideologies, but as pragmatic, local (meaning within lower bureaucratic levels) phenomena that are harnessed to the subordinate institutional (and personal) goals of particular bureaus and actors. It is not mere coincidence that China's most successful and dramatic advances in political citizenship to date—parliamentarianism, rural democratic reforms, legal aid, administrative procedure reforms—emerged in this manner.[61] In the United States, many discoveries regarding the meaning of American citizenship, such as the way citizenship rights are affected by issues of social welfare, racial equality, and universal suffrage, also emerged from pragmatic and local experiments and experiences.[62]

As knowledge of the success of these experiments diffuses through the larger social and political environments, a growing awareness of their commonalities gives rise to new (centralized) meanings and vocabularies—vocabularies that are used to understand and express emerging norms of political citizenship, a dynamic that I earlier referred to as "discursive benchmarking."[63] As noted above, China's new norms of public participation in legislative drafting emerged, not out of a single institutional mind, but out of an accumulation of the experiences and innovations of a decentralized collection of forums—particularly the CLA and lower-level people's congresses.

Moreover, much of this innovation originated as pragmatic solutions to particular, local institutional problems (such as a lack of internal drafting capacities in the case of the CLA) rather than as conscious efforts to promote more political citizenship per se.

In time, however, the pragmatic success of these innovations caused others within China's constitutional and political environments to adapt these innovations to their own institutional needs. In particular, it caused the NPC to extract from these experiences particular norms of public participation that it could use to develop its own democratically based authority within China's larger political environment. Others within that environment, most notably the CCP, seemed to accept, or at least acquiesce to, the claimed authority these norms conveyed. Through this expanding process of adaptation and acceptance, these practices became increasingly embedded in China's evolving conceptions of political legitimacy as new political norms.

China's development of norms of pluralist representation evinces a similar discursive benchmarking process. In addition to interest divergences among China's increasingly assertive and distinct regional and state-corporatist interests, the decentralized experiences of numerous provincial people's congresses have demonstrated delegate independence to engender greater parliamentary authority within both the constitutional structure and the larger political environment. In so doing, the NPC portrayed this development as an inevitable consequence of its constitutionally-mandated democratic character and authority, suggesting an alternative, more pluralistic conception of political representation. In turn, other political institutions such as the CPPCC began promoting representational assertiveness and pluralism as a way of maintaining their own institutional authority. This pragmatic process of adoption and adaptation caused these new norms of representational pluralism to become increasingly embedded in China's evolving conceptions of political legitimacy, displacing claims by Mao of a unitary public good.

Promoting discursive benchmarking. The process of discursive benchmarking is seen in the CLA/NPC's legislative drafting procedures. When the NPC assigns responsibility for drafting a statute to the CLA, the CLA usually delegates responsibility for developing the initial, or preliminary, draft to an outside, specially constituted "drafting group," composed primarily of academics from a number of academic institutions. The group, in consultation with governmental and non-governmental interests, may take several years to research and compile the initial draft. In addition, it may hold conferences and may float particular ideas in the academic and legal press. Once that group completes its preliminary draft, the CLA then solicits written opinions from other departments in the NPC, other constitutional actors (both central and regional), other academics, state corporatist and other public interest associations, and private professionals. After further revisions, the CLA will then hold a number of conferences with representatives from the relevant constitutional, academic, and professional communities to discuss and amend the draft. If these conferences reveal persistent disagreement, the CLA may revise the draft and hold additional rounds of conferences.[64]

Once a suitable draft is completed, it is sent to the NPC Chairmen's Group, which after discussion may send the draft back to the CLA for further revision. Otherwise, the Chairmen's Group places it on the Standing Committee's meeting agenda for vetting. The draft is presented to the floor of the Standing Committee by the bill's institutional drafter (generally the CLA, a special standing committee, or a State Council ministry), and delegates then vet the draft in two distinct forums—first in smaller breakout meetings of delegates called delegate groups (the Standing Committee is subdivided into four delegate groups), and then again on the floor of the entire Standing Committee. Both kinds of vetting are attended by representatives from the bill's drafting organ, who answer questions and address concerns from the delegates. Delegates' comments and concerns are recorded, and the bill, along with records of these vettings, is then sent to the Law Committee (one of the Special Standing Committees) for revision along the principal lines revealed in these discussions.[65]

In the process of revising the draft, the Law Committee again seeks comments from other NPC support services, and from the relevant academic, constitutional, and professional communities. If these comments reveal persistent disagreement, the Law Committee will hold consultative conferences similar to those held by the CLA. Once a suitable revised draft is developed, it is again placed on the

NPC agenda, and again vetted by either the Standing Committee (for ordinary legislation, and under some circumstances basic legislation as well) or the Plenary Session (for basic legislation). If this vetting reveals no serious disagreement among the delegates, the draft will be sent up for a vote. If significant disagreement remains, the bill will go back to the Law Committee for further revision. The disagreement need not be so great as to actually threaten the passage of the bill; as noted above, the dissent of the Standing Committee delegates from Hubei, while clearly not sufficient to threaten the bill's passage, was sufficient to send the draft resolution approving the Three Gorges Dam project back to the Law Committee four times before finally being approved.[66]

If the bill is in the form of a basic law, the Law Committee's revised draft goes to the Plenary Session rather than to the Standing Committee. There, it is introduced to the floor by the institutional drafter and vetted by the delegates in smaller group meetings organized according to province. These vettings are recorded, and the draft is returned to the Law Committee, along with the records of the vettings, for further revision. The Law Committee collects opinions from other constitutional actors, drafts its revisions, and returns the revised bill to the Plenary Session for a vote. In contrast to the situation for ordinary legislation, however, the revised draft basic law is always voted upon before the end of the session (and invariably passes). However, as noted in regard to the 1997 amendments to the Criminal Law, delegate deliberations can have a significant effect on the final content of the legislation.[67]

Thus, initial discussion about emergent legislation is highly decentralized—dispersed by the CLA throughout a diversity of forums in the academic, political, and emergent civil-societal sectors (mainly professional and state-corporatist public-interest organizations). The diverse views and ideas articulated in these forums are then synthesized into a series of drafts, with each successive draft providing a benchmark from which deliberation to the next draft will proceed. As each of these successive benchmarks is produced, new actors are added to the discussion: first the CLA and a select group of academics and/or professionals; then individuals from other relevant academic, professional, and constitutional institutions; then the rest of the NPC support departments; then the Chairmen's Group; then the Standing Committee delegates; and finally, in the case of basic legislation, the Plenary Session delegates. Each successive step in this process (except for bills in the Plenary Session) emphasizes consensus formation and de-emphasizes simple, majoritarian decision-making. This emphasis on consensus is crucial for the kind of bottom-up norm formation that characterizes discursive benchmarking.[68]

Many other aspects of the NPC's parliamentary decision-making, including evaluations of work reports, budgetary reports, and the results of NPC investigations, employ similar, discursive-benchmarking-like processes that involve similar collections of actors.[69] This allows the deliberation of a particular norm that arose in one forum to be continued in other forums that address similar or related matters. For example, pluralist deliberation over appropriate levels of educational spending that arose initially in the context of the State Education Law has been maintained over the years by a subsequent NPC investigation into state educational spending and by the NPC's yearly vetting of the State Council's budgetary and work reports.[70]

Because the NPC's various decision-making procedures, and the discursive methods they engender, frequently involve actors outside the NPC, they also stimulate discussion within China's wider constitutional and political environments. A particularly dramatic example of this can be seen in the pre- and post-enactment history of new criminal trial procedures introduced in the 1996 amendments to the Criminal Procedure Law. Complaints about the Stalinist aspects of China's old criminal adjudication processes (colloquially called "decision before trial") had occasionally been voiced in public forums in China beginning in the late 1980s. The decision to amend the Criminal Procedure Law provided an opportunity for academic reformers involved in the initial drafting of these amendments to introduce provisions providing for more "adversarial" trial procedures into China's criminal justice processes—provisions that promoted direct participation in the trial by the citizen-defendant.[71]

Early dialogue facilitated by the CLA's drafting procedures revealed significant opposition to these provisions, particularly from the Ministry of Public Security (MPS) and the Supreme People's Procuratorate (SPP). Initial vettings before the Standing Committee, on the other hand, showed support for these provisions. This support allowed these provisions to be included, over the MPS's and

SPP's objections, in the final draft of the amendments presented to the NPC Plenary Session in 1996.[72] Subsequent vetting in the Plenary Session further showed strong support for these provisions among the Plenary Session delegates and within the domestic press. At the time of enactment, MPS and SPP opposition to these provisions was most likely too great to allow for the immediate formulation of exact standards of implementation.[73] But even in their inchoate state, these provisions were still sufficient to set a minimum political benchmark that was crucial for allowing, perhaps compelling, the constitutional system to get beyond the issue of whether or not China should adopt a more adversarial criminal trial system, and focus its discourse on questions of what that system should look like in practice.

Establishing this statutory benchmark meant that actors who had originally opposed the introduction of the adversarial system, such as the MPS and the SPP, now had to accept and work within the broad parameters of this system as codified in the amendments if they wanted to have any say over the further refinement of the new criminal trial procedures. Of course, the MPS and the SPP could have simply refused to abide by these statutory provisions.[74] But the wealth of possibilities inherent in the vagueness of the provisions, combined with the inclusive processes that underlie the NPC's power of "statutory interpretation,"[75] encouraged their continued participation in the ongoing discursive benchmarking of these new procedures.

Almost immediately after the passage of these amendments, the CLA, at the behest of the Ministry of Justice, began coordinating the development of a rationalized, interdepartmental set of actors supplementing legislation and implementing regulations that would begin filling in the many lacunae left open in the original draft. This effort involved six constitutional departments, spanning the four principal constitutional branches, and including the MPS and SPP (the other participating departments were the Ministry of Justice, the Supreme People's Court, the Ministry of State Security, and the CLA). This group expanded the dialogue that had been initiated by the earlier drafting process (both the Ministry of State Security and the Chinese Bar were much more involved in the development of these coordinated interpretations than they had been in the development of the initial statutory provisions), which resulted in the "six department provisions," an unprecedented set of coordinated legislation that gave greater concrete meaning to the principle of defendant participation in criminal procedures that was roughly benchmarked in the 1996 amendments.[76]

Whether the MPS and SPP's initial participation in this post-enactment dialogue was strategic (that is, pragmatic) or bona fide is an open question. But in either event, their participation caused a new, more adversarial trial system to become more deeply embedded in the larger regulatory environment, and in their own organizational environments. Most dramatically, the SPP, in the course of its participation, changed from opposing this new system to embracing it as a unique opportunity for it to take its proper place within China's constitutional environment.[77] Participation in this process also caused the MPS to amend its original implementing regulations of the new law to make them much more compatible with the spirit of the new provisions, thus exposing it to the same "runaway legitimation" that we saw operating in the other examples of discursive benchmarking.[78]

Conclusion

China seems to be gradually evolving toward a fuller realization of what political citizenship demands of its public decision-making. This is not to suggest, however, that the mature realization of political citizenship in China is a *fait accompli*. Nevertheless, increasingly pluralist social and political environments are likely to accompany China's present trajectory of economic development and relative social stability. The NPC's institutional architecture and decision-making procedures link China's political development to this organically arising pluralism, and thereby may protect, at least somewhat, China's ongoing evolution toward a more fully realized political citizenship from possible intervening vagaries of individual will.

III | Taiwan

14 | Nationalism versus Citizenship in the Republic of China on Taiwan

Nationalism is that precious possession which enables a state to aspire to progress and a nation to perpetuate its existence.
 —Sun Yat-sen, *San Min Chu I: The Three Principles of the People*

The identification of belonging to a people with membership in an organized political community is the bad trick played by all nationalist ideologies. To conflate principles of national and ethnic belonging with those of democratic citizenship is always explosive and dangerous.
 —Seyla Benhabib, "Democracy and Identity: Dilemmas of Citizenship in Contemporary Europe"

Sun Yat-sen's devotion to nationalism profoundly influenced generations of his successors, both on the mainland and in Taiwan. Yet a key lesson of Taiwan's history over the past fifty years is that Benhabib is right. Democracy and nationalism are not complementary virtues of the state; in fact, nationalism often requires the sacrifice of democracy. Moreover, given the violent opposition of the People's Republic of China to any assertion of Taiwanese nationhood, Sun Yat-sen's nationalism is explosive and dangerous in the most literal sense. This is a lesson that Taiwan is still learning, but the island's contemporary discourse on democracy and national identity reveals a growing consensus favoring a post-nationalist vision of the state, a vision consistent with Habermas's notion of "constitutional patriotism."[1] The niche Taiwan is carving for itself, in which it has found at least temporary respite, is as a state that avoids identification with a nation, but emphasizes instead its political virtues.

As Margaret Somers points out, democratic citizenship emerges from a combination of political culture, civil society, and law.[2] Since 1950, Taiwan's evolution on each of these dimensions has moved the island's people away from their previous role as colonial subjects and toward the status of citizens. Under the banner of Sun Yat-sen's second principle—popular sovereignty—the Taiwanese gradually dismantled the emergency provisions used by the Guomindang government to restrict democracy. In the 1970s and 1980s a serious and committed opposition movement emerged from Taiwan's society, a movement which pushed hard to gain the privileges of citizenship for the Taiwanese. Under pressure from within and without, the legal climate began to change, and institutions that had once served to limit freedom and popular control were transformed. At the same time, the definition of citizenship was redefined, as membership in the state included substantive rights.

Sun Yat-sen's Incoherent Nationalism

Habermas describes nationalism as "a specifically modern phenomenon of cultural integration . . . a form of collective consciousness which both presupposes a reflexive appropriation of cultural traditions that have been filtered through historiography and which spreads only via the channels of modern mass communication. Both elements lend to nationalism the artificial traits of something that is to a certain extent a construct, thus rendering it by definition susceptible to manipulative misuse by political elites."[3] This is an apt description of Chinese nationalism. Indeed, if nationalism was artificial in Europe, where it was born, it was even more so in China, where it was borrowed. Its inauthenticity—and misuse—shows itself most starkly in Taiwan, where the desire to justify various distributions of political power drove passionate, but ultimately fruitless, quests for nationhood.

Although in the late nineteenth century Chinese nationalism mainly took the form of hatred for China's Manchu leaders, Chinese intellectuals soon wedded home-grown xenophobia to theoretical constructs developed in the West. For Sun Yat-sen, who strove throughout his career to justify his political actions in philosophical terms, the nation-state concept was enormously useful, first as a tool to use against the Manchus, then as a weapon against foreign imperialism and internal dissent. In 1924, Sun delivered a series of lectures at Canton in which he summarized and elaborated his Three Principles of the People *(sanmin zhuyi)*. In the three principles, which constitute the Republic of China's ideological touchstone, Sun Yat-sen appropriates the concept of the nation-state for China. Nonetheless, as the 1924 lectures make clear, he was never able to resolve the contradictions inherent in the notion of a Chinese nation-state.

In the first lecture, Sun observes that in the West, the word "nation" has two distinct meanings. It can refer to a race, which is an entity formed by nature, or to a state, which develops through armed force. But in China, he says, and in China alone, "the nation is equivalent to the state."[4] The reason is that the Chinese state—unlike the states of Europe and America—is populated by a racially pure Chinese nation. This idea is in tension from the outset, however, with the undeniable presence in China of non-Han peoples. Sun never resolves this contradiction. Instead, when it is useful to him to conceive of China as a homogeneous nation, he stresses its tradition of assimilating and sinifying non-Han groups. Yet, when he wants to draw the Han together in opposition to outsiders, he reverses course and de-sinifies minority groups. This is most evident in his discussion of the Manchus, whose foreign origins Sun and his contemporaries used to justify the overthrow of the Qing dynasty.

Because the central premise of Sun's lectures on nationalism is that the Chinese nation and state overlap perfectly, he needs to finesse the question of minority nationalities. He does so in two ways in the first lecture. He starts by minimizing their significance. He writes, "The Chinese race totals four hundred million people; of mingled races there are only a few million Mongolians, a million or so Manchus, a few million Tibetans, and over a million Mohammedan Turks. These alien races do not number altogether more than ten million, so that, for the most part, the Chinese people are of the Han or Chinese race with common blood, common language, common religion, and common customs—a single, pure race."[5]

Later, Sun reinforces the idea that the Chinese nation-state is "virtually pure" by proposing an assimilationist view of Chinese identity: "When the Mongols of the Yuan dynasty entered China, they not only failed to destroy the Chinese race but were absorbed by the Chinese . . . The Manchus subjected China and ruled over her for more than two hundred sixty years; they not only did not wipe out the Chinese race, but were, on the contrary, absorbed by them, becoming fully Chinese."[6] In sum, then, the presence of non-Han groups in China does not challenge the nation-state concept because these groups are small, and in any case, political amalgamation and cultural assimilation erase the distinctions between Han and non-Han.

In the long run, however, Sun—like other Chinese thinkers on the subject—is not comfortable with the idea of an assimilationist Chinese identity based on political membership. Race is important to him; what he means by the Chinese race is the Han people, defined by blood. In his third lecture, Sun tries to rally his people against foreign pressure, especially the post–World War I fashion for cosmopolitanism. He appeals to his listeners' instinctual Han solidarity when he asks, "If Chinese should become naturalized British or Americans and help England or America to destroy China, saying that we were but following out the principle of cosmopolitanism, would our consciences, let me ask you, be at rest?"[7]

Similarly, Sun reverses his earlier interpretation of cultural assimilation. No longer is assimilation evidence of the power of Chinese identity to absorb non-Chinese; here it is evidence of the weaknesses of Chinese identity in the face of "foreign" political power. He writes of two Manchu emperors, "K'ang Hsi imposed the ban on certain books, but Ch'ien Lung was more tricky in crushing the national spirit. K'ang Hsi said that he was born of Heaven to be emperor of China and urged the people not to resist Heaven; but Ch'ien Lung wiped out all distinctions between Manchus and Chinese, so that the intellectual class for the most part had after that no more national consciousness. That was bequeathed to the lower classes, but although they knew they ought to kill the Tartars they did not know why. So China's nationalistic ideals have disappeared for hundreds of years, due to the craftiness of the Manchus."[8]

Sun died not long after delivering these lectures, leaving to his successors in the Republic of China (ROC) and the People's Republic of China (PRC) a profoundly problematic view of Chinese nationality. On the one hand, his work offers a blood-based, primordialist definition of the Chinese nation that equates "Chinese" with "Han." Both the PRC and the ROC have used this definition as an important part of their justification for insisting that Taiwan—inhabited mainly by Han people—is an inalienable part of China. As Jia Yibin, a PRC student of Taiwan affairs, has written of the Taiwanese, "Because their bloodlines *(xueyuan)* are Chinese, they are part of the Chinese nation."[9] On the other hand, Sun deployed a political and cultural definition of "Chineseness" to defend the assertion that China's Qing-era borders constituted a coherent nation-state. The minority groups within these boundaries were both too small and too assimilated to challenge the nation's "racial purity." Thus, PRC and ROC governments use this definition to justify their claim to the vast areas of China dominated by non-Han peoples: Tibet, Inner Mongolia, and Xinjiang. The ultimate question—what makes a person Chinese, inclusion in the Han race or inclusion in the Chinese state?—remains unanswered.[10]

Chinese Nationalism on Taiwan

When the ROC government fled to Taiwan in 1949 it brought with it Sun Yat-sen's preoccupation with nationalism, along with his uncertain definition. But over time, the artificiality of the nation-state concept in the Taiwan context became increasingly apparent, forcing adjustments in practice, if not in theory. In keeping with Sun's equation of the ROC state with the "Chinese nation," the ROC defines citizenship in hereditary terms. Its 1930s-era Nationality Law confers citizenship on all persons born to Chinese fathers (or mothers, if the father's identity is uncertain) or on Chinese soil (if both parents are unknown). These provisions—which have never been amended to distinguish between Chinese living under ROC jurisdiction and those in the so-called "Communist areas" or overseas—constitute an ideological pronouncement, not a substantive definition of citizenship. To find out who actually enjoys the *rights* of citizenship—civil, political, and social—we must look to the laws defining eligibility to live, work, vote, and receive government benefits in ROC territory. These laws reveal the unsettled nature of ROC citizenship; they have evolved with Taiwan's changing political conditions and social consensus.

When it first decamped to Taiwan, the ROC government was committed to recovering mainland China from the Communist Party. Consequently, the national identity of the people on Taiwan was uncomplicated: they were citizens of the ROC who happened to occupy the one province remaining under its jurisdiction. Despite Taiwan's rocky adjustment to ROC rule between 1945 and 1949, there was little serious discussion of a separate identity for the island. Instead, Taiwanese found themselves plunged into a whirlwind of activity aimed at cementing their island's identity as the temporary home of "Free China." The ROC maintained a huge standing army that practiced and planned for an attack on the mainland; mandatory conscription ensured that all young men spent at least two years immersed in military preparation. Each year's National Day parade was an extravaganza of anti-communism and military display. School curricula were devoted to promoting ROC nationalism; students memorized Sun Yat-sen's works with the intensity of Confucian scholars, while geography and history classes were devoted entirely to mainland China, with little or no instruction about Taiwan itself.

ROC political institutions, too, reflected the island's subordination to the ROC ideal. The ROC constitution was suspended, opening the door for sweeping restrictions on civil liberties. Central government officials elected on the mainland in 1947 and 1948 were frozen in office because it was impossible to hold elections in their home provinces. Those who could not serve were replaced by their 1940s-era runners-up. Taiwan's ruling party, the Guomindang (GMD), installed two governments—central and provincial—to administer almost exactly the same territory, since eliminating one or the other would have upgraded Taiwan to something more than simply one of China's provinces. Individuals born in other provinces (who made up about 15 percent of Taiwan's postwar population) were over-represented in the national bureaucracy on the theory that this was necessary to ensure "provincial balance." All of these efforts were aimed at a single goal: preserving the fiction that the ROC was the government of all of China, a country of which Taiwan was but one small province.

ROC ideology regarded Taiwan as simply a means to an end, and

ROC leaders gave little thought to the possibility that Taiwan, or the Taiwanese people, might have value as ends in themselves. However, this outlook was sustainable only as long as the goal—mainland recovery—seemed attainable. By the 1970s, few people believed that the ROC would expel the Communist Party from power and reestablish the Republic of China as the sole Chinese government. The PRC was firmly in control of the mainland, a fact increasingly recognized by the international community. In 1971, the ROC found itself pushed out of the United Nations, its seat handed over to the PRC. Recovery of the mainland was out of reach. And once the end itself no longer was feasible, the idea that Taiwan was merely a means to that end lost its appeal. Taiwanese began to demand that their government treat the island as an end in itself.

The collapse of the ROC's original raison d'être left its government with a difficult choice. Either it could continue to impose the ROC fantasy by force, or it could undertake reforms aimed at building a new foundation under the ROC regime—a foundation of democratic participation. For a variety of reasons, the leaders of the ROC government chose the latter strategy. They began to broaden the state's outreach to its people, opening more opportunities in government service to native-born Taiwanese and shifting resources away from military construction and toward economic goals. The ROC's economic accomplishments became the basis of its political appeal as the state relaxed controls on political criticism and allowed an increasingly organized political opposition to take part in electoral competition. The result was a snowballing reform movement; by the mid-1990s, Taiwan's political institutions were entirely democratized.

Despite the many practical flaws and limitations of Taiwan's political system, all significant legal obstacles to full implementation of the ROC constitution were eliminated by 1994. In fact, the constitutional amendment implementing direct presidential elections took Taiwan's democracy beyond its original constitution. The Taiwanese today enjoy freedom of speech and assembly, and all of the ROC's legislative and chief executive offices are subject to free and fair elections. While many practical problems remain in Taiwan's democracy, its government has accepted and even embraced its identity as the "ROC on Taiwan." The goal of melding Taiwan with a democratic

China in the future remains for some, but Taiwan is no longer subordinate to this goal. For example, in 1991, President Lee Teng-hui declared that the ROC would no longer claim jurisdiction over the mainland. Instead, he acknowledged the existence of two Chinese governments, each with jurisdiction over part of the Chinese nation. One of the main accomplishments of the 1996 National Development Conference was a commitment by Taiwan's three leading political parties to put Taiwan's security and well-being ahead of all other policy goals.

The ROC's gradual transformation from an authoritarian state claiming sovereignty over all of China into a democratic state focused on the welfare of Taiwan and its people undermined the feasibility of its Nationality Law. Under the authoritarian institutions originally established on the island, the ROC's antiquated definition of citizenship—which granted "ROC nationality" to all persons with Chinese parents—caused little trouble. Since the substantive rights of citizenship essentially were suspended, formal citizenship could be extended to anyone at very little cost. But the democratization process granted substantive rights to ROC citizens. As a result, extending citizenship to anyone with Chinese ancestors was no longer workable. It was necessary to develop legal mechanisms for excluding PRC residents and overseas Chinese from Taiwan's elections and work force. Citizenship was defined and delimited as the ROC promulgated laws and regulations that—while not changing the formal definition of ROC nationality—limited substantive citizenship rights to a much narrower range of persons.

Laws on immigration and voting rights set the boundaries of substantive citizenship. Under these provisions, only ROC nationals who have permanent household registration in the "Taiwan Areas" of the Republic of China enjoy full citizenship rights.[11] They can live, work, and vote in Taiwan, whereas ROC nationals who do not have permanent household registration in Taiwan cannot. Article 9 of the Immigration Law defines the conditions under which a non-resident ROC national can apply for permanent residency in Taiwan, thereby guaranteeing his or her right to live and work there. Among these conditions are the following: possessing an immediate relative who is a permanent resident, being active in overseas Chinese organizations, investing in the ROC, and having needed job skills. This law makes it clear that Chinese nationality is not the same as ROC citizenship; it does not guarantee one's civil rights in the ROC. Nor does Chinese nationality guarantee political rights. According to Article 12 of the Election and Recall Law, the right to vote and run for office is reserved for permanent (that is, registered) residents of the "Free Areas" of the ROC and former residents living abroad who hold ROC passports. Eligibility for social welfare programs, too, is limited to permanent residents of Taiwan.[12]

The shift in Taiwan's political identity from the temporary home of the ROC to a country in its own right also has a cultural component. Paradoxically, the efforts of both Chinese governments to solidify Taiwan's cultural and historical connections to China proved counterproductive. Instead of convincing the Taiwanese that their fundamental identity is Chinese, these efforts encouraged many Taiwanese to see the island as separate and different from China. One reason for this backlash was the ROC government's insistence on promoting a specific, narrowly defined version of "Chinese" culture. Instead of recognizing the diversity of dialects, cultural practices, and religious traditions that are native to China, ROC leaders sought to impose an elite culture on all Taiwanese. Rather than acknowledging that the Minnan and Hakka languages spoken by most native-born Taiwanese are Chinese dialects, the ROC government demanded that Taiwanese learn Mandarin, which it called "the national language" (guoyu). Taiwanese opera, religion, and other folk practices were similarly denigrated. For many Taiwanese, the lesson was that they were not quite Chinese after all.[13]

The PRC has reinforced this sense of difference. Although Beijing's formal policy is that Taiwan is part of China and its people are Chinese, its behavior undermines its words. The PRC government treats Taiwan as its enemy, maintaining a constant threat of military action against the island. This attitude is not lost on the Taiwanese, who overwhelmingly believe the PRC is more hostile to Taiwan than is any other nation.[14] At the same time, Taiwanese who have traveled to mainland China often find their sense of "Chineseness" diminished. The way of life they encounter on the mainland barely resembles life on Taiwan, and many mainland Chinese treat "Taiwanese compatriots" as foreigners.

Despite the efforts of Sun Yat-sen's successors in the ROC and

PRC leaderships to include Taiwan in an ethnically pure Chinese nation-state, the island's actual experience over the past hundred years has undermined that project. Depending upon how one defines the "nation," Taiwan can be seen either as multi-national (an amalgamation of people whose origins are Minnan, Hakka, and aboriginal along with descendants of immigrants from every mainland province) or as sub-national (one part of a single China). The one category that does *not* work is the ROC on Taiwan as a nation-state. As the Taiwanese political scientist Chiang Yi-hua has explained, advocates of unification and of Taiwan independence use the nationalist approach with equal fervor; nationalism simply cannot resolve the dilemma of Taiwan's identity.[15]

Within Taiwan, the ROC government can no longer sustain the fiction that it represents all of China. Externally, Taiwan cannot assert itself either as "Taiwan," which the PRC violently opposes, or as "China," a mantle which passed long ago to Beijing. The fact remains, however, that the ROC on Taiwan does exist. There is a political entity on the island that administers its territory with the consent of its people. The outside world, for all its denials, tacitly accepts this reality. But this entity cannot claim the title "nation-state." What, then, is the basis of citizenship for the people of Taiwan?

The Changing Meaning of Citizenship in Taiwan

In his essay "Citizenship and National Identity," Habermas reverses the relationship between national identity and citizenship contained in the nationalist conception of the state. He writes, "The nation of citizens does not derive its identity from some common ethnic and cultural properties, but rather from the *praxis* of citizens who actively exercise their civil rights. At this juncture, the republican strand of 'citizenship' completely parts company with the idea of belonging to a prepolitical community integrated on the basis of descent, a shared tradition and a common language."[16] As the nation-state concept lost relevance as an organizing principle for the ROC on Taiwan, the idea of citizenship—of a state justified by its citizens' collective engagement in public life—moved in to fill the vacuum.

Sun Yat-sen envisioned a Republic of China whose legitimacy would rest on three principles: nationalism, democracy, and economic justice. Thus, from the beginning, the ROC's existence did not depend solely upon its status as a nation-state. The democratic component of Sun's ideology and the ROC constitution also served as resources. Initially, these institutions helped to legitimate the regime, but when the regime fell short of its democratic promise, they justified the opposition's reform demands.

The ROC's constitution and ideology both emphasize the central role of democratic procedures and popular sovereignty in establishing the state's legitimacy. Yet amid the chaos, disunity, foreign invasion, and civil war that followed the fall of the Qing dynasty, democracy was sacrificed to keep the state alive. But as the ROC settled in on Taiwan and the military threat subsided, calls for democratization—which never entirely disappeared—grew louder. In 1960, the ROC regime sentenced a GMD intellectual named Lei Chen to ten years in prison for trying to make common cause with Taiwanese politicians who hoped to form an opposition party and contest local elections.

Lei was not the first democracy activist incarcerated on Taiwan, and he certainly was not the last. Yet despite the regime's vigorous efforts to suppress it, the pro-reform movement continued to grow. Indeed, from its inception, democracy was the central demand of Taiwan's political opposition. At the same time, the opposition criticized ROC nationalism, which it said was no more than a rationalization aimed at justifying the GMD's continued rule. As long as the ROC's central mission was mainland recovery, the regime would go on insisting that conditions were not ripe for democratic reform.[17] P'eng Ming-min, an activist intellectual, explicitly rejected the nationalist version of Taiwan's destiny. In his book *A Taste of Freedom* P'eng argued that Taiwan should abandon the notion of the nation-state, adopting instead the concept of a community of shared destiny. He urged the Taiwanese to reject the equation of Chinese ethnic or cultural identity with membership in a Chinese political entity.[18]

Other activists shared P'eng's view. Christopher Hughes analyzes the early issues of the influential dissident magazine *Formosa (Meilidao)* and finds that its authors rejected nationalism in favor of a contractarian view of the state. Hughes writes, "In this view, a state arises when individuals identify with each other due to shared interests, forming a community to protect their territory and to take control of their destiny through democratic government . . . What the [opposition] activists were working towards by the late 1970s, then, was an ideology linking the individual with the political community that reverses the subservience of the individual to the nation-state in Chinese nationalism."[19] In other words, this key group of opposition activists had as their goal the creation of the kind of civic republic that Habermas describes.

Ultimately, the two main players in Taiwan's political arena converged on very similar interpretations of the nature of the state. For its part, the opposition has accepted "Republic of China on Taiwan" as the appropriate name for the political entity representing the people of Taiwan.[20] At the same time, the Guomindang has embraced the idea that ROC legitimacy rests on democracy, and that Taiwan is a "community of shared destiny," as P'eng and others in the opposition wrote so long ago. In the early 1990s, President Lee Teng-hui began speaking of the island's need for *Gemeinschaft (shengming gongtong ti),* or living community, in Taiwan. For Lee, as Hughes explains, "a political community is built by the subjective identification of individuals, rather than objective criteria imposed by ethnicity . . . [and] it is intimately linked by Lee to the idea of popular sovereignty."[21]

Ethnicity also mattered to the early oppositionists; their goal, however, was not to replace ROC nationalism with Minnan nationalism, but to bring about equal justice and democratic participation for all of Taiwan's residents. The idea that Taiwan should become a nation-state in its own right came later, after the opposition's demands for democratic reforms had largely been achieved. Taiwan independence holds great emotional appeal for many Taiwanese, but as a policy prescription, it has been all but abandoned.[22] Likewise, the fact that more than 60 percent of Taiwanese embrace the concept of "New Taiwanese," which explicitly rejects the socio-political categories of "Taiwanese" and "Mainlander," demonstrates the degree to which Taiwanese society is ready to put ethno-nationalism behind it.[23]

The Road Not Taken: Taiwanese Nationalism

When Chinese nationalism failed to legitimate the ROC on Taiwan, the Taiwanese might have chosen to keep "nationalism" and give up

"Chinese," instead of moving toward a post-nationalist vision of the state. In fact, many opposition activists dreamed of building a state on a foundation of Taiwanese nationalism. The vehicle for realizing their dreams was Taiwan independence, a concept that has enjoyed much wider support among political and intellectual elites than among ordinary Taiwanese; few reliable surveys have found more than 10 percent of Taiwanese in favor of immediate independence. But among opposition activists, the idea of separating Taiwan from China forever and building a new nation-state rooted in the experience of the Taiwanese themselves has had considerable appeal. In fact, the lure of a revised ethno-nationalism is so strong that some in the opposition gave independence higher priority than democratization. Julian Kuo points out that one of the central struggles within the opposition in the late 1980s was between those who put democratic procedures first, and those who insisted upon Taiwan independence regardless of the preferences of the Taiwanese people.[24]

The justifications offered for categorizing Taiwan as a nation-state are numerous and complex. Early theorists of Taiwan nationalism, including Shih Ming and Liao Wen-yi, sought to apply to Taiwan the same ethno-cultural definition of the "nation" *(minzu)* that Sun Yat-sen applied to China. They mined Taiwan's past for evidence that the Taiwanese constituted a distinct ethnic and cultural entity, pointing primarily to the island's history of immigration, colonization, and separation from China. This position, while attractive to advocates of Taiwan independence, does not hold up well to historical and theoretical scrutiny. First, it is impossible to deny that the great majority of Taiwanese (about 98 percent) have cultural and ancestral roots on mainland China. The effects of Taiwan's brief (and localized) occupation by Spanish and Portuguese forces were ephemeral, not formative. Japanese influences are discernible, but seem superficial compared with Taiwan's deeply rooted Chinese qualities. Second, as theory, Shih and Liao's work suffers from its essentialist bias and political motivation.

More recently, work by theorists of Taiwanese nationalism has begun to take on a more political coloration. However, even as these authors retreated from the effort to establish an ethno-nationalist basis for a Taiwanese state—tending, as Wu Jui-jen points out, toward territory/citizen nationalism rather than race/culture nationalism —they continued to equate the nation with the state.[25] Wu Nai-teh argues that the Taiwanese people are bound into a nation, not by their blood, but by their shared experience of oppression.[26] A Democratic Progressive Party (DPP) policy document echoes this view: "Deeply scarred by their experience with tyrannical outside rule, Taiwan's people today have a deep wish, a collective will to establish a modern democratic political system, based on their own consent, that will safeguard their freedom and welfare."[27]

The rejection of blood ties as the basis of Taiwan's national identity is even stronger in the work of Chang Mao-kuei and Hsu Hsin-liang, both important anti-GMD thinkers. Chang has written that there is a universal human need for "collective verification," recognition of a community's shared life experience, if societies are to achieve self-respect. As Chiang Yi-hua points out, Chang's perspective closes the door on blood ties as the basis of community, bringing him even closer to the idea that democracy, or popular will, is the basis of the state.[28] Hsu's "rising nation" thesis goes even farther in this direction. He argues that nations arise not because their culture or history is remarkable, but because "they know more than the other nations *(minzu)* of their time and they are more active than other nations of their time."[29] In Hsu's view, Taiwan's economic strength and intellectual attainments make it a rising nation of the twenty-first century.

Taiwan's nationalist intellectuals have come a very long way from their original belief that Taiwan is a distinct nation in the ethno-cultural sense. Still, they cannot free themselves from the quest to justify Taiwan's nationhood, because they want Taiwan to be a state, and they remain in the thrall of the nation-state equation. Thus, instead of searching for a new, non-nationalist basis for the state, these authors look for a new, non-ethnic basis for the nation. It is the liberal thinkers, led by Chen Ch'i-nan, who break out of that trap, rejecting once and for all the "bad trick" of nationalist ideology. Chen argues that the modern state is a "citizen state" *(gongmin guojia)* or "political state" *(zhengzhi guojia)* in which "citizen consciousness" replaces territory or race as its defining characteristic.[30]

These theoretical explorations constitute the explicit justification for the claims of Taiwanese nationalism. Another version of Taiwan's nationhood is rooted in daily life on Taiwan. One potent basis for a common Taiwanese identity is the division of labor between native

Taiwanese and Mainlanders (those who came to Taiwan from mainland China between 1945 and 1949).[31] For decades, Taiwanese were
relegated to the small business and agricultural sectors of Taiwan's
economy, while Mainlanders were disproportionately represented
in government service and in managerial positions in the island's
large industries, most of which were owned by the government or
the GMD. The Taiwanese also suffered discrimination in education,
where their non-standard Mandarin accents and lack of elite connections made admission to the best universities difficult. The native
Taiwanese experience of daily life appeared, at least, to be different
from that of Mainlanders. Taiwanese were taught that their language
and culture were inferior. At the same time, the Taiwanese felt at
home on the soil on which they lived; they could not share the deep
longing for China that many Mainlanders understood to be, not
homesickness, but nationalism. Finally, many of the GMD's opponents believed that Taiwan independence would somehow instanta-
neously expel that party from power.

In sum, there were real social, economic, cultural, and psychological gaps between Taiwanese and Mainlanders, gaps which reinforced
the feeling that Taiwanese were different from Mainlanders, and by
extension, from Chinese. Nonetheless, there were mitigating factors as well, factors which persuaded the majority of islanders that
Taiwanese nationalism provided no better solution to their problems than Chinese nationalism. The most important factors working
against Taiwanese nationalism were (and continue to be) external.
From 1945 to 1990, GMD rule vigorously repressed all discussion of
Taiwan independence and Taiwanese nationalism. In fact, the Taiwan Independence Movement (TIM) was born and grew up outside
of Taiwan, among exiles living abroad. When they returned to Taiwan after the GMD abolished its blacklist of banned dissidents, the
TIM activists found that, while they enjoyed considerable celebrity,
they and their ideas did not mesh well with the people and opinions
on the island. A second external factor working against Taiwanese
nationalism is the PRC, which constantly threatens to use force to
prevent Taiwan from seeking independence.

Internal factors, too, have reduced the attractiveness of Taiwan independence. As we have seen, Taiwan's moderate opposition has always emphasized democracy over nationalism. When the first oppo-

sition party, the DPP, was founded in 1986, its leaders included many opponents of independence, and even some pro-unification Mainlanders. It was only in 1991, after the overseas TIM activists returned to Taiwan and the DPP's main democratization demands were met, that the party reluctantly accepted Taiwan independence as part of its explicit program. The decision proved disastrous at the ballot box; the DPP did not recover from its 1991 setback until nine years later, when its candidate won the 2000 presidential race. The DPP's defeat in 1991 and its ongoing struggle to win more than a third of the vote in national elections have many causes, but its association with independence is an important one. In interviews I conducted in 1999, nearly every DPP leader and legislator mentioned the "burden" that its past advocacy of independence imposes on the DPP. What the party has come to realize is that Taiwanese nationalism does not appeal to mainstream voters in Taiwan, both because they are afraid of the consequences if Taiwan were to declare independence, and because many Taiwanese still cherish an ethnic and cultural identity that is Chinese.

Chiang Yi-hua argues that the reason Taiwanese nationalism fails in Taiwan is that most Taiwanese are not nationalists, but democrats. (He uses the word "liberals.")[32] They are not bound by the assumption that the state must reflect the nation; on the contrary, they believe the state is justified by its ability to serve the people and ensure democracy. This explains the Taiwanese people's overwhelming preference, Chiang argues, for the status quo—in which Taiwan's nationhood is left undecided—over either independence (the embodiment of Taiwanese nationalism) or unification (the embodiment of Chinese nationalism). For many political theorists, this preference for the status quo is a sign of immaturity or indecision; for Chiang, it is evidence of a post-nationalist liberalism.

Chiang's view is substantiated by a 1998 survey-based paper by Liu I-chou. In his poll, Liu disaggregates the concepts of "nation" and "state" by asking respondents three questions: What territory is included in "China" (*Zhongguo*)? What persons does "the Chinese people" (*Zhongguoren*) include? Who has the right to decide Taiwan's future? Liu discovered that Taiwanese tended to answer each of these questions independently. They recognized a strong link between China and Taiwan, both its territory and its people. Half the respondents believed that "China" included both Taiwan and the mainland, and 70 percent thought the "Chinese people" included people living on Taiwan as well as those in mainland China. When it came to politics, however, the respondents were clear that Taiwan should govern itself. Three-quarters of the respondents said only the people living on Taiwan should decide its future, and only 11 percent said the opinions of mainland Chinese should be considered.[33] This result clearly demonstrates that the Taiwanese differentiate between their identity as members of the ethnic, cultural, and historical entity that Sun Yat-sen called the Chinese nation, and their identity as citizens of a political entity which—despite its blurry legal status—they know very well to be a Taiwanese state.

Taiwan's Path to Citizen Republicanism

The failure of Chinese and Taiwanese nationalism to provide a lasting basis for the Republic of China on Taiwan is not itself a sufficient explanation for Taiwan's development into a state based on shared democratic values. As Habermas points out, democratic institutions alone do not make for constitutional patriotism. Summarizing the views of Charles Taylor, he writes: "The principles laid down in the constitution can neither take shape in social practices nor become the driving force for the project of creating an association of free and equal persons until they are *situated* in the horizon of the history of a nation of citizens." Habermas agrees with the caveat that such a political culture "by no means has to be based on all citizens sharing the same language or the same ethnic and cultural origins. Rather, the political culture must serve as the common denominator for a constitutional patriotism."[34]

How, then, did constitutional principles come to be situated in Taiwan's history? Part of the answer lies, ironically, in the ROC government's own propaganda. Sun Yat-sen's tripartite ideology—combining nationalism, popular sovereignty, and economic justice—required the GMD to infuse its propaganda and educational system with democratic as well as nationalistic messages. From the beginning, the GMD's efforts to rationalize its suspension of democratic institutions met with resistance from within and without; Lei Chen, persecuted for attempting to hold the party to its own values, was only one of many martyrs in this cause. Yet, despite the GMD's willingness to repress those who demanded democracy in practice, it could not abandon its rhetorical commitment to democracy. Doing so became even more difficult in the 1970s, when the ROC's only claim to the sympathy of the world (especially the United States, on which it depended for its military modernization and economic growth) was its status as "Free China." The cost of denying democracy increased as the ROC became more vulnerable. Thus, as a result of its efforts to persuade the Taiwanese to embrace its values, the GMD intensified the demand for democracy.

Although the GMD's propaganda activities were not determinative, they did make available to the Taiwanese a broad range of ideas and values for thinking about politics—ideas and values that became part of Taiwan's political culture. As Margaret Somers points out, political culture is one of the factors to be considered in explaining the development of citizenship. She writes, "citizenship cannot be explained by looking for rights granted 'ready-made' by states. Instead, the focus must be on the presence of national universal laws and legal institutions, which under certain conditions of place, political culture and participation could be transformed into rights."[35]

Taiwan's civil society was another contributing factor in the development of citizenship as the basis of the ROC state. Before its GMD-led economic transformation of the 1960s and 1970s, Taiwan resembled the pastoral regions of England that Somers describes: semi-autonomous villages blending industry and agriculture and enmeshed in a dense weave of centuries-old social networks. During the period of Qing rule, Taiwan was largely self-governing; the expression "a small rebellion every three years, a big rebellion every five years" summarized the empire's assessment of its Taiwanese subjects. The Japanese colonial government imposed a much higher degree of administrative penetration on Taiwan, but it, too, built its political institutions on a foundation of existing social networks.

The ROC's economic development strategy reinforced the sense of self-reliance and embeddedness in local networks that characterized Taiwan's rural communities. Under the import substitution and export-oriented industrialization strategies the ROC pursued in the 1950s, 1960s, and 1970s, financial capital for large-scale industrialization was available mainly to state enterprises and firms linked to the

GMD. The entrepreneurs who ran Taiwan's small and medium-sized manufacturing companies were on their own, obtaining financing from informal capital markets and negotiating individual deals with international buyers. The ethnic division of labor was evident in the economic realm: while many Mainlanders became dependents of the state—working in state companies, bureaucratic agencies, or the military—most Taiwanese lived in an economy built on traditional social networks such as families, clans, and villages. Persuaded by the saying, "Better to be a chicken's head than a cow's ass" *(ningwei jitou buwei niuhou)*, the Taiwanese established thousands of tiny manufacturing firms, each of which managed its own international trading relations with little government assistance or involvement.

In addition to these economic developments, Taiwan's robust civil society intersected with politics in local elections that were both frequent and competitive. Beginning in 1950, the ROC government implemented a regular schedule of local elections on Taiwan, including elections at the village, township, county/city, and provincial levels. These elections spawned complex networks, firmly rooted in existing economic, social, familial, and political relationships, aimed at mobilizing votes and distributing the spoils of office. The ROC's emergency provisions prevented non-GMD politicians from forming alternative political parties, but they could not eliminate competition. In practice, the electoral formula used in representative elections—single, non-transferable voting in multi-member districts—encouraged competition. To improve their chances, individual politicians merged their personal political networks into tightly knit local factions that contested elections ferociously, and sought real political and economic stakes. Although most factions cooperated with the GMD most of the time (in exchange for patronage and pork barrel benefits), local politicians owed their loyalty primarily to their factions, and in many cases, they forced the ruling party to reorganize their vital interests. As Kuo explains, "When the center was more powerful and resourceful, central agents tended to prevail. By contrast, when the center was weak and dependent upon elections to sustain its rule, local agents arose."[36]

Elections reinforced the community solidarity and self-reliance that characterized Taiwan's civil society. They also created a sense of expectation and entitlement that nurtured Taiwan's developing citizenship culture. Guomindang organizational theory encouraged Taiwanese to make demands on state representatives, a practice the GMD calls "service." GMD offices in villages and townships are called "service stations" (terminology that elected officials have borrowed for their own district offices), and party officials who work in service stations are classified as "social workers."[37] Wu Nai-teh has argued that a "patronage mentality" was part of the GMD's strategy for ruling Taiwan. According to a 1966 guide to grassroots party organizing, "Our working procedure should be so arranged that we should directly go into the personal problems of the people and help them to solve those problems. Only when we can benefit them practically and immediately can we gain their trust and support."[38] While the GMD's service orientation to some extent created a sense of dependency and subjectivity, rather than citizenship, in combination with other aspects of Taiwan's political economy, the expectation that government should "deliver the goods" helped nurture the idea that ordinary Taiwanese were entitled to make claims against the state, even political ones, and hold the state accountable.

In sum, elections encouraged voters and candidates alike to view themselves as participants in public life. They created interests vis-à-vis the state, and they institutionalized a channel for articulating and asserting those interests. They encouraged Taiwanese to think of their participation in elections and policy-making (at least at the local level) as rights. And as hopes for recovery of the mainland faded, Taiwanese began to pressure their leaders to put Taiwan's own quality of life ahead of nationalistic goals. The dwindling likelihood of unification under the ROC flag also undermined the rationale for preserving the pre-1949 national government, leading many Taiwanese to challenge the electoral system's "glass ceiling." One of the opposition's earliest reform proposals was the replacement of the "thousand year legislature" with a body elected by the people of Taiwan. After the regime agreed to grant that demand in 1990, the opposition began a campaign to amend the constitution to allow popular presidential elections. Its success in this effort made the ROC on Taiwan more democratic than the GMD leaders had ever imagined.

Notes

Contributors

Notes

Introduction: Political Citizenship in Modern China

1. T. H. Marshall, *Citizenship and Social Class* (Cambridge: Cambridge University Press, 1950); *Class, Citizenship, and Social Development* (New York: Doubleday, 1964).
2. For an overview of recent debates, see Bart van Steenbergen, ed., *The Condition of Citizenship* (London: Sage Publications, 1994).
3. On this process of the Chinese borrowing back their own terms, imbued with new meaning, from Japan, see Lydia H. Liu, *Translingual Practice: Literature, National Culture, and Translated Modernity—China, 1900–1937* (Stanford: Stanford University Press, 1995).
4. Sung-chiao Shen and Sechin Y. S. Chien, "Delimiting China: Discourses of 'Guomin' and the Construction of Chinese Nationality in the Late Qing," paper delivered at the conference on "Nationalism: The East Asian Experience," May 25–27, 1999, Academia Sinica, Taipei, p. 5.
5. Ibid., pp. 7–15.
6. Leo Ou-fan Lee, *Shanghai Modern: The Flowering of a New Urban Culture in China* (Cambridge, Mass.: Harvard University Press, 1999), pp. 52–53.
7. Mizoguchi Yūzō, "Chugoku ni okeru *ko, shi* gainen no tenkai" (The evolution of the concepts of *gong* and *si* in China), *Shiso*, no. 669 (1980): 19–38.
8. William T. Rowe, *Hankow: Conflict and Community in a Chinese City, 1796–1895* (Stanford: Stanford University Press, 1989), p. 184.
9. Mary Backus Rankin, *Elite Activism and Political Transformation in China: Zhejiang Province, 1864–1911* (Stanford: Stanford University Press, 1986); Rankin, "Some Observations on a Chinese Public Sphere," *Modern China*, vol. 19, no. 2 (April 1993): 158–182; William T. Rowe, "The Problem of

'Civil Society' in Late Imperial China," *Modern China,* vol. 19, no. 2 (April 1993): 139–157.

10. Zhang Zhongli et al., eds., *Jindai Shanghai chengshi yanjiu* (A study of the modern city of Shanghai) (Shanghai: Shanghai People's Press, 1990), pp. 712–731.

11. R. Bin Wong, "Citizenship in Chinese History," in Michael Hanagan and Charles Tilly, eds., *Extending Citizenship, Reconfiguring States* (Lanham, Md.: Rowman and Littlefield, 1999), pp. 97–122.

12. Andrew J. Nathan, *Chinese Democracy* (New York: Knopf, 1985).

13. Joseph R. Levenson, *Liang Ch'i-ch'ao and the Mind of Modern China* (Cambridge, Mass.: Harvard University Press, 1953); Hao Chang, *Liang Qichao and Intellectual Transition in China, 1890–1907* (Cambridge, Mass.: Harvard University Press, 1971); Philip C. Huang, *Liang Chi-chao and Modern Chinese Liberalism* (Seattle: University of Washington Press, 1972); Zhang Pengyuan, *Liang Qichao yu minguo zhengzhi* (Liang Qichao and Republican politics) (Taipei: Shihuo Publishing Company, 1981); Xiaobing Tang, *Global Space and the Nationalist Discourse of Modernity: The Historical Thinking of Liang Qichao* (Stanford: Stanford University Press, 1996); Peter Zarrow, "Citizenship and Human Rights in Early Twentieth-Century Chinese Thought: Liu Shipei and Liang Qichao," in Wm. Theodore de Bary and Tu Weiming, eds., *Confucianism and Human Rights* (New York: Columbia University Press, 1997); "Liang Qichao and the Notion of Civil Society in Republican China," in Joshua A. Fogel and Peter Zarrow, eds., *Imagining the People: Chinese Intellectuals and the Concept of Citizenship* (Armonk: M. E. Sharpe, 1997), pp. 232–257.

14. Theresa Man Ling Lee, "The Meaning of Citizenship in Late Imperial Chinese Political Discourse: A Century Later," paper prepared for the Conference on Changing Meanings of Citizenship in Modern China, Fairbank Center for East Asian Research, Harvard University, October 29–31, 1999.

15. Michael Schoenhals, "'Non-people' in the People's Republic of China: A Chronicle of Terminological Ambiguity," *Indiana East Asian Working Paper Series on Language and Politics in Modern China,* no. 4 (1994): 1–48.

16. An important contribution in the intellectual history tradition is Fogel and Zarrow, eds., *Imagining the People;* see also Edmund S. K. Fung, *In Search of Chinese Democracy* (Cambridge: Cambridge University Press, 2000). A pathbreaking cultural history that reaches beyond elite circles to address the place of citizenship in Republican-era political rituals is Henrietta Harrison, *The Making of the Republican Citizen: Political Ceremonies and Symbols in China, 1911–1929* (New York: Oxford University Press, 2000).

17. John Fitzgerald, *Awakening China: Politics, Culture and Class in the Nationalist Revolution* (Stanford: Stanford University Press, 1998), pp. 87–92.

18. David Strand, *Rickshaw Beijing: City People and Politics in the 1920s* (Berkeley: University of California Press, 1989).

19. Richard C. Kraus, *Class Conflict in Chinese Socialism* (New York: Columbia University Press, 1981).

20. Ezra F. Vogel, "From Friendship to Comradeship: The Change in Personal Relations in Communist China," *The China Quarterly* (Jan.-March 1965): 54–55.

21. Nathan, *Chinese Democracy.*

22. Dorothy J. Solinger, *Contesting Citizenship in Urban China: Peasant Migrants, the State, and the Logic of the Market* (Berkeley: University of California Press, 1999), p. 1.

23. Margaret M. Pearson, *China's New Business Elite: The Political Consequences·of Economic Reform* (Berkeley: University of California Press, 1997).

1. Gender and the Meaning of Modern Chinese Citizenship

1. A careful reading of the main texts of the Enlightenment in France, England, and the colonies reveals that the nature of the relationship between women and the state remained largely unexamined. Linda Kerber, "The Republican Mother: Women and the Enlightenment—An American Perspective," in *Toward an Intellectual History of Women: Essays by Linda Kerber* (Chapel Hill: University of North Carolina Press, 1997), p. 42. In the case of France, it was not until the Republic that officials took up a problem left wide open by the Revolution: the contradiction between the universal equality of individuals and the exclusion of women from citizenship. In 1870 Jules Ferry made a passionate plea for the education of girls, and it was not until 1880 that the Camille Sée law regarding girls' high schools was passed. Mona Ozouf, *Women's Words: Essay on French Singularity* (Chicago: University of Chicago Press, 1997), pp. 260–261. Mary Wright made a similar point about the entire trajectory of Western ideas being imported into China at once. She described it in terms of the Chinese believing they could "leapfrog over the stages of the development of other countries." "Introduction," in Mary Clabaugh Wright, ed., *China in Revolution: The First Phase, 1900–1913* (New Haven: Yale University Press, 1968), pp. 60–62.

2. The term "knowledge culture" comes from the work of Margaret Somers. It can be briefly defined as a "conceptual site," or "site of knowledge," which "establishes the boundaries of epistemic possibilities within a given historical moment." Margaret R. Somers, "The Privatization of Citizenship: How to Unthink a Knowledge Culture," in Victoria E. Bonnel and Lynn Hunt, eds., *Beyond the Cultural Turn* (Berkeley: University of California Press, 1999), pp. 124–132. I would take issue with Somers's suggestion

that knowledge cultures presuppose epistemic closure. Instead I argue that competing knowledge cultures can coexist, become mutually embedded, and thus give rise to a contested sense of what is historically possible—or desirable.

3. Women such as prostitutes could also serve as symbols of China's degradation. On the uses of women in reformist political discourses in the late Qing and Republican periods, see Gail Hershatter, *Dangerous Pleasures: Prostitution and Modernity in Twentieth Century Shanghai* (Berkeley: University of California Press, 1997), especially pp. 246–248.

4. Rong-qing, Zhang Baixi, and Zhang Zhidong, "Zouding mengyang yuan zhangcheng ji jiating jiaoyu fa zhangcheng" (Memorial on regulations for early training schools and for education on household matters) (January 13, 1904), in Chen Yuanhui, ed., *Zhongguo jindai jiaoyushi ziliao huibian: Xuezhi yanbian* (Compendium of sources on the history of Chinese modern education: The evolution of the educational system; Shanghai: Shanghai jiaoyu chubanshe, 1991), p. 396.

5. Xia Xiaohong, *Wan-Qing wenren funü guan* (The Late Qing literati's view of women; Beijing: Zuojia chubanshe, 1995), pp. 98–99. The author of this statement was Yan Bin, editor of the *Zhongguo xin nüjie zazhi* (Magazine of the New Chinese Women).

6. See, for example, He Xiangning, "Jinggao wo tongbao jiemei" (A warning for my sister compatriots), *Jiangsu*, 4 (June 23, 1903): 144; Xia, *Wan-Qing*, p. 91; Lin Zongsu, "Lin Nüshi Zongsu Nüjiezhong xu" (Ms. Lin Zongsu's discussion of *Wake-up call for women*), *Jiangsu*, 5 (August 23, 1903): 131 [941]. On the suffrage movement in the early years of the Republic, see David Strand, "Citizens in the Audience and at the Podium," Chapter 2 of the present volume.

7. On the distinctions between ideology as "applied," "official," and "in practice," see Dorothy Ko, *Teachers of the Inner Chambers: Women and Culture in Seventeenth-Century China* (Stanford: Stanford University Press, 1994), pp. 17–18.

8. On the stragegy of social naturalism see Somers, "Privatization," pp. 129–130.

9. Guang Zhanyun, Guang Yiyun, and Chen Yuxin, comps., *Zuixin funü guowen duben* (Newest Chinese reader for women), 10 vols. (Fuzhou: Jiaoyu puji she, 1908), "Dayi," pp. 1–2.

10. On the meaning of Republican Motherhood in the United States, see Kerber, *Toward an Intellectual History*, pp. 41–62, 94; in France, see Joan B. Landes, *Women and the Public Sphere in the Age of the French Revolution* (Ithaca: Cornell University Press, 1988), pp. 129–138, and Lynn Hunt, *The Family Romance of the French Revolution* (Berkeley: University of California Press, 1992), pp. 122–123. Hunt uses the term "patriotic motherhood" rather than Republican Motherhood.

11. One of the fundamental differences between the reformists and the radicals lay precisely in their different perspectives on the relationship between motherhood and citizenship. For the most radical female activists in the late Qing period, the two were incompatible. The revolutionary doctor Zhang Zhujun, for example, opposed the idea of marriage since it entailed children, which would keep women from fulfilling their national duties. The radical woman writer Yan Bin also considered the need to work for national salvation to be more pressing than the need to procreate. Xia, *Wan-Qing*, pp. 100–101.

12. Liang Qichao, "Lun nüxue" (On female education), reprinted in Zhu Youhuan, ed., *Zhongguo jindai xuezhi shilao* (Historical materials on the modern Chinese educational system; Shanghai: Huadong Shifan daxue chubanshe, 1986), 2:1.

13. Rong-qing, Zhang, and Zhang, "Zouding mengyang," p. 396.

14. Yalu (Liu Yazi), "Ai nüjie" (A lament for women), *Nüzi shijie* (1904): 1–9. Reprinted in Zhu, *Zhongguo*, 2:2, pp. 577–581.

15. See, for example, Peter Zarrow, "Introduction: Citizenship in China and the West," in Peter G. Zarrow and Joshua A. Fogel, eds., *Imagining the People: Chinese Intellectuals and the Concept of Citizenship, 1890–1920* (Armonk: M. E. Sharpe, 1997), pp. 17–18; Joan Judge, *Print and Politics: "Shibao" and the Culture of Reform in Late Qing China* (Stanford: Stanford University Press, 1996), pp. 79–119.

16. Dan Chen, "Lun funüquan bi yi jiaoyu wei yubei" (Education is necessary as preparation for the revivial of women's rights), *Nüzi shijie*, 4 (1905): 1–3 (reprinted in *Zhu, Zhongguo*, 2:2, pp. 582–584).

17. Liu Sheng, *Nüzi guowen duben* (Chinese reader for girls and women; Shanghai: Shangwu yinshuguan, 1905), pp. 30–31, 33.

18. Xie Chongxie, *Chudeng xiaoxue nüzi xiushen jiaokeshu* (Lower-level elementary female ethics textbook; Shanghai: Zhongguo jiaoyu gailiang hui, 1906).

19. Other early schools include one founded by Liang Qichao and Kang Guangren in 1897 and directed by Li Gui, Tan Sitong's wife, and Jing Yuanshan's Jingzheng nüxue, founded in late 1897. On the early schools see Liao Xiuzhen, "Qingmo nüxue zai xuezhi shang de yanjin ji nüzi xiaoxue jiaoyu de fazhan, 1897–1911" (Late Qing women's education in the context of the evolution of the educational system and the development of women's elementary education, 1897–1911), in Li Yuning, ed., *Zhongguo funü shilun wenji* (Historical essays on Chinese women's history; Taipei: Commercial Publishing, 1992), vol. 2, pp. 224–227. On Aiguo nüxue see Cai Yuanpei, "Aiguo nüxue sanshiwu nian lai zhi fazhan" (The development of the Patriotic Women's School over the last 35 years), *Aiguo nuxuexiao sanshiwu zhounian jinian kan* (Reminiscences on the 35th anniversary of the Patriotic Women's School, reprinted in Zhu, *Zhongguo*,

2:2, pp. 609–610). On Wuben nüshu see Wu Xin, "Wuben nüxue shilüe" (Outline of the history of the Wuben Women's School), *Wuben nüshu* (Wuben Women's School; reprinted in *Zhu, Zhongguo*, 2:2, pp. 589–590).

20. Xia, *Wan-Qing*, p. 88.

21. The Shanghai Zhongguo nüxue hui (Shanghai Chinese Women's Education Association), which was established in 1902 and was closely tied to the Chinese Education Association, for example, was one of the associations that marked the beginnings of the women's rights movement in early twentieth-century China.

22. "Xuebu zouding nüzi shifan xuetang zhangcheng zhe" (The Ministry of Education's memorial on the enactment of regulations for women's normal schools) and "Xuebu zouding nüzi xiaoxue tang zhangcheng" (The Ministry of Education's memorial on the enactment of regulations for women's elementary schools), *Da Qing Guangxu xinfaling, dishisance* (New laws under Emperor Guangxu of the Great Qing Dynasty), vol. 13, 1907, 3.8: 35–47, reprinted in Zhu, *Zhongguo*, 2:2, pp. 657–674. On the importance of the regulations of 1907, see Taga Akigorō, comp., *Kindai Chūgoku kyōiku shi shiryō—Shinmatsu hen* (Historical materials for modern Chinese education—late Qing; Tokyo: Japanese Association for the Advancement of Scholarship, 1972), p. 73.

23. Xia, *Wan-Qing*, p. 89.

24. Liao, "Qingmo," pp. 224–227; Chen Dongyuan, *Zhongguo funü shenghuo shi* (A history of the lives of Chinese women; Shanghai: Shangwu yinshuguan, 1928, reprinted 1937), p. 361.

25. Zhu, *Zhongguo*, 2:2, pp. 632–633; Chen, *Zhongguo*, p. 361.

26. The text was published by the Nanyang guanshuju in Shanghai. Chen Baoquan, a native of Tianjin, attended Kōbun gakuin in Japan and eventually took up the post of director of the Board of Education in China. Gao Buying (1873–1940), the holder of a *juren* degree from Hebei province, went to Japan to study in 1902. After the 1911 Revolution he also took up a position at the Ministry of Education.

27. Advertisements for the *Gongmin bidu chubian* (Citizens' reader, first edition) appeared in each of the bimonthly issues of the *Yubei lixian gonghui bao* (Constitutional Preparation Association Report) from March 13, 1908, until May 2, 1909, when the second edition began to be advertised. From what I could learn at the Shanghai Municipal Library and from scholars in Shanghai, neither of these readers is extant.

28. According to this program, *guomin bidu keben* (citizens' textbooks) should be published in the year 1908. Chi, "Lun jinri wei guomin xiongfei zhi shiqi" (It is now time for citizens to take flight), *Shibao* (September 23, 1908).

29. The one exception I have found is a much later citizens' reader from 1928 which includes a subsection on women in a section entitled "Questions and Answers."

30. Sun Shiyue, *Zhongguo jindai nüzi liuxue shi* (The history of overseas study by Chinese women; Beijing: Zhongguo heping chubanshe, 1995), p. 161. On Chen Hengzhe, see Amy D. Dooling and Kristina M. Torgeson, *Writing Women in Modern China: An Anthology of Women's Literature from the Early Twentieth Century* (New York: Columbia University Press, 1998), pp. 87–89.

31. These commercial publishers included the giants of late Qing publishing, Shangwu yinshuguan and Wenming shuju, both of Shanghai, for example, and some local publishers such as the Jiaoyu puji she of Fuzhou.

32. Xie, *Chudeng*, Lesson 1. Almost precisely the same wording and argument appear in the first lesson of the *Chudeng xiaoxue nüzi guanhua xiushen jiaokeshu* published by the Kexue shuju in Shanghai in 1905. Cited in Luo Suwen, *Nüxing yu jindai Zhongguo shehui* (Women and modern Chinese society; Shanghai: Renmin chubanshe, 1996), p. 145.

33. Xie, *Chudeng*, Lesson 2.

34. "Lun nüxue yi xianding jiaoke zongzhi" (Female education should first set its course objectives), *Dongfang zazhi* (hereafter *DFZZ*), 4: 7 (1908): 129.

35. See Zarrow, "Introduction," on national citizenship, p. 16; and Margaret R. Somers on localized and multiple practices of rights, "Rights, Relationality, and Membership: Rethinking the Making and Meaning of Citizenship," *Law and Social Inquiry,* 19: 1 (Winter 1994): 77.

36. While the term *guomin* had been used since ancient times interchangeably with other compounds designating subject *(chenmin)* in relation to the ruler *(junzhu),* or the common people *(baixing)* or multitude *(limin, lishou,* or *lishu),* in this earlier view the people were the charge of Heaven rather than the participants in a temporal political entity. They existed at a distant remove from the cycles of dynastic rise and decline, deprived of political rights but also free from political concerns and responsibility. It was not until the late Qing period that a new concept of the citizen intimately linked to the nation's destiny arose. See Mizoguchi Yūzō, "Zhongguo minquan sixiang de tese" (Special characteristics of Chinese ideas about popular sovereignty), *Zhongguo xiandaihua lun wenji* (Essays on Chinese modernization; Taipei: Zhongyang yanjiusuo, Jindai shi yanjiu, March 1991), p. 354.

37. As Peter Zarrow has written, the term *guomin* "straddled the distinction between a mere 'national' and a full-fledged 'citizen'"; "Introduction," p. 18.

38. Chen Baoquan and Gao Buying, eds., *Guomin bidu* (Citizens' reader; Shanghai: Nanyang guanshuju, 1905), vol. 1, pp. 1–2.

39. Xu Jiaxing, *Zuixin nüzi xiushen jiaokeshu* (Newest ethical textbook for girls and women; Shanghai: Qunxue she, March–August 1906), p. 3.

40. Lü was the first Chinese woman to head a school, the Beiyang nüzi gongxuetang, and she also served as editor for the Tianjin newspaper *Dagong bao;* Xia, *Wan-Qing,* p. 94.

41. See, for example, "Wuben nüshu zengshe chudeng, gaodeng nüzi xiaoxue guize" (Wuben Women's School adds regulations for lower- and higher-

level elementary education), *Zhili jiaoyu zazhi*, 1: 17: 48–49, reprinted in Zhu, *Zhongguo*, 2:2, pp. 594–595; "Wuben nüshu ji youzhi she yundonghui ji" (Record of the Wuben Women's School and kindergarten athletic meet), *Shibao* (October 17, 1905), reprinted in Zhu, *Zhongguo*, 2:2, p. 600; Chen Xiefen, "Ji Wuben nüxuetang" (Record of Wuben Women's School), *Nübao*, 4 (1902), reprinted in Zhu, *Zhongguo*, 2:2, p. 599.

42. In the lower-level elementary schools, physical education was allotted one-sixth or one-seventh of instruction time (twice the amount devoted to ethics); in upper-level elementary schools one-tenth; and in normal schools one-seventeenth. "Xuebu zouding nüzi xiaoxue tang," pp. 661–665; "Xuebu zouding nüzi shifan," pp. 671–672.

43. Xu, *Zuixin*, p. 3. Another elementary textbook devotes a lesson to the importance of physical activity, citing the authority of Western doctors, and noting the difference between exercises for girls and those for boys; Xie, *Chudeng*, Lesson 16. Both the importance of physical education for girls and this gender specificity are evident in the late Qing production of women's physical education textbooks. One example is a textbook written by a Xu Chuanlin entitled *Nüzi ticao fanben* (Physical education reader for girls). An introduction to the text in *Jiaoyu zazhi* notes that Mr. Xu, an expert on physical education, who had already published a number of books on the subject, tailored this particular textbook to the needs of girls. The reviewer notes that while the Chinese people are generally weak in body *(wenruo)*, this fault is particularly endemic to women and must be changed; "Shaojie piping" (Introduction and criticism), *Jiaoyu zazhi*, 1.2 (XT 1 February 25, 1909): 7 [175].

44. Luo, *Nüxing*, pp. 152–153.

45. The connection between anti-footbinding and women's education was made from the late nineteenth century. As early as 1882 Kang Youwei had made plans to establish an anti-footbinding association in Guangdong. By 1895 several such associations existed in Shanghai, and in 1897 Liang Qichao tied the two issues of footbinding and women's education together in his essay "Bianfa tongyi." Liang suggested that the way to get around the problem of women with bound feet not being marriageable was to create an association in which none of the women members bound their feet, and these women would marry the male members of the association. On this issue, see, for example, Chen, *Zhongguo*, pp. 316–318.

46. This particular song was popularized at the first school for girls and women in Tianjin. Luo, *Nüxing*, p. 154. On the Wuben school and anti-footbinding, see Wu Ruoan, "Huiyi Shanghai Wuben nüshu" (Reminiscences of Shanghai Wuben Women's School), in "Wu Ruoan koushu" (Wu Ruoan's oral history), 1986, reprinted in Zhu, *Zhongguo*, 2:2, p. 603.

47. Liu, *Nüzi*, Lesson 33, p. 9; Lesson 70, p. 20; Lesson 78, p. 22. See also Guang, Guang, and Chen, *Zuixin funü*, vols. 6 and 9.

48. See Liu, *Nüzi*.

49. Xu, *Zuixin*, Lessons 119, 120.

50. Xie, *Chudeng*, Lesson 49.

51. Liu, *Nüzi*, Lesson 17.

52. See, for example, Guang, Guang, and Chen, *Zuixin funü*.

53. Liu, *Nüzi*, Lessons 5–8.

54. Guang, Guang, and Chen, *Zuixin funü*, vol. 5.

55. Ibid.

56. Ibid., vols. 4, 6, 7, 8, 10.

57. Ibid., vols. 7, 10; Xie, *Chudeng*, Lesson 37.

58. Again, this resonates with the ideal of Republican Motherhood. Linda Kerber (*Toward an Intellectual History*, p. 268) has written of republican America that women could claim political participation only so long as they implicitly promised to keep their politics in the service of the men in their family.

59. "Xing nüxue yi" (On promoting women's education), *DFZZ*, 3.13 (1906): 244.

60. Yate (Liu Yazi), "Lun zhuzao guominmu" (Educating mothers of citizens), *Nüzi shijie*, 7 (1904): 1–7 (reprinted in Zhu, *Zhongguo*, 2:2, p. 574). The Spartan mother was also an inspiration for conceptons of republican or patriotic motherhood in America (Kerber, *Toward an Intellectual History*, p. 42) and France. In 1793 a painting by Jean-Claude Nageon entitled *The Spartan Woman* was presented at the Salon in Paris.

61. Xie, *Chudeng*, Lesson 50.

62. Guang, Guang, and Chen, *Zuixin funü*, vols. 4, 6.

63. On the resistance of students from the Patriotic Women's School, see *Subao*, May 8, 1903; on the overseas student organization see Abe Hiroshi, *Chûgoku no kindai kyōiku to Meiji Nihon* (Modern Chinese education and Meiji Japan; Tokyo: Fukumura shuppan kabushiki gaisha, 1990), p. 102.

64. Linda Kerber has demonstrated how allegiance—in the form of joining in boycotts, fund raising, street demonstrations, signing of collective statements—was gradually given as much weight as military service in American definitions of citizenship. Kerber, *Toward an Intellectual History*, p. 92.

65. Guang, Guang, and Chen, *Zuixin funü*, vol. 6.

66. Yate, "Lun zhuzao," p. 575.

67. Guang, Guang, and Chen, *Zuixin funü*, vols. 4, 6. The radical woman Wu Zhiying went so far as to attempt to institutionalize female contributions to the national cause. She advocated the creation of a Nü guomin juan (Female Citizen's Fund) which would allow women to contribute to the repayment of the national debt. Wu called on women to contribute to the fund by saving their money in a Shanghai bank. She drafted regulations for the fund which were distributed throughout the country. Xia, *Wan-Qing*, p. 98.

68. Liang, "Lun nüxue," pp. 869–870.

69. The Board of Education did not even sanction higher education for females until 1913. Luo, *Nüxing*, pp. 158, 348. On Zhang's school and her views on female vocational education see Zhang Zhujun, "Zhang Zhujun zai Aiguo nüxuexiao yanshuo" (Zhang Zhujun's lecture at the Patriotic Women's School), *Jingzhong ribao* (May 2, 1904), p. 3, reprinted in Zhu, *Zhongguo*, 2:2, p. 622. Other schools in this period also included some form of vocational training in women's arts. The Guangdong nüzi baoxianhui shiye xuetang (Female Insurance Association School of Practical Training) and the Aiguo nüxue both established handicraft training institutes, for example; see Xia, *Wan-Qing*, p. 96.

70. Kerber, *Toward an Intellectual History*, p. 91.

71. According to one author, for example, "Westerners . . . say that women are the mothers of citizens." "Lun nüxue yi xianding," p. 130.

72. Authors of the period frequently drew on the *Lienü zhuan* (Biographies of exemplary women) by Liu Xiang (79–8 B.C.E.) of the Han dynasty, for example. These processes of appropriation or historical sedimentation are what Somers calls "narrative causality" in the formation of conceptions of citizenship; "Rights," p. 112.

73. Yang Qianli, ed., *Nüzi xin duben* (New reader for girls and women; Shanghai: Wenming shuju, 1905 [1904]), "Daoyan," p. 2.

74. On these dualities see Prasenjit Duara, "The Regime of Authenticity: Timelessness, Gender, and National History in Modern China," *History and Theory: Studies in the Philosophy of History*, 37:3 (1998): 287–308.

75. Yang, *Nüzi*, vol. 1, Lessons 22, 23, 25.

76. The three specific examples of Meng Mu's maternal rectitude and wisdom which are repeated in different permutations in the textbooks were drawn from two Han texts: the *Lienü zhuan* and the *Hanshi waizhuan* (Master Han's illustrations of the didactic application of the *'Classic of Songs'*) (one example is repeated in the two texts, while two are unique to each of the two texts). Albert Richard O'Hara, *The Position of Woman in Early China According to the Lieh Nü Chuan "The Biographies of Chinese Women"* (Taipei: Meiya Publications, 1971), pp. 39–40; James Robert Hightower, *Han Shih Wai Chuan: Han Ying's Illustrations of the Didactic Application of the "Classic of Songs,"* Harvard-Yenching Institute Monograph Series, vol. XI (Cambridge, Mass.: Harvard University Press, 1952), p. 290. Mencius's mother is not the only maternal exemplar celebrated in these texts. Other righteous Chinese mothers in these materials include the famous Song official Ouyang Xiu's mother, who educated her son to become a famous official despite poverty and the death of her husband. Xie, *Chudeng*, Lessons 44–45. Even after sons had reached official pinnacles, the influence of the mother remained crucial, as demonstrated in the case of the mother of a certain Cui Xuanwei who ensured that her son did not act corruptly in his official capacities. Guang, Guang, and Chen, *Zuixin funü*, vol. 5.

77. Guang, Guang, and Chen, *Zuixin funü*, vol. 6.
78. One of the most important examples of this process of historical appropriation in the late Qing period was Chinese constitutionalism, the larger narrative into which moderate reformers inserted the trope of "women as citizens." These reformers were committed to creating an internationally competitive new nation on the Western model while preserving the power of the dynasty. They therefore sought to integrate foreign ideas like constitutionalism with China's cultural traditions by indigenizing these foreign ideas through references to, for example, China's ancient constitutionalism, *minben* (people as the root of the nation) theory. See Judge, *Print and Politics,* pp. 54–75.
79. Xu, *Zuixin,* Lessons 119, 120.
80. Wu Tao, ed., *Nüzi shifan xiushen xue* (Ethics for female normal students; Beijing: Beijing diyi shuju, 1907), pp. 2–3, 11.
81. Xu, *Zuixin,* Lessons 119, 120.
82. Chen, *Guomin bidu,* vol. 2, pp. 7–8.
83. Guang, Guang, and Chen, *Zuixin funü,* vol. 7, pp. 17–18.
84. For a lesson on eliminating superstition, see, for example, Wu, *Nüzi shifan,* p. 37.
85. Male writers across the political spectrum shared a commitment to eradicating the influence of Buddhism and Daoism. In an essay which appeared in *Nüzi shijie* in 1904, the author (probably Liu Yazi) stated that one of the principal reasons why women's knowledge was blocked was that they had been seduced not only by men but by Buddhists and Daoists. Yate, "Lun zhuzao," p. 574. The radical author using the pen name Jinyi Lover of Freedom (Ai ziyou zhi Jinyi) claims that superstition was a problem endemic to women because of the depth of their affective life. Their misguided feelings and hopes had to be replaced with patriotism, a desire to save the world, and a commitment to revolution. Cited in Chen, *Zhongguo,* pp. 333–334.
86. Xie, *Chudeng,* Lessons 31–32; Guang, Guang, and Chen, *Zuixin funü,* vol. 6; Liu, *Nüzi,* Lessons 56–59, 63–64, pp. 15–18.
87. Liu, *Nüzi,* Lessons 79, 88.
88. From the time of the Roman republic, citizenship was defined in terms of a man's willingness to take up arms to defend the state. J. G. A. Pocock, *The Machiavellian Moment: Florentine Political Thought and the Atlantic Republican Tradition* (Princeton, N.J.: Princeton Universtiy Press, 1975), p. 90. On the connection between militarism and citizenship in the United States, see Kerber, *Toward an Intellectual History,* p. 88.
89. Gao Fengqian, Cai Yuanpei, and Zhang Yuanji, *Zuixin chudeng xiaoxue xiushen jiaokeshu jiaoshou fa* (New primary school textbooks: Methods for teaching elementary ethics; Shanghai: Shangwu yinshuguan, 1906), vol. 3, p. 12.
90. Liu, *Nüzi,* p. 34.

91. Xie, *Chudeng*, Lesson 36; Yang, *Nüzi*, vol. 1, Lessons 8–10.

92. Yang, *Nüzi*, vol. 1, Lesson 19; Xie, *Chudeng*, Lesson 34; Yang, *Nüzi*, vol. 1, Lesson 5.

93. Yang, *Nüzi*, vol. 1, Lesson 25.

94. Ibid., vol. 2, Lesson 6; Lessons 7–9; Guang, Guang, and Chen, *Zuixin funü*, vol. 8.

95. Yang, *Nüzi*, vol. 1, Lessons 13, 16; Guang, Guang, and Chen, *Zuixin funü*, vol. 5; Yang, *Nüzi*, vol. 2, Lessons 3, 4, 10, 11.

96. Guang, Guang, and Chen, *Zuixin funü*, vols. 7, 11.

97. Luo, *Nüxing*, pp. 479–481. This is the reason for Tang Qunying's outrage in 1912; see Strand, "Citizens in the Audience and at the Podium," Chapter 2 of the present volume.

98. Somers sees the meaning of citizenship as arising out of a context of participatory claims in the pluralities of local civil societies; "Rights," p. 65.

2. Citizens in the Audience and at the Podium

1. I think "millions" is reasonable if one includes not only uprisings against the Qing led by Sun Yat-sen and others but the railway recovery movement, the anti-American boycott, and the politics surrounding the establishment of provincial assemblies under the Qing.

2. Henrietta Harrison, *The Making of the Republican Citizen: Political Ceremonies and Symbols in China, 1911–1929* (Oxford: Oxford University Press, 2000), pp. 30–40.

3. I have found Bruce Lincoln's work on the "authorizing capacity" of speech and also the "corrosive" nature of heckling and other contentious responses illuminating. Lincoln, *Authority: Construction and Corrosion* (Chicago: University of Chicago Press, 1994).

4. I have explored the notion of "political aesthetics" as applied to public speaking at greater length in "'Getting Up and Giving a Speech Isn't Easy': Public Speaking, Public Life, and Political Aesthetics in Early Twentieth Century China," Association for Asian Studies annual meeting, March 11, 2000, San Diego.

5. Sun Qimeng, "Yinzi" (Preface), *Yanjian chubu* (Public-speaking Preliminaries) (Shanghai: Shenghuo shudian, 1946), p. 1.

6. Ibid., p. 3. Other examples of anti-glibness sentiments in the *Analects* include: "Someone said, Yung is truly virtuous, but he is not ready with his tongue. The Master said, What is the good of being ready with the tongue? They who encounter men with smartness of speech for the most part procure themselves hatred. I know not whether he be truly virtuous, but why should he show readiness of the tongue?" James Legge, trans. and ed., *The Four Books* (New York: Paragon, 1966), p. 50.

7. Sun Qimeng, "Preface," p. 3.

8. Mu Jinyuan, "Miuxu" (A poor preface), in Richard D. T. Hollister, *Yanshuo xue* (The Science of Public Speaking), Liu Qi, ed. (Shanghai: Shangwu yinshuguan, 1930), p. 1.

9. Ibid., p. 3.

10. J. I. Crump, *Intrigues: Studies of the Chan-kuo Ts'e* (Ann Arbor: University of Michigan Press, 1964), p. 36.

11. Legge, *Four Books,* p. 490.

12. Crump, *Intrigues,* p. 100.

13. See, for example, Ning Wu's memoir of actions taken on behalf of Sun Yat-sen when dispatched to shore up a shaky alliance with Zhang Zuolin in 1921. Ning, by his own account, uses choice phrases and faultless logic to persuade Zhang that rumors of plans to make Sun president are false and planted by common enemies. After hearing Ning out, Zhang can only nod his head and exclaim: "Makes sense, makes sense!" Both the facts of the case and the style of Ning's story suggest continuities with the material analyzed by Crump and discussed above. Ning Wu, "Sun Zhongshan yu Zhang Zuolin lianhe fanZhi jiyao" (A summary of the alliance of Sun Yat-sen and Zhang Zuolin against Zhili), in Shang Mingxuan, Wang Xueqing, and Chen Song, eds., *Sun Zhongshan shengping shiye zhuiyilu* (Recollections of Sun Yat-sen's Lifework) (Beijing: Renmin chubanshe, 1986), pp. 247–301.

14. Kung-chuan Hsiao, *Rural China: Imperial Control in the Nineteenth Century* (Seattle: University of Washington Press, 1960), p. 186.

15. Li Boyuan, *Wenming xiaoshi* (A Short History of Civilization) (Hong Kong: Jindai tushu gongsi, 1958).

16. Ibid., p. 12.

17. Ibid., p. 14.

18. Ibid., p. 15.

19. "Zhongguo jindai yanjiang jianshi" (A short history of modern public speaking in China), in Shao Shouyi et al., eds., *Yanjiang quanshu* (A Complete Book of Public Speaking) (Changchun: Jilin renmin chubanshe, 1991), p. 590 (hereafter *YJQS*). For mention of Kang's Cantonese accent, see Tong Qiang, *Kang Youwei zhuan* (A Biography of Kang Youwei) (Beijing: Tuanjie chubanshe, 1998), p. 133.

20. Kenneth Cmiel, *Democratic Eloquence: The Fight over Popular Speech in Nineteenth-Century America* (Berkeley: University of California Press, 1990), p. 23.

21. See James Polachek, *The Inner Opium War* (Cambridge, Mass.: Council on East Asian Studies, Harvard University, 1992), p. 193; Mary Rankin, *Elite Activism and Political Transformation in China: Zhejiang Province, 1865–1911* (Stanford: Stanford University Press, 1986), p. 5; and *Liang Rengong nianpu changbian* (A Comprehensive Biography of Liang Qichao), ed. Yang Jialuo (Taibei: Shijie shuju, 1972), pp. 15–16, for examples of literati oratory.

22. Li Boyuan, *Civilization*, p. 122.

23. Ibid., p. 125.

24. Bryna Goodman, *Native Place, City, and Nation: Regional Networks and Identities in Shanghai, 1853–1937* (Berkeley: University of California Press, 1995), p. 31.

25. Li Boyuan, *Civilization*, p. 127.

26. Tang Chengye, *Guofu geming xuanchuan zhilüe* (A Sketch of the Guofu's Revolutionary Propaganda) (Taibei: Zhongyang yanjiuyuan sanmin zhuyi, 1985), p. 99.

27. Ibid., p. 100.

28. Ibid. Zhang Park was established in 1882 and became famous not only for its restaurants and theaters but also for the political activities that took place there. See Yu Jianxin, "Cong sijia huayuan dao gongyuan" (From private gardens to public gardens), in Xin Ping, Hu Zhenghao, and Li Xuechang, eds., *Minguo shehui daguan* (An Omnibus of Republican Society) (Fuzhou: Fujian renmin chubanshe, 1991), pp. 959–960.

29. Tang Chengye, *Revolutionary Propaganda*, p. 104.

30. *YJQS*, p. 590.

31. Ibid., p. 592.

32. Min Jie, *Jindai Zhongguo shehui wenhua bianqian lu* (Records of Social and Cultural Change in Modern China), book 2 (Hangzhou: Zhejiang renmin chubanshe, 1998), p. 255.

33. Ibid.

34. Ibid.

35. Ibid.

36. See the many examples of public speaking as a mobilization and communications strategy found in Li Hsiao-ti, *Qingmo de xiaceng shehui qimeng yundong* (Lower Class Enlightenment in the Late Qing Period) (Taibei: Institute of Modern History, 1992), pp. 85, 93, 95, 97, 102–111.

37. See, for example, accounts of Liang Qichao's 1907 speech on the occasion of the founding of his reformist "Political Participation Society" in Tokyo and the mayhem that resulted when the revolutionary Zhang Ji called Liang a "horse fart" and Zhang Ji's comrade Song Jiaoren seized the podium away from Liang. *Comprehensive Biography of Liang Qichao*, p. 250; K. S. Liew, *Struggle for Democracy: Sung Chiao-jen and the 1911 Chinese Revolution* (Berkeley: University of California Press, 1971), p. 86; Peter Zarrow, *Anarchism and Chinese Political Culture* (New York: Columbia University Press, 1990), p. 56.

38. Min Jie, *Records*, p. 256.

39. Ibid.

40. "A Short History," in *YJQS*, p. 589. See also Jonathan D. Spence, *God's Chinese Son: The Taiping Heavenly Kingdom of Hong Xiuquan* (New York: Norton, 1996), pp. 287–288.

41. "Yanshuo de haochu," in *Qiu Jin ji* (A Qiu Jin Anthology) (Shanghai: Shanghai guji chubanshe, 1991), p. 3.

42. Ibid., p. 4.

43. "A Short History," in *YJQS*, p. 588.

44. Ono Kazuko, *Chinese Women in a Century of Revolution, 1850–1950*, ed. Joshua Fogel (Stanford: Stanford University Press, 1989), p. 78.

45. "Tang Qunying," in *Zhongguo funü mingren cidian* (A Dictionary of Famous Chinese Women) (Changchun: Beifang funü ertong chubanshe, 1989), p. 498; Sheng Shusen, Tan Changchu, and Tao Zhi, "Zhongguo nüquan yundong de xianqu Tang Qunying" (Forerunner of Chinese feminism Tang Qunying), *Renwu* (Personalities), 2:72 (1992).

46. Ono, *Chinese Women*, p. 61.

47. Tan Sheying, *Zhongguo funü yundong tongshi* (A General History of the Chinese Women's Movement) (Shanghai: Shanghai shudian, 1990), p. 13 (from the Japan Overseas Chinese Women's Society manifesto). Tang was an officer of the society.

48. Ibid., p. 15.

49. Ibid., p. 21.

50. Liang, "Xinmin shuo," *Liang Qichao wenxuan* (Selected Works of Liang Qichao) (Beijing: Zhongguo guangbo dianshi chubanshe, 1992), p. 102.

51. Li Xisuo and Xu Ning, "Minyuan qianhou (1911–1913 nian) guomin 'canzheng re' pingxi" (A review and analysis of "Political Participation Fever" during the founding of the Republic), *Tianjin shehui kexue* (Tianjin Social Sciences), 2 (1992), p. 52.

52. Chen Dongyuan, *Zhongguo funü shenghuo shi* (A History of the Lives of Chinese Women) (Shanghai: Shanghai shudian, 1928), p. 356.

53. "Tang Qunying," *Zhongguo funü mingren cidian*, p. 499.

54. Chen Dongyuan, *Lives*, p. 357.

55. Li Xisuo and Xu Ning, "Participation Fever," p. 52.

56. Chen Dongyuan, *Lives*, p. 359.

57. Ono, *Chinese Women*, pp. 82–84. Ono thinks that "armed" meant pistol-wielding. See also Jing Shenghong, "Minchu nüquan yundong gaishu" (A general account of the early Republican women's movement), *Minguo chunqiu* (Annals of the Republic), 3 (1995), p. 3.

58. Li Xisuo and Xu Ning, "Participation Fever," p. 52.

59. Chen Dongyuan, *Lives*, p. 57.

60. *Minlibao* (Shanghai), August 25, 1912, and August 30, 1912, in Wang Gengxiong, ed., *Sun Zhongshan shishi xianglu, 1911–1913* (A Detailed Chronology of Sun Yat-sen, 1911–1913) (hereafter *SZSXL*) (Tianjin: Tianjin chubanshe, 1986), pp. 347–348.

61. Wang Canzhi, "Sun Zhongshan yu Beijing Huguang Huiguan" (Sun Yat-sen and the Huguang Hostel), in *Beijing Huguang Huiguan zhigao* (Draft Annals of the Beijing Huguang Hostel) (Beijing: Yanshan chubanshe,

1994). Founded in 1807, the hostel or guild served as a temporary residence for examination candidates but also played host to banquets, weddings, and funerals held by metropolitan officials. With the advent of the Republic, Beijing's hundreds of provincial hostels increasingly assumed the role of political meeting places (p. 29).

62. Tang Chengye, *Revolutionary Propaganda*, p. 23.

63. *Minlibao* (Shanghai), August 31, 1912, in Wang Canzhi, "Sun Yat-sen," p. 30.

64. The single most coherent account of the day's events is found in *Zhongguo ribao* (Beijing), August 26, 1912, p. 2. This version provides the sequence of the two meetings—the Revolutionary Alliance welcome in the morning and the Nationalist Party convention in the afternoon—as well as the two speeches by Sun and the two interventions by the female party members. Unless otherwise indicated, the description of events that day given in this chapter is based on this source.

65. *Minguo yiwen* (Anecdotes of the Republic), vol. 3 (n.p.: Chunfeng wenyi chubanshe, 1993), p. 206.

66. Liew, *Struggle for Democracy*, p. 150.

67. Song Jiaoren, *Wo zhi lishi* (My History), ed. Wu Xiangxiang (Taibei: Zhongguo xiandai shiliao pushu, 1962), pp. 17, 41, 76.

68. Ono, *Chinese Women*, p. 87. Ono provides a brief account of the controversy over women's rights at the August 25 meeting, also based on newspaper accounts.

69. Ibid.

70. Ibid.

71. *Zhengzong aiguobao* (Beijing), August 27, 1912, in Wang Canzhi, "Sun Yat-sen," p. 33.

72. Ibid., pp. 33–34.

73. *Zhengzong aiguobao* (Beijing), August 27, 1912, pp. 3–4.

74. Harrison, *Republican Citizen*, pp. 51–52.

75. *Beijing xinbao*, August 26, 1912, p. 3.

76. *Shenbao* (Shanghai), September 3, 1912, in *SZSXL*, pp. 360–361.

77. Li Xisuo and Xu Ning, "Participation Fever," p. 53.

78. Ibid.

79. Ibid.

80. *Zhongguo ribao* (Beijing), August 25, 1912, p. 2.

81. Kristin Stapleton, *Civilizing Chengdu: Chinese Urban Reform, 1895–1937* (Cambridge, Mass.: Asia Center, Harvard University, 2000), pp. 146–148. See also Harrison, *Republican Citizen*, pp. 76–80, for details on the kinds of clothing women began to wear in public and the political significance of these changes in fashion.

82. Ono, *Chinese Women*, p. 85.

83. For a discussion of the rise of public speaking in the context of other vari-

eties of "political theater," see Joseph W. Esherick and Jeffrey N. Wasserstrom, "Acting Out Democracy: Political Theater in Modern China," in Jeffrey N. Wasserstrom and Elizabeth J. Perry, eds., *Popular Protest and Political Culture in Modern China* (Boulder: Westview Press, 1994), pp. 50–51.

84. Mu Jinyuan, "Poor Preface," p. 6.

85. "A Short History," in *YJQS*, pp. 594–595.

86. On the connection between "reporting" *(zuo baogao)* and *yanjiang*, see Yu Xinyan, "Tantao yixia yanjiang de yishu" (Probing the art of public speaking), in *Yanjiang jingyan tan* (Talks on the Speech-Making Experience) (Beijing: Beijing ribao chubanshe, 1983), pp. 1–2.

87. Han Li, *Yanjiang shu* (The Art of Speech-Making) (Shanghai: Dagongbao daibanbu, 1937), p. 1. The author recalls winning prizes as a student.

88. Ibid., p. 9.

89. "A Short History," in *YJQS*, p. 599.

90. Gong Qichang, *Gongmin jiaoyuxue* (Citizen Education) (n.p.: Zhongzheng shuju, 1948), p. 343.

91. Gu Yaqiu, "Jianzhu sheji yu dushimei zhi guanxi," *Dongfang zazhi* (Eastern Miscellany), 28:5 (March 10, 1931), p. 50.

92. Xu Shilian, "Difang fuwu yu gongmin xunlian" (Local services and citizen training), *Dongfang zazhi*, 23:9 (May 19, 1926), p. 8.

93. Huang Danzai, "Zhongguo nongcun dianhua zhi xianqu" (Forerunner of Chinese rural electrification), *Dongfang zazhi*, 28:31 (November 10, 1931), p. 26.

94. Mu Jinyuan, "Poor Preface," p. 5.

95. E. E. Sheng (pseud.), "Yanshuo wei zuiyao zhi xuewen" (Public speaking is a most important [kind] of learning), *Aiguo bao* (Patriotic Post), Beijing, August 8, 1912, p. 1.

96. Mu Jinyuan, "Poor Preface," p. 6.

97. Huang Yaomin, *Minzhu yundong jianghua* (Talks on Democratic Movements) (n.p.: Qunli shudian, 1947), p. 64.

98. Lincoln (*Authority*, pp. 8–9) in more general terms suggests that "it is through these paired instrumentalities—ideological persuasion and sentiment evocation—that discourse holds the capacity to shape and reshape society itself."

99. For a discussion of the importance of individualism and individual emotion in the Republican era, see Hong-yok Ip, "Liang Shuming and the Idea of Democracy in Modern China," *Modern China*, 17 (1991): 491.

100. Han Li, *Speech-Making*, p. 1.

101. Esherick and Wasserstrom, "Acting Out," p. 52.

102. Zhang Ji, *Zhang Puquan xiansheng quanji* (The Complete Works of Mr. Zhang Ji) (Taibei: Zhongyang wenwu gongying she, 1951), p. 198.

103. "Tang Qunying," *Zhongguo funü mingren cidian*, p. 499.

104. Yu Xinyan, "Probing."

105. "A Short History," in *YJQS,* pp. 657–676. This recent overview of the history of public speaking in China contains an interesting account of the Cultural Revolution as a "strange period" of policy error and lively speech-making.

106. Yang Gaochao and Liu Deqiang, *Yanjiang yishu* (The Art of Public Speaking) (n.p.: Zhejiang renmin chubanshe, 1986), p. 13.

3. Democratic Calisthenics

I am indebted to Cynthia Brokaw, William Kirby, Wendy Larson, Elizabeth Perry, Mary Rankin, and Vivienne Shue for their criticisms and suggestions.

1. David Strand, "Protest in Beijing: Civil Society and Public Sphere in China," *Problems of Communism* (May-June 1990): 2; Elizabeth J. Perry and Ellen V. Fuller, "China's Long March to Democracy," *World Policy Journal,* 8.4 (Fall 1991): 666; R. Bin Wong, *China Transformed: Historical Change and the Limits of European Experience* (Ithaca: Cornell University Press, 1997), pp. 158–164; Mary Rankin, "State and Society in Early Republican Politics," *The China Quarterly,* no. 150 (June 1997); Wen-hsin Yeh, "Commerce and Culture in Shanghai," *The China Quarterly,* no. 150 (June 1997).

2. Lydia H. Liu, *Translingual Practice: Literature, National Culture, and Translated Modernity* (Stanford: Stanford University Press, 1995).

3. Rankin, "State and Society."

4. The term *shimin quan* was widely used. See "Shimin quan yu chunjuan wenti" (Urban citizens' rights and the spring tax problem), *Minguo ribao* (Republican Daily), January 11, 1920; "Shanghai gonggong zujie nashui huarenhui" (Shanghai Ratepayers Association), *Shimin gongbao* (Citizen's Gazette), January 1, 1921; "Ge tuanti huansong wu guwen jiuzhi ji" (Account of each association's send-off on behalf of the five advisers' assuming office), *Shangbao* (Journal of Commerce), May 12, 1921. See also Chen Laixin, "Shanhai kakurō shōkai rengōkai ni tsuite, 1919–1923" (Regarding the Shanghai Federation of Commercial Street Unions), *Kōbe daigaku shigaku nenpō,* 3 (March 1988): 78–98.

5. Reports on these groups and initiatives may be found in Shanghai newspapers *(Shenbao, Minguo ribao, Shangbao)* for 1919–1923, and in the following: Public Record Office, FO 228.3291, Political Intelligence Reports, Shanghai, 1921–1927; Shanghai Archives, Shanghai Municipal Council, Police Daily Reports (hereafter PDR), 1-1-1122 (April-June 1919); 1-1-1126 (April-June 1920); 1-1-1130 (January-March 1921). See also Chen Laixin, "Shanhai kakurō."

6. Guoqi Xu, cited in William Kirby, "The Internationalization of China," *The China Quarterly,* no. 150 (June 1997).

7. Wu Mianbo, "Guang-Zhao gongsuo fengchao shimo ji" (Account of the

Guang-Zhao *gongsuo* struggle) (unpublished ms., 1919), pp. 21, 101; *Shenbao,* September 1, 1919; *Minguo ribao,* September 1, 1918. See also Song Zuanyou, "Yige chuantong zuzhi zai chengshi jindaihua zhong de zuoyong—Guang-Zhao gongsuo chutan" (The function of a traditional organization in urban modernization: A preliminary discussion of the Guang-Zhao *gongsuo*), in Zhang Zhongli, ed., *Zhongguo jindai chengshi: qiye, shehui, kongjian* (Shanghai: Shanghai shehui kexue yuan, 1998), pp. 415–431. Material in this article concerning the Guang-Zhao *gongsuo* first appeared in Bryna Goodman, "Being Public: The Politics of Representation in 1918 Shanghai," *Harvard Journal of Asiatic Studies* (June 2000): 45–88, and is reprinted here with the permission of the editors.

8. One man, Chen Keliang, had been in place for half a century, since the establishment of the *gongsuo* in 1872. Wu, "Guang-Zhao," pp. 79–80; Obituary of Chen Keliang, *North China Herald,* September 27, 1919.

9. Wu, "Guang-Zhao," p. 79, statement of Wen Zongyao. For evidence of meeting practices see also the meeting notes of the Guang-Zhao *gongsuo:* "Guang-Zhao gongsuo yishi bu" 1891–1911 (Record of the Guang-Zhao *gongsuo* meetings); "Guang-Zhao gongsuo yi'an bu," 1912–1914 (Shanghai Municipal Archives, Q-118-12).

10. "Gailiang Guang-Zhao gongsuo zhi yijian" (Opinion concerning the Guang-Zhao *gongsuo* reform), *Minguo ribao,* August 29, 1918.

11. "Guang-Zhao gongsuo gaizu dongshibu zhi zhengyi" (The Guang-Zhao *gongsuo* board of directors reform dispute), *Minguo ribao,* August 26, 1918.

12. See Bryna Goodman, *Native Place, City, and Nation: Regional Networks and Identities in Shanghai, 1853–1937* (Berkeley: University of California Press, 1995), chap. 3.

13. On the native-place associations in the May Fourth movement in Shanghai, see Bryna Goodman, "New Culture, Old Habits: Native-Place Organization in the May Fourth Movement," in Frederic Wakeman and Yeh Wenhsin, eds., *Shanghai Sojourners* (Berkeley: Institute of East Asian Studies, University of California, 1992), pp. 76–107. On the Ningbo *tongxianghui* reform see Goodman, *Native Place,* pp. 224–228; *Ningbo lühu tongxianghui yuebao* (Monthly Journal of the Ningbo Sojourners Association in Shanghai) (Shanghai, 1921).

14. The Commercial Federation, under the leadership of Tang Jiezhi, was already organized as early as February/March 1919, in the context of the North-South peace talks. "Gaige Shanghai zongshanghui zuzhi yi" (Opinion on the Shanghai General Chamber of Commerce reform), *Shenbao,* May 21, 1919; "Shangren duiyu zongshanghui zhi zenan" (Merchants' criticisms of the general chamber of commerce), *Shangbao,* May 11, 1919. See also Xu Dingxin and Qian Xiaoming, *Shanghai zongshanghui shi* (History of the Shanghai General Chamber of Commerce) (Shanghai: Shanghai

shehui kexue yuan, 1991); Zhang Huanzhong, *Shanghai zongshanghui yan-jiu, 1902–1929* (Research on the Shanghai General Chamber of Commerce) (Taibei: Zhishufang, 1996), p. 206; Joseph Fewsmith, *Party, State, and Local Elites in Republican China: Merchant Organizations and Politics in Shanghai, 1890–1930* (Honolulu: University of Hawaii Press, 1985), pp. 55–56; Marie-Claire Bergère, *The Golden Age of the Chinese Bourgeoisie, 1911–1937* (Cambridge: Cambridge University Press, 1986), pp. 136–139.

15. Shanghai zongshanghui tongrenlu (Membership list of the Shanghai Chamber of Commerce) (Shanghai, 1920); "Overthrow of Old Clique in Chamber of Commerce Gives Chinese New Hope," *China Press*, August 22, 1920 (clipping in Sokolsky archives, Hoover Institution, Box 311); Zhang Huanzhong, *Shanghai zongshanghui*, p. 222; Fewsmith, *Party, State*, p. 55.

16. See Shanghai Municipal Council, PDR, 1-1-1122; Chen Laixin, "Shanhai kakuro"; Zhang Huanzhong, *Shanghai zongshanghui; Shanghai Nanjinglu shangjie lianhehui huikan* (n.d.), Shanghai Municipal Archives, QO-13-186; "Chinese Firms Organizing New Chamber of Commerce," *North China Star,* June 27, 1919 (clipping in Sokolsky archives, Hoover Institution, Box 331). I am grateful to Mary Rankin for pointing out that the slogan "no taxation without representation" was used earlier in the Zhejiang and Sichuan railway movements.

17. The question of such representation had been an active issue in Shanghai politics since the Mixed Court Riot of 1905. See Kuai Shixun, "Shanghai gonggong zujie huaguwenhui de shizhong" (Account of the Chinese Advisory Council for the Shanghai International Settlement), *Shanghai shi tongzhiguan qikan,* 1:4 (March 1934): 915–973; Goodman, *Native Place*, pp. 193–194.

18. PDR, 1-1-1123, 1-1-1124; Shanghai Municipal Council, *Annual Report* (Shanghai, 1920); Kuai Shixun, "Shanghai gonggong zujie." This figure of 10,000, as Fewsmith notes, does not appear to be exaggerated. A petition to the Municipal Council in April bore chops of 8,000 merchants. Fewsmith, *Party, State*, p. 58.

19. The Chinese text is reproduced in *Shimin gongbao*, 1 (January 1921): 2–3. The translation which appears here slightly modifies the translation which appeared in the *North China Herald,* June 12, 1920.

20. In 1910 the Shanghai Municipal Council informally recognized a body of fourteen principal "guilds" with which it consulted when matters arose affecting the Chinese community; see Shanghai Municipal Council, *Annual Report of the Shanghai Municipal Council for 1910*, pp. 88, 272–273. This consultative role, particularly of the Ningbo and Shanghai native-place associations, was widely recognized in the foreign community. For example, the Shanghai memoir of O. M. Green, the former editor of the *North China Daily News,* describes the "once all-powerful . . . Canton and Ningbo Guilds" as "representing Chinese public opinion in Shanghai" prior to

1919; O. M. Green, *The Foreigner in China* (London: Hutchinson, 1942), p. 161. See also Goodman, *Native Place*, pp. 152–158.

21. *Shimin gongbao*, 1 (January 1921): 3; *North China Herald,* June 12, 1920.

22. I have slightly modified the translation of the *gongsuo* letter, quoted in the *North China Herald,* June 12, 1920, p. 660, according to the Chinese text of this statement, published in *Shimin gongbao*, 1 (January 1921): 3. See also PDR, V1-1-1130 (June 7, 1920).

23. They are remarkable particularly in view of the fact that Western "representative democracy" in the Shanghai Municipal Council was, as Robert Bickers has recently noted, "a secretive, self-perpetuating oligarchy," scarcely amenable to public inquiry into its representative mechanisms, even within the Western community. The Municipal Council was elected, within a property-based franchise that was highly restrictive and in which certain individuals exercised multiple voting privileges; see Robert Bickers, "Shanghailanders: The Formation and Identity of the British Settler Community in Shanghai 1843–1937," *Past and Present,* 159 (May 1998): 161–211.

24. *Shimin gongbao*, 1 (January 1921).

25. See, for example, "Historic Move Launched as Shanghai Forms Body for Citizens' Convention: Eighty-Three Local Organisations Represented at Initial Meeting of Local Society for Holding of National Conference," *China Press,* August 22, 1920 (clipping in Sokolsky archives, Hoover Institution, Box 311).

26. This movement had some success in terms of charter revision. "Gelu lianhehui zhi guoqu he jianglai" (Past and future of the Street Union Federation), *Shishi xinbao,* August 11, 1920; Yan E'sheng, "Shanghai zongshanghui he shangjie zong lianhehui de ruogan huodong" (Various activities of the Shanghai Chamber of Commerce and the Federation of Commercial Unions) (oral history manuscript, recorded by Hu Zhipan, c. 1960), Shanghaishi Gongshanglian archives. I am indebted to Xu Dingxin for giving me a copy of this manuscript. See also Chen Laixin, "Shanhai kakurō," pp. 80–81.

27. Huo Shouhua and Feng Shaoshan were also active in this movement, though I do not mean to suggest, by noting this, that these Guangdong reformers were the force behind the new Federation. "Gelu lianhehui gaixuan fengchao" (Storm in the Street Union Federation over the election issue), *Minguo ribao,* August 27, 1921; *Shibao,* September 5, 1921; "Gelu shangjie lianhehui zhi xin zuzhi" (The New Street Union Federation), *Shangbao,* September 4, 1921.

28. After the transliteration "de-mo-ke-la-xi," *pingmin zhuyi*, together with *shumin zhuyi*, both, literally, "the doctrine of the common people," were the most common translations for democracy in the May Fourth era. See Edward X. Gu, "Who Was Mr. Democracy? The May Fourth Discourse of

Popular Democracy and the Radicalization of Chinese Intellectuals (1915–1922)," *Modern Asian Studies*, 35.3 (July 2001).

29. Yan E'sheng, "Shanghai zongshanghui"; Chen Laixin, "Shanhai Kakurō," pp. 79–82; Laurent Galy, "Le Guomindang et ses relais dans la société shanghaienne en 1923," *Études Chinoises*, 17.1–2 (1998).

30. PDR, VI-1-1130; *Shenbao*, February 21, 1921; February 22, 1921.

31. On the associational networks underlying the anti-Japanese boycott, see Galy, "Le Guomindang et ses relais."

32. For the Guang-Zhao *gongsuo* crisis, see Goodman, "Being Public." For the Street Unions, see Chen Laixin, "Shanhai kakurō"; for the Chinese Ratepayers' Association, see Kuai Shixun, "Shanghai gonggong zujie."

33. See Rankin, "State and Society," p. 273, regarding the growth and crucial role of the press in the social mobilization of the early Republican era.

34. Translated in PDR, V1-1-1130 (February 22, 1921). Copies of this pamphlet were published in *Xinwenbao, Shenbao,* and *Xin Shenbao* on February 21, 1921.

35. Bryna Goodman, "Politics, Press Rivalries and Reportage: Shanghai Newspaper Culture and What Was Public in the Early Republican Era," conference paper, "Press, Reader and Market in Late Qing and Republican China," Institute for Chinese Studies, University of Heidelberg, October 19–21, 1997.

36. In public disputes, newspapers also served to constitute the public record of events and utterances, against which the truth of particular claims could be assessed. As one party to the Guang-Zhao *gongsuo* dispute reflected, responding to his opponents' reconstructions of events: "The newspapers are still there—there is no way they can cover it up." Wu, "Guang-Zhao," p. 121. The 1919 manuscript history of the Guang-Zhao crisis testifies to the new importance of newspapers and their capacity to represent a new form of public truth. The manuscript is made up of pamphlet and newspaper transcriptions, cobbled together with periodic background explanations and intertextual commentary.

37. See, for example, "Shangren duiyu zongshanghui zhi zenan" (Businessmen's censure of the General Chamber of Commerce), *Shenbao*, May 11, 1919.

38. *Shibao*, September 10, 1919; *North China Herald*, September 13, 1919.

39. The PDR describe Tang as owner of the *Guang-Zhao zhoubao*, V1-1-1125 (February 6, 1920).

40. Bergère, *Golden Age*, p. 137.

41. PDR, V1-1-1130 (January 5, 1921); *Shimin gongbao*, 1 (January 1921).

42. *Shanghai Nanjinglu shangjie lianhehui huikan.*

43. On the *Shangbao*, see Goodman, "Politics, Press Rivalries."

44. It is interesting to note a corresponding effect on institutional record-keeping in this period. Prior to the May Fourth movement, the meeting

records of the Chamber of Commerce provide only brief summations of resolutions taken, with little, if any, mention of the actual discussions that took place. After May Fourth, the discussions appear in greater detail. In this period, Feng Shaoshan proposed taking this increasing spirit of reportage in record-keeping a step further, advocating the literal transcription of everything said at meetings through the introduction at board meetings of secretaries trained in shorthand (Shanghai zongshanghui, "Ben hui yi'anlu," Shanghaishi Shangye Lianhehui archives, 200-1-008, entry of October 14, 1922) at the board of director meetings. (His proposal was defeated as impractical, on the grounds that, because individuals spoke in their local dialects, Chinese could not be uniformly transcribed as English could.)

45. Stephen MacKinnon, "Toward a History of the Chinese Press in the Republican Period," *Modern China*, 23:1 (January 1997): 3–32; Goodman, "Politics, Press Rivalries."

46. Goodman, *Native Place*, pp. 152–158, 220–238.

47. Yu Heping, *Shanghui yu Zhongguo zaoqi xiandaihua* (Chambers of Commerce and China's Early Modernization) (Shanghai: Shanghai renmin chubanshe, 1993). Because of their unusual importance in Chinese history, Chinese chambers of commerce have been a subject of avid study, in contrast to a relative dearth of historiographical interest in European or U.S. chambers of commerce. The voluminous complete archives of the Suzhou and Tianjin Chambers of Commerce have been published. The Shanghai Chamber of Commerce archives have only remained unpublished because of disputes among contesting scholarly units over control of this valuable historical material.

48. *Shanghai Nippo*, November 1, 1918, translated in PDR, V1-1-1120 (November 1 and 2, 1918); *North China Herald*, September 6, 1919; Joshua Fogel, "'Shanghai-Japan': The Japanese Residents' Association of Shanghai," *Journal of Asian Studies* (November 2000).

49. *North China Herald*, September 6, 1919.

50. Galy, "Le Guomindang," notes the difficulty of Guomindang penetration of the Street Union movement.

51. Gu, "Who Was Mr. Democracy?"

52. The Chinese texts are reproduced in *Shimin gongbao*, January 1921. The English translation is quoted from *North China Herald*, June 12, 1920.

53. See Kuai Shixun, "Shanghai gonggong zujie," pp. 970–972.

54. The Chinese City Council, heralded by foreign observers as "the first attempt at purely Chinese municipal representative government," was created as a local self-government project by local gentry merchants, with the approval of Daotai Yuan Shuxun in 1905. Quotation from *North China Herald*, October 20, 1905, cited in Mark Elvin, "The Gentry Democracy in Shanghai, 1905–1914" (D.Phil. diss., University of Cambridge, 1967),

p. 50. See also *Shanghai shi zizhi zhi* (Shanghai Municipal Self-government Gazetteer) (Shanghai, 1915); Goodman, *Native Place*, pp. 198–200. The Chinese City Council functioned in the Chinese city (outside of the foreign settlements) from 1905 until 1914, when it was shut down by Yuan Shikai. In the May Fourth era, it became a nostalgic model for Shanghai self-government.

55. See, for example, Elvin, "The Gentry Democracy," Appendix I: "On the Problem of So-called Unanimous Decisions"; Goodman, *Native Place*, pp. 220–229.

56. Statement of Wen Zongyao, cited in Wu, "Guang-Zhao," pp. 79–80.

57. Ibid., p. 81.

58. Wu, "Guang-Zhao," pp. 37, 79–81.

59. Statement of Hu Yaoting, cited in Wu, "Guang-Zhao," p. 21; Wu, "Guang-Zhao," p. 101; *Shenbao*, August 31, 1918; *Minguo ribao*, September 1, 1918.

60. *Shanghai Gazette*, July 30, 1919 (clipping, Sokolsky archives, Hoover Institution, Box 331). The reference to article 24 in the quotation is mistaken. Article 8 is the relevant regulation. See "Shanghai zongshanghui zhangcheng" (1916), reproduced in Zhang Huanzhong, *Shanghai zongshanghui yanjiu*, Appendix, p. 360.

61. PDR, V1-1-1130, translation of a letter in *Xinwenbao*, *Shenbao*, and *Xin shenbao* of February 21, 1921, signed by the Fuzhou Road Street Union and others.

62. Goodman, "Being Public," p. 79; *Shanghai Gazette*, July 30, 1919.

63. PDR, V1-1-1126 (April 6, 1920).

64. In his 1897 article, "Shuo qun" (On grouping), Liang Qichao advocated the integration of the Chinese people into a united political community through the formation of associations. See Hao Chang, *Liang Ch'i-ch'ao and Intellectual Transition in China, 1890–1907* (Cambridge, Mass.: Harvard University Press, 1971), pp. 95–99. This notion is echoed in Mao Zedong's early writings, which envision the creation of a great union of the popular masses from smaller popular associations. "Minzhong de da lianhe" (Great union of the popular masses), in *Mao Zedong ji* (Collected Works of Mao) (Tokyo, 1974), pp. 57–69 (originally published in *Xiangjiang pinglun*, July 21, July 28, and August 4, 1919). Similarly, Sun Yat-sen's "Three People's Principles" developed the notion of building the nation as a large unified body *(da tuanti)*, not of individuals, but of small groups *(xiao tuanti)*. See Goodman, *Native Place*, p. 258.

65. *Shibao*, September 16, 1918; *Minguo ribao*, September 16, 1918; *Shenbao*, September 16, 1918; Wu, "Guang-Zhao," p. 75.

66. Wu, "Guang-Zhao," p. 89.

67. Ibid.

68. PDR, V1-1-1129 (February 24, 1921).

69. Bergère, *Golden Age;* Fewsmith, *Party, State.*

70. *Shimin gongbao,* 1 (January 1921): 4.

71. All of these associations found it natural to exclude women, even in this era of blossoming Chinese feminism and female suffrage movements. At this time, a few individual women were just beginning to agitate for membership in native-place associations. There were no female members of the Chamber of Commerce or even of the Street Unions (at least as far as may be known from newspaper details of their meetings).

72. Bergère, *Golden Age,* pp. 211–212; Chen Laixin, "Shanhai kakurō," p. 86.

73. Translated in "Chinese Firms Organizing New Chamber of Commerce: People's Organization Launched in Shanghai by 2,700 Concerns Which Charge Old Bodies are not Representative," *North China Star,* June 27, 1919 (clipping in Sokolsky archives, Hoover Institution, Box 331); PDR, V1-1-1122.

74. Goodman, *Native Place,* pp. 121–125.

75. See, for example, *Shishi xinbao,* September 6, 1918; Wu, "Guang-Zhao," p. 65.

76. Wu, "Guang-Zhao," pp. 53–54; *Minguo ribao,* September 1, 1918.

77. The reformers' social commitments were not merely rhetorical. By the end of 1918 they had established six new charitable schools, and additionally a night school for workers. This emphasis precedes the "commoners' education" *(pingmin jiaoyu)* movement of 1919–1924 at Beijing Normal School, a movement which has been attributed to the influence of Dewey. On the "commoners' education movement," see Gu, "Who was Mr. Democracy?"

78. PDR, V1-1-1129 (January 19, 1921); PDR, V1-1-1135 (July 20, 1922); PDR, V1-1-1129 (February 28, 1921); PDR, V1-1-1129 (March 28, 1921); PDR, V1-1-1132 (October 25–28, 1921).

79. PDR, V1-1-1134 (May 22, 1922). Fifty representatives of thirty-two commercial organizations met under the coordination of the Nanjing Road Street Union, where it was resolved that all associations would stop using lightweight copper coins. Included in the meeting were bankers, the Guang-Zhao and Ningbo native-place associations, and the New Federation of Street Unions.

80. PDR, V1-1-1129 (March 28, 1921); PDR, V1-1-1135 (July 18, 1922). When such activities inclined in the direction of communism, the Street Associations disciplined their more radical members. For example, the Shandong Road Street Union warned Dong Licang, President of the Merchants and Laborers Mutual Aid Society, to stop issuing May Day pamphlets or leave the Street Union. PDR, V1-1-1130 (May 5, 1921).

81. In 1919, Mao Zedong listed the various Chinese renderings of democracy *(de-mo-ke-la-xi)* as *pingmin zhuyi, minben zhuyi, minzu zhuyi,* and *shumin zhuyi,* defining them together as an ideology of resistance to oppression. Mao Zedong, "Xiangjiang pinglun chuankan xuanyan" (Manifesto on the

founding of the *Xiang River Review*), July 14, 1919, translated in Stuart R. Schram, ed., *Mao's Road to Power: Revolutionary Writings 1912–1949* (Armonk, N.Y.: M. E. Sharpe, 1992), vol. 1, pp. 318–319. See also the discussion in Gu, "Who Was Mr. Democracy?"

82. PDR, Vl-1-1125 (March 31, 1920). This is related in a letter from Commissioner Yang Cheng to the Federation of Street Unions.

83. PDR, Vl-1-1126 (April 17, 1920). In contrast, the role of Commissioner Yang Cheng, as a representative of the Chinese government, dropped out of public discussion altogether. It is not clear that he played any further role in the procedures.

84. PDR, Vl-1-1126 (April 10 and April 13, 1920); *Shibao*, April 10, 1920; PDR, Vl-1-1126 (April 22, 1920).

85. PDR, Vl-1-1126 (April 17, 1920).

86. Shanghai Shangjie Lianhe Zonghui, "Huaren nashui hui shibai zhi neimu" (The inside story of the Chinese Ratepayers' Association) (pamphlet, 1921), Beijing Library. In the case of Chen Zemin, his alternate name, Chen Huinong, also appeared on the ballot. The authors of the pamphlet were particularly incensed that no discussion was permitted which questioned the appropriateness of modeling the CRA on the foreign Ratepayers' Association.

87. Kuai Shixun, "Shanghai gonggong zujie," pp. 970–972.

88. This is obvious from the rhetoric of the *Shimin gongbao*, which makes continual reference to self-government. See also, for example, "Duiyu jieshou zizhi chankuan zhi xiwang" (Hopes for the nurturance of self-government), *Shangbao*, March 23, 1921; "Huifu zizhi" (Recovering self-government), *Shangbao*, March 12, 1922.

89. Elvin, "Gentry Democracy."

90. The intrusiveness of the International Settlement police may be amply documented by the great utility for this study of the Police Daily Reports.

91. PDR, Vl-1-1122 (May 10, 1919).

92. "Tuanti yundong zaping" (Miscellaneous comments on the group movement), *Shangbao*, March 20, 1922.

93. Bergère, *Golden Age*, pp. 226–227; Rankin, "State and Society," p. 273.

4. Questioning the Modernity of the Model Settlement

I am grateful to the participants in the Harvard Conference, and particularly the editors of this volume, for enriching my understanding of the issues at stake in considering citizenship and helping me refine my own approach to the topic. I also owe debts to Susan Gubar, Dave Thelen, Steve Smith, Wendy Gamber, Barbara Mittler, and Carol Greenhouse, each of whom listened to my ideas and pointed me to useful sources or secondary works. I am especially grateful to two people: first, to Margaret Somers, for discussions about citizenship that influenced me greatly; works of hers such as "Citizenship and the Place of the Public Sphere: Law, Community, and Political Culture in the Transition to Democracy," *American Sociological Review,* 58 (October 1993): 587–620, helped inspire the approach taken in this chapter. Second, Robert Bickers collaborated with me on an earlier project that laid the groundwork for this one. Finally, Prasenjit Duara's work, though originally cited in earlier drafts, is not mentioned in any of the notes to this version. Its effects retain a ghostly presence, though, in the part of my title that alludes to one of his books, *Rescuing History from the Nation: Questioning Narratives of Modern China* (Chicago: University of Chicago Press, 1995).

1. Consider, for example, the following pair of statements (emphasis added). First, from Murphey: "Economically, the institutions, and still more the values, which had grown up in the West with the end of the Middle Ages and reached a full flowering in the nineteenth century, were transplanted to Shanghai . . . [and] the city grew [into] a *modern* commercial, financial, and industrial metropolis," *Shanghai: Key to Modern China* (Cambridge, Mass.: Harvard University Press, 1953), p. 4. Second, from Lee: "Shanghai developed into a *modern* metropolis in only a few decades . . . in the 1930s [it] was already a *modern* city in a country yet to be *modernized,*" *Shanghai Modern* (Cambridge, Mass.: Harvard University Press, 1999), p. 37.

2. Hudson, writing in the late 1920s after a visit to Shanghai, described the International Settlement as having impressed him as a place that was "well organized and *modernly* and efficiently administered." He went on to note, however, that it was "not administered in behalf of the ninety-five percent majority of the population which pays not less than sixty percent of the taxes." He praised as "much more accommodating" the policy "followed in the French Concession [where] *two Chinese [are] on the council [and] Chinese are admitted to the public park.*" The emphasis in these quotes has been added; all of them come from Manley O. Hudson, *The International Settlement in Shanghai and the Mixed and Provisional Courts at Shanghai* (Beijing: Peking Leader Press, 1928, Peking Leader Reprints no. 39), pp. 11–13. Here are excerpts from a November 1924 speech by Sun (again with emphasis added): "Shanghai is our China's *leading place,* but in the concessions, though most residents are Chinese . . . *do we have a voice on the councils? . . . There are even parks . . . that we Chinese can't enter . . .* We are rightfully the rulers of Shanghai, those from foreign lands the guests, yet the guests act like the rulers . . . Oh, what a low position we have, as though we lacked the spirit of *citizens* [guomin]." This comes from "Zhongguo neiluan de yuanyin" (The reason for China's internal chaos), *Sun Zhongshan xuanji* (Sun Yat-sen's Collected Works) (Beijing: Renmin chubanshe, 1956), vol. 2, pp. 899–911, quotations from pp. 908–909.

3. Murphey, *Shanghai: Key to Modern China,* p. 4.

4. One of many recent works that take for granted the status of the nation-state as the quintessential modern political entity is Jürgen Habermas, *The Inclusion of the Other: Studies in Political Theory,* ed. Ciaran Cronin and Pablo De Greiff (Cambridge, Mass.: MIT Press, 1998). See especially pp. 105–

127, in which Habermas draws contrasts with pre-modern city-states and post-national entities of the current era, with their plethora of "post-national" forms of organization. That post-modern and post-national are sometimes used interchangeably further underscores the presumed connection between the things we are thought to be moving beyond today. See also, for another recent statement of the situation focusing on history rather than political theory, Charles Maier, "Consigning the Twentieth Century to History: Alternative Narratives for the Modern Era," *American Historical Review,* vol. 105, no. 3 (June 2000): 807–831, esp. p. 815. Also of relevance, of course, is Benedict Anderson, *Imagined Communities: Reflections on the Origins and Spread of Nationalism* (London: Verso, 1991; rev. version of 1983 orig. ed.).

5. For excellent introductions to various foreign communities in East Asian treaty ports, including Shanghai, see assorted contributions to the new collection edited by Robert Bickers and Christian Henriot, *New Frontiers: Imperialism's New Communities in East Asia, 1842–1953* (Manchester: Manchester University Press, 2000).

6. John K. Fairbank, *Trade and Diplomacy on the China Coast: The Opening of the Treaty Ports* (Cambridge, Mass.: Harvard University Press, 1964); see also Lucian Pye, "How China's Nationalism was Shanghaied," in Jon Unger, ed., *Chinese Nationalism* (Armonk, N.Y.: M. E. Sharpe, 1996), pp. 86–112.

7. This is true of various Chinese works that are cited in Robert A. Bickers and Jeffrey N. Wasserstrom, "Shanghai's 'Dogs and Chinese Not Admitted' Sign: Legend, History and Contemporary Symbol," *The China Quarterly,* no. 142 (June 1995): 444–466; see also, among more recent works, Li Tiangang, "1927: Shanghai shimin zizhi yundong de zongjie" (1927: The culmination of the self-government movement by Shanghai's citizenry), in Wang Hui and Yu Kwok-leung, eds., *Shanghai: Chengshi, shehui yu wenhua* (Shanghai: City, Society, and Culture) (Hong Kong: Hong Kong University Press, 1998), pp. 57–72.

8. Here, I am endorsing the call for more microhistorical analyses of structures of treaty-port inequality of the kind that Bryna Goodman makes in "Improvisations on a Semicolonial Theme, or, How to Read Multiethnic Participation in the 1893 Shanghai Jubilee," *Journal of Asian Studies,* vol. 59, no. 4 (November 2000): 889–926. I find very problematic, however, her implication there that the approach to the International Settlement taken in Bickers and Wasserstrom, "Shanghai's 'Dogs and Chinese Not Admitted' Sign," is very close to that proposed by Fairbank in his work on synarchy and by Pye in "How Chinese Nationalism was Shanghaied." One aim of our 1995 piece was, after all, to draw attention to the serious shortcomings of exactly these discussions of Old Shanghai. And one way we made that point (p. 466) was by calling attention to a symbolic slighting of Chinese residents during the very same Jubilee celebration that is the fo-

cus of Goodman's essay and is discussed in more detail later in this chapter.

9. For a succinct and clear description of Apartheid and the categories around which it was structured, see Roger B. Beck, *The History of South Africa* (London: Greenwood Press, 2000), pp. 125–136. For a fascinating examination of racial categories in the American South, see James Loewen, *The Mississippi Chinese: Between Black and White* (Prospect Heights, Ill.: Waveland Press, 1988; 2nd ed. of 1971 publication). It begins with a quote from an interview with a Baptist minister, who notes that at one point local Chinese were considered "nigras," then later they were called "whites," and Loewen shows how many differences came in the wake of that shift. In the International Settlement, a comparable two-race system was not in place—a point returned to later in this chapter in relation to the status of Japanese in the Settlement. For a stimulating theoretical discussion of the complexity of racial categories and patterns of exclusion in colonial and semi-colonial settings, see Klaus Mühlhahn, "Racism, Culture and the Colonial Laboratory: Rethinking Colonialism," *Asien Afrika Lateinamerika*, vol. 27 (1999): 443–459.

10. For more on this general situation, see Jeffrey N. Wasserstrom, "Where Did the Chinese Government Learn its Authoritarian Ways?", *The Chronicle of Higher Education*, August 4, 2000, p. B8. A clear statement from the time, from one who thought the tutelage process was over, can be found in Hollington Tong, "Chinese Participation in the Italian Concessions in Tientsin," *Millard's Review*, January 24, 1920, pp. 359–361. Tong quotes a Captain Fileti, an Italian official, saying that letting Chinese participate in local affairs "could not have been possible say fifty years ago, when the Chinese knew nothing about modern forms of government and Western ideas, but such is not the case now. They have learned more from Europe of late than we in China have learned from China." An example of a Shanghailander describing very gradual moves toward the need for full Chinese political participation can be found in the following 1915 statement supporting the position that some Shanghairen (merchants, of course) should be allowed to serve as advisers to the SMC: "[A Chinese] Advisory Board . . . will give responsible status to a representative Chinese group just such as we require [and] educate our Chinese fellow-residents into appreciating their *rights of citizenship.*" E. C. Pearse, Chairman of the Shanghai Municipal Council (SMC), March 1915 (emphasis added); quoted in Richard Feetham, *Report of the Honorable Justice Feetham, C.M.G., to the Shanghai Municipal Council*, 3 vols. (Shanghai: North China Daily News, 1931), p. 124. For more on advisory board proposals, see later in this chapter.

11. Many references to the way park access was linked to citizenship in the minds of Shanghailanders and local Chinese alike—probably the most un-

usual of my claims—are cited below. One of the clearest ones, which also draws attention to a setting in which the two main groups that interest me were in direct dialogue, can be found in a speech that a man named Siow Choon-leng gave (in English) at the Annual Meeting of the Ratepayers in 1927. Published in full in *The Municipal Gazette*, April 14, 1927, p. 142, it is worth reading in its entirety if one is concerned with contemporary under-standings of citizenship and the ability of Enlightenment discourse to be appropriated and adapted in appeals to colonial or semi-colonial elites. Ig-noring the question of political representation, it is a wide-ranging plea for Chinese to be able to use the parks, which includes everything from a digression on the etymology of the term "citizen" to an appeal to the no-tion that all members of a community deserve equal rights. That it was given at a gathering at which foreign ratepayers chose representatives to the SMC is, in itself, revealing of the interconnection between park access and political representation.

12. This kind of language opens J. D. Clark, *A Short History of Shanghai* (Shang-hai: Shanghai Evening Post, 1921), p. 1; see also, for nearly identical phrasing, H. O'Shea, "The Birth and Youth of Shanghai," in the booklet *1843—Shanghai—1893: The Model Settlement—Its Birth. Its Youth. Its Jubilee* (Shanghai: Shanghai Mercury, 1893), pp. 1–48. See also O. M. Green's "Introduction" in *Shanghai of Today: A Souvenir Album of Thirty-Eight Van-Dyke Prints of the "Model Settlement"* (Shanghai: Kelly and Walsh, 1927), pp. 7–15, esp. pp. 13–14. Insightful general treatments of this sort of Shanghailander self-image can be found in Kerrie L. Macpherson, *A Wil-derness of Marshes: The Origins of Public Health in Shanghai* (Hong Kong: Ox-ford University Press, 1987); Robert Bickers, *Britain in China: Community, Culture and Colonialism 1900–1949* (Manchester: Manchester University Press, 1999); and Nicholas Clifford, *Spoilt Children of Empire: Westerners in Shanghai and the Chinese Revolution of the 1920s* (Hanover, N.H.: Middlebury College Press, 1991).

13. "The Past, Present and Future of Shanghai," *North China Herald*, May 27, 1881, pp. 497–498.

14. *The Jubilee of Shanghai, 1843–1893* (Shanghai: North-China Daily News, 1893), pp. 1–4 and passim.

15. "Community and Council," *North China Herald*, March 27, 1915, p. 890.

16. John Pal, *Shanghai Saga* (London: Jarrold's, 1963), pp. 17 and 227. On the way in which discourses of hygiene and modernity intertwined with and shaped political arrangements in Chinese treaty ports, see Ruth Rogaski, "Hygienic Modernity in Tianjin," in Joseph W. Esherick, ed., *Remaking the Chinese City: Modernity and National Identity, 1900–1950* (Honolulu: Univer-sity of Hawaii Press, 2000), pp. 30–46.

17. See, for example, the statements by Sun quoted in note 2 above; other examples of related documents are cited in Bickers and Wasserstrom, "Shanghai's 'Dogs and Chinese Not Admitted' Sign."

18. Hesen [Cai Hesen], "Bei waiguo diguo zhuyi zaige bashi nian de Shanghai" (Shanghai's eighty years of exploitation at the hands of foreign imperialists), *Xiangdao Zhoubao* (The Guide), no. 46, November 16, 1923, pp. 352–353.

19. For details on the Public Garden's legendary notice, see Bickers and Wasserstrom, "Shanghai's 'Dogs and Chinese Not Admitted' Sign."

20. The relevant section of this document is quoted in A. M. Kotenev, *Shanghai: Its Municipality and the Chinese* (Shanghai: North-China Daily News and Herald, 1927), p. 157, and in Kotenev, *Shanghai: Its Mixed Court and Council* (Shanghai: North-China Daily News and Herald, 1925), pp. 37–40.

21. On the 1870s, see Chen Sanjing, *Jindai Zhongguo bianju xia de Shanghai* (Shanghai and the Changing Situation of Modern China) (Taibei: Dongda tushu, 1996), pp. 39–40. For the 1920s, here is a sample excerpt from the *Shen Bao:* "The Chinese people living in the International Settlement still cannot participate in municipal governance . . . In 1920 we began a movement for *citizenship rights* [*shimin quan*] . . . that has still not been completed," *Shen Bao,* April 17, 1926. For other *Shen Bao* examples, as well as ones from the *Minguo Ribao,* which sometimes used the term *guomin quan* for "citizenship rights," see Gang Shidong, ed., *Shanghai gonggong zujie shigao* (A History of Shanghai's International Settlement). Gang's work has been an invaluable source to me in writing this chapter. Originally published in the 1930s, it is reproduced in full in the *Shanghai shiliao congkan* series entitled *Shanghai gonggong zujie shigao* (A History of Shanghai's International Settlement) (Shanghai: Shanghai renmin chubanshe, 1980), pp. 299–588.

22. See, for example, the letter signed by several Shanghairen in *North China Herald,* December 9, 1885, p. 658. That similar complaints had been lodged in Chinese newspapers several years earlier than that is clear from the defense of exclusionary rules offered in an editorial on "Chinese and the Public Garden," *North China Herald,* May 13, 1881, p. 456. That editorial claims that the "better class of Chinese probably do not care much about going into the [Public] Garden; they have doubtless taken the matter up because they look upon their exclusion as an affront."

23. See, on this, "The Public Garden," *North China Herald,* November 25, 1885, pp. 600–601; *North China Herald,* December 9, 1885, p. 456; letter to the editor on "Admission of Chinese to Public Parks," in *North China Herald,* May 1, 1926, p. 208.

24. J. B. Powell's lead editorial in *Millard's Review,* January 17, 1920; see also his "And the Municipal Band Plays On!", *China Weekly Review,* April 23, 1927, pp. 193–195. In addition, see his April 28, 1928, *China Weekly Review* editorial: "Shanghai Bows to World Opinion!" Powell begins this piece (which runs from pp. 243–247) with a list of the three main grievances of local Chinese: the Mixed Court, SMC representation, and park rules. He then argues (p. 246): "From a psychological standpoint, the exclusion of

Chinese from the park has probably been responsible for more Chinese animosity against foreigners than some of the larger questions such as Chinese representation on the Council."

25. E. S. Little's comments ran as a letter to the editor of the British-run *North China Herald* and as an article, "Chinese Representation on the Muncipal Council," in the American-run *Millard's Review,* January 10, 1920, pp. 258–261.

26. The petition is reproduced in Kotenev, *Shanghai: Its Municipality and the Chinese,* p. 160; for more on E. S. Little, the petition, and related matters, see *Feetham Report,* pp. 126–128.

27. See, for example, the stinging comment on parks and on local elections in Lewis Gannett, *Young China* (New York: The Nation, 1928), pp. 1–2.

28. Powell, "And the Municipal Band Plays On!"

29. On Powell, see in particular his lead editorial in *China Weekly Review,* April 3, 1926, pp. 106–108; on Cai and Hudson, see the texts by each discussed above.

30. A translation of a wonderfully illustrative sample article (from the October 27, 1883, issue of *Shen Bao,* page 1) is provided in Mark Elvin, *Another History: Essays on China from a European Perspective* (Honolulu: University of Hawaii Press, 1996), p. 177. For general discussions of this phenomenon and further relevant citations, see ibid., pp. 176–191. Other important works dealing with *Shen Bao* and Chinese images of the Settlement include Rudolf G. Wagner, "The Role of the Foreign Community in the Chinese Public Sphere," *The China Quarterly,* no. 142 (June 1995): 423–443; Ye Xiaoqing, "Shanghai before Nationalism," *East Asian History,* no. 3 (June 1992): 33–52; and Barbara Mittler's book on *Shen Bao, A Western Medium Creating Chinese Identity: Metamorphosis of the Newspaper (1872–1912)* (Cambridge, Mass: Asia Center, Harvard University, forthcoming). Also note that, in the same December 9, 1885, letter in the *North China Herald* cited above, which complained about exclusionary park rules, the Shanghairen authors claimed that "a visit to Shanghai" by Chinese from other places was "frequently prompted by a desire to witness" the advanced "method and results of Municipal regulations." The enclave's "self-government" system was looked to "with great interest," they wrote, by many Chinese.

31. *China Weekly Review,* December 4, 1926, p. 75; see also Green, "Introduction," pp. 10–11.

32. Lee, *Shanghai Modern;* Pye, "How Chinese Nationalism was Shanghaied"; and Ye, "Shanghai before Nationalism."

33. Dorothy Borg, *American Policy and the Chinese Revolution of 1925–1928* (New York: MacMillan, 1947); Clifford, *Spoilt Children;* Clifford, "A Revolution Is Not a Tea Party: The 'Shanghai Mind(s)' Reconsidered," *Pacific Historical Review,* vol. 59 (1990): 501–526; Li, *1927;* Tang Zhenchang, "Shimin yizhi yu Shanghai shehui" (Civic consciousness and Shanghai society), in Wang

and Yu, *Shanghai*, pp. 91–112; Chen, *Jindai Zhongguo;* Bryna Goodman, *Native Place, City, and Nation* (Berkeley: University of California Press, 1995); and Lynn T. White, III, "Non-Governmentalism in the Historical Development of Modern Shanghai," in Lawrence J. C. Ma and Edward Hanten, eds., *Urban Development in Modern China* (Boulder, Colo.: Westview Press, 1981), pp. 19–57.

34. Kotenev, *Shanghai: Its Mixed Court and Council,* and Kotenev, *Shanghai: Its Municipality and the Chinese;* Gang, *Shanghai gonggong zujie shigao.*

35. On the Chinese Park, see Bickers and Wasserstrom, "Shanghai's 'Dogs and Chinese Not Admitted' Sign."

36. T. H. Marshall, *Class, Citizenship, and Social Development* (Westport, Conn.: Greenwood Press, 1973); and Hannah Arendt, *Men in Dark Times* (New York: Harcourt, 1968), pp. 81–94. For a sense of the continuing influence of Marshall and Arendt, see "Symposium: The State of Citizenship," *Indiana Journal of Global Legal Studies,* vol. 7, no. 2 (Spring 2000): 447–601, esp. Linda Bosniak, "Citizenship Denationalized," pp. 447–509, which reinforces the points made above about assumptions regarding the quintessential pre-modern, modern, and post-modern political forms.

37. Michael Walzer, "Citizenship," in Terrence Ball, James Farr, and Russell L. Hanson, eds., *Political Innovation and Conceptual Change* (Cambridge: Cambridge University Press, 1989), pp. 211–219; and Carl Brinkman, "Citizenship," in Edwin R. A. Seligman, ed. (Alvin Johnson, associate editor), *International Encyclopedia of the Social Sciences,* vol. 3 (New York: MacMillan, 1937), pp. 471–474. Other good general works on citizenship include Michael Hanagan and Charles Tilly, eds., *Extending Citizenship, Reconfiguring States* (Lanham, Md.: Rowman and Littlefield, 1999).

38. Walzer, "Citizenship"; see p. 217 in particular on protection.

39. *The Politics of Aristotle,* edited and translated by Ernest Barker (London: Oxford University Press, 1958), pp. 92–110, esp. p. 93.

40. For a good sense of how moves toward expanding claims to each of these types of rights intertwined, see the relevant section of the *Feetham Report,* pp. 90–148, in which Chapter V is devoted to "Chinese Residents of the Settlement and the Rule of Law," Chapter VI focuses on "Chinese Representation" (on the SMC), and Chapter VII deals with the "Position of Chinese Under Settlement Administration" (with a section on "Benefits of Municipal Services," in which "parks, schools, and hospitals" are discussed). The reference to citizenship on p. 140, near the end of this classically Marshallian account, is particularly noteworthy.

41. The sexual politics of citizenship (a topic that deserves more attention vis-à-vis Shanghai than I can possibly give it here) and the complex ways in which racial categories and gendered ones often intersect have inspired some very interesting work lately in American history. An excellent entry into this rich literature is Linda Kerber, *No Constitutional Right to Be Ladies:*

Women and the Obligations of Citizenship (New York: Hill and Wang, 1998). See also Glenda Elizabeth Gilmore, *Gender and Jim Crow* (Chapel Hill: University of North Carolina Press, 1996).

42. *Feetham Report,* p. 145, includes the statement that a decision was made in 1928 to charge "a small admission fee" so as to "keep within limits the number of people using the parks and prevent their being overrun by persons of an undesirable class." See also the argument a Shanghailander made the year before the parks were opened to Chinese that is presented in *The Municipal Gazette,* April 14, 1927, p. 142. Mr. W. H. Trenchard Davis warned of the danger that, if exclusionary rules were changed, the grounds would be so "crowded with the scum of this City" that "there would be no room for us or for our real Chinese friends" (i.e., elite Shanghairen).

43. Arendt, *Men in Dark Times,* p. 81.

44. Brinkman, "Citizenship," p. 472.

45. Examples of different ways in which the issue is being rethought can be found in Bosniak, "Citizenship Denationalized," and Habermas, *Inclusion.* For one of many statements that implies that divided citizenship was a problem in the pre-modern era and is again becoming one in the contemporary period, but was not troubling in between, see Hanagan and Tilly, *Extending Citizenship,* p. 5.

46. On the nature of early twentieth-century Chinese national citizenship, along with other chapters in this volume, see Henrietta Harrison's important new study, *The Making of the Republican Citizen: Political Ceremonies and Symbols in China, 1911–1929* (Oxford: Oxford University Press, 2000). For the intertwining of concerns about local and national citizenship, along with previously cited materials, see the *Shen Bao* and *Minguo Ribao* articles from the 1920s reprinted in Gang, *Shanghai,* pp. 529–530, 556, and 588.

47. This point is stressed in Little, "Chinese Representation," and various previously cited editorials by Powell.

48. The materials from the 1893 civic rituals reproduced in *The Jubilee of Shanghai* are relevant here, as is the reference to the "secondary patriotism" of Shanghailanders toward the Settlement in *North China Herald,* June 29, 1906, p. 725.

49. *North China Herald,* June 16, 1870, p. 438.

50. See, for example, the unpaginated "Foreword" in I. I. Kounin, ed., *The Diamond Jubilee of the International Settlement of Shanghai* (Shanghai: Post Mercury Co., 1941).

51. Tang Tsou, "Interpreting the Revolution in China," *Modern China,* vol. 26, no. 2 (April 2000): 205–238.

52. Goodman, *Native Place,* pp. 192–194 and passim; Kotenev, *Shanghai: Its Mixed Court and Council,* p. 37.

53. See, for a sense of this dynamic, *Millard's Review,* December 6, 1919, p. 2,

and "The Shanghai Municipal Council," *Oriental Affairs,* vol. 1, no. 4 (March 1934): 3–4.

54. On town hall meetings, see *China Weekly Review,* December 4, 1926, p. 8.

55. This theme was a constant one running not just through the issues of *Millard's Review* previously cited, but through nearly all of the editions of that periodical published in late 1919 and early 1920. Once that publication was renamed the *China Weekly Review,* it continued to show up in articles and editorials of the mid-1920s written by Shanghailanders and Chinese contributors alike.

56. For a sample reference to the Chinese version of Pye's "How Chinese Nationalism was Shanghaied" (which appeared in the journal *Ershiyi shiji*), see Ye Xiaoqing, "Minzu zhuyi xingqi qianhou de Shanghai" (Shanghai before and after the flourishing of nationalism), in Wang and Yu, *Shanghai,* pp. 31–40.

57. Alexander Woodside, "An Enlightenment for Outcasts: Some Vietnamese Stories," in Jeffrey N. Wasserstrom, Lynn Hunt, and Marilyn B. Young, eds., *Human Rights and Revolutions* (Lanham, Md.: Rowman and Littlefield, 2000), pp. 113–125.

58. "Community and Council," *North China Herald,* March 27, 1915, p. 890.

59. Lest my language seem fanciful here in suggesting that images of pollution mattered in both realms, see *North China Herald,* March 27, 1915. This refers to China as a "land where corruption has scattered its germs by handfuls," while the Settlement has "remained uncorrupt" and "maintained a reputation which any city might envy." See Green, "Introduction," and *North China Herald,* November 25, 1885, pp. 600–601, for particularly vivid examples of Shanghailanders expressing fear of the unhealthy effects of close proximity with Chinese, especially those of the lower orders. For more on this theme, see Rogaski, "Hygienic Modernity," and Macpherson, *A Wilderness of Marshes.*

60. See *The Jubilee of Shanghai,* pp. 38–39, on segregation of audience members; and p. 45 for the *hanjian* reference.

61. Samuel Huntington, "The Clash of Civilizations," *Foreign Affairs,* 72 (Summer 1993): 22–49; for a provocative general look at possible links between colonial practices and later forms of authoritarianism developed by domestic regimes, see Mühlhahn, "Racism, Culture and the Colonial Laboratory."

5. Workers as Citizens in Modern Shanghai

1. Joseph T. Chen, *The May Fourth Movement in Shanghai* (Leiden: E. J. Brill, 1971), p. 194.

2. Wen-hsin Yeh, *The Alienated Academy: Culture and Politics in Republican China*

(Cambridge, Mass.: Council on East Asian Studies, Harvard University, 1990), pp. 132–133.

3. See Shen Yixing, Jiang Peinan, and Zheng Qingsheng, eds., *Shanghai gongren yundongshi* (A history of the Shanghai labor movement) (Shenyang: Liaoning Workers Press, 1991), pp. 28–36; Elizabeth J. Perry, *Shanghai on Strike: The Politics of Chinese Labor* (Stanford: Stanford University Press, 1993), chaps. 2–3.

4. *Shanghai jindaishi* (The modern history of Shanghai) (Shanghai: East China Normal University Press, 1987), vol. 2, pp. 6–7.

5. Chow Tse-tsung, *The May Fourth Movement: Intellectual Revolution in Modern China* (Cambridge, Mass.: Harvard University Press, 1960), pp. 151–152.

6. *Shen bao,* June 9, 1919.

7. *Xinwen bao,* June 7, 1919.

8. *North China Herald,* June 14, 1919, p. 717. Emphasis added.

9. *Shibao,* December 14, 1916.

10. Chow, *The May Fourth Movement,* pp. 38–39.

11. Chen Sanjing, *Huagong yu Ouzhan* (Chinese workers and the war in Europe) (Taipei, 1986), pp. 142–144. On at least two occasions Chinese workers also acted as scabs to break strikes among French dockworkers and gas workers. See Ta Chen, *Chinese Migrations, With Special Reference to Labor Conditions* (Taipei: Chengwen Publishing House, 1967), p. 150.

12. In 1919, major strikes erupted not only all across Europe, but also in the United States, Canada, and Egypt. See, for example, Kenneth McNaught, *The Winnipeg Strike, 1919* (Don Mills, Ont.: Longman, 1974); Francis Russell, *A City in Terror: 1919, the Boston Police Strike* (New York: Viking, 1975); Liam Cahill, *Forgotten Revolution: Limerick Soviet, 1919* (Dublin: O'Brien Press, 1990); David Brody, *The Steel Strike of 1919* (Urbana: University of Illinois Press, 1987).

13. On the May Thirtieth Movement, see Richard Rigby, *The May 30th Movement* (Canberra: Australian National University Press, 1980); and Jeffrey Wasserstrom, *Student Protests in Twentieth-Century China: The View from Shanghai* (Stanford: Stanford University Press, 1991), chap. 4.

14. *Shanghai gongren sanci wuzhuang qiyi* (Shanghai's three workers' armed uprisings), Shanghai Municipal Archives, ed. (Shanghai, 1983), p. 70. Emphasis added.

15. Zhou Shangwen and He Shiyou, *Shanghai gongren sanci wuzhuang qiyi shi* (History of the Shanghai three workers' armed uprisings) (Shanghai: Shanghai People's Press, 1987), p. 2.

16. Roger V. Gould, *Insurgent Identities: Class, Community and Protest in Paris from 1848 to the Commune* (Chicago: University of Chicago Press, 1995), p. 4.

17. Mark Elvin, "The Gentry Democracy in Shanghai, 1905–1914," in Jack Gray, ed., *Modern China's Search for a Political Form* (London: Oxford Uni-

versity Press, 1969), pp. 41–65. Although limited to a minority of the population, the system nevertheless was based upon majority voting by those eligible to participate. For more on the self-government movement of the late Qing period, see Roger R. Thompson, *China's Local Councils in the Age of Constitutional Reform, 1898–1911* (Cambridge, Mass.: Council on East Asian Studies, Harvard University, 1995).

18. *Shibao,* March 18, 1912.

19. Ibid., September 22, 1912.

20. Xu Xiaoqun, *Chinese Professionals and the Republican State: The Rise of Professional Associations in Shanghai, 1912–1937* (New York: Cambridge University Press, 2001), chap. 3.

21. *North China Herald,* May 4, 1912, p. 291; *Shibao,* March 11, August 5, August 12, 1913.

22. Xu Yufang and Ka Xingying, eds., *Shanghai gongren sanci wuzhuang qiyi yanjiu* (Studies of the Shanghai three workers' uprisings) (Shanghai: Zhishi Publishing House, 1987), p. 13.

23. Two major archival collections, culled from the holdings of the Shanghai Municipal Archives, were published for internal circulation *(neibu)* in the 1980s. These are *Shanghai gongren sanci wuzhuang qiyi,* edited by the staff of the Archives and published in 1983; and *Shanghai gongren sanci wuzhuang qiyi yanjiu,* edited by the party history materials committee of the Shanghai Party Committee, and published in 1987.

24. See Perry, *Shanghai on Strike,* pp. 76–81.

25. Si Bingwen, "Li Qihan" (Li Qihan), in *Zhongguo gongren yundong de xianfeng* (Pioneers of the Chinese labor movement) (Beijing: Workers Press, 1983), vol. 2, pp. 149–168.

26. *Shanghai gongren sanci wuzhuang qiyi* (Shanghai, 1983), p. 13.

27. Zhou and He, *Shanghai gongren sanci wuzhuang qiyi shi,* p. 64.

28. *Shanghai gongren sanci wuzhuang qiyi* (Shanghai, 1983), p. 123. In fact, economic grievances were later added to the strike demands (which included a wage hike, establishment of a minimum wage, price controls, an 8-hour work day, no dismissal without just cause, equal pay for men and women, paid maternity leave, etc.), but the core objectives of the strike remained those of toppling the warlords and establishing a new government committed to guaranteeing basic freedoms for its citizens.

29. Gould, *Insurgent Identities,* p. 197.

30. On the importance of the Prussian occupation to the outbreak of the Paris Commune, see Stewart Edwards, *The Paris Commune 1871* (London: Eyre and Spottisworde, 1971), p. 1.

31. Roger L. Williams, *The French Revolution of 1870–1871* (New York: W. W. Norton, 1969), p. 152.

32. On the tension between between federalism and centralism in 1920s China, see Prasenjit Duara, *Rescuing History from the Nation: Questioning*

Narratives of Modern China (Chicago: University of Chicago Press, 1995), chap. 6.

33. On the Enlightenment influence from the May Fourth Movement on, see Vera Schwarcz, *The Chinese Enlightenment: Intellectuals and the Legacy of the May Fourth Movement of 1919* (Berkeley: University of California Press, 1984).

34. Zhou and He, *Shanghai gongren sanci wuzhuang qiyi shi,* p. 98.

35. In the general strike, more than 31 workers and students were killed. In the second uprising, more than 40 workers lost their lives. Ibid., pp. 100, 107.

36. On the Paris Commune, see Gould, *Insurgent Identities,* pp. 154, 187.

37. *Minguo ribao,* December 13, 1926; Zhou and He, *Shanghai gongren sanci wuzhuang qiyi shi,* pp. 115–116.

38. Zhou and He, *Shanghai gongren sanci wuzhuang qiyi shi,* pp. 203–204.

39. Zhou and He, *Shanghai gongren sanci wuzhuang qiyi shi,* pp. 193–194.

40. Karl Marx, "The Civil War in France," in Karl Marx and Frederick Engels, *Selected Works* (New York: International Publishers, 1977), pp. 262, 290–291.

41. *Shanghai gongren sanci wuzhuang qiyi* (Shanghai, 1983), pp. 290–291. As Marx had written, "the Commune . . . filled all posts—administrative, judicial and educational—by election on the basis of universal suffrage of all concerned, subject to the right of recall at any time by the same electors." See "The Civil War in France," pp. 261–262.

42. *Shanghai gongren sanci wuzhuang qiyi* (Shanghai, 1983), p. 440.

43. Ibid., pp. 430–431. As Marx notes of the Paris Commune, "The Commune admitted all foreigners to the honour of dying for an immortal cause . . . The Commune made a German working man its Minister of Labour." See "The Civil War in France," p. 297.

44. Zhou and He, *Shanghai gongren sanci wuzhuang qiyi shi,* p. 291.

45. Zhou and He, *Shanghai gongren sanci wuzhuang qiyi shi,* p. 208.

46. Marx, "The Civil War in France," p. 256.

47. Zhou and He, *Shanghai gongren sanci wuzhuang qiyi shi,* pp. 209–210.

48. In March 1966, a widely touted article in the Communist Party's theoretical journal, *Red Flag,* had introduced the major features of the Paris Commune. See Zheng Zhisi, "Bali gongshe de weida jiaoxun" (The glorious lessons of the Paris Commune), *Hong qi* (Red Flag), no. 4 (March 1966). An English translation appeared in *Peking Review* the following month.

49. *Guojia shi womende, zhengquan shi womende* (The country is ours, political power is ours), February 6, 1967, handbill of the Shanghai Workers' General Headquarters. Emphasis added. In Shanghai Municipal Archives.

50. Originally, the provisional committee of the Commune was to include—in addition to Zhang Chunqiao and Yao Wenyuan—seven representatives from occupational categories: three from the Workers' General Head-

quarters, two peasants, one student, and one member of the party committee revolutionary rebel liaison station. See Li Xun, *Da bengkui: Shanghai
gongren zaofanpai xingwangshi* (The great collapse: a history of the rise and
fall of the Shanghai worker rebels) (Taipei: China Times Publishing Company, 1996), p. 359. Soon, however, these plans were overshadowed by the
debate over factional representation.

51. Shanghai Party Committee, ed., *Yiyue geming zhenxiang* (The true face of
the January Revolution) (Shanghai, 1982).

52. Shanghai Garrison, ed., *Sirenbang zai Shanghai jingying dier wuzhuang shimo*
(The saga of the Gang of Four's management of a second military force in
Shanghai) (Shanghai, 1988). In Shanghai Municipal Archives.

53. A January 30, 1967, editorial in *Red Flag* had noted that Chairman Mao regarded Nie Yuanzi's big-character poster at Peking University as the "manifesto of a Beijing People's Commune of the 1960s." Before the editorial
had been published, Chen Boda had telephoned Zhang Chunqiao to tell
him that Mao was already drawing up a name list for a Beijing Commune.
See Wang Nianyi, *Da dongluan de niandai* (Decade of great turmoil)
(Zhengzhou: Henan People's Press, 1988). As John Starr has noted, Mao's
interest in the Paris Commune seems to have developed out of the polemics surrounding the Sino-Soviet rift. See John Bryan Starr, "Revolution in
Retrospect: The Paris Commune through Chinese Eyes," *The China Quarterly*, no. 49 (January-March 1972), p. 110.

54. Stuart Schram, ed., *Chairman Mao Talks to the People* (New York: Pantheon,
1974), p. 278; Harry Harding, *Organizing China* (Stanford: Stanford University Press, 1981), pp. 251–252.

55. Shanghai Party Committee, ed., *Zhongguo gongchandang Shanghaishi zuzhi-
shi ziliao* (Materials on the organization history of the Shanghai Communist Party) (Shanghai: Shanghai People's Press, 1991).

56. Li, *Da bengkui*, p. 567.

57. Ibid., p. 447. Marx had celebrated the fact that in the Paris Commune "all
officials, high or low, were paid only the wages received by other workers."
Marx, "The Civil War in France," p. 262. During the Cultural Revolution,
however, the rebel workers did not deny themselves other forms of special
compensation in the form of housing, subsidies, and the like.

58. See Elizabeth J. Perry and Li Xun, *Proletarian Power: Shanghai in the Cultural Revolution* (Boulder: Westview Press, 1997), chap. 6, for a discussion
of workers' political involvement after Shanghai's January Revolution of
1967.

59. Stephen Andors, *China's Industrial Revolution: Politics, Planning and Management, 1949 to the Present* (New York: Pantheon, 1977), p. 213.

60. Song Yongyi and Sun Dajin, *Wenhua dageming he tade yiduan sichao* (Heterodox thoughts during the Cultural Revolution) (Hong Kong: Tianyuan
Publishers, 1997), chap. 6; Yang Jianli, ed., *Hongse geming yu heise zaofan*

(Red Revolution and Black Rebellion) (Pleasant Hill, Calif.: Foundation for China in the Twenty-First Century, 1997), p. 84.

61. For a similar conclusion based on another urban case, see Wang Shaoguang, *Failure of Charisma: The Cultural Revolution in Wuhan* (New York: Oxford University Press, 1995), p. 170.

62. *Jinji tongling* (Emergency order), handbill of the Workers' General Headquarters, January 7, 1967. In Shanghai Municipal Archives.

63. See Perry and Li, *Proletarian Power,* chap. 4.

64. Wang Hongwen's political ambitions were evident from the outset. On the eve of the inauguration of the WGH, he told a group of fellow worker rebels, "Rebellion at the municipal level can gain us the mayorship; at the department level, directorships; and at lower levels, factory headships. So what if you're not a party member? I can get you all into the party!" Shanghai Party Committee Cultural Revolution Materials Small Group, ed., *Shanghai "wenhua dageming" shihua* (Historical narrative of the "Great Cultural Revolution" in Shanghai) (Shanghai, 1992), p. 172.

65. To be sure, they could also poke fun at this heritage. Comic strips were used to convey revolutionary messages with a dose of surreal humor. One such comic strip, quoting Marx on the Paris Commune, pictured closeups of a man and woman about to embrace with the following captions: "Look at the Paris Commune . . ." (lips approach); "That was the dictatorship . . ." (noses almost touch); ". . . of the proletariat" (passionate kiss). Bernard E. Brown, *Protest in Paris: Anatomy of a Revolt* (Morristown, N.J.: General Learning Press, 1974), p. 100.

66. Ibid., pp. 78–79, 124, 150; Daniel Singer, *Prelude to Revolution: France in May 1968* (New York: Hill and Wang, 1970), pp. 152–185.

67. For more on these transnational connections, see Klaus Mehnert, *Peking and the New Left: At Home and Abroad* (Berkeley: Center for Chinese Studies, University of California, 1969). On Maoist influences in the Italian protests of this period, see Sidney Tarrow, *Democracy and Disorder: Protest and Politics in Italy, 1965–1975* (New York: Oxford University Press, 1989).

68. As Bernard Brown notes of France, "the May Revolt had indeed changed everything. Vast reforms were announced by the government in all spheres of economic and social life . . . All structures, all values, all authority had been challenged by the revolutionaries, who had struck a responsive chord deep within the nation." Brown, *Protest in Paris,* p. 30.

69. On May 18, the Shanghai Federation of Trade Unions issued the following statement: "Workers in the city have expressed universal concern and sympathy for the patriotism of the students who are demanding democracy, rule of law, an end to corruption, checking inflation, and promoting reform. The municipal council of trade unions fully affirms this." *Foreign Broadcast Information Service: China,* May 22, 1989, p. 91.

70. Roger W. Howard reports a brief effort by students in Changchun to take

their protest to the auto workers, but this attempt came late in the movement (after the declaration of martial law) and lasted only a day or two. See Howard, "The Student Democracy Movement in Changchun," in Jonathan Unger, ed., *The Pro-Democracy Protests in China: Reports from the Provinces* (Armonk, N.Y.: M. E. Sharpe, 1991), pp. 61–62.

71. Shelley Warner, "Shanghai's Response to the Deluge," in Unger, ed., *The Pro-Democracy Protests in China*, pp. 218–227. Warner credits Zhu Rongji with averting "a situation in which Shanghainese turned on each other, which seemed to be developing into a most likely scenario around the 7th of June with sporadic clashes already occurring between workers and students" (p. 230).

72. Shanghai Federation of Trade Unions, ed., *Shanghai gongyun zhi* (Gazetteer of the Shanghai Labor Movement) (Shanghai, 1996), p. 514.

73. Warner, "Shanghai's Response to the Deluge," pp. 230–231.

74. Quoted in Anita Chan and Jonathan Unger, "Voices from the Protest Movement in Chongqing: Class Accents and Class Tensions," in Unger, ed., *The Pro-Democracy Protests in China*, p. 120. See also, for Beijing, Andrew G. Walder and Gong Xiaoxia, "Workers in the Tiananmen Protests: The Politics of the Beijing Workers' Autonomous Federation," *Australian Journal of Chinese Affairs*, no. 29 (January 1993).

75. On worker involvement in the East German case, see Jeffrey Kopstein, "Chipping Away at the State: Workers' Resistance and the Demise of East Germany," *World Politics*, 48 (April 1996): 391–423.

76. Sidney Tarrow, *Power in Movement: Social Movements, Collective Action and Politics* (Cambridge: Cambridge University Press, 1994), pp. 168–169.

77. For an argument about the importance of the worker-intellectual nexus in other cultural settings, see Robert M. Fishman, *Working-Class Organization and the Return to Democracy in Spain* (Ithaca, N.Y.: Cornell University Press, 1990).

78. The classic English-language treatment of this subject is Jean Chesneaux, *The Chinese Labor Movement, 1919–1927* (Stanford: Stanford University Press, 1968).

79. On the activities of students in these events, see Wasserstrom, *Student Protests in Twentieth-Century China*.

80. Changes in the configuration of the political climate—as a result of reform initiatives, intra-elite conflicts, a weakening of the instruments of state repression, and the like—have been identified as key precipitants of large-scale protest movements. See, for example, Charles Tilly, "Social Movements and National Politics," in C. Bright and S. Harding, eds., *Statemaking and Social Movements* (Ann Arbor: University of Michigan Press, 1984), pp. 297–317; Doug McAdam, *Freedom Summer* (Oxford: Oxford University Press, 1988); Charles Brockett, "The Structure of Political Opportunities and Peasant Mobilization in Latin America," *Comparative Politics*, 23

(1991): 253–274; Hanspeter Kriesi, "The Political Opportunity Structure of New Social Movements," *Occasional Paper* (Berlin: Offentlichkeit und Sociale Bewegung, 1991); Hanspeter Kriesi et al., "New Social Movements and Political Opportunities in Western Europe," *European Journal of Political Research*, 22 (1990): 219–244; and Sidney Tarrow, *Power in Movement*, chap. 5.

81. Gerald Marwell and Pam Oliver, *The Critical Mass in Collective Action: A Micro-Social Theory* (New York: Cambridge University Press, 1993); Roger V. Gould, "Collective Action and Network Structure," *American Sociological Review*, 58 (1993): 182–196; Gould, "Multiple Networks and Mobilization in the Paris Commune," *American Sociological Review*, 56 (1991): 716–729; William Gamson, *The Strategy of Social Protest* (Belmont, Calif.: Wadsworth, 1990); Alberto Melucci, *Nomads of the Present* (Philadelphia: Temple University Press, 1989).

82. Gould, *Insurgent Identities*, pp. 205–206.

83. See Bryna Goodman, *Native Place, City, and Nation: Regional Networks and Identities in Shanghai, 1853–1937* (Berkeley: University of California Press, 1995); and David Strand, *Rickshaw Beijing: City People and Politics in the 1920s* (Berkeley: University of California Press, 1989). For arguments that the process was already well under way in the late Qing period, see Mary Backus Rankin, *Elite Activism and Political Transformation in China: Zhejiang Province, 1865–1911* (Stanford: Stanford University Press, 1986); and William T. Rowe, *Hankow: Conflict and Community in a Chinese City, 1796–1895* (Stanford: Stanford University Press, 1989).

84. For a stimulating critique of civil society discussions in the China field, see Frederic Wakeman, Jr., "The Civil Society and Public Sphere Debate: Western Reflections on Chinese Political Culture," *Modern China*, 19 (April 1993): 108–138. A general argument about the importance of links between workers and intellectuals in the development of a civil society can be found in Antonio Gramsci, *The Modern Prince and Other Writings* (New York: International Publishers, 1957), pp. 118–125. On the concept of citizenship, see the special issues of the *International Review of Social History*, 40 (1995), suppl. 3, and of the *International Journal of Urban and Regional Research*, 20 (1996).

85. Martin K. Whyte and William L. Parish, *Urban Life in Contemporary China* (Chicago: University of Chicago Press, 1984); Tiejun Cheng and Mark Selden, "The Origins and Social Consequences of China's *Hukou* System," *The China Quarterly*, no. 139 (September 1994): 644–668.

86. Intellectual influence during the Cultural Revolution was not confined to Red Guards. In the case of Shanghai's worker rebels, the most important source of outside advice came from the Writers' Group, a circle of radical intellectuals with close connections to Zhang Chunqiao and Yao Wenyuan. See Perry and Li, *Proletarian Power*, chap. 2.

87. The lack of cooperation was mutual; in fact, relations between workers and students were sometimes overtly hostile. See *Renmin ribao*, August 8, 1957, and *Chengdu ribao*, July 9, 1957, for descriptions of violent encounters between the two groups. Further discussion of this point can be found in Elizabeth J. Perry, "Shanghai's Strike Wave of 1957," *The China Quarterly*, no. 137 (March 1994).

88. See the relevant chapters in Deborah Davis, Richard Kraus, Barry Naughton, and Elizabeth J. Perry, eds., *Urban Spaces in Contemporary China: The Potential for Autonomy and Community in Contemporary China* (Cambridge: Cambridge University Press, 1995).

89. Gabriella Montinola, Yingyi Qian, and Barry R. Weingast, "Federalism, Chinese Style: The Political Basis for Economic Success in China," *World Politics*, 48 (October 1995): 50–81.

6. The Reassertion of Political Citizenship in the Post-Mao Era

1. Andrew J. Nathan, *Chinese Democracy* (New York: Alfred A. Knopf, 1985).

2. Ibid., p. 127.

3. Roger Thompson, *China's Local Councils in the Age of Constitutional Reform, 1898–1911* (Cambridge, Mass.: Council on East Asian Studies, Harvard University, 1995).

4. Marina Svensson, *The Chinese Conception of Human Rights* (Department of East Asian Languages, Lund University, 1996).

5. Nathan, *Chinese Democracy*, p. 55.

6. Tang Tsou, *The Cultural Revolution and Post-Mao Reforms* (Chicago: University of Chicago Press, 1986), p. xliii.

7. "Fervently Support the Publication of the Article 'Long Live the People' on December 21, 1978," translated in *Chinese Law and Government*, vol. 14, no. 3 (Fall 1981): 19.

8. Sebastian Heilmann, "Turning Away from the Cultural Revolution: Political Grass-roots Activism in the mid-Seventies," Center for Pacific Asia Studies, Stockholm University, Occasional Paper 28, September 1996.

9. Ibid., p. 30.

10. Ibid.

11. Ibid., pp. 31–32.

12. Ba Jin, *Random Thoughts* (Hong Kong: Joint Publications, 1984), p. xvi.

13. Ibid.

14. Ibid.

15. Ibid., p. 103.

16. Ibid., p. 76.

17. Michel Bonnin and Yves Chevrier, "The Intellectual and the State: Social Dynamics of Intellectual Autonomy during the Post-Mao Era," *The China Quarterly*, no. 127 (September 1991): 573.

18. Roger Garside, *Coming Alive: China after Mao* (New York: McGraw-Hill, 1981), pp. 223–225.

19. Yan Hong, "An Account of Democracy Wall in Beijing," *Reference News for the Masses,* no. 3 (February 1979): 2, translated in *Chinese Law and Government,* vol. 13, nos. 3-4 (Fall-Winter 1980–1981): 97–105.

20. Gregor Benton and Alan Hunter, eds., *Wild Lily, Prairie Fire* (Princeton, N.J.: Princeton University Press, 1995), pp. 185, 239.

21. Claude Widor, ed., *Documents of the Chinese Democratic Movement, 1978–80,* 2 vols. (Hong Kong: The Observer Publishers, 1981, 1984).

22. See Merle Goldman, *Sowing the Seeds of Democracy in China* (Cambridge, Mass.: Harvard University Press, 1994).

23. Garside, *Coming Alive,* p. 243.

24. "An Interview with Xu Wenli," translated in *Chinese Law and Government,* vol. 13, nos. 3–4 (Fall-Winter 1980–1981): 131.

25. Lu Lin, "Inauguration and Suspension of the Journal," translated in *Chinese Law and Government,* vol. 13, nos. 3–4 (Fall-Winter 1980–1981): 159.

26. Marina Svensson, "A Hundred Year Long Debate," *China Rights Forum* (Spring 1999): 20–25.

27. "Introducing *April Fifth Forum,*" translated in *Chinese Law and Government,* vol. 13, nos. 3–4 (Fall-Winter 1980–1981): 30–31.

28. "Introducing *Seek Truth Journal,*" translated in *Chinese Law and Government,* vol. 13, nos. 3–4 (Fall-Winter 1980–1981): 32–33.

29. "Introducing *Spring of Peking,*" translated in *Chinese Law and Government,* vol. 13, nos. 3–4 (Fall-Winter 1980–1981): 37–38.

30. "Announcement Soliciting Contributions by China Human Rights [Journal]," translated in *Chinese Law and Government,* vol. 13, nos. 3–4 (Fall-Winter 1980–1981): 61.

31. "China Human Rights Declaration: Nineteen Points," translated in *Chinese Law and Government,* vol. 14, no. 3 (Fall 1981): 21–27.

32. Garside, *Coming Alive,* p. 431.

33. Widor, ed., *Documents on the Chinese Democratic Movement,* vol. 1, p. 421.

34. Ibid., pp. 421–422.

35. Garside, *Coming Alive,* p. 434.

36. Ibid., p. 228.

37. "An Interview with Xu Wenli," translated in *Chinese Law and Government,* vol. 13, nos. 3–4 (Fall-Winter 1980–1981): 138.

38. "Queries on Vice-Premier Deng Xiaoping's Answers to Questions Raised by U.S. Newsmen," *Chinese Law and Government,* vol. 14, no. 3 (Fall 1981): 17.

39. Ming Di, "Democracy in the Show Window," translated in *Chinese Law and Government,* vol. 14, no. 3 (Fall 1981): 112.

40. "An Interview with Xu Wenli," translated in *Chinese Law and Government,* vol. 13, nos. 3–4 (Fall-Winter 1980–1981): 138.

41. Ibid., p. 134.

42. Ibid., p. 135.

43. George Black and Robin Munro, *Black Hands of Beijing: Lives of Defiance in China's Democratic Movement* (New York: John Wiley, 1993), pp. 7–20.

44. "Students of the No. 1 Branch School of Beijing Teachers' College Won a Victory in Their Strike," *Beijing zhi chun,* no. 3 (February 1979), translated in *Chinese Law and Government,* vol. 13, nos. 3–4 (Fall-Winter 1980–1981): 127–128.

45. Garside, *Coming Alive,* p. 219.

46. Ibid., pp. 227–228.

47. Benton and Hunter, eds., *Wild Lily, Prairie Fire,* p. 229.

48. T. C. Chang, C. F. Chen, and Y. T. Lin, comps., *Catalog of Chinese Underground Literatures,* 2 vols. (Taipei: Institute of Current China Studies, 1982), vol. 2, p. 230.

49. Isabella Stasi Castriota Scanderbeg, "Forgotten Champion of the Outcasts," *China Rights Forum* (Fall 1998): 44.

50. Law Research Group, China Human Rights League, "What Actually Happened in Fu Yuehua's Case," translated in *Chinese Law and Government,* vol. 14, no. 3 (Fall 1981): 81–87.

51. "Joint Statement by Seven Journals," translated in *Chinese Law and Government,* vol. 13, nos. 3–4 (Fall-Winter 1980–1981): 74–75.

52. Deng Xiaoping, *Selected Works, 1975–1982* (Beijing: Foreign Languages Press, 1984), pp. 181–182.

53. Ibid., p. 183.

54. Xu Shu, "An Unjust Judgment," translated in *Chinese Law and Government,* vol. 14, no. 3 (Fall 1981): 92–100.

55. Benton and Hunter, eds., *Wild Lily, Prairie Fire,* p. 246.

56. Ibid., p. 240.

57. Black and Munro, *Black Hands of Beijing,* p. 52; Widor, ed., *Documents on the Chinese Democratic Movement,* vol. 2, pp. 75–76.

58. Black and Munro, *Black Hands of Beijing,* p. 53.

59. Benton and Hunter, eds., *Wild Lily, Prairie Fire,* p. 262.

60. Ibid., p. 229; James Tong, "Underground Journals in China, Part II," *Chinese Law and Government,* vol. 14, no. 3 (Fall 1981): 6.

7. Personality, Biography, and History

1. Peter Riesenberg, *Citizenship in the Western Tradition: Plato to Rousseau* (Chapel Hill: University of North Carolina Press, 1992), p. xi.

2. Carol Lee Hamrin and Timothy Cheek, *China's Establishment Intellectuals* (Armonk, N.Y.: M. E. Sharpe, 1986); Merle Goldman with Cheek and Hamrin, eds., *China's Intellectuals and the State: In Search of a New Relationship* (Cambridge, Mass.: Harvard University Press, 1987).

3. The paradox, of course, is that the assignation of "citizen" was far from universal; furthermore, within a nation definitions could vary confusingly,

as James Madison noted—see *The Federalist Papers* (New York: New American Library, 1961), pp. 269–270.

4. Wm. Theodore de Bary, *Asian Values and Human Rights: A Confucian Communitarian Perspective* (Cambridge, Mass.: Harvard University Press, 1998); see also Roger V. Des Forges, "Democracy in Chinese History," in Des Forges, Luo Ning, and Wu Yen-bo, eds., *Chinese Democracy and the Crisis of 1989: Chinese and American Reflections* (Albany: State University of New York Press, 1993), pp. 21–52.

5. Andrew J. Nathan, *Chinese Democracy* (Berkeley: University of California Press, 1985).

6. Merle Goldman, *Sowing the Seeds of Democracy in China: Political Reform in the Deng Xiaoping Era* (Cambridge, Mass.: Harvard University Press, 1994), and Richard Baum, *Burying Mao: Chinese Politics in the Age of Deng Xiaoping* (Princeton, N.J.: Princeton University Press, 1994), both clarify the importance of such an ideological shift among a group of veteran intellectuals, including Hu Jiwei.

7. These sessions began in Beijing in early 1992 and continued the following year, with additional sessions in summer 1994, spring 1996, and early 1999. All quotes, if not otherwise indicated, come from these interviews.

8. See biographical entry in *Zhongguo Xinwen Nianjian 1986* (China Journalism Yearbook 1986) (Beijing: Chinese Social Sciences Press, 1986), p. 362; biographical note in Hu Jiwei, *Xinwen Gongzuo Lunshuoji* (Collected Discussions on Journalism Work) (Beijing: Workers Press, 1989), no page number; "Sishi nian jian san da shi" (Three big matters of forty years), in Li Zhuang, *Wo Zai Renmin Ribao Sishi Nian* (My Forty Years at *People's Daily*) (Beijing: People's Daily Press, 1990), pp. 1–12.

9. Hu was involved with at least eight publications in Chengdu during the 1930s. See *Xinwen Nianjian 1986,* p. 362.

10. The first volume of Hu's memoirs has been published as *Qingchun Suiyue: Hu Jiwei Zishu* (Youthful Years: Memoirs of Hu Jiwei) (Zhengzhou: Henan People's Press, 1999), see chap. 21. At least two additional volumes are planned.

11. Tang Tsou, "Reflections on the Formation and Foundations of the Communist Party-State," in Tang Tsou, *The Cultural Revolution and Post-Mao Reforms: A Historical Perspective* (Chicago: University of Chicago Press, 1986), pp. 259–334.

12. For example, "Liu Shaoqi xinwen guandian shuping" (An assessment of Liu Shaoqi's views on journalism), in Hu, *Collected Discussions,* pp. 96–120; and "'Pingsheng yingde haoqing zai'—huainian Deng Tuo tongzhi" ('Earning lifelong praise for lofty sentiments'—in memory of comrade Deng Tuo), in *People's Daily* History Editorial Group, ed., *Renmin Ribao Huiyilu* (Reminiscences of *People's Daily*) (Beijing: People's Daily Press, 1988), pp. 273–296.

13. See Timothy Cheek, *Propaganda and Culture in Mao's China: Deng Tuo and the Intelligentsia* (Oxford: Clarendon Press, 1997).

14. Tsou, "Reflections," pp. 279, 285.

15. Ibid., p. 277.

16. Ibid.

17. Goldman, *Sowing the Seeds.*

18. See, for instance, "Xinwenfa zhengyi" (On journalism law), in Hu, *Collected Discussions,* pp. 463–477.

19. Xinhua News Agency, English service, September 6, 1980.

20. Goldman, *Sowing the Seeds,* p. 280.

21. Baum, *Burying Mao,* p. 77.

22. Goldman, *Sowing the Seeds,* pp. 93–94.

23. May 17, 1982, p. A3.

24. November 15, 1983, p. A16.

25. Baum, *Burying Mao,* pp. 162–163.

26. See, for instance, Hu's preface "Tan lun 'xinwen ziyou' de ziyou" (On the freedom to discuss 'freedom of the press') and essay "Shehui zhuyi xinwenfa shi xinwen ziyou de baohu fa" (A socialist press law should be a law protecting freedom of the press), in China Journalism Association, ed., *Xinwen Ziyou Lunji* (Essays on Freedom of the Press) (Shanghai: Wenhui Press, 1989).

27. Tenth anniversary meeting of the founding of the Institute of Journalism under the Chinese Academy of Social Sciences, Beijing, October 1988.

28. May 8, 1989.

29. See Goldman, *Sowing the Seeds,* pp. 323–324; and Baum, *Burying Mao,* p. 268.

30. Hu's "Lun fang 'zuo' wei zhu" (On taking opposition to 'leftism' as a key task), in *Lishi de Chaoliu* (The Tides of History) (Beijing: China People's University Press, 1992), pp. 143–157, relates how Shanghai news media came to publicize renewed calls for economic reform that were being suppressed in Beijing. His "Yanlun chuban ziyou bu shi zichan jieji de zhuanli" (The capitalist class doesn't hold the patent on freedom of expression and publication), in Zhao Zhilin, ed., *Fang "Zuo" Beiwanglu* (Memoranda on Guarding against "Leftism") (Taiyuan: Shuhai Press, 1992), pp. 81–86, responds to allegations that freedom of expression is a slogan of the bourgeoisie.

31. Tsou, "Reflections," p. 326.

8. Villagers, Elections, and Citizenship

This chapter benefited from the assistance of many Chinese friends and colleagues, most notably my long-term collaborator, Lianjiang Li. Elizabeth Perry and Peter Gries also offered helpful comments. For generous financial support, I would like to thank the Asia

Foundation, the Ford Foundation, the Henry Luce Foundation, the Research and Writing Program of the John D. and Catherine T. MacArthur Foundation, the Pacific Cultural Foundation, and the Research Grants Council of Hong Kong.

1. Interviews and observation, July 1995 and December 1995.

2. For more on the village of Wangjiacun and the unfolding of a bitter collective complaint there, see Kevin J. O'Brien and Lianjiang Li, "The Politics of Lodging Complaints in Rural China," *The China Quarterly*, no. 143 (September 1995): 756–783.

3. Max Weber, "Citizenship in Ancient and Medieval Cities," in Gershon Shafir, ed., *The Citizenship Debates* (Minneapolis: University of Minnesota Press, 1998), pp. 43–49; Martin Bulmer and Anthony M. Rees, "Conclusion: Citizenship in the Twenty-First Century," in Bulmer and Rees, eds., *Citizenship Today: The Contemporary Relevance of T. H. Marshall* (London: UCL Press, 1996), p. 272; Bryan S. Turner, "Preface," in Turner, ed., *Citizenship and Social Theory* (London: Sage, 1992), p. vii; Bryan S. Turner, "Outline of a Theory of Citizenship," *Sociology*, 24, no. 2 (May 1990): 194, 203; Richard Dagger, "Metropolis, Memory, and Citizenship," *American Journal of Political Science*, 25, no. 4 (November 1981): 714–715.

4. See, among others, T. H. Marshall, *Class, Citizenship, and Social Development* (Westport, Conn.: Greenwood Press, 1976); Thomas Janoski, *Citizenship and Civil Society* (New York: Cambridge University Press, 1998); Turner, "Preface," pp. vii–viii.

5. Kevin J. O'Brien, *Reform without Liberalization: China's National People's Congress and the Politics of Institutional Change* (New York: Cambridge University Press, 1990). But for recent changes, see Murray Scot Tanner, *The Politics of Lawmaking in China: Institutions, Processes, and Democratic Prospects* (Oxford: Oxford University Press, 1999), and Kevin J. O'Brien, "Agents and Remonstrators: Role Accumulation by Chinese People's Congress Deputies," *The China Quarterly*, no. 138 (June 1994): 359–380.

6. Peter Riesenberg, *Citizenship in the Western Tradition* (Chapel Hill: University of North Carolina Press, 1992), pp. xv, 5. "Greek citizenship, in both its Athenian and Spartan forms, in large measure inheres in the countryside" (p. 5).

7. Margaret R. Somers, "Citizenship and the Place of the Public Sphere: Law, Community, and Political Culture in the Transition to Democracy," *American Sociological Review*, 58 (October 1993): 594–598, 603; Margaret R. Somers, "Rights, Relationality, and Membership: Rethinking the Making and Meaning of Citizenship," *Law and Social Inquiry*, 18, no. 1 (Winter 1994): 83.

8. Quoted text in Marc W. Steinberg, "'The Great End of all Government . . .': Working People's Construction of Citizenship Claims in Early Nineteenth-Century England and the Matter of Class," *International Review*

of Social History, 40, suppl. 3 (1995): 22. On conditions conducive to the appearance of citizenship norms (i.e., small size, autonomy, unfragmented power, low residential mobility, civic memory), see Dagger, "Metropolis, Memory, and Citizenship," pp. 721–731.

9. Charles Tilly, "The Emergence of Citizenship in France and Elsewhere," *International Review of Social History,* 40, suppl. 3 (1995): 233; Michael Mann, "Ruling Class Strategies and Citizenship," in Bulmer and Rees, eds., *Citizenship Today,* pp. 125–144.

10. Riesenberg, *Citizenship in the Western Tradition,* p. 176, writes: "Citizenship is today so freighted with notions of individual participation and self-government that we automatically think of it as an intrinsic part of democratic society. In fact, over most of history, considering it as a mechanism of discrimination and reward, it has been compatible with all forms of government." On the exclusion of women, see Linda K. Kerber, "The Meanings of Citizenship," *Journal of American History,* 84, no. 3 (December 1997): 833–854; Ursula Vogel, "Is Citizenship Gender-Specific?" in Ursula Vogel and Michael Moran, eds., *The Frontiers of Citizenship* (New York: St. Martin's Press, 1991), pp. 61–62; Ruth Lister, *Citizenship: Feminist Perspectives* (New York: New York University Press, 1997).

11. On citizenship as full membership, see Marshall, *Class, Citizenship, and Social Development,* p. 84; J. M. Barbalet, *Citizenship* (Minneapolis: University of Minnesota Press, 1988), p. 18. It was the U.S. Supreme Court that defined a citizen as a person who has "the right to have rights." Quoted in Will Kymlicka and Wayne Norman, "Return of the Citizen: A Survey of Recent Work on Citizenship Theory," in Ronald Beiner, ed., *Theorizing Citizenship* (Albany: SUNY Press, 1995), p. 310 n. 6.

12. Kerber, "The Meanings of Citizenship," pp. 833–854; Gershon Shafir, "Introduction: The Evolving Tradition of Citizenship," in Shafir, ed., *The Citizenship Debates,* p. 24. "From the beginning citizenship has meant privilege and exclusion; it is no exaggeration to say that one of its principal functions has been as an agent or principle of discrimination." Riesenberg, *Citizenship in the Western Tradition,* p. xvii.

13. Vogel, "Is Citizenship Gender-Specific?" p. 62.

14. On the three dimensions of citizenship, see Marshall, *Class, Citizenship, and Social Development,* pp. 71–72.

15. For Jiang's comment, see Tanner, *The Politics of Lawmaking in Post-Mao China,* chap. 10. On Zhu's remark to *Time* Magazine, see "Carter Center Delegation Report: Village Elections in China," Atlanta, Georgia, March 2–15, 1998, Appendix 8.

16. Dali L. Yang, "Constitutionalism in China? Congressional Oversight and China's Political Future," paper presented at the "Workshop on Cadre Monitoring and Reward: Personnel Management and Policy Implementation in the PRC," University of California–San Diego, June 6–7, 1998, p. 5.

17. On dissenting vote totals, see Murray Scot Tanner and Chen Ke, "Breaking the Vicious Cycles: The Emergence of China's National People's Congress," *Problems of Post-Communism*, 45, no. 3 (May-June 1998): 41. According to one report, vice-premier Jiang Chunyun met opposition because NPC deputies were disappointed with the amount of background information provided. Michael W. Dowdle, "The Constitutional Development and Operations of the National People's Congress," *Columbia Journal of Asian Law*, 11, no. 1 (Spring 1997): 105. Others have attributed opposition to Jiang's age, his education level, and his association with corruption scandals. Minxin Pei, "'Creeping Democratization' in China," *Journal of Democracy*, 6, no. 4 (October 1995): 71.

18. Ming Xia, "Informational Efficiency, Organizational Development and the Institutional Linkages of the Provincial People's Congresses in China," *The Journal of Legislative Studies*, 3, no. 3 (Autumn 1997): 15; Pei, "'Creeping Democratization,'" p. 71; Ming Xia, *The Dual Developmental State* (Aldershot, U.K.: Ashgate, 2000), pp. 168–172; Tianjian Shi, *Political Participation in Beijing* (Cambridge, Mass.: Harvard University Press, 1997), p. 36.

19. Dowdle, "The Constitutional Development," pp. 104, 106–107. On growing attention to oversight after years of neglect, see Yang, "Constitutionalism in China?" On legislative supervision prior to 1978, see O'Brien, *Reform Without Liberalization*, pp. 77–79.

20. J. Bruce Jacobs, "Elections in China," *The Australian Journal of Chinese Affairs*, no. 25 (January 1991): 188, 190–191. On competition for vice-executive positions, but not chief executives, see Bao Yu'e, Pang Shaotang, and Sun Yezhong, "Guanyu Nanjingshi renmin daibiao dahui de diaocha" (Investigation on the Nanjing city people's congress), in Zhao Baoxu and Wu Zhilun, eds., *Minzhu Zhengzhi yu Difang Renda* (Xi'an: Shaanxi Chubanshe, 1990), p. 104. On limited time for mulling over candidates, see Wang Zimu, "Wanshan xianqu xuanju de ruogan wenti tansuo" (Exploring certain issues in perfecting district and county elections), in Quanguo Renda Changweihui Bangongting Yanjiu Shi, ed., *Lun Woguo Renmin Daibiao Dahui Zhidu Jianshe* (Beijing: Zhongguo Minzhu Fazhi Chubanshe, 1990), pp. 193–194.

21. "The Carter Center Report on Chinese Elections: Observations on the Township People's Congress Elections," January 5–15, 1999, p. 12.

22. For the argument against equal representation, see Xu Chongde and Pi Chunxie, *Xuanju Zhidu Wenda* (Beijing: Qunzhong Chubanshe, 1982), pp. 64–65; Li Youyi, "Lun woguo de xuanju zhidu" (On our country's electoral system), *Renmin Ribao*, November 29, 1957, p. 7; Jacobs, "Elections in China," p. 177. On reform proposals, see Andrew J. Nathan, *China's Transition* (New York: Columbia University Press, 1997), p. 236; Thomas P. Bernstein, "Proposals for a National Voice for Agricultural Interests: A Farmers' Association," prepared for the Conference on Rural China:

Emerging Issues in Development, East Asian Institute, Columbia University, March 31–April 1, 1995, pp. 14–15.

23. This paragraph is drawn from Kevin J. O'Brien and Lianjiang Li, "Chinese Political Reform and the Question of 'Deputy Quality,'" *China Information*, 8, no. 3 (Winter 1993–94): 20–31. See also Nathan, *China's Transition*, p. 236; Bernstein, "Proposals for a National Voice," pp. 14–17.

24. On quotas, "blind elections," nominations, and supplementary selections, see Jacobs, "Elections in China," pp. 188–190, 199; Murray Scot Tanner, "The National People's Congress," in Merle Goldman and Roderick MacFarquhar, eds., *The Paradox of China's Post-Mao Reforms* (Cambridge, Mass.: Harvard University Press, 1999), pp. 119–121; Dowdle, "The Constitutional Development," pp. 37–39; O'Brien, *Reform Without Liberalization*, pp. 129, 168. For a proposal to gradually abolish "capped" deputies, see Wang Zimu, "Wanshan xianqu xuanju," p. 184.

25. Tanner, "The National People's Congress," p. 121. On proposals to begin direct election of NPC deputies, dating back to the Hundred Flowers era, see O'Brien, *Reform Without Liberalization*, pp. 40, 128–129, 230 n. 54; Wu Jialin, "Zenyang fahui quanguo renda zuowei zuigao guojia quanli jiguan de zuoyong" (How to bring into play the NPC as the highest organ of state power), *Xinhua Wenzhai*, no. 12 (December 1980): 49; Feng Wenbin, "Guanyu shehuizhuyi minzhu wenti" (Problems concerning socialist democracy), *Renmin Ribao*, November 24 and 25, 1980, p. 5; Kan Ke, "Quanguo renmin daibiao dahui daibiao ming'e queding yiju tantao" (An approach to determining the number of deputies to the NPC), *Zheng-zhixue Yanjiu*, no. 5 (September 1987): 33; Nathan, *China's Transition*, pp. 235–237. For a proposal to elect provincial congresses through popular balloting, see Jiang Fukun, "Gaige he wanshan minzhu xuanju zhidu" (Reform and improve the democratic electoral system), *Lilun Neican*, no. 9 (September 1989): 10–11.

26. See Jiang Fukun, "Gaige he wanshan minzhu xuanju zhidu," pp. 11–12. On voters "blindly checking one name or another," see Ji Yu, "Guanyu difang renda daibiao suzhi de diaocha yu yanjiu" (Investigation and research on local people's congress deputies' quality), in Zhao and Wu, eds., *Minzhu Zhengzhi yu Difang Renda*, p. 254. On peasant apathy and ballot irregularities, see Kang Fangming, "Guanyu xianxiang zhijie xuanju de jige wenti" (Several issues concerning county and township direct elections), in Zhao and Wu, eds., *Minzhu Zhengzhi yu Difang Renda*, pp. 274, 277–279; also Nie Yunlin, *Zhongguo Shehuizhuyi Minzhu Zhidu de Fazhan he Xiankuang* (n.p.: Hebei Chubanshe, 1988), pp. 250–251. For Western accounts of direct elections in the 1980s, see Brantly Womack, "The 1980 County-Level Elections in China: Experiment in Democratic Modernization," *Asian Survey*, 22, no. 3 (March 1982): 261–277; Jacobs, "Elections in China," pp. 178–188; Barrett McCormick, *Political Reform in Post-Mao China* (Berke-

ley: University of California Press, 1990), pp. 130–156; Andrew J. Nathan, *Chinese Democracy* (Berkeley: University of California Press, 1985), pp. 193–223.

27. "The Carter Center Report on Chinese Elections," p. 4.

28. Shi, *Political Participation in Beijing*, pp. 38–39, 110, 177, 179; Tianjian Shi, "Voting and Nonvoting in China: Voting Behavior in Plebiscitary and Limited-Choice Elections," *Journal of Politics*, 61, no. 4 (November 1999): 1115–1139. On campaigning nearly doubling from 1988 to 1996, see Tianjian Shi, "Mass Political Behavior in Beijing," in Goldman and MacFarquhar, eds., *The Paradox of China's Post-Mao Reforms*, p. 157.

29. O'Brien, "Agents and Remonstrators," pp. 359–380. For reasons why villagers' committees receive more attention than people's congresses, see Allen C. Choate, "Local Governance in China: An Assessment of Villagers' Committees," Working Paper no. 1, The Asia Foundation, San Francisco, p. 7; Tianjian Shi, "Voting and Nonvoting in China," p. 1134.

30. Interviews, Fujian, July–August 1992.

31. Jean C. Oi, "Economic Development, Stability and Democratic Village Self-Governance," in Maurice Brosseau, Suzanne Pepper, and Tsang Shu-ki, eds., *China Review, 1996* (Hong Kong: Chinese University of Hong Kong Press, 1996), p. 137; see also Jean C. Oi and Scott Rozelle, "Elections and Power: The Locus of Decision-Making in Chinese Villages," *The China Quarterly*, no. 162 (June 2000): 513–539. Oi and Rozelle also note that some VCs are "empty shells."

32. On the mentally disturbed, see Jorgen Elklit, "The Chinese Village Committee Electoral System," *China Information*, 11, no. 4 (Spring 1997): 6; International Republican Institute, "Election Observation Report: Sichuan, People's Republic of China," Washington, D.C., November 1998, p. 5.

33. On using foreign criticism to persuade local officials to accept individual voting, see Tianjian Shi, "Village Committee Elections in China: Institutionalist Tactics for Democracy," *World Politics*, 51, no. 3 (April 1999): 408; Wang Zhenyao, "Village Committees: The Basis for China's Democratization," in Eduard B. Vermeer, Frank N. Pieke, and Woei Lien Chong, eds., *Cooperative and Collective in China's Rural Development* (Armonk, N.Y.: M. E. Sharpe, 1998), p. 246. Some provincial regulations indirectly outlaw household voting by stipulating that elections are valid only if 50 percent (or more) of registered voters participate.

34. On changing electoral procedures, see Robert A. Pastor and Qingshan Tan, "The Meaning of China's Village Elections," *The China Quarterly*, no. 162 (June 2000): 490–512; International Republican Institute, "Election Observation Report: Fujian, People's Republic of China," May 1997, Washington, D.C., pp. 2, 5–6. On the Ministry urging open nomination, see Shi, "Village Committee Elections," pp. 405–406; Amy B. Epstein, "Village Elec-

tions in China: Experimenting with Democracy," in U.S. Congress, Joint Economic Committee, *China's Economic Future: Challenges to U.S. Policy* (Washington, D.C.: Government Printing Office, 1996), p. 409.

35. Kevin J. O'Brien and Lianjiang Li, "Accommodating 'Democracy' in a One-Party State: Introducing Village Elections in China," *The China Quarterly*, no. 162 (June 2000): 462–463; Kevin J. O'Brien, "Rightful Resistance," *World Politics*, 49, no. 1 (October 1996): 44; Lianjiang Li and Kevin J. O'Brien, "The Struggle over Village Elections," in Goldman and MacFarquhar, eds., *The Paradox of China's Post-Mao Reforms*, p. 139.

36. See M. Kent Jennings, "Political Participation in the Chinese Countryside," *American Political Science Review*, 91, no. 2 (June 1997): 366, and Xu Wang, "Mutual Empowerment of State and Peasantry: Grassroots Democracy in Rural China," *World Development*, 25, no. 9 (September 1997): 1437; see also Oi, "Economic Development," pp. 129–130; Li and O'Brien, "The Struggle over Village Elections," p. 137; Wang, "Village Committees," pp. 245–246.

37. See Kevin J. O'Brien, "Implementing Political Reform in China's Villages," *The Australian Journal of Chinese Affairs*, no. 32 (July 1994): 51–53; Shi, "Village Committee Elections," p. 394. On peasants' suspicions that outcomes are predetermined, see Epstein, "Village Elections," p. 409.

38. The quoted text and survey data appear in Shi, "Village Committee Elections," pp. 402, 404. Other surveys put the number at a still healthy 5 percent. Personal communication, Lianjiang Li, September 1999.

39. Compiled from Pastor and Tan, "The Meaning of China's Village Elections," table 2. Shi, "Village Committee Elections," p. 386, reports that voters ousted 30 percent of incumbent VC members in the 1995 balloting in Shandong. A Ministry of Civil Affairs official has written that approximately 20 percent of VC chairs are not reelected "in most places." Wang, "Village Committees," p. 251. These sources do not make it clear if ordinary retirement or choosing not to run are included.

40. Jude Howell, "Prospects for Village Self-Governance in China," *Journal of Peasant Studies*, 25, no. 3 (April 1998): 99; see also Wang, "Mutual Empowerment," p. 1437; Epstein, "Village Elections," p. 415; Interviews, Fujian, August 1992; Shandong, August 1994; Tianjin suburbs, July 1998.

41. "Villagers Spurn Communist in Chinese Election," *The Atlanta Journal Constitution*, November 22, 1999, p. A18.

42. See Oi and Rozelle, "Elections and Power," p. 537; Epstein, "Village Elections," p. 413; Melanie Manion, "The Electoral Connection in the Chinese Countryside," *American Political Science Review*, 90, no. 4 (December 1996): 741–745; Li and O'Brien, "The Struggle over Village Elections," p. 140.

43. Interviews, Tianjin suburbs, July 1998; Interviews, Shandong, July 1994. Whether long-term migrants retain their voting rights varies by location.

On the second-class citizenship of urban migrants, see Dorothy J. Solinger, *Contesting Citizenship in Urban China: Peasant Migrants, the State, and the Logic of the Market* (Berkeley: University of California Press, 1999).

44. International Republican Institute, "Election Observation Report: Fujian, People's Republic of China," p. 20.

45. Howell, "Prospects for Village Self-Governance," pp. 99–100.

46. Elklit, "The Chinese Village Committee Electoral System," p. 5; "The Carter Center Delegation to Observe Village Elections in China," March 4–16, 1997, p. 10. On an election committee selecting candidates, and the final election becoming "a ritualized enactment of a foregone conclusion," see Howell, "Prospects for Village Self-Governance," pp. 97–98, 101.

47. Pastor and Tan, "The Meaning of China's Village Elections," p. 19; "Carter Center Delegation Report," p. 7.

48. On culling nominees and potential abuses, see Howell, "Prospects for Village Self-Governance," p. 97; O'Brien, "Implementing Political Reform," p. 55; Elklit, "The Chinese Village Committee Electoral System," pp. 8–9; Daniel Kelliher, "The Chinese Debate over Village Self-Government," *The China Journal*, no. 37 (January 1997): 82.

49. O'Brien and Li, "Accommodating 'Democracy,'" p. 465; Interviews, Hebei, 1993.

50. On limited competition, see Elklit, "The Chinese Village Committee Electoral System," p. 6; Howell, "Prospects for Village Self-Governance," pp. 98–99. In a Muslim village I visited in the Tianjin suburbs in July 1998, primaries were hotly contested but the final election was uncontested. On the lack of "genuine competition" in five 1996 elections in Hunan, see Sylvia Chan, "Research Note on Villagers' Committee Elections: Chinese-Style Democracy," *Journal of Contemporary China*, 7, no. 19 (1998): 513.

51. For two fairly spirited speeches, see Thomas L. Friedman, "It Takes a Village," *New York Times*, March 10, 1998, p. A25; also Pastor and Tan, "The Meaning of China's Village Elections," pp. 22–23. On door-to-door campaigning, see Elklit, "The Chinese Village Committee Electoral System," p. 9; Anne F. Thurston, *Muddling Toward Democracy: Political Change in Grassroots China* (Washington, D.C.: United States Institute of Peace, 1999), p. 28; Choate, "Local Governance in China," p. 9; Wang, "Village Committees," pp. 248–250. Wang states that campaigning is being adopted in "more and more rural areas."

52. Interviews, Tianjin suburbs, July 1998; Thurston, *Muddling Toward Democracy*, p. 28; Epstein, "Village Elections," p. 410; Chan, "Research Note," pp. 512–513.

53. Thurston, *Muddling Toward Democracy*, p. 3; Howell, "Prospects for Village Self-Governance," p. 96; Elklit, "The Chinese Village Committee Electoral System," pp. 10–11; Chan, "Research Note," p. 513.

54. For data from Fujian, Jilin, and Hunan and doubts that the principle of se-

cret voting is well understood, see Pastor and Tan, "The Meaning of China's Village Elections," pp. 24–25, 33, 35; see also Howell, "Prospects for Village Self-Governance," p. 96.

55. "Carter Center Delegation Report," pp. 5–6, 11–12; "The Carter Center Delegation," p. 15; International Republican Institute, "Election Observation Report: Sichuan," p. 11.

56. Thurston, *Muddling Toward Democracy,* p. 30.

57. Pastor and Tan, "The Meaning of China's Village Elections," p. 25. In four Sichuan villages, proxies accounted for 15 to 30 percent of the ballots cast in November 1998.

58. International Republican Institute, "Election Observation Report: Fujian," pp. 26–27; International Republican Institute, "Election Observation Report: Sichuan," p. 11; "The Carter Center Delegation," p. 15. On the Liaoning village and why these practices should be abolished, see Pastor and Tan, "The Meaning of China's Village Elections," pp. 25–26.

59. Kelliher, "The Chinese Debate," p. 82; Li and O'Brien, "The Struggle over Village Elections," pp. 136–139.

60. Interviews by the author and Lianjiang Li, Hebei, October-November 1993, May and August 1994, December 1995; Beijing, January-February 1997.

61. Oi, "Economic Development," p. 136; Oi and Rozelle, "Elections and Power." On party-VC relations, see Kelliher, "The Chinese Debate," pp. 81–85; Howell, "Prospects for Village Self-Governance," p. 101.

62. Turner, "Preface," p. 2; Nick Ellison, "Towards a New Social Politics: Citizenship and Reflexivity in Late Modernity," *Sociology,* 31, no. 4 (November 1997): 699.

63. See Anthony Giddens, *Profiles and Critiques in Social Theory* (Berkeley: University of California Press, 1982), pp. 165, 171–172.

64. Marshall, *Class, Citizenship, and Social Development,* p. 70.

65. These posters were written on white paper (a color associated with death and ill fortune). This gesture attracted the attention of county officials, who investigated the charges and ruled that the balloting should be rescheduled and nominations reopened. See Zhongguo Jiceng Zhengquan Jianshe Yanjiu Hui, *Zhongguo Nongcun Cunmin Weiyuanhui Huanjie Xuanju Yanjiu Baogao* (Beijing: Zhongguo Shehui Chubanshe, 1994), p. 80.

66. Interviews with two Ministry of Civil Affairs officials, Beijing, June 1994.

67. Shao Xingliang et al., "Yi min wei tian" (Regarding the people as sovereign), *Xiangzhen luntan,* no. 4 (April 1994): 10–13.

68. Interview with a Ministry of Civil Affairs official, Beijing, June 1994.

69. Tian Yuan, "Zhongguo nongcun jiceng de minzhu zhilu" (The pathway to grassroots democracy in rural China), *Xiangzhen luntan,* no. 6 (June 1993): 3–4.

70. For more on this strategy, see O'Brien, "Rightful Resistance."

71. Jennings, "Political Participation in the Chinese Countryside," p. 366; Shi, "Village Committee Elections," pp. 403–404. Five percent seems remarkably high. In 1994, the Fujian Bureau of Civil Affairs received 562 election-related complaints and deemed 24 elections invalid. International Republican Institute, "Election Observation Report: Fujian," p. 27.

72. Howell, "Prospects for Village Self-Governance," p. 104; Chan, "Research Note," pp. 519–520; O'Brien, "Rightful Resistance," pp. 31–55. On increased rights consciousness more broadly, see Jennings, "Political Participation in the Chinese Countryside," p. 371; David Zweig, "The 'Externalities of Development': Can New Political Institutions Manage Rural Conflict?" in Elizabeth J. Perry and Mark Selden, eds., *Chinese Society: Change, Conflict and Resistance* (New York: Routledge, 2000).

73. For this term, see Howell, "Prospects for Village Self-Governance," p. 104.

74. See Li and O'Brien, "Villagers and Popular Resistance," and O'Brien, "Rightful Resistance."

75. On the uneven development of citizenship and the importance of local conditions, see Somers, "Citizenship and the Place of the Public Sphere."

76. Li and O'Brien, "Villagers and Popular Resistance," pp. 54–55.

77. For parallels with the past, see Wang Gungwu, "Power, Rights, and Duties in Chinese History," in *The Chineseness of China* (Hong Kong: Oxford University Press, 1991), pp. 165–186; R. Randle Edwards, Louis Henkin, and Andrew J. Nathan, *Human Rights in Contemporary China* (New York: Columbia University Press, 1986).

78. For examples outside China, see James C. Scott, *Domination and the Arts of Resistance* (New Haven: Yale University Press, 1990), pp. 101–106; Daniel Field, *Rebels in the Name of the Tsar* (Boston: Houghton Mifflin, 1976).

79. For an argument that imperial subjects could not make claims on the state, see R. Bin Wong, "Citizenship in Chinese History," in Michael Hanagan and Charles Tilly, eds., *Extending Citizenship, Reconfiguring States* (Lanham, Md.: Rowman and Littlefield, 1999), pp. 98–99.

80. Mi Chu Wiens, "Lord and Peasant: The Sixteenth to the Eighteenth Century," *Modern China*, 6, no. 1 (January 1980): 33.

81. R. Bin Wong, *China Transformed* (Ithaca, N.Y.: Cornell University Press, 1997), pp. 235–237. On resentment over unfair conversion ratios in Shandong of the 1860s and its relationship to tax resistance, see Elizabeth J. Perry, "Tax Revolt in Late Qing China: The Small Swords of Shanghai and Liu Depei of Shandong," *Late Imperial China*, 6, no. 1 (June 1985): 102.

82. Roxann Prazniak, "Tax Protest at Laiyang, Shandong, 1910," *Modern China*, 6, no. 1 (January 1980): 59.

83. Patricia Thornton, "Beneath the Banyan Tree: Popular Views of Taxation and the State during the Republican and Reform Eras," *Twentieth-Century China*, 25, no. 1 (November 1999): 3, 13, 30. Kathryn Bernhardt has noted a similarly complex view of the Republican state in relation to rents: "In its

role as rent dunner, the state was seen as an oppressor, but in its role as the monitor of rents, it was seen as a potential ally." *Rents, Taxes, and Peasant Resistance* (Stanford: Stanford University Press, 1992), p. 229.

84. Sebastian Heilmann, "Turning Away from the Cultural Revolution," Occasional Paper 28, Center for Pacific Asia Studies, Stockholm University, September 1996, p. 34. In the 1950s, land reform and collectivization also gave rise to much reactive violence in the countryside. Elizabeth J. Perry, "Rural Violence in Socialist China," *The China Quarterly*, no. 103 (September 1985): 415–426.

85. Heilmann, "Turning Away from the Cultural Revolution," p. 13; Elizabeth J. Perry, "'To Rebel Is Justified': Maoist Influences on Popular Protest in Contemporary China," paper presented at the Colloquium Series of the Program in Agrarian Studies, Yale University, November 17, 1995, p. 27.

86. To this day, many villagers say that the inclusion offered by Maoist "shock tactics" was both enlightening and empowering. Anti-corruption campaigns, in particular, are often fondly recalled as a means for ordinary peasants to rein in grassroots cadres who transgressed regime norms. See Kevin J. O'Brien and Lianjiang Li, "Campaign Nostalgia in the Chinese Countryside," *Asian Survey*, 39, no. 3 (May-June 1999): 377, 384, 391. On "the imprint of past practices—including those of the Maoist era," see Perry, "'To Rebel Is Justified,'" p. 34.

87. Some county officials use the phrase "return [*huan*] power to the people" analogously when promoting village elections, even though the people have never had the power that is being returned to them.

9. Ethnic Economy of Citizenship in China

1. Both the Ford Foundation and the Carter Foundation, for example, sponsor policy studies on China's village autonomy inside and outside China. Other supporters include the Asia Foundation, the EU Foundation, and the International Republican Institute.

2. See Minxin Pei, "Creeping Democratization in China?" *Journal of Democracy*, 6, 4 (October 1995).

3. For example, Zhang Houan, *Zhongguo tese de nongcun zhengzhi: "xiang-zheng cun-zhi" moshi* (Village politics with Chinese characteristics: the model of "county-government, village-autonomy") (Taipei: Guiguan Press, 1998), pp. 112–116.

4. See Kevin O'Brien, "Rightful Resistance," *World Politics*, 49 (October 1996).

5. See Chih-yu Shih, "Public Citizens, Private Voters: The Meaning of Elections for Chinese Peasants," in C. P. Lin, ed., *PRC Tomorrow: Development under the Ninth Five-Year Plan* (Kaohsiung: National Sun Yat-sen University, 1996), pp. 145–168.

6. I report on interviews in four of these villages in my *Collective Democracy: Political and Legal Reform of China* (Hong Kong: The Chinese University Press of Hong Kong, 1999).

7. For a related discussion on Hong Kong's and Taiwan's practices of democracy, see Fred Y. L. Chiu, "Politics and the Body Social in Colonial Hong Kong," in T. Barlow, ed., *Formations of Colonial Modernity in East Asia* (Durham, N.C.: Duke University Press, 1997), pp. 295–322; Lily Ling and Chih-yu Shih, "Confucianism with a Liberal Face: The Meaning of Democracy for Postcolonial Taiwan," *Review of Politics,* 60, 1 (1998).

8. Franz Schurmann, *Ideology and Organization in Communist China* (Berkeley: University of California Press, 1965).

9. Richard Madsen creatively labels one of these hybrid types as "communist gentry" in his *Morality and Power in a Chinese Village* (Berkeley: University of California Press, 1984).

10. Concerning the nesting of polities in ancient Chinese politics, see Yale H. Ferguson and Richard W. Mansbach, "The Past as Prelude to the Future? Identities and Loyalties in Global Politics," in Y. Lapid and F. Kratochwil, eds., *The Return of Culture and Identity in IR Theory* (Boulder: Lynne Rienner, 1997), pp. 21–44.

11. Dru C. Gladney, *Muslim Chinese: Ethnic Nationalism in the People's Republic* (Cambridge, Mass.: Council on East Asian Studies, Harvard University, 1991), p. 187.

12. See Michael Hunt, "Chinese National Identity and the Strong State: The Late Qing–Republican Crisis," in L. Dittmer and S. Kim, eds., *China's Quest for National Identity* (Ithaca: Cornell University Press, 1993), pp. 62–79.

13. Hong-yuan Chu, *Tongmenghui de geming lilun: "minbao" gean yanjiu* (The revolutionary theory of the allied association: the case of "people's news") (Taipei: Institute of Modern History, Academia Sinica, 1995).

14. Wang Tianxi, *Minzu fa gailun* (On ethnic law) (Kunming: Yunnan People's Press, 1988), pp. 80–95.

15. This anxiety is revealed most vividly in Shi Zhengyi, *Guanyu minzu kexue yu minzu wenti yanjiu* (Regarding the science of ethnicity and studies of ethnic issues) (Beijing: Zhongguo minzu xueyuan chubanshe, 1993), p. 42.

16. Stevan Harrell, "Introduction," in S. Harrell, ed., *Cultural Encounters on China's Ethnic Frontiers* (Hong Kong: Hong Kong University Press, 1996), pp. 3–36.

17. Stevan Harrell, "The History of the History of the Yi," in Harrell, ed., *Cultural Encounters,* pp. 63–91.

18. Norma Diamond, "The Miao and Poison: Interactions on China's Southwest Frontier," *Ethnology,* 27, 1 (1988): 1–25.

19. Ming-ke Wang, "From the Ch'iang Barbarians to Ch'iang Nationality: The Making of a New Chinese Boundary," presented at the International Con-

ference on Imaging China: Regional Division and National Unity, March 19–21, 1998, Taipei.

20. See Yang Houdi, *Zhongguo shaoshu minzu renquan shuyao* (Briefing on minority human rights in China) (Beijing: Peking University Press, 1997).

21. Norma Diamond, "Defining the Miao: Ming, Qing, and Contemporary Views," in Harrell, ed., *Cultural Encounters*, pp. 92–116.

22. Stevan Harrell, "The Role of the Periphery in Chinese Nationalism," presented at the International Conference on Imaging China: Regional Division and National Unity, March 19–21, 1998, Taipei.

23. I visited Kunming in March 1997, October 1997, and March 1998; Dali and Lijiang in October 1997; and Menghai, Xishuangbanna, in March 1998. Dali is a Bai autonomous district; Lijiang, a Naxi autonomous district; and Xishuangbanna, a Dai autonomous district. In total, I saw six villages, five village schools, and three municipal schools, and interviewed cadres at various levels, including those of the autonomous district educational commissions, at the prefecture, county, and village levels, those on medical teams, on-leave staff working as supplemental workers, teachers and local scholars, as well as Yunnan University professors.

24. Bai scholar Li Donghong, who escorted me to Dali and Lijiang, made this observation.

25. Yi scholar Fu Zhizheng, who escorted me to Xishuangbanna and nearby counties, made this observation.

26. Tan Xiaojian, deputy director for Menghai Prefecture, Xishuangbanna Autonomous Dai District, constantly worried that minorities in his region would not be able to catch up.

27. Slogans of this sort abound not only along paved roads, but also along mountain trails.

28. One anonymous teacher in the occupational school, a Han, made this comment. Most of his students were laid off from national farms. We met by chance, and subsequently spent three hours over dinner.

29. Mr. Ding, a Bai scholar affiliated with the local literary association in Xizhou County, provided this analysis.

30. I saw such children wearing heavy packs, exercising to pop music in the morning. When the music was over, they dashed to the roadside to buy watermelon slices. In a different village, little Buddhas were helping to rebuild a temple during school time.

31. Xishuangbanna Education Commission Director Dao, a Dai, believes that Mandarin is the key to development. One should not cling to a language that promises only underdevelopment.

32. Professor Li witnessed a Mosuo son introducing his father as his uncle to tourists who came for the sole purpose of observing his matrilineal family style.

33. Naxi scholar He Pinzheng's comment.

34. Professor Ding's comments.
35. For example, see Richard Maxwell, "Technology of National Desire," in M. Shapiro and H. Alker, eds., *Challenging Boundaries* (Minneapolis: University of Minnesota Press, 1996), pp. 327–358; Ralph A. Litzinger, "Making Histories," in Harrell, ed., *Cultural Encounters*.
36. I visited Wuzhong (now called Litong City), south of Yinchuan, Ningxia, in October 1998. It is a Muslim city within the Ningxia Hui Autonomous Region. I saw five villages, two temples, and two schools in total, and met with numerous village as well as county cadres, people's deputies, municipal directors in charge of civil affairs, education, and religion, and provincial directors in charge of civil affairs.
37. Yang Kaihuang, "Zhonggong zhengquan minzhuhua keneng zhi yanjiu" (Research on the possibility of the democratization of the Chinese Communist regime), in Y. Bai, K. Yang, and C. Shih, eds., *Cunmin zizhi de shijian: lilun, shijian yu fagui* (The experience of village autonomy: theories, practices, and regulations) (Taipei: Guiguan Press, 1998), pp. 3–44.
38. Comment by Mr. Ma, deputy director of the Litong Bureau of Civil Affairs.
39. Comment by Ms. He, director in charge of Gucheng County civil affairs.
40. Comment by Mr. You, party division secretary of Zaoyuan Village. He himself served as a case in point: he replaced the previous secretary before the latter's term was over. His mission was to lead the incoming village director to rebuild the village economy.
41. It was a cultural shock to hear village directors and party division secretaries in Zaoyuan, Wuxing, Jiefang, Huasi, and Nilujiafang speak of the size of their personal incomes the previous year, without any sign of embarrassment.
42. Ms. Ma, a people's deputy of Shangqiao County, made this comment.
43. Mr. Ma, deputy director of the Bureau of Civil Affairs, Yinchuan, made this comment.
44. Mr. Wang, a division chief at the Bureau of Civil Affairs, Yinchuan, made this comment.
45. I first visited the Yongshun areas in September 1996, and then again in September 1997 and June 1998. Yongshun has two major minorities: Tujia and Miao. In total, I saw two villages, two enterprises, and one school which are Tujia; and three villages, three enterprises, and one school which are Miao. My interviewees included village cadres, factory managers, school principals, county cadres, officials from the prefecture and the autonomous district, and, in an extraordinary experience, several ordinary villagers. Yongshun trips were the most physically demanding of all the trips I took in China, for they often required very long walks and mountain climbing in a hot, humid climate.
46. See Shi Zhengyi, *Guanyu minzu kexue*, pp. 52–53.
47. Lucian Pye, *The Spirit of Chinese Politics: A Psychocultural Study of the Authority*

Crisis in Political Development (Cambridge, Mass.: MIT Press, 1968), pp. 50–66.

48. Mr. Shi, 73 years old in 1997, lived in Yongshun, Hunan, throughout his life, and acquired his Miao identity in 1957.

49. Mr. Wang, a Tujia deputy school principal in Yongshun, made this comment.

50. Comments of Mr. Yang, a party division secretary in the Miaozhai Natural Village, Zejia Village.

51. Without exception, every household I visited had a work of calligraphy with five big characters meaning "heaven," "earth," "state," "parents," and "teachers"—the five basic norms Confucius taught, except that "state" served as a substitute for "emperor." This is true of both the Tujia and Miao households I visited.

52. Mr. Sheng, whose relative is a village director, ran away to Guangdong in order to have a third child (his first two were both boys). His sixth sister had moved in with him from a neighboring village at the time of the interview, and was about to give birth to her third child. Her first two were girls. Mr. Sheng is a common villager with whose family I spent three days in total.

53. An anonymous general manager of a private enterprise in Wangcun County, Yongshun, over 70, told of his own experience. He had eight children, and many of them had more than two of their own.

54. Mr. Ma, deputy director of Huasi Village, Wuzhong, made this comment.

55. Mr. Ding made this comment.

56. Mrs. Sheng, age 73, with six children and thirteen grandchildren, made this comment.

57. The distribution of resources is not balanced by any standard. For example, Yongshun Elementary School receives much more than the much poorer school in Diaojin County.

58. I visited Shanmei Village only once in April 1997. Many of the interviews were conducted by my former colleague, Chao-chi Shan, at Chiang Kaishek University in Chiayi, which holds jurisdiction over Ali Mountain County. Dr. Shan left for the United States in January 1998.

59. Mainland Affairs Council, Executive Yuan, *Taihai liang'an guanxi shuoming shu* (Position papers on cross–Taiwan Strait relations) (Taipei: Central Daily News, 1994).

60. For this reason, the Ministry of Education has edited a new volume of supplemental reading for junior high school students. See *Renshi Taiwan: shehui zhang* (Knowing Taiwan: the social chapter) (Taipei: Ministry of Education, 1997).

61. Tzvetan Todorov, *The Conquest of America: The Question of the Other* (New York: Harper Perennial, 1992).

62. Wu Feng, whom Zou people today claim was a corrupt businessman used

by Japanese colonial authorities, is represented in the story as one widely loved by the Zou. Allegedly, Wu Feng wanted to influence Zou people away from using human sacrifice, so he offered his life. Zou people killed him in disguise and were deeply moved by his action after discovering his true identity. It was said that the Zou henceforth evolved into a higher civilization. See Hao-pang Wen, *Lishi de liubian yu duo sheng: "yi ren Wu Feng" yu "sha yun zhi zhong" de renleixue fenxi* (Changeability and multiple voices of history: an anthropological analysis of "Wu Feng, a man of propriety" and "Bell of Sha Tone"), Master's thesis, Graduate Institute of Anthropology, National Taiwan University, Taipei, 1996.

63. Chao-chun Hong, "Caozu jiqi zhengming wei Zouzu" (Rectification of the name Cao to Zou today), *Lianhe bao,* November 7, 1998, p. 8.

64. Yi-chun Kuo, "Saixiazu yu ai heiren xiangjian huan" (Saixia and Black Dwarf met happily), *Lianhe bao,* June 16, 1998, p. 8.

65. Mr. Zhuang, former general secretary of the Society to Promote Tourism, made this comment.

66. Ms. Chuang, a female leader working in Shanmei's Medical Care Office, made this comment.

67. Mr. Wen made this comment.

68. For a similar observation with reference to Muslim societies and discourses, see Dru Gladney, "Representing Nationality in China: Refiguring Majority/Minority Identities," *Journal of Asian Studies,* 53, 1 (1994): 92–123.

10. Do Good Businessmen Make Good Citizens?

Research for this chapter was made possible by a grant from the Smith Richardson Foundation and the United States Institute of Peace. I would like to thank Leslyn Hall, M. Kent Jennings, Pierre Landry, Elizabeth Perry, Shen Mingming, Alan Wachman, Martin Whyte, and colleagues in China for their help and suggestions, and Mark Kugler and Zhu Yuelin for technical advice. None of them should be held responsible for the content of this chapter.

1. On Western state-building, see Reinhard Bendix, *Nation Building and Citizenship* (New York: Wiley, 1964), and Charles Tilly, ed., *The Formation of National States in Europe* (Princeton: Princeton University Press, 1975).

2. R. Bin Wong, *China Transformed: Historical Change and the Limits of European Experience* (Ithaca: Cornell University Press, 1997), p. 101.

3. Michael Mann, "Ruling Class Strategies and Citizenship," in Martin Bulmer and Anthony M. Rees, eds., *Citizenship Today: The Contemporary Relevance of T. H. Marshall* (London: UCL Press, 1996), pp. 125–144.

4. Adam Przeworski and Fernando Limongi, "Modernization: Theories and Facts," *World Politics,* vol. 49, no. 2 (January 1997): 155–183.

5. Martin King Whyte, "Urban China: A Civil Society in the Making?" in Arthur Lewis Rosenbaum, ed., *State and Society in China: The Consequences of Reform* (Boulder: Westview Press, 1992); "Symposium: 'Public Sphere'/ 'Civil Society' In China?," *Modern China*, vol. 19, no. 2 (April 1993), with contributions from Frederic Wakeman, Jr., William T. Rowe, Mary Backus Rankin, Richard Madsen, Heath B. Chamberlain, and Philip C. C. Huang); Jeffrey N. Wasserstrom and Elizabeth J. Perry, eds., *Popular Protest and Political Culture in Modern China* (Boulder: Westview Press, 1994); Timothy Brook and B. Michael Frolic, eds., *Civil Society in China* (Armonk, N.Y.: M. E. Sharpe, 1997).

6. Minxin Pei, "Chinese Civic Associations: An Empirical Analysis," *Modern China*, vol. 24, no. 3 (July 1998): 285–318; Tony Saich, "Negotiating the State: The Development of Social Organizations in China," *The China Quarterly*, no. 161 (March 2000): 124–141.

7. William T. Rowe, *Hankow: Commerce and Society in a Chinese City, 1796–1889* (Stanford: Stanford University Press, 1984).

8. Rowe, *Hankow;* Joseph Fewsmith, *Party, State, and Local Elites in Republican China: Merchant Organizations and Politics in Shanghai, 1890–1930* (Honolulu: University of Hawaii Press, 1985); David Strand, *Rickshaw Beijing: City People and Politics in the 1920s* (Berkeley: University of California Press, 1989).

9. Strand, *Rickshaw Beijing*, p. 101.

10. Fewsmith, *Party, State, and Local Elites in Republican China*, p. 137.

11. Parks M. Coble, Jr., *The Shanghai Capitalists and the Nationalist Government, 1927–1937* (Cambridge, Mass.: Council on East Asian Studies, Harvard University, 1980).

12. Frederick C. Teiwes, "The Establishment and Consolidation of the New Regime, 1949–57," in Roderick MacFarquhar, ed., *The Politics of China: The Eras of Mao and Deng*, 2nd ed. (New York: Cambridge University Press, 1997).

13. Dorothy Solinger, *Chinese Business under Socialism: The Politics of Domestic Commerce in Contemporary China* (Berkeley: University of California Press, 1984).

14. Susan Young, *Private Business and Economic Reform in China* (Armonk, N.Y.: M. E. Sharpe, 1995).

15. Christopher Earle Nevitt, "Private Business Associations in China: Evidence of Civil Society or Local State Power?" *The China Journal*, no. 36 (July 1996): 25–45; Jonathan Unger, "'Bridges': Private Business, the Chinese Government and the Rise of New Associations," *The China Quarterly*, no. 147 (September 1996): 795–819.

16. David Wank, "Private Business, Bureaucracy, and Political Alliance in a Chinese City," *The Australian Journal of Chinese Affairs*, no. 33 (January 1995): 55–71; Margaret Pearson, *China's New Business Elite: The Political*

Consequences of Economic Reform (Berkeley: University of California Press, 1996); and Pearson, "China's Emerging Business Class: Democracy's Harbinger," *Current History,* vol. 97, no. 620 (September 1998): 268–272.

17. Yanqi Tong, "State, Society, and Political Change in China and Hungary," *Comparative Politics,* vol. 26, no. 3 (April 1994): 333–353; see also Baogang He, *The Democratic Implications of Civil Society in China* (New York: St. Martin's Press, 1997).

18. See Gordon White, Jude Howell, and Shang Xiaoyuan, *In Search of Civil Society: Market Reform and Social Change in Contemporary China* (Oxford: Oxford University Press, 1996).

19. Jonathan Unger and Anita Chan, "Corporatism in China: A Developmental State in an East Asian Context," in Barrett L. McCormick and Jonathan Unger, eds., *China after Socialism: In the Footsteps of Eastern Europe or East Asia* (Armonk, N.Y.: M. E. Sharpe, 1996); Bruce J. Dickson, "Cooptation and Corporatism in China: The Logic of Party Adaptation," *Political Science Quarterly,* vol. 115, no. 4 (Winter 2000–2001): 517–540.

20. Nevitt, "Private Business Associations in China"; Unger, "'Bridges.'"

21. Jean C. Oi, "Fiscal Reforms and the Economic Foundations of Local State Corporatism," *World Politics,* vol. 45, no. 1 (October 1992): 99–126; Andrew G. Walder, "Local Governments as Industrial Firms: An Organizational Analysis of China's Transitional Economy," *American Journal of Sociology,* vol. 101, no. 2 (September 1995): 263–301; Karl J. Fields, *Enterprise and the State in Korea and Taiwan* (Ithaca: Cornell University Press, 1995).

22. Peter Evans, *Embedded Autonomy: States and Industrial Transformation* (Princeton: Princeton University Press, 1995); Andrew Nathan, *Chinese Democracy* (Berkeley: University of California Press, 1985); Kevin J. O'Brien, "Chinese People's Congresses and Legislative Embeddedness: Understanding Early Organizational Development," *Comparative Political Studies,* vol. 27, no. 1 (April 1994): 80–107.

23. The percentage of PEA members who sought its help dropped slightly in the more developed areas, from 72.7 to 67.7 percent. I do not have a simple explanation for this discrepancy.

24. Kenneth Jowitt, "Inclusion," in *New World Disorder: The Leninist Extinction* (Berkeley: University of California Press, 1992), pp. 88–120; Jeffrey Pfeffer and Gerald R. Salancik, *The External Control of Organizations: A Resource Dependence Perspective* (New York: Harper and Row, 1978); Christine Oliver, "Strategic Responses to Institutional Processes," *Academy of Management Review,* vol. 16, no. 1 (January 1991): 145–179.

25. *Zhongguo siying jingji nianjian 1996* (China's Private Economy Yearbook 1996) (Beijing: Zhonghua gongshang lianhe chubanshe, 1996), p. 162.

26. Andrew G. Walder, ed., *The Waning of the Communist State: Economic Origins of Political Decline in China and Hungary* (Berkeley: University of California Press, 1995).

27. This is one of the few questions where the level of development influenced cadre responses: in the most developed counties, 57.9 percent of cadres felt their social standing had improved, but only 25.9 percent of those in poorer counties agreed. On a related issue, 93.3 percent of private entrepreneurs and 89.4 percent of officials felt their material lives had improved in the past year.

28. Doug Guthrie, *Dragon in a Three-Piece Suit: The Emergence of Capitalism in China* (Princeton: Princeton University Press, 1999).

29. See Pearson, *China's New Business Elite* and "China's Emerging Business Class"; Wank, "Private Business, Bureaucracy, and Political Alliance in a Chinese City"; and He, *Democratic Implications of Civil Society in China.*

11. Citizenship, Ideology, and the PRC Constitution

This chapter builds on many conversations I had with my teacher William P. Alford. I wish to thank him for his wise advice and unconditional support. I also wish to thank Merle Goldman and Nancy Hearst for painstakingly revising an earlier draft; Elizabeth Perry, Jeffrey Wasserstrom, Minling Yu, and Dongsheng Zang for their comments; and Sung-Chiao Shen for sharing his papers on the Chinese reception of the concept of citizenship.

1. Aristotle, *The Politics,* translated with notes by Ernest Barker (Oxford: Clarendon Press, 1960), p. 105. Harry C. J. Phillips, "Citizenship: An Historical Perspective," *www.curriculum.edu.au/democracy/resource/pd/philipsh.htm.*

2. T. H. Marshall, *Sociology at the Crossroads and Other Essays* (London: Heinemann, 1963), p. 74.

3. The right to strike was written into the 1975 and 1978 constitutions. The 1982 constitution deleted this right.

4. The 1982 constitution was amended in April 1988, March 1993, and March 1999.

5. Earl Warren, quoted in Independent Commission on International Humanitarian Issues, *Winning the Human Race?* (Atlantic Highlands, N.J.: Zed Books, 1988), p. 107.

6. According to one source, the term *gongmin* was formally used in the Election Law of the People's Republic of China, promulgated in 1953, for the first time. See Zhang Qingfu, ed., *Xianfaxue jiben lilun* (Basic theory of constitutional law) (Beijing: Social Science Literature Publishing House, 1999), vol. 2, p. 592.

7. See Sung-Chiao Shen and Sechin Y.-S. Chien, "Delimiting China: Discourses of *Kuomin* and the Construction of Chinese Nationality in the Late Ching," paper read at the Conference on Nationalism: East Asia Experience, May 25–27, 1999, ISSP Academia Sinica, Taipei.

8. Ibid.

9. See, for instance, "Zhaogong shisan nian" (The thirteenth year of Duke

Zhao), *Zuo zhuan* (Zuo's commentaries, a Chinese-English bilingual edition) (Changsha: Hunan Publishing House, 1996), p. 1170.

10. Liang Qichao, "Lun jinshi guomin jingzheng zhi dashi ji Zhongguo zhi qiantu" (On the general trends of competition of modern nations and the future of China), *Liang Qichao xuanji* (Selected writings of Liang Qichao) (Shanghai: Shanghai People's Publishing House, 1984), p. 116.

11. Zhou Enlai, "Characteristics of the Draft Common Program of the People's Political Consultative Conference," *Selected Works of Zhou Enlai* (Beijing: Foreign Languages Press, 1981), vol. I, pp. 368–369.

12. Mao Zedong, *Selected Works of Mao Tsetung* (Beijing: Foreign Languages Press, 1977), vol. V, p. 385.

13. *Zhonghua renmin gongheguo "gongtong gangling" ji xin jiu xianfa huiji, 1949–1970* (Collection of the "Common Program" and the constitutions of the People's Republic of China) (Hong Kong: Beifang Publishing House, 1970).

14. *The Constitution of the People's Republic of China* (Beijing: Foreign Languages Press, 1961, revised translation).

15. *The Constitution of the People's Republic of China* (Beijing: Foreign Languages Press, 1975).

16. *The Constitution of the People's Republic of China* (Beijing: Foreign Languages Press, 1978).

17. The preamble of the 1982 constitution retains the idea of limited class struggle, and Article 34 stipulates deprivation of certain people's political rights, but it is not clear who these people are. *The Constitution of the People's Republic of China* (Beijing: Foreign Languages Press, 1982).

18. Ibid., chapter 2.

19. See T. H. Marshall, *Citizenship and Social Class and Other Essays* (Cambridge: Cambridge University Press, 1950), pp. 10–14.

20. Mao Zedong, "Zai bajie sanzhong quanhui shang de jianghua" (Speech at the Third Plenary Session of the CCP Eighth Central Committee), *Mao Zedong sixiang wansui* (Long live Mao Zedong thought) (Beijing, 1969).

21. Deng Xiaoping, "Muqian de xingshi he renwu" (Current situation and tasks), *Deng Xiaoping wenxuan* (Selected works of Deng Xiaoping) (Beijing: People's Publishing House, 1983), pp. 203–237.

22. Zhang Qingfu, ed., *Xianfaxue jiben lilun*, vol. 2, pp. 742–743.

23. For instance, Article 35 of the 1982 constitution provides that citizens of the People's Republic of China enjoy freedom of speech, of the press, of assembly, of association, of procession, and of demonstration, while Article 51 provides that the exercise by citizens of the People's Republic of China of their freedoms and rights may not infringe upon the interests of the state, of society, and of the collective, or upon the lawful freedoms and rights of other citizens.

24. *Jiancha ribao* (Procuratorial daily), March 6, 1999.

25. Ibid.

26. For instance, between 1979 and 1999, in addition to revising and promulgating the 1982 constitution and three constitutional amendments, the National People's Congress and its Standing Committee have made 333 laws and decisions on issues related to the law, an average of 16 pieces of legislation annually. The State Council drafted more than 700 administrative regulations, formulating an average of nearly 40 administrative laws annually. Local people's congresses and their standing committees formulated more than 6,000 local laws, averaging over 300 pieces of legislation annually. Ministries and commissions under the State Council and municipal and local governments drafted more than 30,000 administrative regulations, an average of 1,500 per year. Liu Han and Li Lin, "20 Years of Development of the Chinese Legal System: Achievements and Outlook," *Qiushi* (Seeking truth) (December 1998), translated text, *FBIS,* January 16, 1999.

27. By the end of 1998, China had a total of 3,556 people's courts and nearly 290,000 court officers, of which 130,000 were judges. There were 3,846 people's procuratorates and 221,514 procuratorate officers, of which 159,638 were prosecutors. From 1993 to 1997, courts nationwide settled a total of 22,417,744 criminal, civil, economic, administrative, and maritime cases in their first hearing, with an average annual increase of 11.47 percent. Liu Han and Li Lin, "20 Years of Development."

28. Minxin Pei, "Citizens v. Mandarins: Administrative Litigation in China," *The China Quarterly,* no. 152 (1997): 833.

29. Ibid.

30. Article 7 of the Administrative Reconsideration Law of the PRC (promulgated on April 29, 1999).

31. Michael Ignatieff, "The Myth of Citizenship," in Ronald Beiner, ed., *Theorizing Citizenship* (Albany: State University of New York Press, 1995), pp. 53–77.

32. Liang Xiaosheng, *Zhongguo shehui gejieceng fenxi* (An analysis of social strata in China) (Beijing: Jingji ribao chubanshe, 1997); Li Tongwen, ed., *Zhongguo minsheng baogao: Zhongguo shehui gejieceng de xianzhuang yu weilai* (A report on the lives of the Chinese people: the current situation and the future of social strata in China) (Beijing: Jincheng chubanshe, 1998); Min Xia, "From Camaraderie to the Cash Nexus: Economic Reforms, Social Stratification and Their Political Consequences in China," *Journal of Contemporary China,* 8(21) (1999): 345–358.

33. The household registration system was legalized by the Household Registration Regulations of the PRC issued in 1958. Article 10 of that law stipulated that citizens in rural areas must have permission to move to cities.

34. Preamble and Article I of the 1982 constitution.

35. Michael Walzer, "The Problem of Citizenship," in *Obligations: Essays on Disobedience, War, and Citizenship* (Cambridge, Mass.: Harvard University Press, 1970), p. 226.

36. Sung-Chiao Shen and Sechin Y.-S. Chien, "Delimiting China," p. 3.

37. See Liang Qichao, "Xinmin shuo" (On the new citizen), *Liang Qichao xuanji,* pp. 211–212.

12. Law and the Gendered Citizen

The author would like to thank Bina Agarwal, William Alford, Judy Brown, Mindy Fried, and Andrew Rainer for their comments on this chapter.

1. Cass R. Sunstein, "Why Markets Don't Stop Discrimination," in Sunstein, *Free Markets and Social Justice* (Oxford: Oxford University Press, 1997), pp. 151–167.
2. T. H. Marshall, *Class, Citizenship, and Social Development* (New York: Anchor, 1965).
3. Cass R. Sunstein, "On Property and Constitutionalism," in *Perspectives on Property Law,* ed. R. Ellickson, C. Rose, and B. Ackerman (Boston: Little, Brown, 1995), pp. 88–101.
4. Margaret Somers, "Citizenship and the Place of the Public Sphere: Law, Community, and Political Culture in the Transition to Democracy," *American Sociological Review,* 58, no. 5 (1993): 587–614.
5. Ibid.
6. Sally E. Merry, "1994 Presidential Address: Resistance and the Cultural Power of Law," *Law and Society Review,* 29, no. 1 (1995): 14–20.
7. Lon L. Fuller, "The Forms and Limits of Adjudication," *Harvard Law Review,* 92 (1978): 357.
8. Merry, "1994 Presidential Address," pp. 14–20.
9. Hope Lewis, "Between 'Irua' and Female Genital Mutiliation: Feminist Human Rights Discourse and the Cultural Divide," *Harvard Human Rights Journal,* 8 (1995): 1–51. See also Angela P. Harris, "Race and Essentialism in Feminist Legal Theory," *Stanford Law Review,* 42 (1990): 581.
10. Sharon K. Hom, "Law, Ideology, and Patriarchy in China," *International Review of Comparative Public Policy,* 4 (1992): 174.
11. Ann Jordan, "Human Rights, Violence Against Women, and Economic Development (The People's Republic of China Experience)," *Columbia Journal of Gender and Law,* 5 (1996): 216–272.
12. Lucy A. Williams and Margaret Y. K. Woo, "The 'Worthy' Unemployed: Societal Stratification and Unemployment Insurance Programs in China and the United States," *Columbia Journal of Transnational Law,* 33, no. 3 (1995): 510–511.
13. Delia Davin, *International Migration and Contemporary China* (London: Mac-Millan, 1999), p. 138; Christina Gilmartin and Tan Lin, "Where Have All the Rural Women Gone? Marriage Migrations in Contemporary China," in *Gender Transformations in East Asia,* ed. E. Chow and C. K. Lee (New York: Routledge, forthcoming).

14. Official figures reported that in 1996, the police arrested 14,709 people in 8,290 trafficking cases, involving 1,928 trafficking groups. As a result, 10,503 victims, including 1,563 children, were rescued. Unofficial figures are much higher. "Suppression of Trafficking in Women," *China Rights Forum* (Spring 1999): 42.

15. The trafficking of women has developed into a lucrative international trade spanning all the way to Vietnam. See Samantha Marshall, "Double Crossing: They Don't Say 'I Do' These Kidnap Victims Taken From Vietnam," *The Wall Street Journal,* August 3, 1999, pp. A1, 8.

16. With the market reforms has also come a declining trend of women in formal politics. Thus, women's participation declined from 22.6 percent to 21.3 percent from the Fourth National People's Congress to the Seventh National People's Congress. In 1997, at the Fifteenth National Party Congress, there were only 8 women out of the 193 delegates (constituting 4.01 percent) and no women on the 22-member Central Committee. See "The Third and Fourth National Report on the Implementation of the Convention on the Elimination of All Forms of Discrimination Against Women: China," paper by Professor Chen Mingxia, China Academy of Social Sciences (on file with the author). China has 3 women ministers and 14 women vice-ministers in the central government, 23 women vice-provincial governors, and 375 women mayors or deputy mayors of its 640-odd cities.

17. Economic reform and the resultant increase in wage variations have also contributed to further increases in gender-based wage differentials. See also Margaret Maurer-Fazio, Thomas G. Rawski, and Wei Zhang, "Inequality in the Rewards for Holding Up Half the Sky: Gender Wage Gaps in China's Urban Labour Market 1988–1994," *The China Journal,* no. 41 (January 1999): 55–88.

18. "China to Help More Unemployed Women Find Jobs," Xinhua News Agency, June 18, 1998.

19. Elisabeth Rosenthal, "In China 35-plus and Female = Unemployable," *New York Times,* October 13, 1998, p. A1.

20. These biases run so deep that women seem to share their culture's low opinion of themselves. Hence, Yang Xiyuan, a retired lawyer in Beijing, confided: "I met women who'd been laid off from a textile factory who were given new jobs in a bank, but they learned too slowly. They were all in their 40's, so their reactions were not very quick. They just couldn't do it fast enough." Ibid.

21. Li Xiaohua, "Family Violence and the Legal Guarantee and Consummation of Our Women's Human Rights," *Hubei Faxue,* no. 5 (1995): 1–11.

22. In 1996 divorces rose to 1.13 million, compared to 389,000 in 1980. "Chinese Women Lose Out in Divorce Under Current Laws," Agence France-Press, October 31, 1997.

23. Dorothy J. Solinger, *Contesting Citizenship in Urban China* (Berkeley: University of California Press, 1999), p. 279.

24. Pun Ngai, "Becoming *Dagongmei* (Working Girls): The Politics of Identity and Difference in Reform China," *The China Journal*, no. 42 (July 1999): 2.

25. Emily Kao, "Holding More Than Half the Sky: Women Lawyers and Gender Discrimination in China," Third-year paper, Harvard Law School, on file with the author.

26. Elisabeth Rosenthal, "Women Suicide Rate Puzzles China," *New York Times*, January 24, 1999, p. A2. The female suicide rate in rural China has made China's rate the highest in the world. Some 56 percent of the world's female suicides—about 500 a day—occur in China.

27. 1982 Constitution of the People's Republic of China, Art. 48; 1986 Civil Code, Art. 105.

28. Women's Rights Law, Arts. 28, 29, and 43; 1980 Marriage Law, Art. 13.

29. Women's Rights Law, Arts. 28 and 31; Inheritance Law, Art. 9.

30. Women's Rights Law, Arts. 41–44; 1980 Marriage Law, Art. 31.

31. Women's Rights Law, Art. 44.

32. 1980 Marriage Law, Art. 27, stipulates: "Within one year of delivery and during pregnancy, the man cannot petition for a divorce."

33. Arts. 13 and 14, "Concerning the People's Court Adjudication of Property Divisions in a Divorce."

34. The 1995 Labor Law elaborates that "in recruiting workers, it is prohibited to refuse to recruit women or to raise criteria of enrollment for women based on gender reasons, except for types of work and posts identified by the state as unsuitable for women." The Women's Rights Law stipulates that "no employer units shall fire women workers or unilaterally revoke their labor contract on the grounds of their marriage, pregnancy, maternity leave, or nursing."

35. For example, Regulations Concerning Labor Protection of Women Workers (1988); Regulations Concerning Health Care of Women Workers and the Methods Concerning Maternity Insurance of Enterprise Workers for Trial Implementation (1995).

36. "China Considers Sexual Harassment Law," Deutsche Press-Agentur, July 5, 1998.

37. 1982 Constitution, Art. 49.

38. In 1989, the State Council issued the Circular on Resolutely Cracking Down on the Abduction and Sale of Women and Children. In 1991, the Standing Committee of the Seventh NPC adopted at its 21st Session the Decision to Punish Criminals Guilty of Abducting, Selling, and Kidnapping Women and Children and the Decision to Severely Punish Prostitution. The 1997 Revised Criminal Code punishes those who force women and children into prostitution with imprisonment ranging from five to ten years, and in circumstances resulting in injury or death, the sentence is life or the death penalty. See 1997 PRC Criminal Code, Arts. 301, 358, 359.

39. Traffickers are punishable by imprisonment for five to ten years plus a fine. In cases involving more than three women or children, the punishment is ten years to life. 1997 PRC Criminal Code, Art. 240. Traffickers who commit "especially serious crimes" are to be sentenced to death in addition to confiscation of property. 1997 PRC Criminal Code, Art. 241. Buyers are punished by three years in prison, criminal detention of one to six months, or "public surveillance," analogous to probation. Officials who fail to rescue trafficking victims may be sentenced to "less than five years' imprisonment or criminal detention." 1997 PRC Criminal Code, Arts. 242, 257 (forcible interference with marriage subject to not more than two years' imprisonment, Arts. 358, 359, 360).

40. Women's Rights Law, Art. 22.

41. This is based on my interviews with Chinese scholars such as Xu Anqi of the Shanghai Academy of Social Sciences and Chen Mingxi of the Chinese Academy of Social Sciences. See also Ann D. Jordan, "Human Rights, Violence Against Women, and Economic Development (The People's Republic of China Experience)," *Columbia Journal of Gender and Law,* 5 (1996): 216–272; Ma Yuan, ed., *Jianjue Zhizhi He Xiaochu Dui Funü De Baoli* (Resolutely Stop and Eliminate Violence Against Women) (Beijing: Renmin fayuan chubanshe, 1997).

42. Ronald C. Keith, "Legislating Women's and Children's 'Rights and Interests' in the PRC," *The China Quarterly,* no. 149 (March 1997): 29.

43. Women's Rights Law, Art. 48.

44. 1980 Marriage Law, Art. 25.

45. "Supreme People's Court Report" as delivered by Supreme People's Court President Ren Jianxin at the Fourth Session of the Eighth National People's Congress on March 12, 1996, *BBC Summary of World Broadcasts,* April 9, 1996, p. 26.

46. See *Zhonghua Renmin Gongheguo Faguanfa* (People's Republic of China Law on Judges) (1995).

47. *Zhonghua Renmin Gongheguo Lüshi Fa* (People's Republic of China Law on Lawyers) (1996).

48. "Supreme People's Court Report" as delivered by Supreme People's Court President Ren Jianxin at the Fourth Session of the Eighth National People's Congress on March 12, 1996, *BBC Summary of World Broadcasts,* April 9, 1996, p. 26.

49. Ibid., p. 23.

50. In interviews conducted in 1998 by the author, Chinese judges affirmed that courts will not step in even to advise against an unfair negotiated settlement.

51. *Zhongguo Falü Nianjian 1996* (China Law Yearbook) (Beijing: Falü chubanshe, 1996); *Zhongguo Falü Nianjian 1989* (Beijing: Falü chubanshe, 1989).

52. *Zhongguo Falü Nianjian 1996,* p. 958.

53. *Renmin Fayuan Nianjian 1992* (People's Court Yearbook) (Beijing: Renmin fayuan chubanshe, 1995), p. 258.

54. These statistics come from *Zhongguo Falü Nianjian* for the years 1988–1995. The percentage increase of civil cases was calculated by the author. But see also Ethan Michelson, "Guest Editor's Introduction," *Chinese Law and Government*, 31, no. 5 (September-October 1998): 17, citing *Zhongguo Falü Nianjian* for the years 1987 to 1997.

55. These statistics also come from *Zhongguo Falü Nianjian* for the years 1988–1995. The percentage of civil cases that were resolved by mediation was calculated by the author.

56. See the chart compiled by Ethan Michelson, "Guest Editor's Introduction," p. 17, citing *Zhongguo Falü Nianjian* for the years 1987 to 1997.

57. Elisabeth Rosenthal, "A Day in Court, and Sometimes Justice, for Chinese," *New York Times*, April 27, 1998, pp. A1, 6.

58. See Higher People's Court Training Center, ed., *Zhongguo Shenpan Anli Yaolan 1996* (Overview of Tried Cases in China 1996) (Beijing: Zhongguo renmin daxue chubanshe, 1997).

59. Individual male plaintiffs constituted 51 of the civil cases. The remainder of the 140 civil cases were filed by companies, village committees, research institutes, and otherwise, group plaintiffs (e.g., 2,004 farmers). Ibid.

60. An encouraging sign that courts may be increasingly used even for labor cases is seen in Shanghai. In Shanghai, one of the busiest and most liberal courts nationwide, civil cases filed in 1995 increased from 1994 by 10.28 percent. Of these cases, marriage and family disputes increased by 5.05 percent; labor disputes increased by 51.91 percent; housing and property disputes increased by 31.61 percent. *Zhongguo Falü Nianjian 1996*, p. 696.

61. Li Weisha, "Analysis of Female Plaintiffs in Divorce Cases," *Chinese Sociology and Anthropology*, 21 (Spring 1989): 84–93.

62. These interviews were conducted by the author pursuant to a grant by the National Science Foundation and the Research, Scholarship, and Development Fund of Northeastern University Law School.

63. Davin, *International Migration*.

64. H. Richard Hartzler, *Justice, Legal Systems, and Social Structure* (Port Washington, N.Y.: Kennikat Press, 1976), p. 15.

65. Fuller, "The Forms and Limits of Adjudication," pp. 263–265.

66. Jerome A. Cohen, "Reforming China's Civil Procedure," *The American Journal of Comparative Law*, 45 (1997): 794.

67. Case No. 2, *Zhongguo Shenpan Anli Youguan: 1996 Nian Minshi Shenpan* (Chinese Tried Cases: 1996 Civil Cases) (Beijing: Zhongguo renmin daxue chubanshe, 1997).

68. See William P. Alford, "Tasselled Loafers for Barefoot Lawyers: Transformation and Tension in the World of Chinese Legal Workers," *The China Quarterly*, no. 141 (March 1995): 22. The United States, by contrast, had

896,000 lawyers for its nearly 260 million people in 1995. See Kenneth F. Boehm and Peter T. Flaherty, "Legal Disservices Corp.: There are Better Ways to Provide Legal Aid to the Poor," *Policy Review,* no. 74 (1995): 17–24.

69. "White Paper: 'The Situation of Chinese Women,'" reported by Xinhua News Agency, June 3, 1994, in *BBC Summary of World Broadcasts,* June 10, 1994.

70. In 1994 the Ministry of Justice announced plans to establish a nationwide legal aid system, and formally established the Ministry's Legal Aid Center in 1996 to oversee the development of such programs. At present, there are other legal aid programs in Wuhan and Guangzhou, for example. Although the Ministry of Justice listed the development of legal aid as a central goal under its Ninth Five-year Plan, the central government remains noncommittal as to how much funding it is willing to provide to support legal aid. See Benjamin Liebman, "Legal Aid in China and Public Interest Law," *Texas International Law Journal,* 34 (1999): 211; see also Luo Qizhi, "Legal Aid Practices in the PRC in the 1990s—Dynamics, Contents, and Implications," Occasional Papers/Reprints Series in Contemporary Asian Studies, no. 4 (1997): 141.

71. In 1995, of the 4,889,353 cases filed, lawyers reportedly participated in just 863,574. See *Zhongguo Falü Nianjian 1996,* pp. 957, 975.

72. 1991 Civil Procedure Code, Art. 53. Art. 54 also specifies that "litigants of one party involving many people in a joinder may name a representative to handle the litigation," and Art. 55 provides that "a court may issue a public notice explaining the case and litigant request and notify those who have the right to join the litigation to register with the people's court within a prescribed period."

73. As Benjamin Liebman in a recent article on class action points out, "[Class action] is attractive to Chinese litigants who historically are less inclined to assert individual rights against the state." Benjamin Liebman, "Class Action Litigation in China," *Harvard Law Review,* 111 (1998): 1540.

74. The Legal Center provides free legal counseling to women clients by manning a telephone hotline, as well as by bringing "impact litigation" on behalf of women. As of 1997, the Center provided consultation to nearly 3,000 clients through the hotline, letters, and in-person consultation, and litigated more than 60 cases for its clients. The kinds of problems that the Center receives are indicative of the problems facing Chinese women today. Of the litigated cases, 55 percent involved marriage and family matters, 10 percent involved labor, 9 percent involved violence (including domestic violence, assault, and rape), 10 percent involved housing and medical compensation matters, and the remaining 16 percent involved miscellaneous matters.

75. These women worked 14 hours a day in a Beijing textile mill for a boss who beat them and kept them locked in the factory, and they were left

without pay when the factory went bankrupt. When the labor bureau refused to give relief, the Legal Center filed the case in court, and in February of 1998, the court ordered the factory to pay back the salaries that were owed. Bay Fang, "New Class Struggle: Lawsuits Serve Interests of the Masses—and Beijing," *Far Eastern Economic Review,* March 19, 1998, pp. 24–25.

76. The Center's work is funded by foreign sources and impacted by its interaction with foreign lawyers and law students, such that, for example, the Center for Women's Law Studies and Legal Services of Peking University is even using the term "impact litigation."

77. Case No. 123, Higher People's Court Training Center, ed., *Zhongguo Shenpan Anli Yaolan 1996.*

78. Jude Howell, "The Struggle for Survival: Prospects for the Women's Federation in Post-Mao China," *World Development,* 24, no. 1 (1996): 129–143.

79. Art. 3 of the Women's Rights and Interests Law refers both to the specific responsibilities of the Women's Federation and to the organizational responsibility of the "whole society" inclusive of state organs, social organizations, enterprises, institutions, and "autonomous mass organizations."

80. Akhil Gupta and James Ferguson, "Beyond 'Culture': Space, Identity, and the Politics of Difference," in *Culture, Power, and Place: Explorations in Critical Anthropology,* ed. A. Gupta and J. Ferguson (Durham: Duke University Press, 1997), p. 37, citing Edward Said, "Zionism from the Standpoint of Its Victims," *Social Text,* 1: 7–58.

81. Patricia Ewick and Susan S. Silbey, *The Common Place of Law: Stories from Everyday Life* (Chicago: University of Chicago Press, 1998).

13. Constructing Citizenship

1. Murray Scot Tanner, *The Politics of Lawmaking in Post-Mao China: Institutions, Processes, and Democratic Prospects* (Oxford: Clarendon Press, 1999).

2. See, for example, Li Zuxing, "Jiaqiang Zhuanmen Weiyuanhui Zai Lifa Shenyi Zhong de Zuoyong," *Zhongguo Faxue,* no. 3 (1997): 51ff. (arguing that the NPC should reduce the CLA's influence over legislative development because of its lack of substantive competence).

3. See, for example, Peng Zhen, "Zai Zhongyang Zhengfa Weiyuanhui Kuoda Huiyi Shang de Jianghua," in National People's Congress Standing Committee General Office Research Department, ed., *Zhonghua Renmin Gongheguo Quanguo Renmin Daibiao Dahui Wenxian Ziliao Xuanbian 1949–1990* (Beijing: Zhongguo Minzu Fazhi Chubanshe, 1990), pp. 582–584; Cai Dingjian, *Zhongguo Renda Zhidu,* 3rd ed. (Beijing: Shehui Kexue Wenxian Chubanshe, 1996), p. 416; Michael Dowdle, "The Constitutional Development and Operations of the National People's Congress," *Columbia Journal of Asian Law,* 11 (1997): 21–25.

4. Dowdle, "Constitutional Development," p. 43.

5. "Dog Lovers Angry at Fee," *South China Morning Post,* December 1, 1994, p. 6.

6. Zhiyue Bo, "Managing Political Elites in Post-Deng China," paper delivered at the Workshop on Cadre Monitoring and Reward: Personnel Management and Policy Implementation in the PRC, University of California Institute on Global Conflict and Cooperation, San Diego, June 6–7, 1998.

7. Interview with Professor Stanley Lubman of Stanford Law School. New York, October 1999.

8. "Seeds of Change," *Far Eastern Economic Review,* September 30, 1999, p. 22.

9. B. Michael Frolic, "State-led Civil Society," in Timothy Brook and B. Michael Frolic, eds., *Civil Society in China* (Armonk, N.Y.: M. E. Sharpe, 1997), pp. 46–67; quotation from p. 53.

10. Ibid.; see also Baohei Zhang, "Corporatism, Totalitarianism, and Transitions to Democracy," *Comparative Political Studies,* 27 (1994): 108–136.

11. Frolic, "State-led Civil Society," p. 59; Anita Chan, "Revolution or Corporatism? Workers and Trade Unions in Post-Mao China," *The Australian Journal of Chinese Affairs,* no. 29 (January 1993): 58–59; Colin Crouch, "Pluralism and the New Corporatism: A Rejoinder," *Political Studies,* 31 (1983): 456–458.

12. Gordon White, Jude Howell, and Shang Xiaoyuan, *In Search of Civil Society: Market Reform and Social Change in Contemporary China* (Oxford: Clarendon Press, 1996), p. 63.

13. Tanner, *The Politics of Lawmaking,* pp. 145, 167–203.

14. Sek Hong Ng and Malcolm Warner, *China's Trade Unions and Management* (New York: St. Martin's Press, 1998), pp. 61–62. See also Dowdle, "Constitutional Development," pp. 59–63 (discussing the NPC's largely autonomous role in determining the composition of legislative drafting groups).

15. White, Howell, and Shang, *In Search of Civil Society,* p. 62.

16. Ibid., p. 52. See also Anita Chan and Irene Nørland, "Vietnamese and Chinese Labour Regimes: On the Road to Divergence," *The China Journal,* no. 40 (January 1998): 173; Tony Saich, "Discos and Dictatorship: Party-State and Society Relations in the People's Republic of China," in Jeffrey N. Wasserstrom and Elizabeth J. Perry, eds., *Popular Protest and Political Culture in Modern China* (Boulder: Westview Press, 1994), p. 253.

17. Qizhi Luo, "Legal Aid Practices in the PRC in the 1990s—Dynamics, Content, and Implications," *Occasional Papers/Reprint Series in Contemporary Asian Studies,* no. 4 (1997): 56–61.

18. Interviews with MOJ officials (Beijing, April 1996); Canadian diplomatic personnel (Beijing, April 1996); and American diplomatic officials and persons from the ACLA (Beijing, September 1994). See also Luo, "Legal Aid Practices," pp. 40–41 (noting objections by the "legal profession" to particular legal aid provisions in the draft Lawyers Law).

19. Ibid., p. 157 n. 198 (citing interview with ACLA official). See also "Lüshi Canyu Lifa de Xin Qidian," *Zhongguo Lüshi,* no. 9: (1996): 7; "Lawyers Lobby for Clearer Rules to Protect Defenders," *South China Morning Post,* June 23, 1998 (Internet edition).

20. Tanya S. J. Selvaratnam, "Backseat Driver: Steering Chinese Women's Voices Through the 1990s," *Journal of Law and Politics,* 12 (1996): 108.

21. Interview with Wan Exiang, founder and director of the Wuhan Center for the Protection of the Rights of Disadvantaged Citizens. Wuhan, May 1997.

22. Murray Scot Tanner, "Organization and Politics in China's Post-Mao Lawmaking System," in Pitman Potter, ed., *Domestic Law Reform in Post-Mao China* (Armonk, N.Y.: M. E. Sharpe, 1994), pp. 76, 79.

23. Dowdle, "Constitutional Development," pp. 8–11, 34–35.

24. Ibid., pp. 32–33; Tanner, *The Politics of Lawmaking,* pp. 135–205.

25. Susan Shirk, *The Political Logic of Economic Reform in China* (Berkeley: University of California Press, 1993), pp. 149–196.

26. Dowdle, "Constitutional Development," p. 29.

27. Cai, *Zhongguo Renda Zhidu,* p. 280; Dowdle, "Constitutional Development," pp. 35–36.

28. Ibid., p. 39.

29. Tanner, "Organization and Politics," pp. 63, 86; Tanner, *The Politics of Lawmaking,* p. 80.

30. Dowdle, "Constitutional Development," pp. 34–35.

31. Ibid., p. 11. See also Tanner, *The Politics of Lawmaking,* pp. 75–93.

32. Dowdle, "Constitutional Development," pp. 9–11, 33, 96. See also Shirk, *Political Logic,* pp. 116–128 (noting strong political preference for consensus building in China's political environment).

33. See articles discussed in Zhe Sun, "The Remaking of the National People's Congress in China: 1979–1999" (Ph.D. diss., Columbia University, 1999), pp. 366–370; Dowdle, "Constitutional Development," pp. 19 n. 82, 32 n. 149, 34 n. 162.

34. See generally Sun, "The Remaking of the National People's Congress," pp. 361–374.

35. "Deputies Reject Revisions in Rare Show of Dissent," *Hong Kong Standard,* March 15, 1997 (Internet edition).

36. "Wo You Butong Yijian," *Fazhi Ribao,* March 16, 1996, p. 1; "Conference Urged to Play Political Role," *South China Morning Post,* March 3, 1996 (Internet edition).

37. Tanner, "Organization and Politics," pp. 76, 79, 80.

38. "NPC Sets Regulations for Sessions," *China Daily,* March 1, 1996, p. 2; Bo, "Managing Political Elites."

39. "Forget About Hotels and Roads, Spend the Money on Children's Education, Say Deputies," *South China Morning Post,* March 15, 1999 (Internet edition); Dowdle, "Constitutional Development," pp. 9–11, 35–36, 102–

103; "Laid-Off Women Besiege Shanghai Hotline," *South China Morning Post,* March 13, 1999 (Internet edition); "'Our Voices Have Been Heard,' Says Private Sector Boss," *South China Morning Post,* March 15, 1999 (Internet edition); "State Firm Managers Demand More Pay," *South China Morning Post,* March 15, 1999 (Internet edition); "Expert Tells of Patient Rage," *South China Morning Post,* March 8, 2000 (Internet edition).

40. Dowdle, "Constitutional Development," pp. 22–23. See also Peter L. Strauss, "From Expertise to Politics: The Transformation of American Rulemaking," *Wake Forest Law Review,* 31 (1996): 477–478 (noting that this is true for most parliaments).

41. Mark Barenberg, "Democracy and Domination in the Law of Workplace Cooperation: From Bureaucratic to Flexible Production," *Columbia Law Review,* 94 (1994): 833–834; Kevin J. O'Brien, "Rightful Resistance," *World Politics,* 49 (1996): 31. See also William E. Nelson, *The Fourteenth Amendment: From Political Principle to Judicial Doctrine* (Cambridge, Mass.: Harvard University Press, 1988); Michael Dowdle, "The Descent of Antidiscrimination: On the Intellectual Origins of the Current Equal Protection Jurisprudence," *New York University Law Review,* 66 (1991): 1165–1232.

42. Dowdle, "Constitutional Development," pp. 22–23.

43. Peng Zhen, *Peng Zhen Wenxuan* (Beijing: Renmin Chubanshe, 1991), pp. 607–608.

44. "More Direct Elections Ruled Out," *South China Morning Post,* May 20, 1995, p. 7; "Li Urges Development of Rural Democracy," *South China Morning Post,* March 10, 1999 (Internet edition).

45. Tianjian Shi, *Political Participation in Beijing* (Cambridge, Mass.: Harvard University Press, 1997); Kevin J. O'Brien, "Villagers, Elections, and Citizenship" (Chapter 8 of this volume); Chan, "Revolution or Corporatism?" p. 57; Bo, "Managing Political Elite." See also Andrew J. Nathan and Tianjian Shi, "Cultural Requisites for Democracy in China: Findings from a Survey," *Daedalus,* 122 (1993): 95–123 (finding Chinese citizenry more or less as satisfied with opportunities for political input as the citizens of several Western European nations).

46. Shirk, *Political Logic,* pp. 82–91.

47. See, for example, Xueguang Zhou, "Unorganized Interests and Collective Action in Communist China," *American Sociological Review,* 58 (1993): 54–73 (describing the phenomenon in the context of labor relationships in China).

48. Frolic, "State-led Civil Society"; White, Howell, and Shang, *In Search of Civil Society,* pp. 51–52; Chan, "Revolution or Corporatism?" pp. 57–58. See also John W. Meyer and Brian Rowen, "Institutional Organization: Formal Structure as Myth and Ceremony," *American Journal of Sociology,* 83 (1991): 356–357.

49. Anita Chan, "Emerging Patterns of Industrial Relations in China—and the

Rise of Two New Labor Markets," *China Information*, 9, no. 4 (1995): 56–59; Richard Baum, "The Fifteenth National Party Congress: Jiang Takes Command?" *The China Quarterly*, no. 153 (1998): 141–156; "'Toothless Tiger' Telling It Like It Is," *South China Morning Post*, March 12, 1999 (Internet edition); "Laid-off Women Besiege Shanghai Hotline," *South China Morning Post*, March 13, 1999 (Internet edition).

50. Dowdle, "Constitutional Development," pp. 120–123. See also Dennis Wrong, *Power: Its Forms, Bases, and Uses* (New Brunswick, N.J.: Transaction Publishers, 1995), pp. 8–10, 126–128 (noting how the simple reputation for having power can provide a sufficient basis for exercising actual power over persons who believe the reputation).

51. Bo, "Managing Political Elite." See also Dowdle, "Constitutional Development," pp. 106–108.

52. Lin Feng, *Constitutional Law in China* (Hong Kong: Sweet and Maxwell Asia, 2000); Xin Chunying, *Zhongguo Falü Zhidu Jiqi Gaige/Chinese Legal System and Current Legal Reform* (Beijing: Falü Chubanshe, 1999), pp. 373–378.

53. Herbert A. Simon, *Administrative Behavior: A Study of Decision-Making Processes in Administrative Organizations* (New York: The Free Press, 1997), pp. 55–71; Strauss, "From Expertise to Politics," pp. 747–748.

54. Simon, *Administrative Behavior*, pp. 65–66.

55. James Q. Wilson, *Bureaucracy: What Government Agencies Do and Why They Do It* (New York: Basic Books, 1989), pp. 298–301; Kay Lehman Schlozman and John T. Tierney, *Organized Interests and American Democracy* (New York: Harper and Row, 1989), pp. 271–272.

56. Lawyers Committee for Human Rights, *Opening to Reform? An Analysis of China's Revised Criminal Procedure Law* (New York: Lawyers Committee for Human Rights, 1996), pp. 5–18; "State Firm Managers Demand More Pay," *South China Morning Post*, March 15, 1999 (Internet edition).

57. Ronald Inglehart, *Modernization and Postmodernization: Cultural, Economic, and Political Change in 43 Societies* (Princeton: Princeton University Press, 1997), p. 151; Randall P. Peerenboom, "What's Wrong with Chinese Rights? Toward a Theory of Rights with Chinese Characteristics," *Harvard Human Rights Journal*, 6 (1993): 29–57.

58. See also Peter L. Berger and Thomas Luckman, *The Social Construction of Reality: A Treatise in the Sociology of Knowledge* (New York: Irvington Publishers, 1980), pp. 92–103.

59. Wilson, *Bureaucracy*, pp. 31–112.

60. Zhou, "Unorganized Interests."

61. Dowdle, "Constitutional Development," pp. 20–21; Luo, "Legal Aid Practices"; Amy B. Epstein, "Village Elections in China: Experimenting with Democracy," in U.S. Congress, Joint Economic Committee, *China's Economic Future: Challenges to U.S. Policy: Study Papers* (Washington, D.C.: Government Printing Office, 1996), pp. 403–422; O'Brien, "Villagers,

Elections, and Citizenship." Information on the regional and local experimental roots of China's ongoing efforts to develop more participatory norms of administrative procedure comes from the author's discussions with NPC research staff and academic scholars, participation in internationally funded administrative law development projects, and a six-month residency in the China Securities Regulatory Commission.

62. Frederick A. O. Schwarz, "States and Cities as Laboratories of Democracy," *The Record of the Association of the Bar of the City of New York*, 54 (1999): 157–165.

63. Charles F. Sabel, "Bootstrapping Reform: Rebuilding Firms, the Welfare State, and Unions," *Politics and Society*, 23 (1995): 5–48; Charles F. Sabel, "Learning by Monitoring: The Institutions of Economic Development," in Neil Smelser and Richard Swedberg, eds., *Handbook of Economic Sociology* (Princeton: Princeton-Sage, 1994), pp. 137–165. See also Brook K. Baker, "Beyond MacCrate: The Role of Context, Experience, Theory, and Reflection in Ecological Learning," *Arizona Law Review*, 36 (1994): 287–356.

64. Dowdle, "Constitutional Development," pp. 63–77.

65. Ibid., pp. 78–81.

66. Ibid., p. 77 (discussing the Three Gorges Dam resolution).

67. Liu Renwen, "Xulun," in Ou Yangtao, Wei Kejia, and Liu Renwen, eds., *Zhonghua Renmin Gongheguo Xin Xingfa Zhuyi yu Shiyong* (Beijing: Renmin Fayuan Chubanshe, 1997), pp. 10–11.

68. Dowdle, "Constitutional Development," pp. 63–81. See also Edgar Schein, *Process Consultation* (Reading, Mass.: Addison-Wesley, 1988), pp. 72–73 (emphasis on how voting works against consensus formation); Berger and Luckman, *Social Construction of Reality*, pp. 61–67 (role of consensus formation in construction of new social knowledge).

69. Dowdle, "Constitutional Development," pp. 90–104.

70. Ibid., pp. 102–103; "Forget About Hotels and Roads, Spend the Money on Children's Education, Say Deputies," *South China Morning Post*, March 15, 1999 (Internet edition).

71. Lawyers Committee for Human Rights, *Opening to Reform*, pp. 52–56.

72. Ibid., p. 18. See also "Xingsufa Xiugaian Shouge Jieguanyi," *Fazhi Ribao*, February 3, 1996, p. 1.

73. Lawyers Committee for Human Rights, *Opening to Reform*, p. 18.

74. "Tongyi Guize: Lüshi Canyu Xingshi Susong de Xin Fabao," *Zhongguo Lüshi*, no. 4 (1998).

75. The NPC's power of "legislative interpretation" allows the Standing Committee to promulgate supplemental legislation—what in the United States would be called "remedial legislation"—for basic laws passed by the Plenary Session and other statutes. It is not, as is sometimes suggested, a usurpation of the judiciary's independent authority to decide cases. Dowdle, "Constitutional Development," pp. 81–85.

76. *Renmin Ribao,* January 21, 1998, p. 1. Additional information regarding this development was provided to the author in October 1999 by Wei Luo, director of Technical Services at the Washington University School of Law Library; Danny Dingying Xu, legal translator for Allen and Overy; and Ping Yu of the University of Washington Law School.

77. Interview by the author with Mr. Liu Renwen, senior researcher at the Institute of Law, Chinese Academy of Social Sciences. Beijing, May 1996.

78. "Tongyi Guize." See also O'Brien, "Rightful Resistance."

14. Nationalism versus Citizenship on Taiwan

1. Christopher Hughes was the first to elaborate the term "post-nationalism" in the Taiwan context. See Christopher Hughes, *Taiwan and Chinese Nationalism: National Identity and Status in International Society* (London: Routledge, 1997), especially chapter 5.

2. Margaret R. Somers, "Citizenship and the Place of the Public Sphere: Law, Community, and Political Culture in the Transition to Democracy," *American Sociological Review,* 58:5 (October 1993): 609.

3. Jürgen Habermas, "Citizenship and National Identity," in *Theorizing Citizenship,* ed. Ronald Beiner (Albany: SUNY Press, 1995), p. 257.

4. Sun Yat-sen, *San Min Chu I: The Three Principles of the People,* trans. Frank W. Price (Shanghai: China Committee, Institute of Pacific Relations, 1927), p. 6.

5. Ibid., pp. 11–12.

6. Ibid., p. 23.

7. Ibid., p. 70.

8. Ibid., pp. 64–65.

9. Jia Yibin, *Lun Taidu* (On Taiwan independence) (Beijing: Tuanjie Chubanshe, 1993), p. 54.

10. For a study of how the coexistence of primordialist and assimilationist definitions of Chinese identity has affected relations between Taiwan and the PRC, see Shelley Rigger, "Competing Conceptions of Taiwan's Identity: The Irresolvable Conflict in Cross-Strait Relations," *Journal of Contemporary China,* 6: 15 (1997): 307–317.

11. The Immigration Law of the Republic of China defines the "Taiwan Areas" as Taiwan, Penghu, Kinmen, Matsu, and other territories controlled by the ROC. The Election and Recall Law uses the term "Free Areas." An English translation of the ROC Immigration Law is available at the Web site of the Ministry of the Interior *(www.moi.gov.tw).* An English translation of the Election and Recall Law is available in John F. Copper, *Taiwan's Mid-1990s Elections: Taking the Final Steps to Democracy* (Westport, Conn.: Praeger, 1998), pp. 193–225.

12. ROC law grants more rights to permanent residents of Taiwan than to

other Chinese nationals, but it grants even fewer rights to non-Chinese. For example, the requirements for a non-national to obtain permanent residency in Taiwan are more burdensome than those applied to Chinese nationals. In addition, residents of the "Communist areas" are subject to special restrictions.

13. Alan Wachman, *Taiwan: National Identity and Democratization* (Armonk, N.Y.: M. E. Sharpe, 1994), p. 85.

14. In May 2000, 76 percent of Taiwanese said they thought Beijing was hostile toward the ROC government, and 56 percent said they thought it was hostile toward the people of Taiwan. Mainland Affairs Council Web site: *www.mac.gov.tw/english/POS/890623/8906e_7.gif.* Accessed February 21, 2001.

15. Chiang Yi-hua, "Dangqian Taiwan Guojia Rentong Lunshu zhi Fanxing" (Theories of national identity in contemporary Taiwan: a reflection), paper presented to the Chinese Political Science Association, Taipei, January 24, 1998, pp. 2–16, passim.

16. Habermas, "Citizenship and National Identity," pp. 258–259.

17. Much attention has been given to the Taiwan independence movement, but the fact is that Taiwan's political opposition adopted that position only recently, and reluctantly. Until the 1990s, political activists on Taiwan stressed democratization, while the Taiwan independence movement was headquartered in the United States and Japan.

18. P'eng Ming-min, *A Taste of Freedom: Memoirs of a Formosan Independence Leader* (New York: Holt, Rinehart and Winston, 1972), p. 244.

19. Hughes, *Taiwan and Chinese Nationalism,* p. 39.

20. The Democratic Progressive Party (DPP) made this decision at a party meeting held on May 8, 1999.

21. Hughes, *Taiwan and Chinese Nationalism,* p. 98.

22. The DPP's first successful presidential candidate, Chen Shui-bian, campaigned on a promise not to seek independence unless Taiwan were under military attack.

23. Mainland Affairs Council summary of public opinion surveys, September 29, 1999: *www.mac.gov.tw/english/pos/880913/8808e_7.gif.*

24. Kuo Cheng-liang, *Minjindang Zhuanxing zhi Tong* (The DPP's painful transformation) (Taipei: Tianxia Cultural Publishing, 1998), p. 63.

25. Wu Jui-jen, quoted in Chiang Yi-hua, "Dangqian Taiwan Guojia Rentong Lunshu zhi Fanxing," p. 13.

26. Wu Nai-teh, "Provincial Origin Consciousness, Political Support and National Identity," in Tien Hung-mao, ed., *Ethnic Relations and National Identity (Zuqun Guanxi yu Guojia Rentong)* (Taipei: Institute for National Policy Research, 1993), p. 44.

27. "'Taiwan is Taiwan, China is China': A Pratical *[sic]* Basis for a New Re-

lationship" (Taipei: Democratic Progressive Party Central Headquarters, 1994), p. 4.

28. Chiang Yi-hua, "Dangqian Taiwan Guojia Rentong Lunshu zhi Fanxing," p. 14.

29. Quoted in ibid., p. 14.

30. Ibid., p. 18.

31. Marshall Johnson, "Classification, Power, and Markets: Waning of the Ethnic Division of Labor," in *Taiwan: Beyond the Economic Miracle,* ed. Denis Fred Simon and Michael Y. M. Kau (Armonk, N.Y.: M. E. Sharpe, 1992), pp. 69–100, passim.

32. Chiang Yi-hua, "Dangqian Taiwan Guojia Rentong Lunshu zhi Fanxing," pp. 38–39.

33. Liu I-chou, "Taiwan Minzhong de Guojia Rentong—Yige Xin de Celiang Fangshi" (The Taiwanese people's national identity—a new survey method), paper presented to the Chinese Political Science Association, Taipei, January 24, 1998, p. 10.

34. Habermas, "Citizenship and National Identity," pp. 263–264.

35. Somers, "Citizenship and the Place of the Public Sphere," p. 611.

36. Julian Kuo (Kuo Cheng-liang), "The Reach of the Party-State: Organizing Local Politics in Taiwan" (Ph.D. diss., Yale University, 1995), p. 45.

37. Ibid., p. 41.

38. Quoted in Wu Nai-teh, "Provincial Origin Consciousness, Political Support and National Identity," p. 52.

Contributors

Bruce Dickson is Associate Professor of Political Science and International Affairs, George Washington University. He is the author of *Democratization in China and Taiwan: The Adaptability of Leninist Parties* (1997), coeditor of *Remaking the Chinese State: Strategies, Society, and Security* (2001), and Associate Editor of the journal *Problems of Post-Communism*.

Michael William Dowdle is Associate Professor of Law, City University of Hong Kong. Among his recent publications is "The Constitutional Development and Operations of the National People's Congress," *Columbia Journal of Asian Legal Studies* (1997), and "Preserving Indigenous Paradigms in an Age of Globalization: Pragmatic Strategies for the Development of Clinical Legal Aid in China," *Fordham Journal of International Law* (2000).

Merle Goldman is Associate of the Fairbank Center for East Asian Research, Harvard University. She is the author of *Sowing the Seeds of Democracy in China: Political Reform in the Deng Xiaoping Era* (1994) and coauthor with John K. Fairbank of *China: A New History,* enlarged edition (1998).

Bryna Goodman is Associate Professor of History, University of Oregon. She is the author of *Native Place, City, and Nation: Regional Networks and Identities in Shanghai, 1853–1937* (1995).

Joan Judge is Associate Professor of History, University of California, Santa Barbara. She is the author of *Print and Politics: "Shibao" and the Culture of Reform in Late Qing China* (1996) and "Talent, Virtue, and the

Nation: Chinese Nationalisms and Female Subjectivities in the Early Twentieth Century," *American Historical Review* (2001).

Kevin J. O'Brien is Professor of Political Science, University of California, Berkeley. He is the coauthor of "Selective Policy Implementation in Rural China," *Comparative Politics* (1999), and "Accommodating 'Democracy' in a One-Party State: Introducing Village Elections in China," *The China Quarterly* (2000).

Elizabeth J. Perry is Rosovsky Professor of Government and Director of the Fairbank Center for East Asian Research, Harvard University. She is the author of *Challenging the Mandate of Heaven: Social Protest and State Power in China* (2001).

Judy Polumbaum is Associate Professor, School of Journalism and Mass Communication, University of Iowa. She writes on mass media, freedom of expression, culture, and sports in China.

Shelley Rigger is Brown Associate Professor of Political Science, Davidson College. She is the author of *Politics in Taiwan: Voting for Democracy* (1999) and *From Opposition to Power: Taiwan's Democratic Progressive Party* (2001).

Chih-yu Shih is Professor of Political Science, National Taiwan University. His most recent publications include *State and Society in China's Political Economy* (1995), *Collective Democracy* (1999), and *Reform, Identity, and Chinese Foreign Policy* (2000).

David Strand is Professor of Political Science, Dickinson College. He is the author of *Rickshaw Beijing: City People and Politics in the 1920s* (1993) and coeditor of *Reconstructing Twentieth-Century China: State Control, Civil Society, and National Identity* (1998).

Jeffrey N. Wasserstrom is Associate Professor of History, Indiana University. His most recent books are *Human Rights and Revolutions* (2000) and *Chinese Femininities/Chinese Masculinities: A Reader* (2001).

Margaret Y. K. Woo is Professor of Law, Northeastern University School of Law. In 1997, she was named the law school's Distinguished

Professor of Public Policy. Professor Woo has published and spoken widely on China's legal reforms, as well as on domestic legal issues involving Asian Americans and gender equality in America.

Yu Xingzhong is Assistant Professor of Government and Public Administration, The Chinese University of Hong Kong. He is the author of "The Constitution of a Civil Order," *Investigation of Culture* (1997), and "The Authority System and the Chinese Constitution," *Hong Kong Journal of Social Sciences* (1995).

Harvard Contemporary China Series

New Perspectives on the Cultural Revolution
Edited and with an Introduction by
William A. Joseph, Christine P. W. Wong, and David Zweig

From May Fourth to June Fourth: Fiction and Film in
Twentieth-Century China
Edited by Ellen Widmer and David Der-Wei Wang

Engendering China: Women, Culture, and the State
Edited by Christina K. Gilmartin, Gail Hershatter,
Lisa Rofel, and Tyrene White

Zouping in Transition:
The Process of Reform in Rural North China
Edited by Andrew G. Walder

The Paradox of China's Post-Mao Reforms
Edited by Merle Goldman and Roderick MacFarquhar